TAPESTRY

THE
TAPESTRY
GRAMMAR

A Reference for
Learners of English

TAPESTRY

The **Tapestry** program of language
materials is based on the concepts
presented in *The Tapestry of
Language Learning: The Individual
in the Communicative Classroom* by
Robin C. Scarcella &
Rebecca L. Oxford.

❖

Each title in this program focuses on:

❖

Individual learner strategies and
instruction

❖

The relatedness of skills

❖

Ongoing self-assessment

❖

Authentic material as input

❖

Theme-based learning linked to task-
based instruction

❖

Attention to all aspects of
communicative competence

TAPESTRY

THE TAPESTRY GRAMMAR

A Reference for Learners of English

Alice H. Deakins

Kate Parry

Robert R. Viscount

Heinle & Heinle Publishers
A Division of Wadsworth, Inc.
Boston, Massachusetts, 02116, USA

The publication of *The Tapestry Grammar* was directed by the members of the Heinle & Heinle Global Innovations Publishing Team:

Elizabeth Holthaus, ESL Team Leader
David C. Lee, Editorial Director
John F. McHugh, Market Development Director
Lisa McLaughlin, Production Editor

Also participating in the publication of this program were:

Publisher: Stanley J. Galek
Assistant Editor: Kenneth Mattsson
Manufacturing Coordinator: Mary Beth Lynch
Full Service Project Manager/Compositor: PC&F, Inc.
Interior Design: Maureen Lauran
Cover Design: Maureen Lauran

Manufactured in the United States of America.

ISBN: 0-8384-4122-X

Heinle & Heinle Publishers is a division of Wadsworth, Inc.

10 9 8 7 6 5 4 3 2 1

This book is dedicated to
the memory of
ROBERT L. ALLEN

WELCOME TO TAPESTRY

*E*nter the world of Tapestry! Language learning can be seen as an ever-developing tapestry woven with many threads and colors. The elements of the tapestry are related to different language skills like listening and speaking, reading and writing; the characteristics of the teachers; the desires, needs, and backgrounds of the students; and the general second language development process. When all these elements are working together harmoniously, the result is a colorful, continuously growing tapestry of language competence of which the student and the teacher can be proud.

This volume is part of the Tapestry program for students of English as a second language (ESL) at levels from beginning to "bridge" (which follows the advanced level and prepares students to enter regular postsecondary programs along with native English speakers). Tapestry levels include:

Beginning
Low Intermediate
High Intermediate
Low Advanced
High Advanced
Bridge

Because the Tapestry Program provides a unified theoretical and pedagogical foundation for all its components, you can optimally use all the Tapestry student books in a coordinated fashion as an entire curriculum of materials. (They will be published from 1993 to 1995 with further editions likely thereafter.) Alternatively, you can decide to use just certain Tapestry volumes, depending on your specific needs.

Tapestry is primarily designed for ESL students at postsecondary institutions in North America. Some want to learn ESL for academic or career advancement, others for social and personal reasons. Tapestry builds directly on all these motivations. Tapestry stimulates learners to do their best. It enables learners to use English naturally and to develop fluency as well as accuracy.

Tapestry Principles

The following principles underlie the instruction provided in all of the components of the Tapestry program.

Empowering Learners

Language learners in Tapestry classrooms are active and increasingly responsible for developing their English language skills and related cultural abilities. This self direction leads to better, more rapid learning. Some cultures virtually train their students to be passive in the classroom, but Tapestry weans them from passivity by providing exceptionally high interest materials, colorful and motivating activities, personalized self-reflection tasks, peer tutoring and other forms of cooperative learning, and powerful learning strategies to boost self direction in learning.

The empowerment of learners creates refreshing new roles for teachers, too. The teacher serves as facilitator, co-communicator, diagnostician, guide, and helper. Teachers are set free to be more creative at the same time their students become more autonomous learners.

Helping Students Improve Their Learning Strategies

Learning strategies are the behaviors or steps an individual uses to enhance his or her learning. Examples are taking notes, practicing, finding a conversation partner, analyzing words, using background knowledge, and controlling anxiety. Hundreds of such strategies have been identified. Successful language learners use language learning strategies that are most effective for them given their particular learning style, and they put them together smoothly to fit the needs of a given language task. On the other hand, the learning strategies of less successful learners are a desperate grab-bag of ill-matched techniques.

All learners need to know a wide range of learning strategies. All learners need systematic practice in choosing and applying strategies that are relevant for various learning needs. Tapestry is one of the only ESL programs that overtly weaves a comprehensive set of learning strategies into language activities in all its volumes. These learning strategies are arranged in six broad categories throughout the Tapestry books:

Forming concepts
Personalizing
Remembering new material
Managing your learning
Understanding and using emotions
Overcoming limitations

The most useful strategies are sometimes repeated and flagged with a note, "It Works! Learning Strategy . . ." to remind students to use a learning strategy they have already encountered. This recycling reinforces the value of learning strategies and provides greater practice.

Recognizing and Handling Learning Styles Effectively

Learners have different learning styles (for instance, visual, auditory, hands-on; reflective, impulsive; analytic, global; extroverted, introverted; closure-oriented, open). Particularly in an ESL setting, where students come from vastly different cultural backgrounds, learning styles differences abound and can cause "style conflicts."

Unlike most language instruction materials, Tapestry provides exciting activities specifically tailored to the needs of students with a large range of learning styles. You can use any Tapestry volume with the confidence that the activities and materials are intentionally geared for many different styles. Insights from the latest educational and psychological research undergird this style-nourishing variety.

Offering Authentic, Meaningful Communication

Students need to encounter language that provides authentic, meaningful communication. They must be involved in real-life communication tasks that cause them to *want* and *need* to read, write, speak, and listen to English. Moreover, the tasks—to be most effective—must be arranged around themes relevant to learners.

Themes like family relationships, survival in the educational system, personal health, friendships in a new country, political changes, and protection of the environment are all valuable to ESL learners. Tapestry focuses on topics like these. In every Tapestry volume, you will see specific content drawn from very broad areas such as home life, science and technology, business, humanities, social sciences, global issues, and multiculturalism. All the themes are real and important, and they are fashioned into language tasks that students enjoy.

At the advanced level, Tapestry also includes special books each focused on a single broad theme. For instance, there are two books on business English, two on English for science and technology, and two on academic communication and study skills.

Understanding and Valuing Different Cultures

Many ESL books and programs focus completely on the "new" culture, that is, the culture which the students are entering. The implicit message is that ESL students should just learn about this target culture, and there is no need to understand their own culture better or to find out about the cultures of their international classmates. To some ESL students, this makes them feel their own culture is not valued in the new country.

Tapestry is designed to provide a clear and understandable entry into North American culture. Nevertheless, the Tapestry Program values *all* the cultures found in the ESL classroom. Tapestry students have constant opportunities to become "culturally fluent" in North American culture while they are learning English, but they also have the chance to think about the cultures of their classmates and even understand their home culture from different perspectives.

Integrating the Language Skills

Communication in a language is not restricted to one skill or another. ESL students are typically expected to learn (to a greater or lesser degree) all four language skills: reading, writing, speaking, and listening. They are also expected to develop strong grammatical competence, as well as becoming socioculturally sensitive and knowing what to do when they encounter a "language barrier."

Research shows that multi-skill learning is more effective than isolated-skill learning, because related activities in several skills provide reinforcement and refresh the learner's memory. Therefore, Tapestry integrates all the skills. A given Tapestry volume might highlight one skill, such as reading, but all other skills are also included to support and strengthen overall language development.

However, many intensive ESL programs are divided into classes labeled according to one skill (Reading Comprehension Class) or at most two skills (Listening/Speaking Class or Oral Communication Class). The volumes in the Tapestry Program can easily be used to fit this traditional format, because each volume clearly identifies its highlighted or central skill(s).

Grammar is interwoven into all Tapestry volumes. However, there is also a separate reference book for students, *The Tapestry Grammar,* and a Grammar Strand composed of grammar "work-out" books at each of the levels in the Tapestry Program.

Other Features of the Tapestry Program

Pilot Sites

It is not enough to provide volumes full of appealing tasks and beautiful pictures. Users deserve to know that the materials have been pilot-tested. In many ESL series, pilot testing takes place at only a few sites or even just in the classroom of the author. In contrast, Heinle & Heinle Publishers have developed a network of Tapestry Pilot Test Sites throughout North America. At this time, there are approximately 40 such sites, although the number grows weekly. These sites try out the materials and provide suggestions for revisions. They are all actively engaged in making Tapestry the best program possible.

An Overall Guidebook

To offer coherence to the entire Tapestry Program and especially to offer support for teachers who want to understand the principles and practice of Tapestry, we have written a book entitled, *The Tapestry of Language Learning. The Individual in the Communicative Classroom* (Scarcella and Oxford, published in 1992 by Heinle & Heinle).

A Last Word

We are pleased to welcome you to Tapestry! We use the Tapestry principles every day, and we hope these principles—and all the books in the Tapestry Program—provide you the same strength, confidence, and joy that they give us. We look forward to comments from both teachers and students who use any part of the Tapestry Program.

Rebecca L. Oxford
University of Alabama
Tuscaloosa, Alabama

Robin C. Scarcella
University of California at Irvine
Irvine, California

TO THE TEACHER

*T*his book is a new approach to English grammar for students learning English as a second or foreign language. It is new in the following respects. First, we have built it on a coherent linguistic theory which takes into account the constant interplay between form and function. This constitutes the "warp" in the "tapestry" of our title. Second, it reflects the actual use of language in communication, especially the use of the students for whom it is intended. This constitutes the "weft" of our "tapestry."

Our first principle provides a context for explaining the problematic areas of English. Our second principle has guided us in deciding which problems to focus on. These problems are primarily common sources of error (e.g., the verb system), but for more advanced students, we have included information on how to use the resources of English grammar for structuring their discourse. Consequently, it is unlikely that all the chapters will be appropriate for any one student. Those who are making basic errors should concentrate on Chapters 2, 3, 4, 8, and possibly 5 and 7. Those who need to develop their accuracy and range can be directed to Chapters 6 and 9-14. Chapter 1 is intended as an introduction to the whole book.

Our illustrations and exercises are taken, for the most part, from material written by students—whole essays or substantial portions of them. We have selected these essays not only for the structures that they illustrate but also for their intrinsic interest. They represent a number of themes that are important to students learning English: problems of getting an education, nostalgia for places left behind, difficulties in coping with a rapidly changing world. These essays will, we hope, present a model that students will see as attainable and will make it easier to build the teaching of grammar into larger communicative projects. We would urge, in particular, that the passages be used to stimulate the students' own writing and that exercises similar to those we provide be developed from what they themselves produce.

We should point out that where a passage has been heavily adapted for the purpose of constructing an exercise, we have printed a correct version in Appendix 2. These correct versions can be used as answer keys, but students should be made aware that there is often more than one correct answer.

While our primary focus is on writing, we also consider spoken English. Chapter 2, in particular, discusses speaking and pays special attention to the differences between formal and informal discourse. It is illustrated from genuine conversations taken from published sources. We have also, throughout the book, inserted notes on **When You're Talking,** in which we point out ways in which written and spoken English differ.

As additional aids, we have added notes on **When You Are Writing,** which direct attention to common errors, and **Learning Strategies,** which introduce tips on how to learn particular rules and lists. In keeping with other books in the Tapestry Series, we acknowledge that different people have different learning styles, so we suggest as wide a variety of strategies as possible, and we have supplemented our verbal explanations with figures and charts for the benefit of those who are more visually oriented.

We have not attempted to be comprehensive in this book, but we have, we believe, covered all the grammar that students need to know in order to communicate successfully in English, and we have focused attention and provided practice on those points that we know, from experience, cause particular difficulty.

TO THE STUDENT

*G*rammar is not the first thing you should think about when you are communicating in English. It is more important to know what you want to say and to find the words for saying it. However, you then need to think about the rules for arranging those words and for signaling the relationships between them. It is those rules that we try to explain in this book.

In any language, grammatical rules govern both speech and writing, but the rules are not always the same for the two methods of communication. You are usually more aware of the rules in writing because written mistakes are noticed more (and corrected more often) than spoken ones, and, of course, as a writer you have more opportunity to correct yourself. So throughout the book, we have included notes on **When You're Talking,** which point out ways in which speech and writing differ, and notes on **When You Are Writing,** which point out particular problems that you should check for when you are editing.

Editing, in general, should be thought of as a late stage in the writing process. If you want to write a good essay, first you need to concentrate on what you want to say. At this early stage, when you are getting your ideas in order, you should not bother much about grammar. Later, when you have worked out what to say, you will be writing a draft of your essay, which you may show to your classmates and your teacher. On the basis of their comments, you will probably change your essay by adding, dropping, or rearranging information. It is not until you have done all this that you are ready to concentrate on editing.

At the editing stage, you will need to look carefully at the words you have chosen and how you have arranged them in sentences and paragraphs. You need to check that they not only say precisely what you mean but that they also do not contain grammatical errors that would distract your readers and make it difficult for them to see your point. That is when you will need to use this book.

If you are reading this book, you already know a lot about English grammar, and you probably need to work on only a few problem areas. These will be different for different individuals and will depend in part on what your first language is.

How do you identify what you need to work on? You may already know that you have particular problems with English, or your teacher may tell you what they are. In this book, we state at the beginning of each chapter the topics covered in the chapter. For example, if you know that you find English verb forms difficult, go to Chapter 8 ("Verbs with Tense: Active"); Sections 2.1 and 3.4 give specific information on verb forms. Similarly, if you know you have problems with articles, go to Chapter 5 ("Noun Phrases: The Basic Structure"); articles are explained in Section 3.1. If you don't know how to name the problem you have and therefore can't look it up, read Chapter 1 for the basic vocabulary, and then go to the table of contents.

At the end of each chapter, you will find student essays that have been adapted as exercises, and, for those that have been changed considerably, we provide correct versions in Appendix 2. You can use these exercises after you have read a chapter to reinforce what you have learned, and you can check your answers against the correct versions. (In a number of cases, there is more than one correct answer although we only give one—that is, the one the writer originally used.) Alternatively, you can do the exercises and check your answers before you read a chapter in order to see whether you need to study it or not. Either way, after doing the exercises we provide, you should be sure to apply the principles you have just been practicing to your own writing. In this way, you can learn to take control over the final step of the writing process: editing.

ACKNOWLEDGMENTS

Our greatest helpers in writing this book have been our students. We would like to thank all those we have taught at Hunter College and Kingsborough Community College, both of the City University of New York; at William Paterson College in New Jersey; and at Nanjiing University in China. Our special thanks go to the students whose essays are quoted here.

For our understanding of the systems which make up the English sentence, we are indebted to Robert L. Allen, whose inspired teaching made us fascinated with the beauty and power of the English sentence.

We would also like to thank the many colleagues and friends who have helped us with their advice and comments. We especially thank Clifford Hill and Franklin Horowitz for their focus on discourse and Pamela Martin for her work on phrasal verbs. We cannot mention by name all who have helped us, but we particularly acknowledge Diana Bowstead, Shawn Harrison, Darlene Larson, and Jean McConochie. Kathleen Keller, then of St. Martin's Press, gave us considerable encouragement at an early stage of the book's preparation, and the readers' comments that she collected for us were especially valuable. David Lee and Ken Mattsson at Heinle & Heinle have also been enormously supportive, and the comments of the readers they recruited for us have helped us a great deal. We would like to acknowledge, too, the series editors, Rebecca Oxford and Robin Scarcella, whose imagination and breadth of vision have provided a home for a book that differs in many respects from traditional grammars.

We would also like to thank Patricia Byrd (Georgia State University), Marta Dmytrenko-Ahrabian (Wayne State University), Nancy Herzfeld-Pipkin (San Diego State University), Kathy Leffel (University of Alabama), Madalyn Marabella (Texas Intensive English Institute), Eileen Prince (Northeastern University), Melanie Schneider (Beloit College), and Melissa Tawalbeh (University of Findlay), who gave helpful comments during the development of the manuscript. We would also like to thank the students of Diana Bowstead (Hunter College), Kate Goodspeed (University of Architecture and Surveying, Nanjing, China), Shawn Harrison (University of Illinois, Urbana), Jean McConochie (Pace University), Jacqueline Milligan (State

ACKNOWLEDGMENTS

University of New York at Buffalo), and the staff at The Writing Center at Hunter College for piloting sections of the manuscript.

Finally, our undying gratitude goes to our families. We have neglected them sadly while writing this book, and we thank them, especially our spouses, Roger Deakins and Barbara Gonzales, for their patience and loyal support.

In writing this book, we have drawn on the following published sources:

Algeo, John. 1988. "The Tag Question in British English: It's Different, I'n' It?" *English World-Wide* 9:2 171–191.

Allen, Robert L. 1966. *The Verb System of Present-Day American English.* New York: Mouton Publishers.

———. 1972. *English Grammars and English Grammar.* New York: Charles Scribner's Sons.

Cameron, Deborah, Fiona McAlinden, and Kathy O'Leary. 1989. "Lakoff in context: the social and linguistic functions of tag questions" in *Women in Their Speech Communities.* Edited by Jennifer Coates & Deborah Cameron. New York: Longman, 74–93.

Carterette, Edward C., and Margaret Hubbard Jones. 1974. *Informal Speech: Alphabetic & Phonemic Texts With Statistical Analyses And Tables.* Berkeley: University of California Press.

Celce-Murcia, Marianne, and Diane Larsen-Freeman. 1983. *The Grammar Book: An ESL/EFL Teacher's Course.* Cambridge: Newbury House Publishers.

Frost, David. 1971. *The Americans.* London: Heinemann.

Halliday, A. K., and Ruqaiya Hasan. 1976. *Cohesion in English.* New York: Longman.

Pinter, Harold. 1976. "The Dumb Waiter," in *Plays: One.* London: Eyre Methuen.

Quirk, Randolph, Sidney Greenbaum, Geoffrey Leech, and Jan Svartvik. 1985. *A Comprehensive Grammar of the English Language.* New York: Longman.

Santoli, Al. 1988. *New Americans: An Oral History.* New York: Ballantine Books.

Thoreau, Henry David. 1966. *Walden and Civil Disobedience.* Edited by Owen Thomas. New York: W. W. Norton & Company.

PASSAGES

Note: An asterisk indicates that the passage has been altered by the deliberate inclusion of errors, choices, or blanks. Correct versions of these passages are printed in Appendix 2. For most of these passages, two numbers are given: The first refers to the page of the exercise, the second to the page of the correct version.

PASSAGES

CONTENTS

2   *Asking and Answering Questions*   *11*

3   *Making Statements: The Minimal English Sentence*   *37*

7 *Pronouns*   *153*

8 *Verbs with Tense: Active*   *177*

9 Verbs with Tense: Passive   225

10 Verbals and Verbal Phrases   243

Sixteen Basic Terms

1

CHAPTER

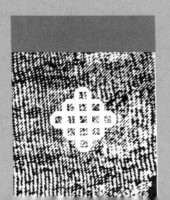

*T*o talk about grammar, you have to know certain grammatical terms, but you do not have to know very many. In this chapter, we present the 16 terms that we have found necessary for explaining how a sentence works.

English sentences are all variations of a basic structure, which you can think of as a series of positions. You need to know what these positions are, which of them have to be filled, and what kinds of unit they can be filled with. The terms we present here are the names of the positions and the names of the units that go in them.

So that you can see what we are talking about, we will be giving examples taken from the following essay. First, read the essay as a whole; as you see, it is a thoughtful consideration of a student's experience of learning English—perhaps your experience was like it.

Passage 1-A　　　　　　　　**LEARNING ENGLISH**

by Kioko Miura

I sometimes question myself, "How many years have I been learning English?" I am shocked when I count because I have been learning English more than eight years. Unfortunately, I'm not satisfied with my English skills, and simultaneously I have a question, "What was I learning for eight years in
5　English classes in Japan?"

English was and is one of the main subjects at junior and high school in Japan. My first experience of the English language started when I was in the first grade of junior high school. I was really excited by learning the language because I felt like I would explore an unknown world. The first lesson was
10　that I followed a teacher's voice saying "A, B, C . . . " and basic conversation. Even though I was confused by those brand-new things, I was certainly learning something.

But my interest in English was being diminished day by day by English teachers. Our teachers required us to memorize grammatical formulas and
15　meanings of words. Memorizing seemed to be the only way of learning English. I had to memorize at least twenty words a week, and the teachers gave us a quiz once a week to know how many words we remembered. In the midterm and final examination, they copied a few sentences from the

2

20 textbook and erased one or two of the original words. We were ordered to fill in those blanks with exactly the same words as the textbook. There was no exception. Consequently, we had to memorize a whole chapter to pass the examination. After the examination, I used to forget everything. Thus, I didn't learn anything. . . .

25 In New York, I realized that I had to practice English instead of memorizing to pass the examination. The "English" that I learned in Japan didn't help much in New York. Of course, I might have tried to improve by myself, but I didn't even want to think about English. English for me was tedious memorization. I don't want to blame English education in Japan, but as long as English teachers are not concerned with the importance of
30 practical English rather than forcing students to memorize the textbook, they will continue making victims like me. Recently, CUNY [City University of New York] has opened a campus in the Hiroshima prefecture of Japan. English education has been changing, and Japanese students are having the opportunity to learn "real" English. I hope that I am the last victim of the out-
35 dated education system.

1. SUBJECTS, PREDICATES, ADVERBIALS

The sentences in the essay above can each be divided into at least two parts, a **subject** and a **predicate.** For example:

SUBJECT	PREDICATE
I	sometimes question myself.
English	was and is one of the main subjects at junior and high school in Japan.
I	hope that I am the last victim of the out-dated education system.

In written English, every sentence must have a subject and a predicate, so we will talk in this book about a **subject position** and a **predicate position.**

A sentence that has only these two positions filled is grammatically complete, but all writers frequently use two other positions as well, one before the subject and one after the predicate. These are called **adverbial positions,** and the groups of words that go in them are called **adverbials.** For example:

ADVERBIAL	SUBJECT	PREDICATE	ADVERBIAL
Even though I was confused by those brand-new things,	I	was certainly learning something.	

ADVERBIAL	SUBJECT	PREDICATE	ADVERBIAL
	My first experience of the English language	started	when I was in the first grade of junior high school.
After the examination	I	used to forget everything.	

Some students see these four positions more easily if they are shown graphically, so we mark the subject position of any particular sentence with a box and the predicate with an arrow, as follows:

I   sometimes question myself.

English   was and is one of the main subjects at junior and high school in Japan.

I   hope that I am the last victim of the out-dated education system.

Then we show how adverbials are added in the abverbial positions by marking each off with parentheses, as follows:

(Even though I was confused by those brand-new things,) I was certainly learning something.

My first experience of the English language started (when I was in the first grade of junior high school.)

(After the examination) I used to forget everything.

(If you need to know more about the subject, predicate, and adverbial positions, see Chapter 3.)

2. NOUNS, NOUN PHRASES, AND PRONOUNS

The subject position is nearly always filled with either a **noun phrase** or a **pronoun.** Noun phrases are explained in detail in Chapters 5 and 6 and pronouns in Chapter 7, but here is a summary of the most important points.

Noun phrases are built around **nouns,** that is, words that name anything you can think of as separate from other things—for example, people, places, things, actions, ideas. The number of nouns is infinite, because people keep making up new ones as they think of new things, and you will probably find that most of the new words you learn are nouns. They are usually identified in dictionaries by <u>n</u> in italics.

Most nouns in English have two different forms, a **singular** form, meaning only one, and a **plural** form, meaning more than one. The singular form is the one you can look up in a dictionary, and you can usually make the plural form by adding an -s. Below is a list of noun phrases, all of which are used in the subject position in the essay you have just read; the noun that each phrase is built around is underlined:

> my first <u>experience</u> of the English language
> our <u>teachers</u>
> English <u>education</u>
> <u>victims</u> like me

Of the underlined nouns, *experience* and *education* are singular, while *teachers* and *victims* are plural.

The pronouns that are used in the subject position are *I, we, you, he, she, it,* and *they.* The last four, *he, she, it,* and *they,* usually replace noun phrases—that is, they tell a reader to think of a noun phrase that has been mentioned already. *He, she,* and *it* replace singular noun phrases, while *they* replaces plural ones. For example, in Paragraph 3 of the essay above, Miura has written:

> In the midterm and final examinations, *they* copied a few sentences from the textbook . . .

Miura has used *they* to replace the noun phrase, *the teachers.* In other positions, other pronouns are used; a complete list of pronouns that can replace noun phrases is given in Chapter 7.

3. ADJECTIVES

Adjectives are identified in dictionaries by the letters <u>adj.</u> in italics. You will often find them in noun phrases, before the noun, where their function is to describe the noun. In the noun phrases below, the adjectives are underlined:

> an <u>unknown</u> world
> <u>grammatical</u> formulas
> <u>tedious</u> memorization

You may also find an adjective on its own in the predicate of a sentence.

Adjectives are discussed in Chapter 7, and you can find out about how to use them in the predicate position in Chapter 11.

4. VERBS, EXPANDED VERBS, AND AUXILIARIES

The predicate position can be filled in a number of different ways. The important point is that every predicate must begin with a <u>verb</u>. Verbs, like nouns, are identified in dictionaries, usually by the letter <u>v.</u> in italics, and they usually describe actions or states.

4.1 Simple Verbs

A simple verb consists of only one word. It is the word you find in the dictionary, with perhaps an *-s* or an *-ed* added. (How and why you need to change the form of a simple verb is explained in Chapter 8, Section 2.) The sentences below have predicates that begin with simple verbs. The verb in each case is underlined:

> My first experience of the English language <u>started</u> when I was in the first grade of junior high school

> Our teachers <u>required</u> us to memorize grammatical formulas and meanings of words

> I <u>hope</u> that I am the last victim of the out-dated education system

4.2 Expanded Verbs and Auxiliaries

Frequently you will use an **expanded verb**—that is, a verb preceded by one or more **auxiliaries.** The first auxiliary in an expanded verb is in several ways the most important: It shows what time you are talking about, it must often agree with the subject, and it controls the form of the auxiliary or verb that follows. The essay above includes many expanded verbs; we list some of them below, underlining the auxiliaries and marking the first one with an *X:*

X
<u>have been</u> learning

X
<u>was</u> confused

X
<u>was being</u> diminished

X
<u>has been</u> changing

The auxiliaries that can go first in an expanded verb are a small group. They are listed in Chapter 2, Figure 2-1, and in Chapter 8, Figure 8-4.

6

4.3 Verbs and Tense

The verbs that begin predicates always show **tense;** that is, they tell the reader what time to think about. In English, the verbs show two time frames, the present period (which you can think of as NOW) or some time in the past (which you can think of as THEN). For example, throughout the first paragraph of the essay above Miura uses present tense verbs:

> I sometimes <u>question</u> myself . . .
> I <u>am</u> shocked when I <u>count</u> . . .

These verbs show us, her readers, that we should think of the present time, that is NOW.

In the next paragraph, however, Miura moves into the past tense:

> My first experience of the English language <u>started</u> . . .
> I <u>was</u> really excited . . .

These verbs tell us that we should think of some time in the past, THEN; and she explains which time in the past she means by saying,

> When I <u>was</u> in the first grade of junior high school . . .

English has no future tense, so when Miura has something to say about the future she uses present tense verbs together with the auxiliary *will:*

> As long as English teachers <u>are</u> not concerned with the importance of practical English rather than forcing students to memorize the textbook, they <u>will continue</u> making victims like me.

By using *will*, she shows that she is making a prediction.

5. VERBALS AND VERBAL PHRASES

Verbs do not always have tense. For example, when a verb ends in *-ing* and has no auxiliary in front of it, it tells us nothing about what time to think of, and the same is true of a verb that has no ending added and has the word *to* in front of it. We call such verbs **verbals.** A verbal is often followed by a noun phrase or an adverbial, or maybe both. We call this combination a **verbal phrase;** it looks just like a predicate, except that the verb does not have tense.

Each of the following sentences from Passage 1-A contains a verbal phrase; we have underlined it and written the verbal that it begins with in italics:

> I was really excited by <u>*learning* the language</u> because I felt like I would explore an unknown world.

Our teachers required us *to memorize* grammatical formulas and meanings of words.

LEARNING STRATEGY

Remembering New Material: Linking new material with familiar concepts helps you remember.

Traditional grammar books refer to verbals by a number of different names. A verbal introduced by *to* is traditionally called an **infinitive.** One that ends in *-ing* is called a **gerund** or a **present participle,** depending on what position it is in. A third kind of verbal that ends in *-d, -t,* or *-n* is called a **past participle** or sometimes a **passive participle.** We are not, however, using these terms because we find that they cause confusion. The different kinds of verbals and verbal phrases are discussed fully in Chapter 10.

6. INDEPENDENT CLAUSES, SUBORDINATE CLAUSES, AND SUBORDINATORS

A subject and a predicate together form what is called an **independent** or **main clause.** An independent clause can stand by itself as a sentence, beginning with a capital letter and ending with a period. This fact makes it different from a **subordinate clause,** which is a subject and a predicate introduced by a word called a **subordinator**—that is, a word such as *although, because, when, which,* or *that.* (Lists of subordinators are given in Chapter 3, Section 1.2, Chapter 4, Section 2, and Chapter 6, Section 2.3.) A subordinate clause can only be part of a sentence; it cannot stand on its own. For example, the following clause is not complete by itself:

Even though I was confused by those brand-new things, . . .

We are still waiting for the rest of the sentence, which must be an independent clause. Here it is:

. . . I was certainly learning something.

In this sentence, the subordinate clause is in the front adverbial position, as many subordinate clauses are, but they can also be used in other positions. (See Chapters 3, 4, 6, and 11 for more about independent and subordinate clauses.)

Prepositional phrases all begin with **prepositions**, such as *in, on, of, out of,* or *in addition to.* What follows the preposition is usually a noun phrase or a verbal phrase in which the verbal has an *-ing* ending. Some examples from the above essay are as follows. (The preposition in each case is underlined.)

<u>for</u> eight years
<u>of</u> the English language
<u>by</u> English teachers
<u>instead of</u> memorizing to pass the English examination

8. SUMMARY

For quick reference, we list below all of the 16 terms discussed in this chapter.

adjective	preposition
adverbial	prepositional phrase
auxiliary	pronoun
expanded verb	subject
independent (main) clause	subordinate clause
noun	subordinator
noun phrase	verb
predicate	verbal phrase

Once you understand these terms, you have the essential tools for using this book. You do not have to read all the chapters in sequence, but you can use them in the order in which you need them.

Asking and Answering Questions

2

CHAPTER

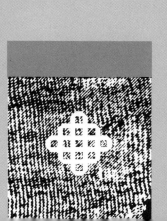

*W*hen you ask and answer questions in English, you are using two different systems—one, grammatical; the other, social. Grammatically, English has four different ways to form questions. Socially, people use questions not only to request information but also to indicate the relationship between the speakers. In this chapter, we discuss the structure of English questions and answers and also two aspects of relationships that are relevant to questions. Is the relationship formal or informal? Is it polite or impolite?

The conversations we use as examples took place in both informal and formal situations. Those headed "informal speech" are from conversations between college students, and those headed "formal speech" are from television interviews.

INFORMAL SPEECH

Conversation 2-1

A You don't like baseball?
B No.
C Don't you?
A Yeah. I like baseball.
C Which other sports do you like to watch?
A I like football. Basketball once in a while.
B You like to watch football games?
A Yeah. I like to be at them.
C Do you like to watch them in person?
A Yeah. Except it's always so noisy.

> —in *Informal Speech* by Edward C. Carterette and Margaret Hubbard
> Jones, University of California Press, 1974

Conversation 2-2

A I'm taking psychology myself with Mister Esgate.
B How do you like him?
A Oh, he's all right. He's a pretty nice guy.
B When did you graduate?
A It must have been four years ago. Yeah, it was four years ago.
B You know Verna Walker?
A Yeah. I knew her in school.
B How'd you like it there? How long did you go there?
A I went three years. I enjoyed it very much. And then when I graduated, I went to the University of Miami.
B You went where?
A University of Miami.

> —in *Informal Speech*

FORMAL SPEECH

Conversation 2-3

Frost   In that Chicago speech you asked what is the best definition of love. What would you say was the best definition?

Luce   Oh, did I give one in the speech?

Frost   Yes, you did.

Luce   What was it?

Frost   Well, luckily I did read the speech. You said, "Friendship with desire," didn't you?

Luce   Oh, yes, yes, yes. Love in my view is friendship with, if you prefer, desire, or lust, or sex.

Frost   Any of them will do.

Luce   But the durable component of love is friendship. Because obviously you can make love physically only if there is contact between bodies. You can love only if there is contact through love between hearts and minds. And bodies wear themselves out, and so does the desire. But what remains is the heart and the mind.

　　　—in *The Americans,* interview with Clare Boothe Luce by David Frost, Heinemann, 1971

1. CONSTRUCTING QUESTIONS

There are four types of questions: yes/no, *wb*-(information), rising intonation, and tag.

1.1 Yes/No Questions

Constructing yes/no questions requires several decisions: selecting the appropriate auxiliary, placing the auxiliary in front of the subject, and using the correct form of the verb. In the examples below, we underline both the auxiliary and the verb.

　　　The yes/no question model:

AUXILIARY	SUBJECT	VERB	
<u>Do</u>	you	<u>have</u>	a job?
<u>Would</u>	you	<u>want</u>	to be a psychologist?
<u>Have</u>	you	<u>been</u>	up there?
<u>Are</u>	you	<u>going</u>	to be a teacher?

1.1a Selecting the Auxiliary in Yes/No Questions

There are 20 auxiliaries, in four groups, which are used in yes/no questions. The auxiliaries carry many different kinds of information. Among other functions, the **modals** express politeness. (See Chapter 8, Section 4 for a discussion of the meaning of the auxiliaries.)

FIGURE 2-1   Auxiliaries in Yes/No Questions

DO	MODAL	HAVE	BE**
do*	will/would	have*	am*
does*	can/could	has*	is*
did	shall/should	had	are*
	may/might		was*
	must		were*

*For subject–auxiliary agreement rules, see Chapter 8, Section 3.3.
**The BE group are often verbs, not auxiliaries, but they shift in questions exactly like auxiliaries.

LEARNING STRATEGY

 Remembering New Material: Practicing aloud helps you remember more effectively.

Practice naming the groups of auxiliaries and saying out loud the members of the group, i.e, "The DO group: *do, does, did.* The MODAL group: *will, would; can, could; shall, should; may, might, must,*" etc.

Hidden Auxiliaries

A yes/no question is a variation of a statement. The statement may contain a visible auxiliary.

	AUXILIARY	SUBJECT	AUXILIARY	PREDICATE
1.		Any of them	<u>will</u>	<u>do</u>.
	<u>Will</u>	any of them		<u>do</u>?
2.		You	<u>can</u>	<u>love</u> only if there is contact through love between hearts and minds.
	<u>Can</u>	you		<u>love</u> only if there is contact through love between hearts and minds?

AUXILIARY	SUBJECT	AUXILIARY	PREDICATE
3.	It		<u>was</u> four years ago.
Was	it		four years ago?
4.	He		<u>'s</u> a pretty nice guy.
<u>Is</u>	he		a pretty nice guy?

If a statement does not have a visible auxiliary, the auxiliary will always be *do, does,* or *did.* We call these the "hidden" auxiliaries. In forming a yes/no question from a statement, you do not drop or add anything except *do, does,* or *did.*

AUXILIARY	SUBJECT	AUXILIARY	PREDICATE
1.	Bodies		<u>wear</u> themselves out.
<u>Do</u>	bodies		<u>wear</u> themselves out?
2.	He		<u>likes</u> baseball.
<u>Does</u>	he		<u>like</u> baseball?
3.	I		<u>enjoyed</u> it very much.
<u>Did</u>	I		<u>enjoy</u> it very much?
4.	I		<u>gave</u> one in the speech.
<u>Did</u>	I		<u>give</u> one in the speech?

NOTE The verb changes its form when you take out the hidden auxiliaries *does* and *did: likes* becomes *does like, enjoyed* becomes *did enjoy,* and *gave* becomes *did give.* The tense is shown by the auxiliary.

HAVE and DO

The three forms of DO (*do, does,* and *did*) and HAVE (*have, has,* and *had*) function as both auxiliaries and verbs. When they are acting as verbs, they contain the hidden auxiliaries *do, does,* and *did.*

AUXILIARY	SUBJECT	PREDICATE
1.	I	<u>do</u> all my housework. (Adapted from Passage 4-C)
<u>Do</u>	I	<u>do</u> all my housework?
2.	Every boarder	<u>had</u> to bring up her luggage to her room after she arrived. (Passage 3-A)
<u>Did</u>	every boarder	<u>have</u> to bring up her luggage to her room after she arrived?

In British English, HAVE by itself can fill the auxiliary position in a yes/no question.

British English:	<u>Have</u>	you		any tea?
	<u>Have</u>	you	<u>got</u>	any tea?

American English:	Do	you		have any tea?
	Have	you	got	any tea?

Shall

Shall is used more often in British than in American English. In yes/no questions, *shall I/we* expresses the speaker's desire and asks for confirmation from the listener. *Shall I/we* is used to make an offer or to make a suggestion about a shared activity.

Shall	I	open	the window?	[I want to open the window. Do you want me to do it?]
Shall	we	go?		[I want to go. Are you ready?]

1.1b Placement of the Auxiliary in Yes/No Questions

In yes/no questions, the auxiliary is usually in front of the subject. When the yes/no question is negative, *n't* (contracted *not*) is attached to the auxiliary. In formal or emphatic speech, *not* can occasionally remain after the subject.

FIGURE 2-2   Positive and Negative Yes/No Questions

AUXILIARY	SUBJECT	(ADVERBIAL)	PREDICATE
Positive yes/no questions (both informal and formal speech)			
Do	you		like to watch them in person?
Can	you		remember who your heroes were as a child?
Would	you		like me to teach you how to swim?
Have	you	ever	been surfing here?
Is	it		a good place to work?
Were	your parents		strict?
Negative yes/no questions (both informal and formal speech)			
Don't	you		find that encouraging?
Didn't	you		like high school?
Don't	their consciences	somehow	affect them?
Isn't	politics		the price we pay for civilization?
Couldn't	it		be that what you characterize as the evils of the modern age are just endemic in every age?
Formal or emphatic speech only			
Are	they	not	afraid of some kind of punishment?

WHEN YOU'RE TALKING

In informal conversation, you will hear yes/no questions without auxiliaries. If a nonnative speaker uses this pattern regularly in formal speech, however, it is considered a serious error.

Absent Auxiliary

[are]	You <u>going</u> to major in accounting?
[have]	You ever <u>done</u> any surfing?
[do]	You <u>prefer</u> Florida or California?

1.1c Verb Forms in Yes/No Questions

The verb form depends on the auxiliary. The rules for auxiliary–verb agreement are rigid. A mistake in auxiliary–verb agreement is considered serious. (See Chapter 8, Section 3.4 for a full discussion.)

FIGURE 2-3

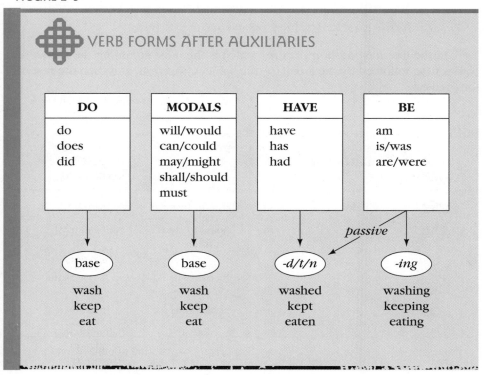

VERB FORMS AFTER AUXILIARIES

DO	MODALS	HAVE	BE
do	will/would	have	am
does	can/could	has	is/was
did	may/might	had	are/were
	shall/should		
	must		

base	base	-d/t/n	-ing
wash	wash	washed	washing
keep	keep	kept	keeping
eat	eat	eaten	eating

passive

Remembering New Material: Making a picture in your mind of models and charts helps you understand.

Look carefully at each arrow, making a picture in your mind. Then close your eyes and look at the picture in your mind. Say aloud what you see. Without checking with the model, write down what you see in your mind. Then check with the model and correct your arrow, if necessary. Repeat aloud your correction.

1.2 *Wh*-(information) Questions

When you are asking for more information than "yes" or "no," you must use one of a set of *wh*-words that ask for different kinds of information: <u>who</u>, <u>what</u>, <u>where</u>, <u>when</u>, <u>why</u>, <u>how</u>, <u>which</u>, and <u>whose</u>. The *wh*-words can also introduce phrases which ask for more specific information: <u>what kind of . . .</u>, <u>which other . . .</u>, <u>how many . . .</u>, etc. *Wh*-questions have two patterns.

1.2a Wh-questions (Not About the Subject)

In the first *wh*-question pattern, which is the most common, the *wh*-word comes first, followed by the auxiliary, the subject, the verb, and then the rest of the predicate.

FIGURE 2-4   *Wh*-questions (Not About the Subject)

QUESTION WORD	AUXILIARY	SUBJECT	PREDICATE	UNKNOWN INFORMATION
<u>Who</u>*	do	you	have for history?	[people]
<u>What</u>	are	you	going to study there?	[things/ideas]
<u>When</u>	did	you	graduate?	[time]
<u>Where</u>	were	you	born?	[place]
<u>Why</u>	do	you	like kids?	[reason]
<u>How</u>	did	you	like it?	[method/ quality/ quantity]

FIGURE 2-4   (continued)

Wh-PHRASE	AUXILIARY	SUBJECT	PREDICATE
Phrases beginning with *wh*-words ask for more specific information.			
What high school	did	you	go to?
What kind of classes	are	you	taking?
How many words a minute	can	you	type?
Which other sports	do	you	like to watch?
How many years	have	I	been studying English?

*Note on *who(m)*

In formal speech, *whom* is sometimes used instead of *who*.

Informal:	Who do you have for history?
Formal:	Whom do you have for history? (correct but rare)
Informal:	Who did you give it to?
Formal:	To whom did you give it? (correct but rare)

WHEN YOU'RE TALKING

Be sure you do not add a pronoun to your question that duplicates the information you are asking for.

INCORRECT:	Which other sports do you like to watch them?
CORRECT:	Which other sports do you like to watch?

1.2b *Wh*-questions About the Subject

The second, less frequent pattern for *wh*-questions occurs when the unknown information is the subject of the question.

FIGURE 2-5   *Wh*-questions About the Subject

QUESTION WORD = SUBJECT	AUXILIARY	PREDICATE
What		happened to you?
Who		watches television?
Who	's	got a purse? ['s is contracted has.]
Who	's	talking? ['s is contracted is.]

Note: When *who* is asking about an unknown person or persons, it takes a singular verb.

WHEN YOU'RE TALKING

1. In informal speech, you will hear native speakers ask information questions without auxiliaries. In formal speech, however, it is considered an error to omit the auxiliary.

QUESTION WORD	ABSENT AUXILIARY	SUBJECT	PREDICATE
Where	[are]	you	going?
When	[are]	you	going?
What	[are]	you	going to study there?
How	[are]	you	doing in psychology?
Which other sports	[do]	you	like to watch?

2. In informal speech, you will also hear auxiliaries contracted and attached to the *wh*-words. When the following word is *you*, the contracted *d* can sound like "j" as in *just* or *judge*. When the following word is *they*, the *d* may be lost or sound like "ed." It is important to realize that some form of the auxiliary is present, even in a reduced form.

QUESTION WORD/ AUXILIARY	SUBJECT	PREDICATE
Where'd	you	go to high school?
What'd	you	say your name was?
How'd	you	like it there?
What'd	they	do to it?

3. In informal speech, to ask for information you may not have heard correctly, use one of the *wh*-words with rising intonation.

> I went to the University of Miami last year.
> You went <u>where</u>?
> University of Miami.

> Do you know Sherry Abels?
> Sherry <u>who</u>?
> Abels.
> No.

> —in *Informal Speech*

1.3 Rising Intonation Questions

Any statement can be turned into a question. This can be done by rising intonation at the end of the statement. A rising intonation question occurs more frequently in informal than in formal speech.

INFORMAL SPEECH

Conversation 2-4

A You don't like baseball?
B No.
C Don't you?
A Oh, yeah. I like baseball.
C Which other sports you like to watch?
A I like football. Basketball once in a while.
B You like to watch football games?
A Yeah. I like to be at them.
> —in *Informal Speech*

FORMAL SPEECH

Conversation 2-5

Frost About a year ago, I think it was, I remember putting to one of your countrymen the question, "Would you mind if your daughter wanted to marry a man not of your race?" Would it worry you if she married a white man, or would you be happy, or indifferent?
Jones I wouldn't be happy about it, no. I don't think it's an unusual statement that I'm making. I'm sure most people want to see their own line, their own culture, continued.
Frost You wouldn't be happy about it?
Jones Not especially, no.
> —in *The Americans,* interview with LeRoi Jones by David Frost

1.4 Tag Questions

Tag questions are more common in British and British-related Englishes than in American English. They are complicated in both their structure and their functions.

1.4a Structure of Tag Questions

Tag questions have two structural dimensions: their form and their intonation.

The Form of Tag Questions

Tag questions are formed by adding the appropriate auxiliary and pronoun to the end of a statement. The auxiliary will either be present in the statement or be *do, does,* or *did.* The pronoun in the tag is a substitute for the subject of the statement. Positive statements have negative tags; negative statements have positive tags.

FIGURE 2-6　The Forms of Positive and Negative Tag Questions

STATEMENT	TAG AUXILIARY	PRONOUN
Positive statement/negative tag		
You have heard of it,	haven't	you?
It was marvelous,	wasn't	it?
That would be chaos,	wouldn't	it?
They keep coming back,	don't	they?
He teaches sociology,	doesn't	he?
Negative statement/positive tag		
You can't be politically independent,	can	you?
It wouldn't be that interesting,	would	it?
She didn't know what to do with herself,	did	she?

In tags following compound pronouns, there are two patterns. Compound pronouns about things—*everything, anything, something, nothing*—have *it* in a tag. Compound pronouns about people—*everyone, everybody, anyone, anybody, someone, somebody, no one, nobody*—have *they* and a plural verb in a tag.

FIGURE 2-7   Tags with Compound Pronouns

About things

Everything is ready,   isn't   it?

Nothing is ready,   is   it?

About people

Everybody is ready,   aren't   they?

Nobody is ready,   are   they?

WHEN YOU'RE TALKING

1. When you use a tag question following a statement with *there* as the subject, be sure to use *there*, not *they*, in the tag.

   There isn't any left, is there?
   There are some more, aren't there?

2. Some regional dialects of English have an invariant tag, often *isn't it?* or *is it?* in the spoken language. This is not acceptable in standard British or American English.

   INCORRECT: They mended the road, isn't it?
   CORRECT: They mended the road, didn't they?

The Intonation of Tag Questions

Tag questions can end with either a rising or a falling intonation pattern on the tag.

They're coming, aren't they?

They're not coming, are they?

They're coming, aren't they?

They're not coming, are they?

1.4b Functions of Tag Questions

Tag questions are difficult to interpret and use because their main function is to signal relationships between people. The way they do this varies by nation, region, and even social class. The variations and uses of tag questions are not yet well understood.

To understand tag questions, you need to pay particular attention to their form and their intonation.

- Form: A negative tag can have either a positive or negative answer; a positive tag expects a negative answer.

- Intonation: It can be rising or falling.

Other voice features that can influence the interpretation of tags are pitch, stress, volume (loudness and softness), speed, and intensity. Variation in voice can make the same tag question polite or impolite.

Tag questions can be arranged in three categories along a continuum from polite to impolite:

POLITE		IMPOLITE
Confirming/ Inviting/ Softening	Requesting Information	Dominating

Confirming, Inviting, Softening Tags

A confirming tag follows a statement that is expected to be true. It requests confirmation of the content of the statement. It can also invite participation in the conversation. It's a nice day, isn't it?

An inviting tag is a strong social device for initiating or encouraging conversation. It expects a response. That wasn't a bad test, was it?

A softening tag reduces the force of a statement or request. It gives the person addressed more room for personal opinion. Open the door, would you?

Requesting Information Tags

A requesting information tag with a rising pitch is a polite request for information. The answer may be either positive or negative. The same tag with a different intonation, however, may be less polite. The exam is next Tuesday, isn't it? You did your homework, didn't you?

Dominating Tags

A dominating tag question follows a statement that the speaker expects the addressee to agree with. Indeed, the information is considered obvious. In its weakest form, it expects polite, humble agreement. In its strongest form, it discourages participation and cuts off conversation. It is a put-down. <u>You will be on time tomorrow, won't you? This essay is a mess, isn't it?</u>

FIGURE 2-8   The Functions of Tag Questions

EXAMPLES	STATEMENT	TAG	INTONATION ON TAG	FUNCTION
Confirming/inviting/softening tags				
It's a nice day, isn't it?	pos	neg	down ⬊	invites agreement
That wasn't a hard exam, was it?	neg	pos	down ⬊	and participation
Open the door, would you?			up ⬈	softens request
Requesting information tags				
The exam is next Tuesday, isn't it?	pos	neg	up ⬈	polite request for information
You did your homework, didn't you?	pos	neg	down ⬊	can be demanding and less polite
The exam isn't next Tuesday, is it?	neg	pos	up ⬈	tentative and deferential
You didn't do your homework, did you?	neg	pos	down ⬊	can be accusatory
Dominating tags				
You will be on time tomorrow, won't you?	pos	neg	down ⬊	discourages participation
You haven't finished your work, have you?	neg	pos	down ⬊	accusation
This essay is a mess, isn't it?	pos	neg	down ⬊	insult

WHEN YOU'RE TALKING

1. Listen carefully to how native speakers use tag questions, but be cautious about using them yourself.
2. In casual American speech, you will hear another common tag: <u>you know</u>. Like the other tags, its functions are complicated. It can express both speaker confidence and certainty or various kinds of uncertainty. <u>You know</u> does not usually expect an answer.

    It all depends. You never know until you get on the boat. <u>You know</u>.

    Yeah. That's for sure.

    You should avoid <u>you know</u> in formal speech.

3. In the classroom, you will hear another tag: <u>okay</u>? When teachers are presenting complicated material, they sometimes check whether students have understood by using the tag question <u>okay</u>? with rising intonation. If you have understood, nod your head or do nothing. If you want more information, raise your hand.

1.5 Rhetorical Questions

Sometimes people ask questions they do not expect to be answered. These are called rhetorical questions. They are structured like questions but function as strong statements.

Conversation 2-6

Frost   Well, I'd be delighted to debate [capital punishment] with you because I think if capital punishment does deter that's a very powerful argument in its favor. We had a tremendous debate on the subject in England recently. But nobody could point to any place in the world where it could be proved that capital punishment deters. . . .

Leibowitz   Statistics don't mean a thing. <u>You want me to prove that capital punishment deters</u>? I've got the official court records right here. It'll only take a minute to read what the defendant said, that he didn't kill because he didn't want to go to the hot seat. . . .

—in *The Americans,* interview with Judge Samuel Leibowitz by David Frost

WHEN YOU ARE LISTENING

You will occasionally hear rhetorical questions both in conversation and in the classroom. The person asking the question does not expect an answer from you. If you think a question might be rhetorical, pause a second before you answer. If the person continues to talk, the question was rhetorical.

2. ANSWERING QUESTIONS

Questions may be answered in a variety of ways. Often the answer is not structurally related to the question.

2.1 Yes/No Questions

Yes/no questions may be positive or negative. Positive yes/no questions can be answered positively, negatively, or neutrally. In informal speech, a positive answer is often "yeah." Formal speech requires "yes." The following figure shows how some positive yes/no questions were answered in informal and formal speech.

FIGURE 2-9   Answering Positive Yes/No Questions

QUESTION	ANSWER POSITIVE, NEGATIVE, OR NEITHER
Informal Speech	
Can you surf?	Yeah. Well, not with a board.
Have you ever been surfing here?	Yeah. I've surfed here.
Do you surf?	No. Not here. I wouldn't.
Would you like me to teach you how to swim?	Oh. They tried.
Formal Speech	
Did I give one in the speech?	Yes, you did.
Is it a good place to work?	Yes, for me it's a great place to work.
Do you think marriage will change?	I think it's changing very rapidly.
Would you say that Martin Luther King was the black leader you respected the most?	No, I wouldn't.
Would it be right to say that the gene is to the human makeup as the thread in my suit is to the suit?	No, the best way to look at it is that a gene is like a sentence in an encyclopedia.
Can you remember who your heroes were as a child?	Mostly sporting figures.
Have people said that specifically?	The links are very tenuous.

CHAPTER 2: ASKING AND ANSWERING QUESTIONS

Negative yes/no questions contain an expectation on the part of the speaker that the answer will be negative. Therefore, it is especially important to answer negative questions clearly, particularly if your answer is <u>not</u> negative. The following figure shows how some negative yes/no questions were answered in informal and formal speech.

FIGURE 2-10   Answering Negative Yes/No Questions

QUESTION	NEGATIVE ANSWER
Informal Speech	
Did<u>n't</u> you go anywhere special?	No, but I'm going tomorrow to Disney.
Do<u>n't</u> you like challenges?	I like challenges, but not when they're like that.
Formal Speech	
Wo<u>n't</u> the market take care of our choices?	The short answer is no.

QUESTION	POSITIVE ANSWER
Informal Speech	
Do<u>n't</u> you like baseball?	Yeah. I like baseball.
Did<u>n't</u> you like high school?	I liked high school, but I liked the idea of college better.
Formal Speech	
Is<u>n't</u> that brilliant?	Marvelous.
Do<u>n't</u> you find that encouraging?	Yes, I think we have learned from that.
Do<u>n't</u> you agree that in a democracy the majority has the right to rule, admittedly with generosity, with tolerance?	We think that in Newark.

WHEN YOU'RE TALKING

Because negative yes/no questions anticipate a negative answer, be sure that your listener understands your answer, especially if it is positive. Native speakers often expand an answer to avoid ambiguity.

Haven't you finished yet?

UNCLEAR ANSWERS	CLEAR ANSWERS
No.	No, I haven't.
Yes.	Yes, I have.

2.2 *Wh*-(information) Questions

The answers to *wh*-questions can be either fragments or complete sentences. Even answers that are complete sentences often contain ellipses, that is, missing information which is supplied by the larger context. In the following conversations, the fragments are underlined, and the ellipses are filled in in square brackets.

INFORMAL SPEECH

Conversation 2-7

C   Which other sports do you like to watch?
A   I like [to watch] football. <u>Basketball once in a while</u>.

Conversation 2-8

B   How'd you like it there? How long did you go there?
A   I went [there] three years. I enjoyed it very much. And then when I graduated, I went to the University of Miami.
B   You went where?
A   <u>University of Miami</u>.

   —in *Informal Speech*

FORMAL SPEECH

Conversation 2-9

Frost   What is being happy, really?
Williams   I don't know [what being happy is]. Does anyone? I think that the greatest happiness is felt in moments of great tenderness between two people. Isn't that about as much as we know?
Frost   Is it that any one person yearns to communicate with another and it's only in those moments of love that they can most deeply communicate? Why are those the peaks of happiness?
Williams   <u>Because we all have a great desire to escape from ourselves and to feel joined to another human being</u>.
Frost   Why do we like to escape from ourselves?
Williams   <u>Because to be alone is to be lonely</u>. <u>Unless you're a writer and you have your typewriter</u>.

   —from *The Americans,* interview with Tennessee Williams by David Frost

2.3 Rising Intonation Questions

Rising intonation questions are infrequent. Rising intonation on a positive statement is open to either a positive or negative reply. Rising intonation on a negative statement anticipates a negative reply.

INFORMAL SPEECH

Conversation 2-10

B You like to watch football games?
A <u>Yeah</u>. I like to be at them.

A You do<u>n't</u> like baseball?
B <u>No</u>.

— in *Informal Speech*

FORMAL SPEECH

Conversation 2-11

Frost You would<u>n't</u> be happy about it?
Jones <u>Not</u> especially, <u>no</u>.

—from *The Americans,* interview with LeRoi Jones by David Frost

2.4 Tag Questions

The most common tag question is a positive statement followed by a negative tag. It anticipates a positive answer, which may be either direct or implied. The answer can also be negative.

2.4a Positive Statement/Negative Tag

Positive Answer

INFORMAL SPEECH

Conversation 2-12

A Mister Poole sponsors that thing, <u>doesn't he</u>?
B <u>Uh hum</u>.
C Mister Poole?
B He's a real good teacher.
C He teaches sociology, <u>doesn't he</u>?
B <u>Sociology one and two</u>.

— in *Informal Speech*

FORMAL SPEECH

Conversation 2-13

Hopper If a person can prove that they're addicted to heroin or any of those drugs, let them go to the drugstore and be able to purchase it. Let them see a doctor. Let them see a psychiatrist. They're sick. And, like, they're a problem to society.

Frost   But you would make a criminal out of the pusher if heroin became available by prescription only, <u>wouldn't you</u>?

Hopper   <u>Well, if it was legalized</u>.

—in *The Americans,* interview with Dennis Hopper by David Frost

Negative Answer

Conversation 2-14

Frost   Where is home for you now? It's Paris more than here, <u>isn't it</u>?

Baldwin   <u>Oh, no, I left Paris a long time ago</u>.

—in *The Americans,* interview with James Baldwin by David Frost

2.4b Negative Statement/Positive Tag

You will occasionally hear a negative statement followed by a positive tag. This combination anticipates a negative answer.

Negative Answer
INFORMAL SPEECH

Conversation 2-15

A   You don't waste around, <u>do you</u>?
B   <u>No</u>. Well, you know. Things happen.

—in *Informal Speech*

FORMAL SPEECH

Conversation 2-16

Frost   But you're <u>not</u> suggesting that there would be issue [a baby] in the case of every time that a couple made love anyway, <u>are you</u>?

Sheen   <u>No, no, no, of course not</u>. Not any more than every time I talk I make sense.

—in *The Americans,* interview with Fulton J. Sheen by David Frost

The answer to a negative tag question can sometimes be positive.

Positive Answer
INFORMAL SPEECH

Conversation 2-17

A   About three weeks ago it was in the newspaper. This lady, she's been blind for sixty years of her whole life, and just one day she woke up and she could see.

B Yeah. I read about that.

A It was really fascinating.

B She did<u>n't</u> know what to do with herself, <u>did she</u>?

A <u>I know</u>. She started looking at everything and wondering what it oh it was really wonderful.

> —*in Informal Speech*

FORMAL SPEECH

Conversation 2-18

Frost You ca<u>n't</u> be politically independent, <u>can you</u>?

Jones <u>Yes, you can</u>.

> —in *The Americans*, interview with LeRoi Jones by David Frost

---

WHEN YOU'RE TALKING

1. Because tag questions are hard to hear, listen carefully for them in conversations where politeness is particularly important.

2. Because tag questions are complicated in both structure and function, they can be difficult to understand correctly and to answer clearly, even for native speakers.
   - Be sure that you understand what is being asked. Ask for clarification if you need to.
   - Be sure that your answer is clear to your hearer. Your hearer will be expecting either a positive or negative answer. But you may not answer as expected, so be sure that your answer has been understood. Native speakers often elaborate an answer following a tag to avoid misunderstanding.

ACTIVITIES

I. Asking Yes/No Questions (to the teacher)

As a class activity, ask your teacher yes/no questions, which he or she will answer honestly. Keep the list of auxiliaries (Figure 2-1) in front of you, and check off each auxiliary as you use it. Do not use any auxiliary more than once, and try to use the whole set. Be sure to put the auxiliary in front of the subject, but don't worry about the form of the verb. You may want to prepare your questions in small groups.

2. Asking Yes/No Questions (to other students)

On a small piece of paper, write down the name of a famous dead person. Tape the name on a classmate's forehead or on the back of their shirt so that the classmate doesn't see the name. Your classmate will do the same to you. Walk around the room and ask yes/no questions to each of your classmates about the name on you until you have discovered who you are.

Then write down some of the questions that you asked. Check them against the yes/no question figures. Did you place the auxiliary in front of the subject? (Figure 2-2) Have you used the correct form of the verb? (Figure 2-3)

3. Asking Questions About an Occupation

On a small piece of paper, write down the name of an occupation. Tape it to a classmate's forehead or on the back of their shirt so that the classmate doesn't see the name. Your classmate will tape one to you. Walk around the room and ask questions about the occupation taped to you. You may ask any questions except "What do I do?" or "What is my occupation?"

When you have discovered your occupation, write down some of the questions you asked. Check them against the question figures, Chapter 2, Sections 1.1 and 1.2. Did you begin with a *wh*-word? If so, was the auxiliary next? (Figure 2.2) If not, was the auxiliary first? Have you used the correct form of the verb? See Figure 1.3.

4. Asking Questions About an Object

Bring to class an unusual object that your classmates will probably not recognize. Your classmates can ask you any question except, "What is it?" or "What is it used for?" The person who guesses correctly is the next person to present an object to the class.

5. Asking Questions About a Letter

Bring to class a letter you have received from outside the United States. Work with a partner. Your partner has to duplicate in the space provided on the next page all the information on the envelope, without seeing it, by asking you questions about it. When you have finished, check that the information that your partner has written down is correct.

FIGURE 2-11 An Envelope to Fill In

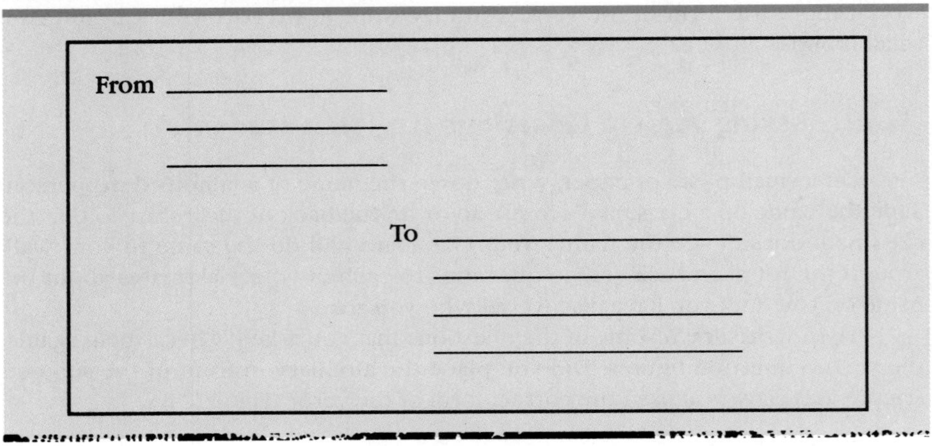

Write down some of the questions that your partner asked. Check the questions with the question tables. Are the auxiliaries placed correctly? Is the verb form correct?

6. Constructing a Questionnaire

Construct a questionnaire to discover information about a classmate's childhood. You can ask questions about family size, siblings, grandparents, education, holidays, etc. Interview several of your classmates. Your teacher may ask you to write a composition using some of the information you have learned.

7. Asking Questions About Learning English

Read Passage 1-A about learning English. Write down some questions that you can ask a partner about how they learned English. Check your questions against the question tables. Interview your partner and write a short paragraph using the information you have learned.

8. Questions in Classrooms

Listen for questions that are asked in your other classes. Write down five that were asked by the teachers and five that were asked by students. Bring them to class. Discuss in small groups the questions that were asked. What kinds of questions were asked? Which were the hardest to understand? Can your group figure out why? Were there any that you did not understand? Can your group figure out what was wanted?

9. Identifying Questions

In the following dialogue taken from Harold Pinter's play *The Dumb Waiter*, the questions have been punctuated with periods, not question marks. Identify the questions and change the periods to question marks. Your teacher may read it aloud for you. Listen to the intonation on the questions.

Passage 2-A

> *A discussion between two men waiting in a room for instructions from their boss.*

Ben   What's that.
Gus   I don't know.
Ben   Where did it come from.
Gus   Under the door.
Ben   Well, what is it.
Gus   I don't know.

> *They stare at it.*

Ben   Pick it up.
Gus   What do you mean.
Ben   Pick it up!

> *Gus slowly moves towards it, bends and picks it up.*

What is it.
Gus   An envelope.
Ben   Is there anything on it.
Gus   No.
Ben   Is it sealed.
Gus   Yes.
Ben   Open it.
Gus   What.
Ben   Open it!

> *Gus opens it and looks inside.*

What's in it.

> *Gus empties twelve matches into his hand.*

Gus   Matches.
Ben   Matches.
Gus   Yes.
Ben   Show it to me.

> *Gus passes the envelope. Ben examines it.*

CHAPTER 2: ASKING AND ANSWERING QUESTIONS

> Nothing on it. Not a word.

Gus That's funny, isn't it.

Ben It came under the door.

Gus Must have done.

Ben Well, go on.

Gus Go on where.

Ben Open the door and see if you can catch anyone outside.

Gus Who, me.

Ben Go on.

> *Gus stares at him, puts the matches in his pocket, goes to his bed, and brings a revolver from under the pillow. He goes to the door, opens it, looks out, and shuts it.*

Gus No one.

> *He replaces the revolver.*

Ben What did you see.

Gus Nothing.

Ben They must have been pretty quick.

> *Gus takes the matches from pocket and looks at them.*

Gus Well, they'll come in handy.

Ben Yes.

Gus Won't they.

Ben Yes, you're always running out, aren't you.

Gus All the time.

Ben Well, they'll come in handy then.

Gus Yes.

Ben Won't they.

Gus Yes, I could do with them. I could do with them too.

Ben You could, eh.

Gus Yes.

Ben Why.

Gus We haven't got any.

Ben Well, you've got some now, haven't you.

> —in *Plays: One* by Harold Pinter, Methuen, 1976, pp. 139–141

Making Statements: The Minimal English Sentence

3

CHAPTER

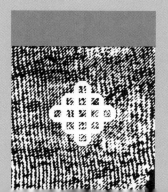

*T*he written English sentence has a subject and a predicate as its core. In all writing, the simple core is often expanded by the addition of adverbials. In speech, you can use one of these units, such as a predicate or an adverbial, as an independent unit. In writing, however, one of these alone is a fragment, a piece of a sentence. In order to punctuate correctly and avoid fragments, you need to be able to recognize subjects, predicates, and adverbials.

"Sister Ida" is a student essay that contains a variety of sentence adverbials as well as subjects and predicates.

Passage 3-A **SISTER IDA**

by Rita Law

The Ursuline Convent School is a boarding school in the U.K. When I finished my junior year in high school, I went there to continue my education.

On my first day at the Ursuline Convent School, I met Sister Ida. She was a dorm mistress for the 6th and 7th year seniors and was also in charge
5 of the school uniform. She was about 60 and was short and skinny.

Every boarder had to bring up her luggage to her room after she arrived. While I was unpacking in my room, I heard her voice from the hallway asking people to go out to listen to the rules about school uniforms. After her announcement, she asked me how I felt about leaving home. I did
10 not answer the question because I was too poor in English at that time. I was very embarrassed because all my dorm mates were watching me. After a half minute of silence, she put her hands on my shoulders. She said that I would be fine in the coming days.

We always had an hour free before study time after school. That day I
15 did not go out. I was looking in my dictionary to check every word I did not know. When Sister Ida passed in the hallway, she told me to see her in her room. She took out a short story book and told me that she wanted to give me an English lesson three times a week.

When I was in my senior year, she became my dorm mistress. Every
20 night when she came in and said goodnight, she would ask me to tell her what I did during the day or if I was homesick. From our conversation, she would correct my mistakes.

The day I left the U.K. after my graduation, she kissed me at the taxi stand and said, "God bless you" in her soft voice. Tears filled my eyes. I will
25 never forget such a good teacher and friend.

1. IDENTIFYING THE PARTS OF THE SENTENCE

1.1 The Basic Sentence

The only required units of a written English sentence are a subject and a predicate. These form the core of the sentence. To indicate the subject, we have put a box around it. To indicate the predicate, we have put an arrow above it.

SUBJECT	PREDICATE
The Ursuline Convent School	is a boarding school in the U.K. (Passage 3-A)
I	went there to finish my education. (Passage 3-A)
Every boarder	had to bring up her luggage to her room. (Passage 3-A)
Tears	filled my eyes. (Passage 3-A)

With the exception of commands and quotations, every written English sentence must have at least one subject and predicate, which together make up an **independent clause** (or **main clause**). It is called an independent clause because it can stand by itself as a sentence beginning with a capital letter and ending with a period. It is also called a main clause because it usually contains the main information in the sentence.

1.1a Identifying the Subject

You need to be able to find the subject so that you can check for three problems: fragments, run-ons, and subject–verb agreement. How do you know what the subject is? You can find the subject of a basic sentence in any one of three ways.

Sentence Topic
You can ask yourself, "What is the sentence about?" The topic of the sentence is often the subject of the main clause.

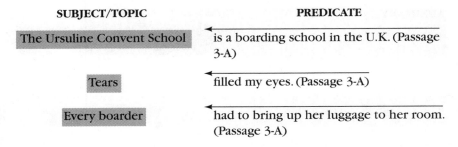

SUBJECT/TOPIC	PREDICATE
The Ursuline Convent School	is a boarding school in the U.K. (Passage 3-A)
Tears	filled my eyes. (Passage 3-A)
Every boarder	had to bring up her luggage to her room. (Passage 3-A)

Sometimes, however, the subject and the topic are not the same.

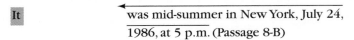

It	was mid-summer in New York, July 24, 1986, at 5 p.m. (Passage 8-B)

Who or *What* Question

You can sometimes ask yourself a *who* or *what* question about the subject.

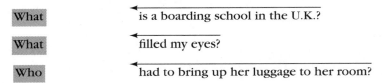

What	is a boarding school in the U.K.?
What	filled my eyes?
Who	had to bring up her luggage to her room?

In some sentences, however, this will not work.

The next thing I did was to look for a job to support myself. (Passage 6-B)

The question "What was the next thing I did?" will not produce the subject of the sentence.

Yes/No Question Test

You can always identify the subject of a sentence by making a yes/no question. (See Chapter 2, Section 1.1 for constructing yes/no questions.) The yes/no question test is particularly useful for identifying long or complicated subjects. Sometimes the question may sound awkward, however, because it would not occur in natural speech.

AUXILIARY	SUBJECT	AUXILIARY/ BE VERBS	PREDICATE

1. The next thing I did was to look for a job to support myself. (Passage 6-B)

	The next thing I did	was	to look for a job to support myself.
Was	the next thing I did		to look for a job to support myself?

AUXILIARY	SUBJECT	AUXILIARY/ BE VERBS	PREDICATE

2. The annual paper budget for each teacher is about 400 sheets for each class. (Passage 5-A)

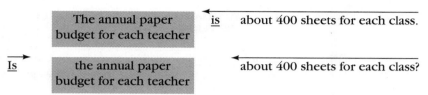

	The annual paper budget for each teacher	is	about 400 sheets for each class.
Is	the annual paper budget for each teacher		about 400 sheets for each class?

3. The remaining members and sisters, wives, mothers, and daughters of the arrested gathered together to solve some of the problems. (Passage 14-H)

	The remaining members and sisters, wives, mothers, and daughters of the arrested	gathered together to solve some of the problems.
Did	the remaining members and sisters, wives, mothers, and daughters of the arrested	gather together to solve some of the problems?

• The subject of a sentence is whatever is (1) between the auxiliary position in a statement and the auxiliary position in the yes/no question (The main verbs *am, is, are, was,* and *were* work just like auxiliaries.)

AUXILIARY	SUBJECT	AUXILIARY/ BE VERBS	PREDICATE
	There	is	one place in the world that I would like to visit again. (Passage 7-B)
Is	there		one place in the world that I would like to visit again?

or (2) between *do, does,* or *did* in the question and the verb in the statement.

	Tears	filled my eyes.
Did	tears	fill my eyes?

Occasionally, you will find a short word or phrase before the main verb. The word will often end in *-ly*. Ignore the word or phrase when you make a yes/no question. (See Chapter 11, Section 1a for a list of the common words and phrases that occur before the verb.)

AUXILIARY	SUBJECT	AUXILIARY/ BE VERBS			PREDICATE
	I	can	clearly	recall	how she looked and what she said. (Passage 4-A)
Can	I		clearly	recall	how she looked and what she said?
	She		always	wore	nice clothes. (Passage 4-A)
Did	She		always	wear	nice clothes?

WHEN YOU ARE WRITING

When you use the yes/no question to find a subject, it is not important that you have the "correct" auxiliary or the "correct" verb form in your question. You can find the subject even if you use the "wrong" auxiliary or verb form.

1.1b Finding the Predicate

The predicate of the basic sentence is what remains after you have identified the subject.

SUBJECT	PREDICATE
The Ursuline Convent School	is a boarding school in the U.K. (Passage 3-A)
The next thing I did	was to look for a job to support myself. (Passage 3-A)
The remaining members and sisters, wives, mothers, and daughters of the arrested	gathered together to solve some of the problems. (Passage 14-H)

1.2 The Expanded Sentence

Writers often expand the independent/main clause (Subject and Predicate) by adding information at the beginning or at the end of the sentence. **Sentence adverbials** are words or groups of words that add information to the entire subject and predicate. The following examples are taken from passage 3-A.

ADVERBIAL	SUBJECT	PREDICATE	ADVERBIAL
(That day)	I	did not go out.	
(After a half minute of silence,)	she	put her hands on my shoulders.	
(When Sister Ida passed in the hallway,)	she	told me to see her in her room.	
	Every boarder	had to bring up her luggage to her room	after she arrived.

To check whether a sentence has a sentence adverbial, see if there are any words that can shift from the front to the end of the sentence or from the end to the front without changing the meaning. To do this, consider the sentence by itself, in isolation from other sentences before or after it. The following examples from Passage 3-A show how sentence adverbials move.

ADVERBIAL	SUBJECT	PREDICATE	ADVERBIAL
(That day)	I	did not go out.	
	I	did not go out	(that day.)
(After a half minute of silence,)	she	put her hands on my shoulders.	
	She	put her hands on my shoulders	(after a half minute of silence.)
(When I finished my junior year in high school,)	I	went there to continue my education.	
	I	went there to continue my education	(when I finished my junior year in high school.)

ADVERBIAL	SUBJECT	PREDICATE	ADVERBIAL
	Every boarder	had to bring up her luggage to her room	(after she arrived.)
(After she arrived,)	every boarder	had to bring up her luggage to her room.	

In the above examples, think of the subject and predicate as the stable core of each sentence and the adverbial as the unit that can move around the core.

Once you have shifted any sentence adverbials from the beginning to the end of a sentence, the next unit in the sentence is almost always the subject.

2. USING SENTENCE ADVERBIALS

Sentence adverbials occur in all kinds of writing. Because of punctuation conventions, you need to recognize them, particularly when they are at the beginning of a sentence. Sometimes a comma is optional following a sentence adverbial, but sometimes it is required.

2.1 Kinds of Sentence Adverbials

You will find several kinds of sentence adverbials: single words, noun phrases, prepositional phrases, verbal phrases, and subordinate clauses. Because of punctuation conventions, the verbal phrase and the subordinate clause are the sentence adverbials that writers particularly need to recognize.

ADVERBIAL	SUBJECT	PREDICATE
• Single words (Nowadays,)	I	try to minimize the hours of sleep and prepare classes. (Passage 4-C)
• Noun phrase (That day,)	I	did not go out. (Passage 3-A)
• Prepositional phrase (From our conversation,)	she	would correct my mistakes. (Passage 3-A)

ADVERBIAL	SUBJECT	PREDICATE

• Verbal phrase

(To be
successful,) | it | is important to know how to use time
well. (Passage 4-B)

• Subordinate clause

(When I was in
my senior year,) | she | became my dorm mistress.

2.1a Verbal Phrase as Sentence Adverbial

A **verbal phrase** is a single word or phrase that begins with a verb without tense, i.e., a **verbal.** (See Chapter 10.) The verbal may be preceded by a **subordinator.** (See Section 2.1b below.)

ADVERBIAL	SUBJECT	PREDICATE
(Hoping to find food or simply soda bottles,)	the old man	was rummaging through the garbage pail. (adapted from Passage 5-B)
(While working as a shop assistant,)	Tedesse	learned a great deal about controlling her temper. (adapted from Passage 10-A)

2.1b Subordinate Clause as Sentence Adverbial

A **subordinate clause** has a subject and a predicate introduced by a **subordinator,** a word that signals that the clause cannot stand alone as an independent clause. A subordinate clause must be inside a larger sentence.

SUBORDINATE CLAUSE	INDEPENDENT CLAUSE
(When I finished my junior year in high school,)	I went there to continue my education.

Here is a list of the most frequently used subordinators for sentence adverbial clauses. Whenever you begin a clause (a Subject and a Predicate) with one of these words, it becomes a subordinate clause. You must attach a subordinate clause to an independent clause (another Subject and Predicate) that does not begin with one of these words:

after	in case	whatever
although	inasmuch as	when
as	no matter what	whenever
as if	now that	where
as . . . as	once	whereas
as though	since	wherever
because	so that	whether . . . or not
before	though	whichever
even though	unless	while
if, even if	until	whoever

2.2 Punctuating Sentence Adverbials

Following a sentence adverbial, a comma is sometimes optional, sometimes required.

2.2a Optional Commas

Short sentence adverbials—single words, noun phrases, or prepositional phrases—at the beginning of a sentence do not require commas after them, but it is never wrong to use a comma. If the adverbial is three words or more, put a comma after it.

Nowadays, I try to minimize the hours of sleep and prepare classes. (Passage 4-C)

That day I did not go out. (Passage 3-A)

From our conversation, she would correct my mistakes. (Passage 3-A)

2.2b Required Commas

In written American English, use a comma after a sentence adverbial at the beginning of a sentence if it is long, if it is a verbal phrase, or if it is a subordinate clause. (British English is more flexible about omitting commas after a short subordinate clause.)

* long:

The day I left the U.K. after my graduation, she kissed me at the taxi stand and said, "God bless you" in her soft voice. (Passage 3-A)

* verbal phrase:

Hoping to find food or simply soda bottles, the old man was rummaging through the garbage pail. (Passage 5-B)

* subordinate clause:

American:

As Sister Ida passed in the hallway, she told me to see her in her room. (Passage 3-A)

British:

When I read I like to be alone.

—in *A Comprehensive Grammar of the English Language* by Randolph Quirk *et al.,* Longman, 1985, p. 1082

WHEN YOU ARE WRITING

At the editing stage, look for a sentence adverbial at the beginning of each sentence.

Can you shift any group of words from the front of the sentence to the end without changing the meaning? If the answer is yes, ask yourself three questions:

1. Is it long?
2. Is it a verbal phrase?
3. Does it begin with a subordinating conjunction?

If the answer to any of these questions is yes, put a comma after the sentence adverbial. Remember that it is never an error to put a comma after an adverbial at the beginning of a sentence.

2.3 Functions of Sentence Adverbials

Sentence adverbials have many different functions. Front adverbials can set the scene for an event and tie the text together. End adverbials often give information about place, manner, time, reason, or purpose.

2.3a Adverbials at the Beginning of a Sentence

Setting the Scene
Front adverbials can tell the reader about the time and place of an event.

ADVERBIAL	SUBJECT	PREDICATE
(When I finished my junior year in high school,)	I	went there to finish my education. (Passage 3-A)
(On my first day at the Ursuline Convent School,)	I	met Sister Ida. (Passage 3-A)

Tying the Text Together

Front adverbials can show how one sentence is connected to the previous one.

Every boarder had to bring up her luggage to her room after she arrived. <u>While I was unpacking in my room</u>, I heard her voice from the hallway asking people to go out to listen to the rules about school uniforms. <u>After her announcement</u>, she asked me how I felt about leaving home.

<u>When I was in my senior year</u>, she became my dorm mistress. <u>Every night when she came in and said goodnight</u>, she would ask me to tell her what I did during the day or if I was homesick. <u>From our conversation</u>, she would correct my mistakes. (Passage 3-A)

2.3b Adverbials at the End of a Sentence

Information about place, manner, time, reason, or purpose is often found at the end of a sentence. That is, sentence adverbials at the end often answer the questions *where, how, when,* or *why.*

SUBJECT	PREDICATE	ADVERBIAL
Every boarder	had to bring up her luggage to her room	(<u>after she arrived</u>.) (Passage 3-A)
I	was very embarrassed	(<u>because all my dorm mates were watching me</u>.) (Passage 3-A)

3. AVOIDING FRAGMENTS

LEARNING STRATEGY

Managing Your Learning: Focusing on one point at a time will help you edit your writing.

A fragment is a piece of a sentence, not a complete sentence. Fragments are common in both informal and formal speech. In writing, however, they are unusual. Although professional writers use them occasionally, fragments are almost always considered serious errors in student writing.

In the following conversations, the fragments are underlined.

INFORMAL SPEECH

Conversation 3-1

A What street do you live on?
B Foothill. [Do] you know where the police station is? Where the city hall is?
A Yeah.
B Right around the corner from there.

　　　　—in *Informal Speech*

FORMAL SPEECH

Conversation 3-2

Williams I'm very personal as a writer, yes. I don't mean to be, I just am. Unavoidably.
Frost Which is the most personal of your plays?
Williams Perhaps *Camino Real.*
Frost Why do you pick that?
Williams It was sort of a statement of my own philosophy, a credo.
Frost What is your credo?
Williams That romanticism is absolutely essential. That we can't really live bearably without a good deal of it. It's very painful, but we need it.
Frost By romanticism do you mean fantasy?
Williams A certain amount of that and the ability to feel tenderness toward another human being. The ability to love.

　　　　—in *The Americans,* interview with Tennessee Williams by David Frost

3.1 Identifying Fragments

The first step in eliminating fragments in your writing is learning to recognize them. The best fragment test is a little complicated to learn but is very helpful.

First, find any adverbials at the beginning of your "sentence." Put them at the end.

ADVERBIAL	SUBJECT	PREDICATE	ADVERBIAL
(From our conversation,)	she	◄ would correct my mistakes. (Passage 3-A)	
	She	◄ would correct my mistakes	(from our conversation.)

ADVERBIAL	SUBJECT	PREDICATE	ADVERBIAL
(When I finished my junior year in high school,)	I	← went there to continue my education. (Passage 3-A)	
	I	← went there to continue my education	(when I finished my junior year in high school.)

Next, see if you can turn what is left into a yes/no question. In English, every independent clause (Subject and Predicate) can be turned into a yes/no question. (For information on constructing yes/no questions, see Chapter 2, Section 1.1.)

AUXILIARY	SUBJECT	AUXILIARY	PREDICATE
	She	would	← correct my mistakes.
Would →	she		← correct my mistakes?
	I		← went there to continue my education.
Did →	I		← go there to continue my education?

If you can make a yes/no question without dropping or adding anything except *do, does,* or *did,* you have a complete sentence. If you cannot make a yes/no question, you have a fragment.

WHEN YOU ARE WRITING

When you use the yes/no question test to check for a fragment, it is not important that you use the "correct" auxiliary or the "correct" form of the verb. You can identify a fragment even if you use the "wrong" auxiliary or verb form.

3.2 Correcting Fragments

In student writing, fragments are often sentence adverbials, noun phrases, predicates, or parts of predicates that have been punctuated as if they were sentences; that is, they begin with a capital letter and end with a period. In the following examples, the fragments are underlined. One possible way to correct the fragment is suggested. Often there are several ways to fix a fragment. The examples were found in or constructed from student writing.

3.2a Adverbial Fragments

An adverbial fragment is usually a subordinate clause that needs to be attached to a neighboring independent clause.

INCORRECT: I noticed the first time when he started to work that tenants from the building liked him. <u>Despite the fact that he didn't speak English perfectly and sometimes it was hard to understand words which he pronounced the wrong way</u>.

CORRECT: I noticed the first time when he started to work that tenants from the building liked him, despite the fact that he didn't speak English perfectly and sometimes it was hard to understand words which he pronounced the wrong way.

3.2b Noun Phrase Fragments

• A noun phrase needs to be attached to an independent clause.

INCORRECT: Shanghai is the leading industrial and commercial city of China. <u>And also the most important foreign trade center</u>.

CORRECT: Shanghai is the leading industrial and commercial city of China and also the most important foreign trade center.

• A noun phrase sometimes needs a *wh*-word removed in order to become a sentence. (See Chapter 6, Section 2.3 for a discussion of *wh*-words.)

INCORRECT: My boss <u>who</u> is one of those people who likes everything perfect.

CORRECT: My boss is one of those people who likes everything perfect.

3.2c Predicate Fragments

Several kinds of fragments involve predicates.

- Some languages do not require every sentence to have a subject. Speakers of those languages sometimes leave out the subject of a sentence. In written English, however, every predicate must have a visible subject. Most often, *it* or *there* needs to be added.

INCORRECT: In Columbia is a class that teaches you religion and all about God.

CORRECT: In Columbia there is a class that teaches you religion and all about God.

- A second kind of predicate fragment needs to have a verb with tense, usually a form of BE, added to it.

INCORRECT: Sometimes, she picks out another's defects, and she mimics another's way of talking. Her character diametrically opposed to mine.

CORRECT: Sometimes, she picks out another's defects, and she mimics another's way of talking. Her character is diametrically opposed to mine.

INCORRECT: In the class there two ladies that are very good cooks.

CORRECT: In the class there are two ladies that are very good cooks.

- A third kind of predicate fragment needs to have a subject and verb added to it.

INCORRECT: Sonia saw me as a spoiled child. That I was very possessive with my mom.

CORRECT: Sonia saw me as a spoiled child. She thought that I was very possessive with my mom.

3.2d "Extra Information" Fragments

Extra information added at the end of the predicate is sometimes punctuated as if it were a sentence. These fragments need to be attached to the previous main clause by placing a comma in front of them.

- a list as example

INCORRECT: Most people don't have enough money to afford a mechanic just for the simple basic needs of a car. For instance, changing the motor oil and the oil filter or just cleaning the carburetor.

CORRECT: Most people don't have enough money to afford a mechanic just for the simple basic needs of a car, for instance, changing the motor oil and the oil filter or just cleaning the carburetor.

- *wh*-clause

INCORRECT: All these influences of French, Spanish, and Dutch are reflected in the language the folks speak. <u>Which is Papiamento</u>.

CORRECT: All these influences of French, Spanish, and Dutch are reflected in the language the folks speak, which is Papiamento.

- *-ing* verbal phrase

INCORRECT: It is one of the world's great ports. <u>Lying south of the mouth of the Yangtze River</u>.

CORRECT: It is one of the world's great ports, lying south of the mouth of the Yangtze River.

WHEN YOU ARE WRITING

If you write fragments that you cannot identify, check a piece of your own writing in the following way. For every group of words that begins with a capital letter and ends with a period, ask yourself these questions:

1. Does it begin with a group of words that could be moved to the end without changing the meaning? If it does, you have found a sentence adverbial. Move the adverbial to the end.
2. Can you now make a yes/no question without deleting or adding anything but *do, does,* or *did?* If so, you have a sentence.
3. If you cannot make a yes/no question, check your fragment to see what is missing.
   a. Can it be attached to a neighboring sentence?
   b. Do you need to add something to it? Or take something out?
4. If you add something or take something out, start at step 2 again.

 ACTIVITIES

I. Identifying Subjects and Predicates

In the following sentences, identify the subjects and predicates by placing a box around the subject and drawing an arrow above the predicate. If you have any difficulty finding the subject, use the yes/no question test. The first sentence has been done for you. Check your work with a partner or your teacher.

a. The Ursuline Convent School is a boarding school in the U.K.

b. I was very embarrassed because all my dorm mates were watching me.

c. She said that I would be fine in the coming days.

d. Tears filled my eyes.

e. I will never forget such a good teacher and friend.

2. Identifying Subjects

In the following paragraph, identify the subject of each sentence by drawing a box around it. If you need to, use the yes/no question test. The first one has been identified for you. Check your work with a partner, a small group, or your teacher.

Passage 3-B   **NIGHT SCENE**

by Jocelyn Cruz

The soaked black road was shiny and slick from the rain. The light was reflecting off the glossy pavement. The red lights from the back of the cars and the white bright headlights from the front were beaming down the highway. The dim yellow street lamp glared from above the road and hit the

5   roofs of the cars. All the lights seemed to streak down the highway, leaving a mix of colors on the road. The light seemed like a blur because it reflected against the wet puddles. I was keeping an eye on one spot of the road which was a huge puddle. A van drove over the spot I was observing. It seemed like a splash resembling droplets of light.

LEARNING STRATEGY

Managing Your Learning: Practicing what you already know keeps your progress steady.

3. Identifying Adverbials

In the following sentences, identify all the sentence adverbials by placing parentheses around them. The first sentence has been done for you.

You may want to work individually first, then check with a partner and finally with your teacher.

a. (When I finished my junior year in high school,) I went there to continue my education.

b. On my first day at the Ursuline Convent School, I met Sister Ida.

c. Every boarder had to bring up her luggage to her room after she arrived.

d. While I was unpacking in my room, I heard her voice from the hallway asking people to go out to listen to the rules about school uniforms.

e. After her announcement, she asked me how I felt about leaving home.

f. I was very embarrassed because all my dorm mates were watching me.

g. After half a minute of silence, she put her hands on my shoulders.

h. That day I did not go out.

i. When Sister Ida passed in the hallway, she told me to see her in her room.

j. When I was in my senior year, she became my dorm mistress.

k. Every night when she came in and said goodnight, she would ask me to tell her what I did during the day or if I was homesick.

l. From our conversation, she would correct my mistakes.

m. The day I left the U.K. after my graduation, she kissed me at the taxi stand and said, "God bless you" in her soft voice.

4. Punctuating Sentence Adverbials

Identify the sentence adverbials in the following paragraph. Put commas where they are needed. Which commas are optional and which are required?

You may work individually or in pairs. Be sure you discuss your work with a partner or in a small group. Check with your teacher.

Passage 3-C   **MY NEIGHBORHOOD**

by Fanny Chung

In the kitchen of the front apartment downstairs a woman is standing in front of the sink washing vegetables. On the other side something is cooking in a saucepan on top of the stove. I think it is stewed chicken because I can smell it. She is probably making traditional Italian food. She is
5   working diligently to prepare the dinner. I think she works in an office because she is dressed in a nice blouse and a skirt. She is probably just home from work. In another moment she is out of my sight. After a few seconds she is there again. This time she is talking on a wireless telephone supported by one of her shoulders. To save time her experienced hands are continuously
10 cutting the carrots and tomatoes.

5. Punctuating Sentence Adverbials

Identify the sentence adverbials in the following essay. Put commas where they are needed. Which commas are required and which are optional?

Work first individually, then discuss your work with a partner or small group. Check with your teacher. (For a correct version of this passage, see Appendix 2.)

Passage 3-D   **OUR LANGUAGES AND CUSTOMS**

by Freddy Sampson

When people immigrate to the United States they might consider themselves Americans. This does not mean that they should forget their own language and customs. Because customs and language are inherited through the passage of time and past generations they should not be dismissed lightly.

5   The primary customs that any immigrant coming into the U.S. should hold dear are their own. It makes no sense to change your ideas and beliefs if you think they are right. When it comes to your language two languages are better than one. If you speak two languages you could get special privileges when applying for some jobs. Having your own language and customs could

10   be beneficial.

The fact that you must learn the American language and customs is acceptable. They should be assimilated to your own customs and language, not used to replace them. Since there are no perfect customs or languages to dismiss your own customs or language for those of the U.S. would be a fatal

15   mistake. Because knowledge is power you should not throw it away once you have it.

Your language and customs are a part of you, your parents, their parents, and so on. They are the roots on which your past is built. No person or country should take them away from you.

6. Identifying Subjects (advanced)

In Activity 5, you have identified sentence adverbials. Now identify the subjects of the independent clauses, and draw a box around each subject, as we have done in the example at the top of page 57. Many of the subjects are long and complicated. If you have difficulty, use the yes/no question test. Draw a box around each subject.

Work first by yourself. Then discuss your work with a partner or small group. Be sure you check with your teacher.

(When people immigrate to the United States,) they ← might consider themselves Americans. (Passage 3-D)

7. Placing Sentence Adverbials

In the following paragraphs taken from an essay, the front sentence adverbials have been removed and replaced by a blank. The sentence adverbials are listed following the essay. Match the adverbials and the sentences by writing the adverbials in the blanks. (One of the adverbials must be used twice.) Add commas where they are needed.

You may work individually or with a partner or small group. Check with your teacher. You may also start in class and finish at home. (For a correct version of this passage, see Appendix 2.)

Passage 3-E **A VALUABLE EXPERIENCE**

by Than Than Oo Ma

(1) _____ my class teacher called me in and reminded me that I was not only going to represent my elementary grade but also my school's name. I went to sleep early that night, thinking and dreaming about the first prize.

5 (2) _____ my parents took me to the City Hall, where I had to compete with other students. The huge stage and the many people frightened me. (3) _____ my knees were shaking and my voice was trembling. I was unable to face all kinds of eyes: smiling eyes, curious eyes, jealous eyes, quiet eyes. Those eyes made me lose control.

10 (4) _____ I realized that all my hope was gone. (5) _____ I saw my teacher's angry, reddish face. She yelled at me in front of the other students. "What have you done to me? What have you done to the school? You are a useless student."

(6) _____ my mom cheered me up. She said there was

15 nothing that I couldn't do. I could even make a rod of iron into a fine, small needle. Nevertheless, (7) _____ I decided I must get the prize the next year.

(8) _____ I won the prize. (9) _____ I wasn't afraid to face all those eyes. I could control myself very well as a result of my

20 experience the previous year.

(10) _____ I received big hugs, sweet smiles, and many kisses from my fifth grade class teacher, my parents, and also my fourth grade teacher. The prize, on which I had spent two years of my strength and energy, was in my hand.

25   My picture is hanging in the school library among the other honor students. (11) _____ I remember the day that I lost the prize and the day that I won it.

SENTENCE ADVERBIALS

on the way home	when I arrived on the stage
every time I see that picture	at the end of that day
the following year	after finishing my performance
before the competition that night	the next day
when I came down from the stage	at that time

8. Recognizing Fragments

The following essay is divided into "sentences," each beginning with a capital letter and ending with a period. But a number of them are not grammatical sentences; they are fragments. Identify the fragments by underlining them.

If you need to, use the yes/no question test. If you can make a yes/no question without dropping or adding anything but *do, does,* or *did,* you have a complete sentence.

Correct the fragments that you find and check your work with a partner, then the teacher.

Passage 3-F   **MY COUSIN SONIA**

by Pilar Gonzales

(1) The relationship between my cousin Sonia and me has changed a lot in the last three years.

(2) When I was young. (3) I admired my cousin Sonia. (4) Because she was the model that I always had as I grew older. (5) She was a good daughter
5   and a very good student. (6) She came to study here in the U.S. and got a master's degree in language. (7) She married a professional man and had a beautiful wedding. (8) Their first child was born after five years of marriage. (9) I saw her life as the perfect model.

(10) Sonia saw me as a spoiled child. (11) That I was very possessive
10   with my mom. (12) Also that I didn't know how to behave around adults. (13) Because I was always embarrassing my mom.

(14) Now our relationship has changed. (15) She sees me as an adult and responsible person. (16) We talk about things that are important in a marriage, and I still admire her very much.

9. Recognizing and Correcting Fragments

The following paragraph contains two fragments. Correct them by attaching them to a neighboring main clause or by adding what is missing. If you are not sure whether or not you have found a fragment, use the yes/no question test. Check your work with a partner.

Passage 3-G　　　　　**MY MOTHER**

by Wilda Ramirez

My mother's name is Margarita. She is tall. She has green eyes and her hair is dirty blond. She was the third child of six in her family. When she was seventeen years old, in 1953, she had to work to help support her family. She was working as a cashier at the gas station, but at the same time she was in
5　high school. Four years later a wife.

Although she has a full-time job working at a factory in Kearny. She is also an excellent housewife and mother: cooking, cleaning, taking care of three children's education and going to the mall with us.

10. Recognizing and Correcting Fragments

The following essay contains 14 fragments. Correct them by attaching them to a neighboring main clause or by adding what is missing. If you are not sure whether or not you have found a fragment, use the yes/no question test. You can do this exercise over several class meetings. Always check your work with a partner or your teacher. (For a correct version of this passage, see Appendix 2.)

Passage 3-H　　　　　**CURAÇAO**

by Sou Chang

Curaçao is the island where I was born. Is situated just to the north of the Venezuelan coast. Curaçao had some French influence. Actually, if one looks at the name Curaçao, is of French origin. Later in history when the slave trade flourished, it became a Dutch colony. Up to the present is still a
5　Dutch colony.

All these influences of French, Spanish, and Dutch are reflected in the language the folks speak. Which is Papiamento. Is a mixture of all the languages mentioned and is also mixed with Portugese and Indonesian. Although Papiamento is spoken, the official language is Dutch.

10   The people from the island are so warm and friendly. The population consists of descendants of the original Indians from the island. As well as descendants of slaves, Portugese, Jews, Chinese, and Dutch. All these races get along well with each other. The people of the island are very helpful. If one is stuck with some problem, the people are ready to help out. The

15   people on the island like to make one feel at home.

One thing I also miss is waking up in the morning with the birds singing at my window. I grew up on a farm in Curaçao. In the morning I would wake up smelling fresh brewed coffee, fresh baked eggs, and toast. Later I would take a morning walk barefoot in the countryside. The plant life

20   on our farm is typically tropical. We have coconut trees and big mushroom-shaped trees. Which give shade against the lovely scorching tropical sun.

A legendary site in the harbor of Curaçao is the Floating Market. It consists of Venezuelan boats. The merchants are there every morning selling and praising the fresh tropical fruits. Such as papayas, oranges, bananas,

25   pineapples, and others. They also have vegetables. Such as tomatoes and cucumbers. There are also the fishermen selling their fish. Such as red snapper and shellfish, especially conch. The city made marble tables for them at the shore so they can display their goods. To make the scene more colorful, the merchants extend some multicolored drapes over their heads and tables.

30   They use the drapes as a roof. To protect them from the tropical sun.

Curaçao is a simple and yet colorful and happy island. I miss the island. Whenever I think of Curaçao, brings back those nice and fond memories of the island. But one day I will take a long vacation. Go back. Relax. And I will enjoy every bit of it.

(fragments created by the authors)

Connecting Clauses

CHAPTER 4

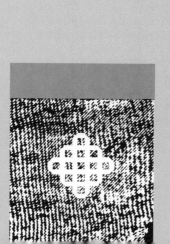

When you write in English, you create a series of independent clauses, like this:

Subject Predicate   Subject Predicate   Subject Predicate

You probably have some adverbials as well, like this:

Adverbial Subject Predicate Adverbial Subject Predicate Adverbial

To make clear where one sentence ends and another begins, English has conventions for punctuation. Professional writers sometimes break these conventions, but student writers are expected to follow them.

To discuss how to connect clauses, we use examples from the following passage.

Passage 4-A   **HER WORDS**

by Ayako Nakashizuka

I don't remember her name, but I can clearly recall how she looked and what she said.

Four years ago, just after I had come to New York from Japan, I went to an English school. I had never lived in a foreign country before, so it was a new experience for me to have classmates who were from different countries. The class I attended was an elementary one. Actually, I couldn't speak or understand English at all. All I could do was some reading.

She was there as the oldest student in my class. She always wore nice clothes; they were in good taste and looked expensive. She looked gracious in those clothes, not only because she was tall like a fashion model but also because she walked beautifully. I enjoyed seeing her clothes every day. I found out why she wore those nice clothes. She said she was running a clothes shop with her husband. She was from Russia and was studying English for her business.

One day, two students in my class started guessing each other's age, and soon other students too began to guess each other's age. Most students were in their teens or twenties; only she was in her forties. After everyone had told their own age, she looked at our faces with a warm smile and said joyously, "Oh, children!" Since the expression was new to me, it made me excited and pleased.

In my country, every man and woman seems to believe that younger women are always better than older women. Men are eager to marry younger women even if the men are quite elderly. A company attempts to hire younger women. If you read Japanese newspapers, you will be surprised by classified ads which read, "Hiring women under twenty-six years of age"; surprisingly, this "twenty-six" could be even younger, such as "twenty-two." Can you believe that a twenty-five year old woman could say, "I envy you. You are younger than me," to a twenty-two year old woman! I can say that every woman in my country worries about getting old and is almost scared by it.

Her words released me from the "must-be-young disease." She may not remember me since I was a very quiet student, nor does she know her words are still alive in my heart and have changed my thinking. I think it will be fun to say, "Oh, children!" to a sixty-year old person when I am eighty.

Two years after I had quit going to the English school, I happened to see her carrying a lot of clothes in her arms. She still walked beautifully and graciously. She didn't notice me, but I said "thank you" to her in my mind.

1. CONNECTING INDEPENDENT CLAUSES

There are five ways to connect independent clauses in modern English. The first three described below are used in both informal and formal writing. The last two are found mainly in formal writing. We have used the letter **S** to represent the subject of an independent clause and the letter **P** to represent the predicate.

1.1 With Periods (SP. SP.)

The basic way to link two independent clauses is to put a period between them. The content of the clauses shows how they are related.

> She said she was running a clothes shop with her husband. She was from Russia and was studying English for her business. (Passage 4-A)

Not using any punctuation between two independent clauses produces a **run-on** (or fused) **sentence.** This a serious error. It can be corrected with a period.

INCORRECT: She said she was running a clothes shop with her husband she was from Russia and was studying English for her business.

CORRECT: She said she was running a clothes shop with her husband. She was from Russia and was studying English for her business.

1.2 With Commas and Coordinators (SP, + SP.)

Another common way to combine two independent clauses is to use a comma and a **coordinator.** The plus sign (+) in SP, + SP. represents one of the coordinators.

> I don't remember her name, <u>but</u> I can clearly recall how she looked and what she said. (Passage 4-A)

1.2a The Coordinators

There are seven coordinators:

for, and, nor, but, or, yet, so.

The first letters of the coordinators together spell FANBOYS. First write down the letters F-A-N-B-O-Y-S in a column, then fill in the words.

1.2b Punctuating the Coordinators

When you are joining two independent clauses with a coordinator, you must also use a comma. Not doing so produces two errors.

Comma Splice
Using only a comma between two independent clauses is called a **comma splice.** This is a serious error.

> INCORRECT: I don't remember her name, I can clearly recall how she looked and what she said.

> CORRECT: I don't remember her name**,** <u>but</u> I can clearly recall how she looked and what she said. (Passage 4-A)

Although in some languages it is correct to link several independent clauses together with commas (SP, SP, SP, SP.), this is rare in modern English. A comma followed by *and* must precede the last independent clause.

> Bands are playing, singers are singing**,** <u>and</u> the whole crowd is enjoying the ride. (Passage 5-C)

Omitted Comma
Using only a coordinator without a comma between two independent clauses is considered an error unless the two clauses are both very short.

> INCORRECT: Almost all the expensive clothes had alarms attached to them <u>but</u> there were small items like underwear, stockings, and scarves that could be slipped out easily.

CORRECT: Almost all the expensive clothes had alarms attached to them, <u>but</u> there were small items like underwear, stockings, and scarves that could be slipped out easily. (Passage 10-A)

WHEN YOU ARE WRITING

And is used in lists as well as between independent clauses. In lists of two items, do <u>not</u> put a comma before *and*.

apples and oranges

In lists of more than two items, a comma is usually used before *and* in American English but not in British English.

American: apples, oranges, and bananas
British: apples, oranges and bananas

(For more about compounding, see Chapter 14.)

1.2c Using the Coordinators (FANBOYS)

The Meaning of the Coordinators
The coordinators express the most basic ways of relating ideas expressed in independent clauses. Four are both formal and informal; three are mainly formal.

INFORMAL AND FORMAL	FORMAL
and	
but	yet
so	for
or	nor

Adding: *and*

One day, two students in my class started guessing each other's age, <u>and</u> soon other students too began to guess each other's age. (Passage 4-A)

Contrasting: *but* and *yet*

I don't remember her name, <u>but</u> I can clearly recall how she looked and what she said. (Passage 4-A)

We struggle during our entire life to leave an inheritance to our children, <u>yet</u> we are unable to transmit to them our knowledge, our experience, and our wisdom. (Passage 7-G)

Concluding: *so*

I had never lived in a foreign country before, <u>so</u> it was a new experience for me to have classmates who were from different countries. (Passage 4-A)

Giving alternatives: *or* and *nor*

Either we get an education to learn and develop the skill that will be later applied, <u>or</u> we learn on site. (Passage 10-C)

She may not remember me since I was a very quiet student, <u>nor</u> does she know her words are still alive in my heart and have changed my thinking. (Passage 4-A)

Note: Nor requires inversion. That is, following *nor,* the auxiliary comes before the subject.

Stating reason or purpose: *for*

Witness the present Mexican war, the work of comparatively a few individuals using the standing government as their tool, <u>for</u>, in the outset, the people would not have consented to this measure. (14-C)

Beginning a Sentence with a Coordinator

It is increasingly acceptable to begin sentences with coordinators, particularly *and, but, so,* and *yet.* But in formal writing, use transition words such as *however* to begin a sentence.

With a box of popcorn in my hand, I listened to my cousin telling me about the places she visited and the people she met while she was in Europe. <u>But</u> I was distracted when I noticed an old man from afar off. (Passage 5-B)

The Galapagos Islands are on the equinoctial line. This gives the idea of very torrid, hot weather. <u>However</u>, this is not so; thanks to the cold Humboldt current, the weather is springlike. (Passage 14-A, Part 2)

WHEN YOU ARE WRITING

When you are editing your writing, you must check the borders between your independent clauses.

1. If you have two independent clauses separated only by a comma, either change the comma to a period and capitalize the first word of the next sentence or add a coordinator (FANBOYS) after the comma.
2. If you have used a coordinator (FANBOYS) between two independent clauses, the coordinator (FANBOYS) should be preceded by a comma unless both clauses are very short.
3. If you have trouble recognizing an independent clause (SP), use the yes/no question test. (See Chapter 3, Section 3.1 on how to use the yes/no question test.)

- If you say the yes/no question aloud, your voice will probably go up at the end of your first independent clause. That is where you must check your punctuation. If you can make another yes/no question out of what follows, you have two independent clauses.
- When you use the yes/no question test for editing your writing, it is not important that you use the "correct" auxiliary or verb form.

1.3 With Periods and Transition Words or Phrases (SP. T, SP.)

Relationships between ideas are often expressed by more specific words than the coordinators. These are called **transition words or phrases.** (Some of these are also called **conjunctive adverbs.**)

The class I attended was an elementary one. <u>Actually</u>, I couldn't speak or understand English at all. (Passage 4-A)

1.3a Some Transition Words and Phrases

Following is an alphabetized list of some of the most common transition words and phrases in English. Because there are so many of them, it is not possible to give a complete list.

FIGURE 4-1   Some Transition Words and Phrases in Alphabetical Order

above all*	at the same time	in addition*	nevertheless*
accordingly*	besides	incidentally	next
actually	certainly	in conclusion*	on the contrary*
additionally*	consequently	in consequence*	on the other hand
after all	even so	in contrast*	otherwise*
afterwards	eventually	indeed*	similarly
again	finally	in fact	specifically*
also	first	in other words	so
alternatively*	for example	in particular	still
apparently	for instance	in spite of that	that is
as a	for this reason	instead	them
consequence*	fortunately	in that case	therefore*
as a result*	further	in the meantime	thus*
as an	furthermore*	likewise*	to conclude*
illustration*	hence*	meanwhile	undoubtedly
at any rate	however*	moreover*	

*Used mainly in formal writing

1.3b Functions of Transition Words and Phrases

Transition words show more specifically than coordinators how the ideas of two independent clauses are related. Below are some of the most widely used, listed according to meaning. The transition words and phrases found mainly in formal writing have been starred.

FIGURE 4-2 Some Transition Words and Phrases According to Meaning

ADDING (*and*)	CONTRASTING (*but*)	CONCLUDING (*so*)
additionally*	at any rate	accordingly*
also	even so	as a result*
besides	however*	as a/in consequence*
further	in contrast*	consequently*
furthermore*	in spite of that	in conclusion*
in addition	instead	for this reason
in the same way	nevertheless*	hence*
likewise	on the contrary*	therefore*
moreover*	on the other hand	thus*
similarly	otherwise	to conclude*
	still	

COMPARING	ADDING ADDITIONAL DETAIL		SUMMARIZING
by comparison	as an illustration*	in other words	briefly
equally	for example	in particular	in a word
in the same way	for instance	specifically*	in brief
likewise	indeed*	that is	in short
similarly	in fact		in summary*
			to summarize*

INDICATING SEQUENCE (LOGICAL)		EXPRESSING OPINION
first(ly), second(ly), third(ly) . . .	then	actually
	above all	apparently
next	in conclusion	certainly
finally	to illustrate	(un)fortunately
lastly	that is	of course
		undoubtedly

FIGURE 4-2   (continued)

INDICATING SEQUENCE IN TIME			
SAME TIME	**EARLIER TIME**	**NOW**	**LATER TIME**
at the same time	before that	at this time	after that
concurrently*	earlier	at present*	afterwards
simultaneously*	first	now	in the future
	formerly*	nowadays	later
	previously*	these days	next
			soon
			subsequently*
			then

LEARNING STRATEGY

Testing Hypotheses: To make sure you understand some small differences in meaning, check with a native speaker.

WHEN YOU ARE WRITING

1. There are subtle differences between transition words and phrases on the same list. If you are unsure about the precise meaning of a transition word or phrase, check your dictionary or consult a native speaker.
2. When you are writing formally, you should use some of the starred transition words and phrases. But be careful. If you use too many in one piece of writing, it sounds pompous and may annoy your reader.

1.4 With Semicolons and Transition Words or Phrases (SP; T, SP.)

This is a variation of the previous pattern: SP. T, SP. A semicolon (;) before a transition word or phrase is used occasionally in formal writing to indicate that the independent clauses are closely related.

　　　The class I attended was an elementary one; <u>actually</u>, I couldn't speak or understand English at all. (Passage 4-A)

NOTE　When a transition word or phrase precedes an independent clause (SP), it is usually followed by a comma. If it "interrupts" a clause, however, it must be preceded and followed by a comma.

> I don't like to read. However, I do like to write. (Passage 4-E)

> I don't like to read. I do, however, like to write.

WHEN YOU ARE WRITING

When you are writing formally, you should use some transition words and phrases in addition to the coordinators. Whenever you have used a transition word or phrase to join two independent clauses, check the following two points.

1. Is the transition word or phrase preceded by a period (.) or a semicolon (;)? If so, it is correct.
2. If all you have is a comma (,), change it to a semicolon (;).
3. Is the transition word or phrase followed by a comma? If not, add one.

1.5 With Semicolons (SP; SP.)

The last and least frequent way to join two independent clauses is with a semicolon only. This occurs occasionally in formal writing when the content of the two independent clauses is very similar.

> Most students were in their teens or twenties; only she was in her forties. (Passage 4-A)

FIGURE 4-3

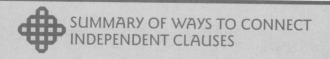

SUMMARY OF WAYS TO CONNECT INDEPENDENT CLAUSES

There are only five ways to connect independent clauses. The first three occur in both informal and formal writing. The last two occur mainly in formal writing. You **must** use one of these patterns at every border between two independent clauses.

1. **SP. SP.** A common pattern used in all writing.

> I enjoyed seeing her clothes every day. I found out why she wore those nice clothes. (Passage 4-A)

FIGURE 4-3   (continued)

2. **SP, + SP.** Another common pattern used in all writing. The plus sign (+) stands for one of a small set of short connecting words called coordinators. Together, their first letters spell *FANBOYS.*

for, and, nor, but, or, yet, so

I had never lived in a foreign country before, <u>so</u> it was a new experience for me to have classmates who were from different countries. (Passage 4-A)

3. **SP. T, SP.** *T* stands for a transition word or phrase. Some transition words and phrases are found in both formal and informal writing, others only in formal writing.

The class I attended was an elementary one. <u>Actually</u>, I couldn't speak or understand English at all. (Passage 4-A)

4. **SP; T, SP.** This is a formal variation of pattern (3). It is used occasionally in formal writing.

The class I attended was an elementary one; <u>actually</u>, I couldn't speak or understand English at all. (Passage 4-A)

During the interview the accent problem came out again; <u>however</u>, she promised to help me get a job. (Passage 6-B)

5. **SP; SP.** This pattern is used infrequently in formal writing when the ideas in the two independent clauses are closely connected.

Most students were in their teens or twenties; only she was in her forties. (Passage 4-A)

2. CONNECTING INDEPENDENT AND SUBORDINATE CLAUSES

All writers regularly use combinations of independent and subordinate clauses. Subordinate clauses, like independent clauses, have a subject and a predicate; however, subordinate clauses begin with **subordinators** (also called **subordinating conjunctions**). In the following examples, the subordinate clauses are underlined and the subordinators are in italics.

Four years ago, <u>just *after* I had come to New York from Japan</u>, I went to an English school. (Passage 4-A)

Men are eager to marry younger women <u>*even if* the men are quite elderly</u>.

A company attempts to hire younger women. <u>*If* you read the Japanese newspapers</u>, you will be surprised by classified ads which read, "Hiring women under twenty-six years of age"; surprisingly, this "twenty-six" could be even younger, such as "twenty-two." (Passage 4-A)

Here is a list of the most common subordinators that begin adverbial clauses.

FIGURE 4-4   Adverbial Subordinators

after	in case	whatever
although	inasmuch as	when
as	no matter what	whenever
as if	now that	where
as . . . as	once	wherever
as though	since	whereas
because	so that	whether . . . or not
before	though	whichever
even though	unless	while
if, even if	until	whoever

Any independent clause can be preceded or followed by an adverbial clause. It may also be "interrupted" by one.

Men, *even if* they are quite elderly, are eager to marry younger women. (Passage 4-A)

2.1 Punctuating Adverbial Clauses

The punctuation of an adverbial clause depends on whether it precedes or follows the independent clause. In American English, a subordinate clause at the beginning of a sentence is usually followed by a comma. (For information about how to identify sentence adverbials, see Chapter 3, Section 1.2.)

adverbial

After everyone had told their own age **,** she looked at our faces with a warm smile and said joyously, "Oh, children!" (Passage 4-A)

adverbial

Since the expression was new to me **,** it made me excited and pleased. (Passage 4-A)

In contrast, subordinate clauses that follow the independent clause are not usually preceded by a comma unless they are very long.

adverbial

Men are eager to marry younger women *even if* the men are quite elderly. (Passage 4-A) *adverbial*

She looked gracious in those clothes, <u>not only *because* she was tall like a</u> <u>fashion model but also *because* she walked beautifully.</u> (Passage 4-A)

2.2 Using Adverbial Clauses

An adverbial clause at the beginning of a sentence often indicates how the ideas of the two neighboring sentences are related. That is, it can function the same way as transition words and phrases.

One day, two students in my class started guessing each other's age, and soon other students too began to guess each other's age. Most students were in their teens or twenties; only she was in her forties. <u>*After* everyone had</u> <u>told their own age</u>, she looked at our faces with a warm smile and said joyously, "Oh, children!" <u>*Since* the expression was new to me</u>, it made me excited and pleased. (Passage 4-A)

WHEN YOU'RE TALKING

You will hear *though* used at the end of a sentence to indicate a contrast.

A   [If] You make one little adding mistake on the first day. . . . It just throws everything all off.
B   I like it [accounting] <u>though.</u> I like intricate things like that.

   —in *Informal Speech*

Though is rarely used in this way in writing. *Although* is never used in this way.

WHEN YOU ARE WRITING

If you have used *although*, ask yourself these questions:

1. Have you put a comma after it? If so, you have made a mistake. *Although* is always a subordinator, never a transition word.
2. Have you used *but* in the same sentence? If you have, cross out one or the other because they mean the same thing.

In order to punctuate your writing correctly, you must know the differences among the following three lists.

FIGURE 4-5

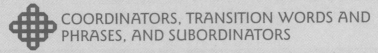

COORDINATORS, TRANSITION WORDS AND PHRASES, AND SUBORDINATORS

1. Coordinators (FANBOYS)

   for, and, nor, but, or, yet, so

   I don't remember her name, <u>but</u> I can clearly recall how she looked and what she said. (Passage 4-A)

   *Punctuation: **SP, + SP.** Coordinators <u>almost always</u> have commas <u>before</u> them.

2. Some transition words and phrases

actually	finally	indeed
additionally	first	in the meantime
also	for example	meanwhile
apparently	for instance	moreover
as a result	fortunately	next
at any rate	furthermore	nevertheless
besides	hence	on the other hand
certainly	however	so
consequently	in addition	then
even so	in contrast	therefore
eventually	in fact	thus

   The class I attended was an elementary one. <u>Actually</u>, I couldn't speak or understand English at all. (Passage 4-A)

   The class I attended was an elementary one; <u>actually</u>, I couldn't speak or understand English at all.

   *Punctuation: **SP. T, SP.** or **SP; T, SP.** Transition words usually have commas immediately after them.

3. Subordinators for sentence adverbial clauses

after	in case	whatever
although	in as much as	when
as	no matter what	whenever
as if	now that	where
as . . . as	once	wherever
as though	since	whereas
because	so that	whether . . . or not
before	though	whichever
even though	unless	while
if, even if	until	whoever . . .

   <u>Since</u> the expression was new to me, it made me excited and pleased. (Passage 4-A)

   *Punctuation: **Adverbial . . . , SP.** Subordinators <u>never</u> have commas immediately after them.

LEARNING STRATEGY

Remembering New Material: Using color coding or cards that you can sort can help you remember long lists.

Copy each word from the three lists onto a different card. Mix the cards. Then sort the cards into three piles like the original lists. Check your piles against the lists.

Some of the coordinators, transition words and phrases, and subordinators are similar in meaning. When you use one from either set (1) or (2) (see Figure 4-6 below), you usually do not need another one from the same set.

FIGURE 4-6   Coordinators, Transition Words and Phrases, and Subordinators with Similar Meanings

COORDINATORS	TRANSITION WORDS AND PHRASES	SUBORDINATORS
1. but yet	however nevertheless on the other hand otherwise even so	although even though even if
2. so for	as a result consequently then therefore thus	because since

WHEN YOU ARE WRITING

1. If you have used a connector from one set, do not use another from the same set. Be especially alert for *but* and *although* in the same sentence.
2. Check the punctuation around your connector. The three columns are punctuated differently.

1. Using Coordinators

Write down the seven coordinators. Choose three and use them to connect three pairs of sentences that you write about a topic you choose or one your teacher suggests. Check your punctuation. Exchange your paper with a partner and check his or her punctuation.

2. Using Transition Words and Phrases

Write down seven transition words and phrases. Choose three and use them to connect three pairs of sentences that you write about a topic you choose or one your teacher suggests. Check your punctuation. Exchange your paper with a partner and check his or her punctuation.

3. Understanding Transition Words and Phrases

Find three transition words and phrases in your reading. Copy as many sentences as you need to understand why the writer used that particular transition word or phrase. Bring your sentences to class and discuss in a small group which transition words and phrases are most common. Looking at particular examples, explain why you copied the sentences you did. What ideas are being expressed by the transition words and phrases?

4. Understanding Difficult Transition Words and Phrases

In a small group, discuss which transition words and phrases you feel comfortable using and which you do not. Make a list of the difficult ones. Each student should take at least one from the list. Look for uses of these transitions in your listening, reading, or a dictionary, or consult a native speaker. Bring back some examples of their use and discuss them with your group.

5. Using Adverbial Subordinators

Write down seven subordinating conjunctions that begin sentence adverbials. Choose three and use them in three sentences about a topic you choose or one suggested by your teacher. Check your punctuation. Exchange your paper with a partner and check his or her punctuation.

6. Sorting Coordinators, Transition Words and Phrases, and Subordinators

Rearrange the following words into three lists:

a. coordinators (FANBOYS)
b. transition words and phrases
c. subordinators for sentence adverbial clauses

after	unless	additionally
however	until	although
yet	consequently	and
instead	because	moreover
finally	nevertheless	in other words
indeed	but	in conclusion
since	before	whenever
so that	finally	if
while	or	therefore

Check your lists with a partner or a teacher.

7. Selecting Coordinators, Transition Words, and Subordinators

Fill in the blanks in the following essay with appropriate coordinators, subordinators, or transition words or phrases. You will find a list at the end of the essay. You will need to use some of the listed words more than once. You can do this with a partner. Check with other groups. Discuss any differences in the way you use the connectors. (For a correct version of this passage, see Appendix 2.)

Passage 4-B   **HOW TO USE TIME WELL**

by Chun Ling Tsien

Time goes in only one direction—forward. It moves from the past to the present, from the present to the future. People live in today, reflect about yesterday, and anticipate the tomorrow that is about to come. _____ people want to be successful, it is very important for them to know how to
5   use time well.

The first way to use time well is not to delay doing something until some future time. This is a terrible habit—procrastination. _____ you have a tendency toward procrastination, you are always doing yesterday's jobs today, _____ tomorrow you are doing today's

10   unfinished work. _____, you cannot catch up. _____, I was
supposed to finish two compositions for today,_____ I only did one.
Today I must not only accomplish my today's homework, _____ also
I shall write one composition which should have been finished yesterday.
_____, I still have only as much time as the day before.

15   _____, there is too much homework to be done today.

The second way is to be against time. Many people complain that they
have no time to do this or that. _____, _____ you check
what you have done all day long, you will find you have done a lot of things
which were not necessary. _____, were you reading magazines or

20   books while taking a bus or train? Did you call someone up or talk with
somebody without a purpose? _____ the first question is answered
"no" and the second question "yes," I could say that you wasted a lot of
precious time _____ you could do something on the train,
_____ it was not necessary to call somebody or talk with somebody.

25   _____, it is very important to make a schedule _____ you
want to keep on time. This weekly schedule may not solve all your problems,
_____ it will force you to realize what is happening to your time.

I have had tremendous success with this method. After making a
schedule, I followed it each day. I gradually stopped postponing the chores

30   that faced me. My life became far less complicated, _____ each day
was easier to face. _____, the schedule should be reasonable,
_____ it was also not easy for me to follow this one. It was filled in
first with committed time—eating, sleeping, dressing, school, etc.
_____ I decided to put in a good, regular time for studying. I was

35   sure to set aside enough time to complete work that I was normally assigned
each week. _____, I didn't forget to set aside enough time for
relaxation. One day, I determined to put away my homework which would
be handed in to my teacher the next morning _____ I was extremely
tired. I raised my head and stared at my schedule. I could see that it

40   contained what I had written in my heart. I changed my mind and continued
doing my homework. _____, _____ I wanted to be lazy, my
schedule gave me power and confidence to reach my aim.

_____, a person cannot buy time. _____ we should catch up with time from the beginning to the end. _____ a person

45   uses time completely and well, he will be more successful than others.

above all	for example	now
and	for instance	of course
as a result	however	so
because	if	then
but	in a word	thus
by the way	in conclusion	when
	in fact	

8. Punctuating Sentences Correctly

Working first alone, then in pairs or a group, punctuate the following passage using commas, semicolons, periods, and capital letters where needed. Discuss any differences you have in your punctuation. You may begin in class and finish at home, or work over several days in class. (For a correct version of this passage, see Appendix 2.)

Passage 4-C   **MY WORK**

by Hye Soo Han

I have been doing four different kinds of work for two years

First I have my own retail shop for men's wear in Flushing I work from Wednesday through Sunday until 8 p.m. I pick the style of clothes and order them directly from companies choosing the style of clothes and color is a

5   very difficult and important job for me I have to finish ordering fall and winter clothes before March I try to buy good quality clothes for a good price which will appeal to my customers' tastes I display all my merchandise myself the conduct of retail business is not that easy but I'm enjoying my work

10   My second job is being a housewife my husband is a typical Korean type of man typical Korean husbands don't do housework such as cooking dishwashing cleaning and laundry they think housework is the duty of wives and wives should be submissive my husband has changed a little in the U.S. but he is still not really helpful with housework sometimes he just helps me

15   vacuum my home and do laundry therefore I'm always doing all the housework I have a 10-month-old baby girl she always scatters her toys and things all over the house I make a constant effort to put the rooms to rights but that is not easy to do

     The third job is school work I'm taking four classes this semester all of

20   the classes that I'm taking require a lot of work I'm a foreigner so I need more time to prepare for classes but I don't have enough time to study homework and exams cause a lot of pressure all the time nowadays I try to minimize my hours of sleep and prepare classes however I feel too tired and it is hard to concentrate on studying

25   My last job is being a mother this work is the most difficult work taking care of a baby is the hardest job that I have ever done feeding changing diapers giving a bath and soothing a crying baby all require love Tuesday is the only day I spend all day with my baby I feel very sorry for my baby she is a good girl she takes kindly to any strangers

30   Nowadays I feel the limitations on my ability to do four kinds of work together I feel too tired to do all the work at the same time I don't know which work I should give up but I feel it is absolutely right to keep my baby

         (punctuation removed by the authors)

9. Punctuating Sentences Correctly

Working first alone, then with a partner or a group, punctuate the following passage using commas, semicolons, periods, and capital letters where needed. Discuss any differences you have. (For a correct version of this passage, see Appendix 2.)

Passage 4-D   **DIFFERENCES BETWEEN PARENTS' AND CHILDREN'S EDUCATION**

                     by Nini Myint

     In order to live in this modern world education is one of the most important things for us there are many kinds of education and many ways of teaching every generation might have different educational systems but they all have the same purpose moreover there was a time that education was not

necessary but as time goes by things have changed in Burma there were
many kinds of changes and differences

During my father's generation the education system was very different
from my generation back in those days most schools were provided by the
British in those days people had a better education than nowadays because
teachers had different ways of teaching most of the students were taught by
British native teachers therefore they spoke better English and had high
standards in English also they began learning English in primary school
furthermore all of the subjects were taught in English the schools' rules were
strictly followed and they had punishment for every little thing

In my generation the educational system was far different from my
father's for example all the subjects were taught in Burmese except for
English I myself and other students from my generation started to learn
English in the fifth grade in the fourth and eight grades the final exams are
given by the state board of education and in the tenth grade the exam is the
nation-wide exam in each grade we must pass every subject otherwise we
must repeat that particular grade therefore it is really hard to graduate from
high school after tenth grade we can enter college in the old days there was
no limit in choosing any major or professional field that we wanted things
are not easy in my generation the students have fewer opportunities to learn

10. Correcting Errors In Punctuation

The following passage is an early draft. Edit the passage by correcting the
punctuation and making other changes you think are needed. Compare your
editing with a partner or a group. (See Appendix 2 for one of several correct ways
to edit this passage.)

Passage 4-E   **JOSÉ**

by José Mazariegos

My name is José I came to the United States seven years ago, I've gone
from the fifth grade in public school, to junior high, to high school and now
to college. I think this has been a great achievement for me and it will be an
even greater achievement if I make it through college and get my degree.

5   About myself I'm five feet five I weigh one hundred and twenty seven pounds, I'm eighteen years old, I live with my mother, my brother, and my sister. All of them speak two languages our first language is Spanish we speak this language at home and all the times that we're together.

      Writing seems easy for me even though I don't do a very good job of it,
10   I do like to write, I think that if they gave me a choice between writing a lot and reading a lot, I would choose writing, even though I have problems with spelling forming paragraphs, or being clear about the major point in my essay I tend to confuse the person reading it, instead of having my thoughts in writing clear.

11. Combining Independent and Subordinate Clauses

Combine the following independent clauses into a paragraph. Your sentences should contain a variety of main and subordinate clause combinations. There are many acceptable ways to do this.

Passage 4-F   **SHANGHAI**

by Paifei Kong

a. Shanghai is the biggest city of China.

b. It has an area of about 6,200 square kilometers.

c. The city has a population of about 12.3 million people.

d. It has a monsoon climate.

e. There are four seasons.

f. The weather in Shanghai is comparable to that in Washington, D.C.

g. The living conditions in Shanghai are not as good as in America.

h. Most apartments and offices used by foreign residents are well heated in winter and air conditioned in summer.

i. No private house in the city is heated or cooled, except for the hotels and other places where tourists live.

12. Combining Independent and Subordinate Clauses

Combine the following independent clauses into a paragraph. Your sentences should contain a variety of main and subordinate clause combinations. There are many acceptable ways to do this.

Passage 4-F **SHANGHAI (Part 2)**

by Paifei Kong

   a. Shanghai is the leading industrial and commercial city of China.

   b. It is also the most important foreign trade center.

   c. It is one of the world's largest ports.

   d. It lies south of the mouth of the Yangtze River.

   e. About half of China's foreign commerce passes through this city.

   f. The city also has an international airport.

   g. Rail lines connect it to other cities.

13. Combining Independent and Subordinate Clauses

Combine the following independent clauses into a paragraph. Your sentences should contain a variety of independent and subordinate clause combinations. There are many acceptable ways to do this. Compare your work with a partner. Pick out some sentences that seem especially good. Discuss why you like them.

Passage 4-G **WINTER IN MONGOLIA**

by Julie Gao

   a. It was the winter of 1980.

   b. The winter in Inner Mongolia was extremely cold and windy.

   c. The trees had been mostly cut down by the wood factories.

   d. All the grass had died out by the beginning of winter.

   e. There wasn't any snow.

   f. The exposed dead grass roots and the strong wind made the place look deserted.

   g. One night, there was a snow storm.

   h. I was scared at first.

   i. I heard the wind screaming like a hungry wolf.

   j. I saw the snow flakes that were as big as duck's feathers.

   k. I thought the snow would bury the house and me along with it by the next morning.

Noun Phrases: The Basic Structure

5

CHAPTER

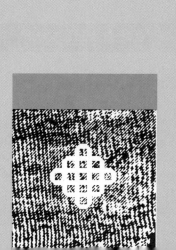

*N*ouns are words that we use to name whatever we think or talk about. Your dictionary will tell you whether a given word is a noun (you will find the letter <u>n</u> or the word <u>noun</u> printed in italics between the word you have looked up and the definition), but it will not tell you how the word is put together with other words to form a **noun phrase.**

In the passage below, each noun phrase is underlined and the noun that is the core of the phrase is in italics.

Passage 5-A

A STARVING EDUCATION SYSTEM

by Jacek Gzik

What is <u>*education?*</u> It is teaching or training <u>a person's *mind*</u> or <u>*character*,</u> <u>the main and basic *program*</u> <u>to achieve one's goal in life</u>. Almost everybody knows how important it is to be well educated because very often <u>the *future*</u> depends on <u>one's *education*</u>.

5   <u>These *days*</u> <u>the education *system*</u> <u>in the USA</u> is "starving." <u>The school *districts*</u> are slicing <u>*budgets*</u>. One by one <u>*districts*</u> are cutting <u>foreign *languages*</u>, <u>art and music *classes*</u>, and even <u>after-school *sports*</u>. <u>Class *sizes*</u> are expanding, and <u>the school *year*</u> is getting shorter. Every one of <u>these *trends*</u> is about to get worse, as <u>the *states*</u> must choose between <u>extra *cops*</u>, <u>extra *classrooms*</u>,

10   <u>health *care*</u> or <u>*welfare*</u>, <u>higher *taxes*</u> or less of everything else.

<u>Many *teachers*</u> are teaching without <u>any *textbooks*</u> at all. Those that they absolutely need they pay for from <u>their own *pockets*</u>. <u>The annual paper *budget*</u> <u>for each teacher</u> is about <u>400 *sheets*</u> for <u>each *class*</u>. If <u>a *teacher*</u> has <u>five *classes*</u> and about <u>25 *students*</u> in each class, and each of them uses <u>one</u>

15   <u>*sheet*</u> <u>a *day*</u>, <u>the *teacher*</u> will run out of <u>*paper*</u> in about <u>four *weeks*</u>. If <u>class *sizes*</u> are expanding, <u>*teachers*</u> cannot be effective with <u>30 or more *students*</u> in <u>a *class*</u>. In <u>some *cities*</u> <u>*children*</u> <u>who live within two miles of school</u> are no longer qualified for <u>bus *service*</u>. <u>Many *companies*</u> <u>that supply the schools with milk</u> have stopped delivering <u>*milk*</u> unless <u>their *bills*</u> are paid.

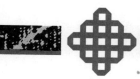

1. PARTS OF NOUN PHRASES

A noun phrase has positions for four different units:

| determiner | premodifier | noun | postmodifier |

In a **simple noun phrase,** only two of these positions are filled: the **determiner** and **noun** positions. These positions are the main focus of this chapter. In an **expanded noun phrase,** either or both of the **premodifier** and **postmodifier** positions are filled as well. Expanded noun phrases are discussed briefly here, but for full information on premodifiers and postmodifiers see Chapter 6.

Below is a list of simple noun phrases from the essay above. The filler of the determiner position is marked with a right-angled arrow, and the noun with an asterisk:

the	future *		each	class *
one's	education *		a	teacher *
these	days *		four	weeks *
many	teachers *		their	bills *

There are a number of words that can fill the determiner position. In addition, the determiner position is sometimes filled by zero—that is, no word at all. The above passage includes the following examples; to make the point clear we have shown how the determiner position is filled by writing *0:*

0	education *		0	teachers *
0	budgets *		0	milk *
0	paper *			

You may find it confusing to think of a position as filled by zero, but a zero determiner has a particular meaning—it is not just nothing. That meaning is explained below.

Between the determiner and the noun, you can put one or more **premodifiers,** that is, words that give more information about the core noun. Gzik has filled the premodifier position in the following phrases; we have marked the position with a straight arrow pointing forward to the core noun to show how that noun and the premodifier are related to each other:

the	school	districts *		0	bus	service *
0	foreign	languages *		their	own	pockets *
0	higher	taxes *				

The fourth position in a noun phrase is for a **postmodifier,** that is, for a phrase or clause that also gives information about the core noun, usually information that identifies it more precisely. Gzik has used the following examples:

the　main　and　basic　program　to achieve one's goal in life

the education　system　in the USA

0　children　who live within two miles of school

Postmodifiers, as you see, are relatively long, and each usually includes a noun phrase in itself. The first of the three examples above includes this one, for instance:

one's　goal　in life

It is a complete noun phrase, with its own postmodifier, and that postmodifier includes still another noun phrase:

0　life

So a number of noun phrases can be packed inside each other, like Chinese boxes. Here is the same example, with all the noun phrases that are in it diagrammed:

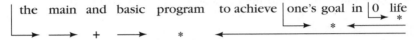

the　main　and　basic　program　to achieve one's goal in 0 life

2. THE CORE NOUN

2.1 Singular and Plural Forms of Nouns

The most important unit in a noun phrase is the core noun. You need to know whether that noun is **singular,** meaning only one, or **plural,** meaning more than one.

2.1a Regular Plurals

Plural nouns are usually marked by adding an -*s* to the singular form (that is the form listed in the dictionary) in one of the ways shown in Figure 5-1.

FIGURE 5-1　How to Mark Regular Nouns as Plural

Add -*s* alone:	This is the regular way, used for most nouns
	e.g., day/days, district/districts, language/languages, teacher/teachers

FIGURE 5-1 (continued)

Add -es:	This is used for nouns that already end in -s as well as for ones that end in -ch, -sh, -x, or -z e.g., class/class<u>es</u>, tax/tax<u>es</u> It is also used for many nouns that end in -o e.g., hero/hero<u>es</u>, tomato/tomato<u>es</u>
Drop -y and add -ies:	This is used for nouns that end in a consonant (b, c, d, f, g, etc.) followed by -y. The -y is removed and -ies added. e.g., city/cit<u>ies</u>, company/compan<u>ies</u>
Drop f and add -ves:	This is used for some, but not all, nouns that end in -f. e.g., half/hal<u>ves</u>, knife/kni<u>ves</u>, wife/wi<u>ves</u>.

WHEN YOU'RE TALKING

The -s at the end of regular plural nouns is pronounced in different ways, sometimes like a hiss, sometimes like a buzz, depending on the sound immediately before the -s. This ending is not always easy to hear, but native speakers of standard English never leave it out entirely, and you should try to pronounce it distinctly in your own speech.

2.1b Irregular Plurals

Some of the most common nouns of English are <u>irregular</u> because their plural forms are not made by adding one of the -s endings listed in Figure 5-1. These irregular nouns are shown in Figure 5-2, with the singular form on the left and the plural form on the right. You should never add an -s to any of these plural forms.

FIGURE 5-2 Nouns with Irregular Plural Forms

SINGULAR	PLURAL	SINGULAR	PLURAL
man	men	mouse	mice
woman	women	louse	lice
child	children	foot	feet
ox	oxen	goose	geese
person	people*	tooth	teeth

* You may add an -s to *people,* but then it means something different: *a people* is a culturally identified group like a tribe or a nation, and *peoples* means several such groups.
  The regular plural *persons* is sometimes used, but only in formal and legal use.

2.1c Foreign Plurals

Many less common English nouns come from other languages, and so their plurals are formed in various ways, according to the rules of those languages. You are most likely to come across these nouns in academic writing. A list of examples is given in Figure 5-3.

FIGURE 5-3   Nouns with Foreign Plural Forms

SINGULAR	PLURAL	SINGULAR	PLURAL
criterion	criteria	hypothesis	hypotheses
phenomenon	phenomena	parenthesis	parentheses
stimulus	stimuli	thesis	theses
syllabus	syllabi	bacterium	bacteria
formula	formulae	continuum	continua
vertebra	vertebrae	cirriculum	curricula
analysis	analyses	datum*	data
basis	bases	medium	media
crisis	crises	memorandum	memoranda

* This singular form is never used, and the plural is often treated as singular.

2.1d Invariant Plurals

A number of nouns have the same form for both singular and plural. These include names of nationalities that end in -ese and many names of animals. A list of examples is given in Figure 5-4.

FIGURE 5-4   Nouns with Identical Singular and Plural Forms

NAMES OF NATIONALITIES	NAMES OF ANIMALS
Chinese	antelope
Japanese	deer
Portuguese	fish
Swiss	sheep
Vietnamese	shrimp

LEARNING STRATEGY

Managing Your Learning: You can learn difficult details by writing the information on cards and placing the cards where you can see them often.

Write out boldly and clearly on a card or slip of paper the singular and plural forms of any noun that causes you trouble, e.g., *child/children*. Stick the card or paper in a place where you will see it often, for example, on the bathroom mirror.

WHEN YOU ARE WRITING

When you use plural nouns in writing, ask yourself these questions:

1. Is it a regular noun? If it is, have you added the *-s?* It is easy to forget the *-s,* especially if you do not hear it or pronounce it clearly.
2. If it is an irregular noun, have you used the correct plural form? Look it up in a dictionary if you are not sure.

2.2 Countable and Uncountable Nouns

A second thing you need to know about the core noun is whether it is **countable** (or **count**) or **uncountable** (or **non-count**).

Countable nouns name things that are thought of (in English) as individuals and that can therefore be counted. For example, *teacher* is a countable noun because you can count two, three, four, or more *teachers;* similarly you can count *sheets (of paper),* as Gzik does in Passage 5-A. Countable nouns can also name more abstract things—that is, things that you cannot actually see or touch, such as *ideas* or *problems.* All countable nouns can be made plural.

Uncountable nouns name things that are thought of as stuff rather than as separate individuals. Examples are *paper* and *milk,* both mentioned in Gzik's essay. Uncountable nouns also often name activities (whether physical or mental), like *memorization* (see Passage 1-A), or conditions, like *silence* (in Passage 3-A) or *confidence* (in Passage 4-B). Uncountable nouns are always singular in form.

It is not always possible to tell from its meaning whether a particular noun is countable or uncountable. When you are not sure, use a dictionary: most dictionaries mark countable nouns with a *C* and uncountable ones with a *U.* The information is important because it tells you which articles or quantifiers you can use with that noun.

2.3 Collective Nouns

Some nouns are singular in form (they have no *-s* ending), but they are often thought of as plural in meaning. A common example is *family.* Because a family includes several people, it is appropriate, though not compulsory, to treat the word as if it were a plural noun when you mean the people in the family. For example, in Passage 7-E, Khorramian writes:

The little girl's family <u>wasn't</u> lucky.

She has used a singular verb correctly after a singular noun (see Chapter 8, Section 2.3). But it would be equally correct to say:

The little girl's family <u>weren't</u> lucky.

This would suggest more strongly that none of the individuals in the family was lucky.

Nouns of this kind are called **collective** nouns. A list of common ones is given in Figure 5-5.

FIGURE 5-5   Common Collective Nouns

army	community	department	gang	majority
audience	company	family	generation	population
class	couple	food	government	senate
committee	crowd	furniture	jury	team

2.4 Coordinated Core Nouns

Occasionally you may put two core nouns in a single noun phrase, joining them together with *and* or *or*. Gzik has done so in the following phrase; in diagramming it, we mark the position of the joining word with a plus sign:

a person's mind <u>or</u> character
* + *

Other examples that appear in this book include the following:

your ideas <u>and</u> beliefs (Passage 3-D)
* + *

0 power <u>and</u> confidence (Passage 4-B)
* + *

When you have a coordinated noun phrase in the subject position of a sentence, you have to decide whether to treat it as singular or plural so that you can make the verb that follows agree with it. (See Chapter 8, Sections 2.3 and 3.3.) If you use *and* as the joining word, the whole noun phrase is considered plural, even if the separate nouns are singular.

Power and confidence <u>are</u> important for success.

If you use *or*, the noun phrase is considered singular when both of the separate nouns are singular, and plural when they are plural:

A man's mind or character <u>is</u> more important than his looks.

If you join a singular and a plural noun with *or*, treat the phrase as being the same in number as the noun that is nearest to the verb.

<u>Is</u> your brother or your sisters coming?

Either your brother or your sisters <u>are</u> coming.

2.5 Adjectives Used as Nouns

Sometimes a word that is usually used as an adjective (and is described in the dictionary as such) can be used after *the* as the core noun of a noun phrase. Two examples appear in this sentence from Passage 5-B:

> Why should we be so reluctant or hesitant in helping people that are unfortunate, especially if <u>the unfortunate</u> are <u>the homeless</u>?

The words *unfortunate* and *homeless* are usually adjectives, but when used as the core of a noun phrase like this they mean "unfortunate people" and "homeless people." That is why the verb in the clause *(are)* is plural.

3. THE DETERMINER POSITION

3.1 Articles

Most commonly the determiner position in a noun phrase is filled by an **article**, that is, one of the following:

a
an
the
0 (i.e., zero—no word at all)

If you do not know which article to use, you should ask yourself a series of questions. The questions are shown in Figure 5-6 on the next page. Here is an explanation of each question.

Question 1: Does the reader know which one or ones you mean by the noun?
In English, you use the word *the* to indicate that readers or listeners know the particular thing(s) or person(s) that you are talking about. They might know for any of the following reasons:

1. There is only one in the world, e.g., "<u>the</u> sun."
2. There is only one in the physical environment that you are talking about, e.g., "<u>the</u> library" when you are talking about your college.
3. The noun names a socially recognized institution and is used to describe the institution in general rather than a particular example of it, e.g., "<u>the</u> family."

CHAPTER 5: NOUN PHRASES: THE BASIC STRUCTURE

FIGURE 5-6

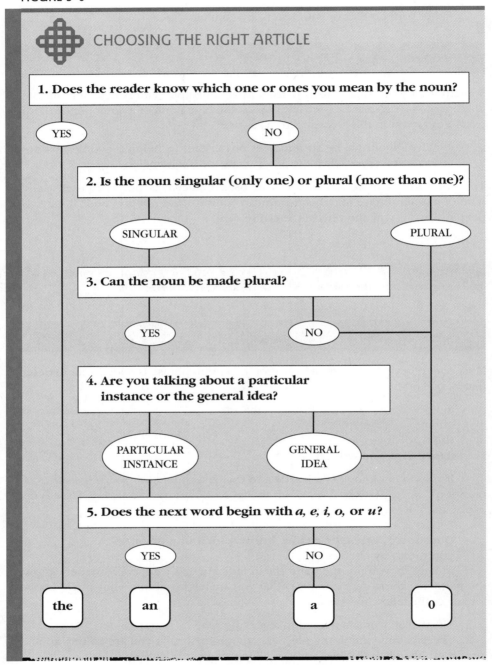

4. You have already mentioned the thing(s) or person(s) in question, e.g., in Passage 5-A, "a teacher" is mentioned in line 14; then, when that person is mentioned again in line 16, she or he is described as "the teacher."

5. Though you have not actually mentioned the thing(s) or person(s) in question, your reader can assume from what you have said that they must be there. For example, in Passage 5-A, Gzik introduces his topic "the education system in the USA," and then mentions "the school districts." He can assume that we know which school districts he means and that we are thinking about them already because they are an essential part of the education system he is talking about.

6. You define whatever you are talking about in the noun phrase itself, usually in the postmodifier. That is exactly what Gzik does in the phrase "the education system in the U.S.A."; the words *in the U.S.A.* explain which education system he means. (The name, "the U.S.A." is another example of the same thing: It is an abbreviation for "the United States of America.")

Question 2: Is the noun singular (only one) or plural (more than one)?

This is a straightforward question, but remember that most plural nouns must be marked by an *-s* at the end.

Question 3: Can the noun be made plural?

Uncountable nouns cannot be made plural (they have no plural form), so if the noun you are using is uncountable, the answer to this question is no.

Question 4: Are you talking about a particular instance or the general idea?

There are some nouns in English that can be thought of as either countable or uncountable, but there is a difference of meaning between the two. When you treat these nouns as countable (that is, you make them plural, or you use them in the singular form with the article *a* or *an*), you tell your reader or listener to think of **particular instances;** when you treat them as uncountable (that is, you keep them singular, but you do not use *a* or *an*), you tell your reader or listener to think of **a general idea.** For example, in Passage 4-B, Tsien discusses "time":

> If people want to be successful, it is very important for them to know how to use time well.

Notice that the noun *time* is singular, and the determiner in front of it is zero: the noun is treated as uncountable, and so we know that Tsien is thinking about time in general. But see what she does a few paragraphs later:

> I decided to put in a good, regular time for studying.

Here, in the noun phrase "a good, regular time," *time* is again singular, but it is preceded by *a:* it is treated as countable. In this way, Tsien indicates that she is thinking of a particular time, one that can be distinguished from other times, such as those she set aside for eating and sleeping.

The nouns that have both a general and a particular meaning are often **abstract** nouns; that is, they name things that cannot be seen or touched, like activities or conditions or ideas. Some common examples are *love, life, death, war,* and *peace,* and most nouns ending in *-ation* or *-ism* are abstract ones.

Some **concrete** nouns, i.e., ones that name things you can see and touch, can also be used as either countable or uncountable. An example from Passage 5-A is *paper.* Here Gzik uses it to refer to stuff, so he correctly treats it as uncountable. But the word can also refer to things made of paper, specifically to newspapers or to essays or articles that are written on paper; when used in this way the noun is treated as countable, so that you can talk about "a paper" or "many papers." Similarly the names for many foodstuffs can be either countable or uncountable: When you talk about "chicken," you refer to the meat, but when you talk about "a chicken," you refer to an individual bird.

Question 5: Does the next word begin with *a, e, i, o,* or *u?*

This is an easy question, but you should know that it concerns pronunciation rather than spelling: the sounds spelled with *a, e, i, o,* or *u* (namely, **vowel** sounds) are hard to say after the article *a,* so *an* is used instead to make the pronunciation easier. Examples from passages in this book include "<u>an</u> unknown world" (Passage 1-A), "<u>an</u> English lesson" (Passage 3-A), and "<u>an</u> imbalance of 'Yin' and 'Yang'" (Passage 14-E). Also, words that begin with *h* have *an* rather than *a* in front of them if the *h* is not pronounced. For example, in Passage 3-A, Law correctly writes "<u>an</u> hour." Similarly, since the question is one of pronunciation, words that begin with *u* do not have *an* before them if the *u* is pronounced like "you." For example, you should say or write "<u>a</u> university."

In writing Passage 5-A, Gzik had to decide which article to use with each of his noun phrases. To help himself reach a decision, he might have used the chart given above, asking himself the questions as shown below. We put a question mark in the determiner position for each example because that is the question that he had to decide.

EXAMPLE: <u>?</u> education (line 1)

Q Does the reader know which one or ones you mean by the noun?
A No, because I am only just beginning and am introducing a topic that is new to my reader.

This would have led him to the next question.

Q Is the noun singular (only one) or plural (more than one)?
A Singular, because I have added no *-s.*

So he would have gone on to the next.

Q Can the noun be made plural?

A Not usually, though you could talk about *educations* if you meant different kinds of education.

This answer suggests that he should probably go down to *0*, but to make sure he could have gone on to the next question:

Q Are you talking about a particular instance or the general idea?

A Here's the answer, because I'm not talking about just one kind of education but about education in general.

That would have led him down to *0*, making the whole noun phrase "education."

> **EXAMPLE:** ? main and basic program to achieve one's goal in life (line 2)

Q Does the reader know which one or ones you mean by the noun?

A Yes, because I define the program I am talking about. That is, I say what kind of program it is, one "to achieve one's goal in life," and there can be only one "main and basic program" of this kind.

This would have led him to *the*.

> **EXAMPLE:** ? foreign languages (line 7)

Q Does the reader know which one or ones you mean by the noun?

A No, because there are many foreign languages, and I have not said which ones I mean.

So he would have moved on to the next question:

Q Is the noun singular (only one) or plural (more than one)?

A Plural. The *-s* shows that I am talking about several of them.

This would have led him to *0*.

> **EXAMPLE:** ? welfare (line 10)

Q Does the reader know which one or ones you mean by the noun?

A No, because this is not an idea I have mentioned before, and anyway I am not talking about a particular <u>one.</u>

So he would have asked the next question:

Q Is the noun singular (only one) or plural (more than one)?

A Singular. There is no *-s* on *welfare*.

And the next one:

Q Can the noun be made plural?

A No, it cannot. People never talk about *welfares*.

So he would have concluded that the correct article to use here is *0*.

CHAPTER 5: NOUN PHRASES: THE BASIC STRUCTURE

EXAMPLE: ? teacher (line 14)

Q   Does the reader know which one or ones you mean by the noun?
A   No, because I have not mentioned any particular teacher yet.

So he would have moved on to the next question:

Q   Is the noun singular (only one) or plural (more than one)?
A   Singular. I am only talking about one teacher.

And to the next:

Q   Can the noun be made plural?
A   Yes, definitely. There could be any number of teachers, although I am only talking about one.

And the next:

Q   Are you talking about a particular instance or the general idea?
A   A particular instance. I can see in my imagination one individual teacher.

This would have led to the last question:

Q   Does the next word begin with *a, e, i, o,* or *u?*
A   No. *Teacher* begins with *t.*

So finally he would have arrived at *a.* That would make the whole noun phrase "a teacher."

EXAMPLE: ? paper (line 16)

Q   Does the reader know which one or ones you mean by the noun?
A   No, because I have said nothing about paper so far.

So, on to the next question:

Q   Is the noun singular (only one) or plural (more than one)?
A   Singular, because I have added no *-s.*

This would have led to the next:

Q   Can the noun be made plural?
A   Yes it can, because we can talk about the papers that we read or write.

This answer suggests a difficulty, because Gzik was not talking about the kind of paper that has writing on it (i.e., a paper that you write for class or a newspaper), but the kind of paper that is blank. The next question would have helped him focus on the problem:

Q   Are you talking about a particular instance or the general idea?
A   I am not talking about any particular paper, but about the stuff in general.

In this way, he would have arrived at *0,* making the whole noun phrase "paper."

By using the questions on the chart in this way, you can solve most of your article problems. You cannot solve them <u>all</u>, for there remain a few exceptions which have to be learned individually as you come across them. Also, the choice of article depends a great deal on what you, as a speaker or writer, know, and on what you expect your reader or listener to know. Finally, the rules for proper nouns—that is, names of people, places, and institutions—are different. See the explanation below.

Try to be aware of articles as you read. If you come across any that surprise you, use the questions on the flowchart to figure out how the writer could have arrived at that article. If the questions fail to lead you to the article that has actually been used, you may have come across an exceptional core noun. Make a note of it and ask an English-speaking friend about it. You will find, in fact, that there are few articles that the flowchart does not explain.

(For practice in using the flowchart, see Activities 2, 3, 4, and 5 at the end of this chapter.)

WHEN YOU'RE TALKING

The article *a* is often not pronounced clearly; it may sound like little more than a grunt. But native speakers of English rarely, if ever, make a mistake on this point, so listen carefully for it.

Articles with Names

The general rule for names is that they have a zero article, e.g., Bob, Susan, China, Mount Everest, Peru. Some categories of names, however, are used with *the*. Those categories are shown in Figure 5-7.

FIGURE 5-7   Names with *the*

Names that are expanded noun phrases with postmodifiers
>   the Bay of Bengal, the Cape of Good Hope, the Gulf of Mexico, the United Kingdom of Great Britain and Northern Ireland, the United States of America

Plural names of countries and regions
>   the Carolinas, the Midlands, the Netherlands

Groups of islands
>   the Bahamas, the Seychelles, the Windward Islands

FIGURE 5-7 (continued)

Ranges of mountains or hills

the Alps, the Appalachian Mountains, the Himalayas, the Rockies

Rivers, seas, oceans, canals

the Amazon, the Atlantic, the Caribbean, the Yellow River, the Zambesi

Public institutions and buildings*

the Forbidden City, the Grand (Hotel), the Great Mosque, the Metropolitan Museum, the Taj Mahal

Ships

the Intrepid, the Mayflower, the Titanic, the Victory

Newspapers

the China Daily, the Daily Mail, the New York Times, the Observer, the Uganda Argus, the Washington Post

* But not usually churches or cathedrals, or colleges

e.g., Canterbury Cathedral, Riverside Church

3.2 Demonstratives

The determiner position can also be filled by a **demonstrative,** that is, a word that you use to "point" at something. There are four demonstratives that are used as determiners: *this, that, these,* and *those.* They all, like *the,* indicate that the reader or listener already knows about whatever is named by the core noun, usually because it has just been mentioned. Which of the four you should choose depends (a) on whether the core noun is to be thought of as being nearby or relatively far away and (b) on whether the core noun is singular or plural. See Figure 5-8.

FIGURE 5-8 Demonstratives

	SINGULAR	**PLURAL**
Near	this	these
Far	that	those

In the essay at the beginning of this chapter, Gzik uses one demonstrative:

these days (line 5)

These indicates the days we are living in now, that is, at the time Gzik was writing his essay.

In the following examples, you can see from the context how the demonstratives introduce nouns that the reader can be expected to know about.

> On my first day at the Ursuline Convent School, I met Sister Ida. . . . <u>That</u> day I did not go out. (Passage 3-A)

> She always wore nice clothes; they were in good taste and looked expensive. She looked gracious in <u>those</u> clothes . . . (Passage 4-A)

> . . . it is very important to make a schedule if you want to keep on time. <u>This</u> weekly schedule may not solve all your problems, but it will force you to realize what is happening to your time. (Passage 4-B)

> In order to live in <u>this</u> modern world education is one of the most important things for us . . . During my father's generation the education system was very different from my generation. Back in <u>those</u> days most schools were provided by the British . . . (Passage 4-D)

3.3 *the other, another, other*

You can use these expressions in the determiner position to tell your readers or listeners to think of more of the kind of thing that you have already been talking about. The difference between *the other, another,* and *other* is the same as the difference between *the, a,* and *0* (zero article).

the other
This means "you know the one(s) I mean, because I have told you about the first of the set already, and now I am telling you about the remaining one(s)."

> My house, which stood at the corner of <u>the widest street</u>, was on the most exciting street in that town. *The other* streets in the town were so narrow that people always went to the widest street to buy or sell things. (Passage 14-G)

another
This simply tells us to think about one more but implies that it is not the only one left.

> In one corner of the airport there was <u>a small room</u> with a sign that said "Monetary Change," and next to this was *another* room with a sign that said "Tour Information." (Passage 8-B)

other
This is used when the core noun that follows is plural. It indicates not just one more, but several more.

No private house in the city is heated or cooled, except for the hotels and _other_ places where tourists live. (Passage 4-F)

Other can also be used in the premodifier position after a possessive or a quantifier:

[In the day care center] I looked after babies, and I shared duties with two _other_ teachers. (Passage 10-C)

3.4 Possessives

You can also fill the determiner position of a noun phrase with a **possessive.** The possessive tells your reader who or what the thing named by the core noun belongs to—that is, who "possesses" it. The possessives include the following pronouns. (See Chapter 7.)

my	**his**	**our**	**its**
your	**her**	**their**	**one's**

In addition, you can turn any noun phrase into a possessive by adding _'s_ (the punctuation mark is called an **apostrophe**), or if the noun phrase is a regular plural and so already ends in an -_s,_ add only the apostrophe, to make _s'_. (You may also add just an apostrophe if the noun phrase is singular but ends in an -_s_ and is difficult to pronounce with another -_s_ after it, e.g., "Moses' teachings.")

The first paragraph of Passage 5-A contains several noun phrases that begin with possessives:

What is education? It is teaching or training _a person's_ mind or character, the main and basic program to achieve _one's_ goal in life. Almost everybody knows how important it is to be well educated because very often the future depends on _one's_ education.

Notice that the possessive ending is added to a complete noun phrase, which has a core noun and a determiner of its own (and may include a premodifier too). An example is "a person's mind or character." The noun phrase, "a person," is packed in the determiner position of another noun phrase:

a person 's mind or character

Notice, however, that the whole phrase is still about "mind or character" rather than about "a person." It is the core noun that is the most important.

Other examples of possessives include the following, all taken from passages in this book. Notice the placement of the apostrophe in each case.

men's wear (Passage 4-C)

my customers' tastes (Passage 4-C)

my uncle's backyard (Passage 5-D)

Ueli Gerber's soul (Passage 7-D)

the islands' flora and fauna (Passage 14-A)

WHEN YOU ARE WRITING

When you make a noun phrase into a possessive, ask yourself these questions:

1. Is the noun singular or plural?
2. Have you added an *-s?*
3. Have you put the apostrophe in the right place?

Remember that the apostrophe should be **before** the *-s* on a singular noun and after the *-s* on a regular plural one.

3.5 Quantifiers

Quantifiers are words that show how many or much you are talking about of whatever you name in the core noun. Many quantifiers fill the determiner position. Others can be called **predeterminers** because they can go at the front of a noun phrase, before a determiner. In the explanation below, we show which these are by putting *(the, etc.)* after the word in question.

The quantifiers can be divided into four groups: **definite, indefinite, negative,** and **comparative.**

3.5a Definite Quantifiers

Definite quantifiers give an exact idea of how many or what proportion you are talking about. They include all numbers and the words *both, either, all, each,* and *every.*

Numbers

Using a number in the determiner position is the most exact way of expressing quantity, but you can only do it with countable nouns. See the following examples from Passage 5-A:

If a teacher has *five* classes and about <u>25 students</u> in each class, and each of them uses <u>*one* sheet</u> a day, the teacher will run out of paper in about *four* weeks.

Any number can also be put into the premodifier position with a determiner in front of it. The determiner is usually one of those that says "You know the one(s) I mean"—i.e., *the, this, that, these,* or *those.* In Passage 8-D, for example, Tang is telling a story about a definite time in the past:

> [My mother] rejected my request [for a pencil case] because she didn't want to spoil me and she would not spend money on those luxury things. I was really mad and cried. *The next two weeks* I didn't eat my breakfast and tried to save money to buy the pencil case . . .

Large numbers have the article *a* in front of them if the numbers themselves are singular:

$$100 = \underline{a} \text{ hundred}$$
$$1000 = \underline{a} \text{ thousand}$$
$$1,000,000 = \underline{a} \text{ million}$$

The noun following the number, however, is always plural:

a hundred <u>years</u>

Also, the words *hundred, thousand,* etc., are not given plural endings:

$$200 = \text{two hundred (no } \text{-}s)$$
$$5000 = \text{five thousand}$$
$$10,000,000 = \text{ten million}$$

And the noun following the number is still plural:

ten million <u>years</u>

WHEN YOU ARE WRITING

It is customary to write small numbers (ten and below) as words, but larger numbers (11 upwards) are generally written as numerals.

---

both (the, etc.)

Both can be either a determiner or a predeterminer. It means "a whole set of two." In his essay on the Galapagos Islands, Zaldumbide uses it as a determiner:

> We find two kinds of iguanas on the islands, the sea iguana and the land iguana. This is the only place in the world where *both* <u>iguanas</u> can be seen at the same time. (Passage 14-A, Part 2)

Both is often used in a coordinated noun phrase that contains two items. For example, we can infer from what Gzik tells us in his essay that:

In American schools nowadays, *both* the children *and* the teachers are suffering.

In this case, *both* indicates not that there are two individuals (i.e., two children), but that there are two groups, the children and the teachers. Using *the* in the determiner position after *both* helps to make that clear.

either (the, etc.)

Either means "<u>one</u> of a set of two." It usually introduces a coordinated noun phrase. The coordinating word is always *or*.

> If you see an iguana in the Galapagos Islands it may be *either* a sea iguana *or* a land iguana.

all (the/these, etc.)

All can be used with either countable or uncountable nouns. Use it in the determiner position to refer to the whole of something or a whole set of individuals:

> *All* life ends in death.
> *All* men (and women) are mortal.

However, you will not usually want to make such sweeping generalizations. More often, you will want to use *all* as a predeterminer and put a determiner after it to restrict the set. For example:

> I display *all my* merchandise myself. . . . [My husband] is still not really helpful with housework . . . Therefore I'm always doing *all my* housework. (Passage 4-C)

> The population [of Curaçao] consists of descendants of the original Indians from the island as well as descendants of slaves, Portuguese, Jews, Chinese, and Dutch. *All these* races get along well with each other. (Passage 3-H)

> This weekly schedule will not solve *all your* problems, but it will force you to realize what is happening to your time. (Passage 4-B)

each, every

These two determiners mean the same as "all," but they can only be used with <u>singular</u> nouns. For example, in Passage 5-A, Gzik talks about "the annual paper budget for <u>each</u> teacher," that is, each individual one within an unknown number of teachers. Similarly, in Passage 4-A, Nakashizuka writes:

> In my country *every* man and woman seems to believe that younger women are always better than older women.

Her emphasis is on all the men and women of Japan as individuals, so she uses "<u>every</u> man and woman" in the singular, thus telling us to think about them as separate people. The fact that they are all separate individuals makes it more remarkable that they all think the same thing.

WHEN YOU ARE WRITING

When you use *each* or *every*, ask yourself this question: Have you put an *-s* on the noun that follows it? If you have, cross it off.

3.5b Indefinite Quantifiers

These are inexact expressions for quantities. The emphasis of each is different, and there are important restrictions on the type of noun used with each of them.

Quantifiers That Can Be Used with Both <u>Countable and Uncountable</u> Nouns

any

Any has a rather specialized meaning: "more than none, however small a number or amount, and it does not matter which one(s)." The word is most often used in questions or negative statements:

> Fortunately for us, we did <u>not</u> have *<u>any</u> friends or relatives* in Western Europe or the U.S. (Passage 9-A)

Without any means the same as *with no:*

> Many teachers are teaching <u>without *any* textbooks at all</u>. (Passage 5-A)

some

Some suggests a number or quantity, but not a particularly large one.

> Although Han gul is much more commonly used in Korea these days, we have kept *<u>some</u> Chinese loanwords*. (Passage 9-C)

> I went to the first room to exchange my dollars for Spanish currency and to get *<u>some</u> information*. (Passage 8-B)

Some cannot be used after a negative word like *not* or *without*. Use *any* instead.

a lot of/lots of

You can use either *a lot of* or *lots of* to indicate a large quantity. Both are informal and are not recommended in academic writing. However, there are examples in many of the essays cited in this book:

> If you check what you have done all day long, you will find you have done *<u>a lot of</u> things which were not necessary*. (Passage 4-B)

> In six months I would be making *<u>lots of</u> money*, I thought. (Passage 6-B)

> Even the action of taking hold of something demands complete concentration

and *a lot of* exercise, until the child is able to control its movements without any observance. (Passage 8-E)

Quantifiers That Can Only Be Used with <u>Countable</u> Nouns

a couple of (the, etc.)

A couple of means technically just two, but people often use it vaguely to mean two or more:

There are *a couple of* things I want to tell you.

This use is informal, so it is better to avoid it in writing.

a few

A few means more than two but not many more. For example:

In the mid-term and final examination, [our teachers] copied *a few* sentences from the textbook and erased one or two of the original words. (Passage 1-A)

You can use *a few* with *not* ("not a few"), but then it means "many"!

several

Several suggests more than *a few* but still not a large number. For example, in describing political repression in Poland in the early 1980s, Stanislawska writes,

There were *several* cases in the city where fathers were arrested and mothers lost their jobs. (Passage 14-H)

You cannot use *several* with *not*.

many

Many indicates a large number:

Many teachers are teaching without any textbooks at all. (Passage 5-A)

It can be used in questions:

Are there *many* Asian students in your school?

And it can be used with *not* to indicate only a few:

At that time, there were not *many* Asian students in our high school. (Passage 13-D)

Many can be used after *the* (in the premodifier position) in just the same way as a number can. For example, in Passage 5-B, Saintilien has written:

With a box of popcorn in my hand, I listened to my cousin telling me about *the many* places she visited and the people she met while she was in Europe.

By using *the* as the determiner and *many* as a premodifier, she tells us two things: She is talking about all the places she visited, and there were many of them.

Quantifiers That Can Only Be Used with <u>Uncountable</u> Nouns

a little

A little indicates a small quantity of something that is uncountable. For example, we can say, from the information that Gzik gives us in Passage 5-A:

Teachers in schools are given *a little* <u>paper</u> for their classes, but it is not enough.

A little is not common in writing. You are more likely to come across it when you are talking. It can also be used with *not* ("not a little") to mean a lot, but that use is formal.

a great deal of

You can use the expression *a great deal of* to describe a large quantity of something that is uncountable, and so you can avoid the informal *a lot of.* For example, the sentence from Passage 8-E that is quoted above could be edited in this way:

Even the action of taking hold of something demands complete concentration and *a great deal of* <u>exercise</u>, until the child is able to control its movements without any observance.

3.5c Negative Quantifiers

Some of the quantifiers you can use in the determiner position have a negative meaning:

no

No can be used with both singular and plural nouns, and it can also be used with uncountable ones. It negates the whole noun phrase that it introduces, so it is not usually used in a sentence that already has *not.* It is used correctly in the following examples:

We were ordered to fill those blanks with exactly the same words as the textbook. There was <u>*no* exception</u>. (Passage 1-A)

In the old days there was <u>*no* limit in choosing any major or professional field that we wanted</u>. (Passage 4-D)

After that interview, I started looking for my own job. I went to a dozen places with <u>*no* results</u>. (Passage 6-B)

In informal writing and in speech, people often use *not . . . any* instead of *no,* as Liney does in the following example:

Life has been easy for me here. Unlike my mother, I do <u>not</u> have <u>any</u> responsibilities but my school work . . . (Passage 7-C)

WHEN YOU ARE WRITING

You should never use *no* with *any*. So check when you use either word: If you have written *no any,* cross out the *any* or change the *no* into *not.*

---

neither (the, etc.)

Neither means "not one out of a set of two." Like *either,* it usually introduces a coordinated noun phrase, but in this case the coordinator is *nor:*

Neither parents *nor* teachers are happy about the state of education today.

few

Few means a small number, but its emphasis is negative: It means "not many at all" or "only a few." For example, in Passage 5-D, Lam tells us about the rural area where his grandfather lived:

The country was calm and elegant with *few* people living there.

Few can only be used with plural countable nouns. It is formal, so in informal writing or in speech use *not . . . many* instead.

little

Little means a small amount, and its emphasis is also negative. For example, in Passage 8-D, Tang tells us how thrifty her mother was, so we can say:

Her mother spent *little* money on luxuries.

Little can only be used with uncountable nouns, and it is quite formal. If you want to be less formal, use *not . . . much* instead, as Tang does:

The food which [a Chinese housewife] buys should be healthy food and should *not* cost *much* money. (Passage 8-D)

3.5d Comparative Quantifiers

It is possible to express the relationships between different numbers or quantities, using comparative words in the determiner position. These words are *most, more, less, fewer,* and *enough.*

most

When *most* is used in the determiner position, it means considerably more than half of the number or quantity in question. For example:

Most students were in their teens or twenties; only she was in her forties. (Passage 4-A)

more

In Passage 4-C, Han writes about how difficult it is for her to do her school work, and she implicitly compares her situation to that of native speakers of English. They can do their assignments more quickly than she can:

> All of the classes that I'm taking require a lot of work. I am a foreigner, so I need *more* time to prepare for classes . . .

Time is uncountable, but *more* can also be used with plural countable nouns. For example, Gzik tells us in Passage 5-A that class sizes are expanding, so we can say:

> Now there are *more* children in each class.

less

The comparison between Han and her classmates could be expressed in negative terms:

> All of the classes that Han is taking require a lot of work. But her American-born classmates need *less* time to prepare than she does.

But if we want to put the comparison about class sizes negatively, we should not use *less,* because *less* is supposed only to be used with uncountable nouns. To be correct, we should use *fewer* instead.

> Before, there were *fewer* children in each class.

However, the language is changing on this point. Native speakers often use *less* now with plural nouns.

enough

A different kind of comparison is made with *enough.* If you put *enough* in the determiner position in front of a noun, you are saying that the amount of whatever you are talking about is the same as the amount that is needed for a particular purpose. In describing how she organized her time, for instance, Tsien tells us:

> I was sure to set aside *enough* time to complete work that I was normally assigned each week. However, I didn't forget to set aside *enough* time for relaxation. (Passage 4-B)

Here she uses *enough* with an uncountable noun, but it can also be used with plural countable ones.

5.3e Summary of Quantifiers

In Figure 5-9, we summarize when you can use which quantifier.

FIGURE 5-9   Quantifiers

	WITH SINGULAR COUNTABLE NOUNS	WITH PLURAL NOUNS	WITH UNCOUNTABLE NOUNS	IN FORMAL WRITING
Definite quantifiers				
one	yes	no	no	yes
two, three, etc.	no	yes	no	yes
both (the, etc.)	no	yes	no	yes
either (the, etc.)	yes	yes	yes	yes
all (the, etc.)	no	yes	yes	yes
each	yes	no	no	yes
every	yes	no	no	yes
Indefinite quantifiers				
any	yes	yes	yes	yes
some	no	yes	yes	yes
a lot of/lots of	no	yes	yes	no
a couple of (the, etc.)	no	yes	no	no
a few	no	yes	no	yes
several	no	yes	no	yes
many	no	yes	no	yes
a little	no*	no	yes	yes
Negative quantifiers				
no	yes	yes	yes	yes
neither (the, etc.)	yes	yes	yes	yes
few	no	yes	no	yes
little	no	no*	yes	yes
Comparative quantifiers				
more	no	yes	yes	yes
less	no	no†	yes	yes
fewer	no	yes†	no	yes
most	no	yes	yes	yes
enough	no	yes	yes	yes

* *Little* is also used as an adjective meaning "small." In that sense, it can be used in the premodifier position with both singular and plural countable nouns, e.g., "a little bird," "some little birds."

† *Less* is now often used with plural countable nouns, even though it is not formally correct. *Fewer* is therefore becoming rare.

1. Using a Dictionary to Find Out About Nouns

For this activity, use a good dictionary, such as the *Oxford Advanced Learner's Dictionary of Current English* or the *Longman Dictionary of Contemporary English*. Preferably with a partner, look up each of the nouns that is listed in the chart below and, using information from the dictionary, fill in the blank spaces. Some of the spaces have been filled in for you.

SINGULAR	PLURAL	COUNTABLE/ UNCOUNTABLE
appendix		countable
beer	beers	either
cloth		
no singular	clothes	
discrimination		
distinction		
divorce	no plural	
electricity		
exercise		
fungus		
furniture		
happiness		uncountable
life		
marriage		
medicine		
prejudice		
problem		
tuition		

Now look closely at the definitions of those nouns that can be either countable or uncountable. What is the difference in meaning between the countable and the uncountable use in each case? Discuss this question with your classmates and your teacher.

2. Recognizing Determiners

In Passage 5-B, put a circle around every determiner that you can find, and write in a zero (0) in front of every noun phrase that has a zero article. (You should put in 16 zeros.) Compare notes with your classmates, and then use Figure 5-6 and the accompanying discussion to explain the writer's use of *the, a, an,* or *0.*

Passage 5-B   **THE HOMELESS**

by Michelle Saintilien

My cousin and I were coming home late one night from the movies. With a box of popcorn in my hand, I listened to my cousin telling me about the many places she visited and the people she met while she was in Europe. But I was distracted when I noticed an old man from afar off. Dressed in
5   tattered clothing, he was rummaging through a garbage pail, hoping to find food or simply soda bottles. I felt sorry for him. It was horrible the way I was filling my stomach with popcorn, and there he was, probably dying of starvation. As we approached him, I was going to hand him the box of popcorn, but my cousin forcefully pulled me away before I had a chance. I
10   never questioned her action. I knew she was just thinking about my safety.

Why should we be so reluctant or hesitant in helping people that are unfortunate, especially if the unfortunate are the homeless . . .? With wistful eyes, homeless men and women walk up and down the subway cars asking the riders to offer them money for food. Some passengers are willing to give
15   them a little pocket change. Others just look at the homeless with pity or disgust. I offer them some money when I have any, but at other times I can only turn my head away and thank God that I am not in their shoes.

3. Choosing the Right Article

In Passage 5-C, all the articles (*the, a,* or *an*) that the writer originally used have been replaced by blanks, and a blank has also been put in where the writer used a zero article. Underline the core noun that follows each blank and use Figure

5-6 to decide which article to put in. Write the article in the blank, using the sign *0* if you think it should be zero. Since the passage is rather long, your teacher may ask you to do the first two paragraphs as a group activity and then to do the rest at home.

(For a correct version of this passage, see Appendix 2. Note that for some of the blanks, there is more than one possible answer, depending on what is meant.)

Passage 5-C　　　**QUEBEC CITY**

by Honorata Lewicka

Quebec City is (1) _____ most joyful place that I have ever been to. Let me take you for (2) _____ one-day tour around Quebec.

(3) _____ day starts at 8 a.m., in (4) _____ small room up on (5) _____ fifth floor of (6) _____ private hotel. (7) _____ sun is very bright, (8) _____ air is clean; it will be (9) _____ great day. From (10) _____ windows we can see (11) _____ St. Lawrence river, which is full of (12) _____ white dots. (13) _____ little dots are (14) _____ ships and boats on (15) _____ river seen from (16) _____ distance. Across (17) _____ river is (18) _____ colorful spread: red, white and green. You have to look very closely to see that (19) _____ red spots are (20) _____ roofs of (21) _____ houses, (22) _____ white ones are (23) _____ houses themselves, and there are (24) _____ green trees all around them.

First we take (25) _____ ride outside of Quebec City, to (26) _____ country where we can see (27) _____ farms and animals that are not in (28) _____ city. We stop at (29) _____ farm where you can buy (30) _____ freshly picked strawberries, or you can pick them for yourselves. We pay for (31) _____ baskets and start to pick (32) _____ strawberries, and we are allowed to eat them while we pick. These strawberries have (33) _____ soil on them, but they taste great.

After that we go back to (34) _____ hotel to wash up and to change our clothes. We are set to take (35) _____ boat ride for a few hours. As we step on (36) _____ boat, (37) _____ atmosphere is very friendly and enjoyable. There are many musicians and singers, clowns and artists. (38) _____ bands are playing, (39) _____ singers are singing, and (40) _____ whole crowd is enjoying (41) _____ ride.

When we get back from (42) _____ ride, it is 10 p.m. We take (43) _____ walk along (44) _____ streets where (45) _____ festival is in progress. (46) _____ streets are full of (47) _____ talented people: (48) _____ musicians and singers,

(49) ____ store owners, and (50) ____ people who enjoy walking and listening to others perform.

30   All of us are having (51) ____ good time. At about midnight, we walk back to our hotel where we can get some rest for (52) ____ next day.

4. Choosing the Article for Style

In the following passage, you are again asked to fill in the articles. In this case, however, you will find that the answers are less clear-cut. In a few places, either *a* or *the* would be correct, but the stylistic effect is different: The choice of *a* suggests that the information is new to the reader, whereas *the* suggests that the reader is in the picture already. Identify the places where there is a choice and discuss with your friends or classmates and/or with a native speaker of English which article you prefer and why.

(For a correct version of this passage, see Appendix 2, but remember that the choices made in that version are not always the only possible ones.)

Passage 5-D   **MY UNCLE'S BACKYARD**

                  by Wan Lam

        I liked my uncle's backyard. Although it was not big, it was beautiful and tranquil. It was in (1) ____ back of (2) ____ two-story Spanish style house, located in (3) ____ countryside of Hong Kong.

        (4) ____ countryside was calm and elegant with few people living
5   there. (5) ____ group of (6) ____ houses was built along (7) ____ tiny river. There was (8) ____ small waterfall with (9) ____ water running from (10) ____ top of (11) ____ hill into (12) ____ river. There were many trees on (13) ____ side of (14) ____ river, grown so strongly that their huge amount of (15) ____ roots anchored (16) ____ soil tightly and extended in all directions.
10 My uncle's house was among those houses; and his backyard was facing (17) ____ river. My uncle and I spent most of (18) ____ time together in (19) ____ backyard when I was (20) ____ child. Thus, it was more than (21) ____ backyard.

        (22) ____ backyard was surrounded on three sides by (23) ____ fences
15 which extended from one side of (24) ____ house to (25) ____ other end. It didn't occupy (26) ____ large area, but it was big enough for (27) ____ children to play. (28) ____ ground was covered with (29) ____ long greenish grass; it was so fresh that I wanted to put my nose deep in (30) ____ grass in

order to breathe (31) ____ air and enjoy (32) ____ smell. It gave me (33)

20   ____ sense of refreshment.

In addition, there was (34) ____ number of (35) ____ colorful flowers along (36) ____ fences on two sides; (37) ____ tulips, (38) ____ daisies, (39) ____ lilies, (40) ____ sunflowers, and (41) ____ roses all showed off their pretty dresses to attract one another. (42) ____ flowers were beautiful and

25   attractive with (43) ____ butterflies dancing on them.

5. Editing Articles in Your Own Writing

Take a piece of your own writing, or exchange your writing with a partner. Underline all the articles used in it and insert *0* wherever there is a zero article. Then check each article, using the questions in Figure 5-6. Discuss any difficult cases with your partner, other classmates, and your teacher.

6. Possessives: Placing the Apostrophe

The following sentences, taken from various passages in this book, have the possessives in them underlined. In each case, the apostrophe has been omitted, and you are asked to insert it in the right place.

1. The first lesson was that I followed <u>a teachers</u> voice saying "A, B, C. . . ." (Passage 1-A)

2. [Sonia] came to study here in the U.S. and got <u>a masters</u> degree in language. (Passage 3-F)

3. If you have a tendency toward procrastination, you are always doing <u>yesterdays</u> jobs today, and tomorrow you are doing <u>todays</u> unfinished work. (Passage 4-B)

4. During <u>my fathers</u> generation the education system was very different from my generation. (Passage 4-D)

5. He wants to arrange <u>his sons</u> and <u>daughters</u> marriages. They are a big family . . . (Passage 8-C)

6. During <u>Stalins</u> era in the forties and fifties, knowledge of western languages was a real problem [in Poland] because it could cause a lot of trouble. (Passage 9-A)

7. In this restaurant <u>at least three countries</u> cultures were blended in one place. (Passage 8-H)

8. At the end of his journey, near <u>the castles</u> gate, [the oldest son] saw a dwarf who asked him for a crust of bread. (Passage 9-E)

7. Using Articles and Quantifiers
"I went to the market and I bought . . ."

This is a game to be played with a group of people. You can divide the group into two teams which play alternately and compete to lose the fewest points.

The first player, from Team 1, begins by naming something that he or she bought in the market. For example:

I went to the market and I bought a donkey.

The second player, from Team 2, repeats this and adds another item:

I went to the market and I bought a donkey and some apples.

The third player, from Team 1 again, adds yet another :

I went to the market and I bought a donkey, some apples, and three radios.

Continue alternating between the teams until someone makes a mistake. If the person forgets one of the items, their team loses one point; but if they use the wrong quantifier or article, their team loses two points.

At the end of the game, your teacher may ask you to write down the whole list of things that you "bought."

8. Choosing an Appropriate Quantifier

The following sentences are taken from various essays in this book. The quantifiers have been taken out and replaced by blanks. For each blank, make a list of all the quantifiers that could be placed there, and mark with an asterisk (*) the one that you think is best. (In many cases there is only one possibility, but in some cases there are several.) When you have finished, compare your choices with what the writers of the essays actually used.

1. I sometimes question myself, "How _____ years have I been learning English?" (Passage 1-A)

2. I was looking in my dictionary to check _____ word I did not know. (Passage 3-A)

3. The merchants extend _____ multicolored drapes over their heads and tables. (Passage 3-H)

4. One day, _____ students in my class started guessing each other's age, and soon _____ students too began to guess each other's age. (Passage 4-A)

5. _____ people complain that they have _____ time to do this or that. However, if you check what you have done all day long, you will find that you have done _____ things which were not necessary. (Passage 4-B)

6. Nowadays I feel the limitation of my capability to do _____ kinds of work together. I feel too tired to do _____ the work at the same time. (Passage 4-C)

7. During my father's generation the education system was very different from my generation. Back in those days _____ schools were provided by the British. . . . Things are not easy in my generation. The students have _____ opportunities to learn. (Passage 4-D)

8. What if a housewife neglects her housekeeping job for _____ days? Most likely, she will not be kicked out by her husband. (Passage 7-A)

9. I see my uncle's house, small but comfortable, very old-fashioned looking without bathroom and electric kitchen, surrounded by the forest on _____ side and fields of corn on _____ one. (Passage 7-B)

10. I went to the first room to exchange my dollars for Spanish currency and to get _____ information. A nice woman explained to me that the tour information office and _____ marketplaces were closed because it was the weekend. (Passage 8-B)

9. Editing for Style

In the following sentences, the writers have used the informal quantifiers *a lot of* or *lots of*. Edit each sentence by substituting an appropriate and more formal quantifier.

1. All of the classes that I'm taking require <u>a lot of</u> work. . . . I don't have enough time to study homework, and exams give me <u>a lot of</u> pressure. (Passage 4-C)

2. Several days ago, I read an interesting article in the newspaper. It was a correspondence column by a housewife. She was writing that <u>a lot of</u> married women were working these days and the media had implied that just being a housewife was out of date. (Passage 7-A)

3. There is one place in the world that I would like to visit again. It is a magic place—a small village in southeastern Poland where I spent <u>a lot of</u> time growing up. (Passage 7-B)

4. During Stalin's era in the forties and fifties, knowledge of western languages was a real problem [in Poland] because it could cause <u>a lot of</u> trouble. (Passage 9-A)

5. I would like to introduce the Korean writing system because <u>lots of</u> people think that Korean, Chinese, and Japanese have the same writing systems. Chinese and Japanese have similar writing systems, but the Korean one is different. (Passage (9-C)

Expanded Noun Phrases

CHAPTER 6

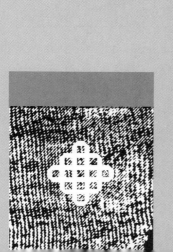

*I*n an **expanded noun phrase,** either or both of the **premodifier** and **postmodifier** positions are filled. (See Chapter 5.) In the following passage, all the expanded noun phrases are underlined and the core noun of each is in italics:

Passage 6-A   **THE GREAT CULTURAL REVOLUTION**

by Yin Yan Zhang

Twenty-six years ago, the unprecedented *Great Cultural Revolution* swept across all *parts* of China. This campaign was created by some *statesmen* whose aim was to realize their political ambition of owning the right to rule the whole of China by praising Chairman Mao. During this campaign,
5 *students* traveling from one place to another cried *slogans* such as "Long live Chairman Mao" and "Class struggle is a key link." Meantime, they, along with workers, peasants and soldiers, learned Mao's works as the supreme *instruction* and took part in the so-called revolutionary *criticism* in which they criticized the authorities and some old people who had contributed most of their lives
10 to Chinese liberation.

In some expanded noun phrases, only the premodifier position is filled, in addition to the determiner and the core noun:

| the supreme instruction
└──→ ────→   *

In other cases, by contrast, only the postmodifier position is filled, in addition to the determiner and the core noun:

| all parts of China
└──→ * ←────

| some statesmen   whose aim was to realize their political ambition of
| owning the right to rule the whole of China by praising
| Chairman Mao
└────→   *   ←──────────────

In some noun phrases, both the premodifier and the postmodifier positions may be filled:

| the so-called revolutionary criticism   in which they criticized the
| authorities and some old people
| who had contributed most of their
| lives to Chinese liberation
└────────────────────→   *   ←────

All these postmodifiers have other noun phrases packed inside them. (See

120

the explanation of how noun phrases are packed inside each other in Chapter 5, Section 1.)

1. PREMODIFIERS

The premodifier position enables you to describe or identify the core noun that you are talking about more exactly. Three kinds of words are used as premodifiers: adjectives, verbals, and nouns.

1.1 Adjectives

Adjectives are identified in dictionaries by the letters <u>adj.</u> in italics. They include words that describe size (e.g., *big, small*), color (e.g., *blue, red*), general appearance (e.g., *ugly, beautiful*), and other attributes that a person or a thing might have (e.g., *intelligent, clumsy, wonderful, fat*).

In writing Passage 3-F, Gonzales has used several adjectives in the premodifier position:

> [My cousin Sonia] married a <u>professional</u> man and had a <u>beautiful</u> wedding . . . I saw her life as the <u>perfect</u> model . . . Sonia saw me as a <u>spoiled</u> child . . . [but now] she sees me as an adult and <u>responsible</u> person.

1.1a Singular and Plural Adjectives

English adjectives do <u>not</u> have different forms for singular and plural, so you should never add an *-s* ending to one. (In this respect, English is different from many other European languages.) So, for example, the adjectives in the passage about Cousin Sonia would remain the same even if the nouns were plural:

<u>professional</u> men   <u>beautiful</u> weddings   <u>perfect</u> models
<u>spoiled</u> children   <u>responsible</u> people

1.1b Using Qualifiers with Adjectives (*very*, etc.)

You can qualify any adjective—that is, make its meaning stronger or weaker—by putting a **qualifier**, such as *very*, in front of it. Look at this example from Passage 2-C:

> [My cousin Sonia] was a <u>good</u> daughter and a <u>very good</u> student.

The combination of *very* plus adjective, e.g., *very good,* is a kind of adjective phrase.

WHEN YOU ARE WRITING

Inexperienced writers often use qualifiers unnecessarily, especially *very*. When you edit your work, check each use of *very* and delete the word if you do not need it.

WHEN YOU'RE TALKING

English has many words that can be used to qualify adjectives. The following are used in speech but not usually in writing:

a bit	darn(ed)*	plain	right
awful(ly)	kind of	pretty	sort of
bloody*	mighty	real(ly)	terribly
damn(ed)*			

The ones with the asterisk (*) are mild swear words.

WHEN YOU ARE READING

You will see a number of other words used as qualifiers, particularly in academic writing. These qualifiers usually end in *-ly*. They include:

about	in no way	particularly	rather
almost	merely	partly	scarcely
entirely	nearly	perfectly	somewhat
especially	not at all	practically	thoroughly
fairly	only	quite	vitally
hardly			

Note that *too* is not a qualifier. It is part of a comparative construction (see Chapter 11, Section 3.4) and should never be used in place of *very*.

1.1c Comparative Adjectives

All adjectives can be made **comparative** so that you can say how one thing or person compares with another. Comparative adjectives are formed in the following ways:

- For **short adjectives,** the comparative form is made by adding *-er* to the base (i.e., the word you find in the dictionary). Figure 6-1 gives the comparative forms of some common adjectives:

FIGURE 6-1 Comparative Forms of Short Adjectives

BASE	COMPARATIVE
big	bigger
early	earlier
great	greater
happy	happier
hard	harder
small	smaller

Notice that when an adjective ends in a single consonant, as *big* does, you double the consonant before adding *-er.* If it ends in a *y,* as *early* and *happy* do, you change the *y* to *i* when you add *-er.*

Notice also that two of the most common English adjectives have highly irregular forms, as shown in Figure 6-2:

FIGURE 6-2 Comparative Forms of *good* and *bad*

BASE	COMPARATIVE
good	better
bad	worse

- For **long adjectives** (ones that are three or more syllables), you make the comparative form by putting *more* in front of the base adjective. Thus, instead of an adjective, you use an adjective phrase. Examples are given in Figure 6-3:

FIGURE 6-3 Comparative Forms of Long Adjectives

BASE	COMPARATIVE
beautiful	more beautiful
difficult	more difficult
horrible	more horrible

WHETHER YOU'RE TALKING OR WRITING

Be careful not to use *more* together with an adjective that is already comparative in form. For instance, you may occasionally hear "more better," but this is considered a bad mistake in standard English.

Using Comparative Adjectives

The comparative form of an adjective (as well as a base adjective with *more* in front of it) always implies a comparison with other things or people. For example, in Passage 5-A, Gzik writes:

> Every one of these trends is about to get worse, as the states must choose between extra cops, extra classrooms, health care or welfare, <u>higher taxes</u> or less of everything else.

In the phrase "higher taxes," Gzik is comparing future taxes with past ones and suggesting that there may be an increase in the amount of taxes people have to pay.

It is unusual, however, to find a comparative adjective as a premodifier in a noun phrase. More often you will find one in the predicate (in the **complement** position—see Chapter 10) when the noun it describes is in the subject. For example, look at the first part of the sentence quoted above:

SUBJECT	**PREDICATE**
Every one of these trends	is about to get <u>worse</u> . . .

In the complement position, a comparative adjective is usually at the core of an adjective phrase that has a postmodifier beginning with the preposition *than*. For example, in Passage 4-A, Nakashizuka writes:

> In my country every man and woman seems to believe that younger women are always *better* <u>than older women</u> . . .

This kind of adjective phrase is hardly ever used as a premodifier. (For a full explanation of how to use it as a complement, see Chapter 11.)

1.1d Superlative Adjectives

All adjectives can also be made **superlative** so that you can describe a thing or person as being in the top or bottom position in a ranked group. Superlative adjectives are formed in the following ways:

- For **short adjectives,** the superlative form is made by adding *-est* to the base (i.e., the word you find in the dictionary). Figure 6-4 gives the superlative forms of some common adjectives:

FIGURE 6-4   Superlative Forms of Short Adjectives

BASE	SUPERLATIVE
big	biggest
early	earliest
great	greatest
happy	happiest
hard	hardest
small	smallest

Notice that when a base adjective is made superlative, it is modified in the same ways as it is when made comparative.

Again, the adjectives *good* and *bad* have highly irregular superlative forms, as shown in Figure 6-5.

FIGURE 6-5   Superlative Forms of *good* and *bad*

BASE	SUPERLATIVE
good	best
bad	worst

Be careful when using *worse* or *worst.* They are often confused.

• For **long adjectives** (ones that are three or more syllables), you make the superlative form by putting *most* in front of the base adjective. Examples are given in Figure 6-6:

FIGURE 6-6   Superlative Forms of Long Adjectives

BASE	SUPERLATIVE
beautiful	most beautiful
difficult	most difficult
horrible	most horrible

Using Superlative Adjectives

A superlative adjective describes the noun it goes with as being in the top or bottom position in a group. It assumes that the group has been ranked with respect to the quality named by the adjective.

Since only one individual (or set of individuals) can be at the top or bottom, it identifies whatever you are talking about. For this reason, you should nearly always put *the* in the determiner position before a superlative adjective. Then you should usually add a postmodifier to define the group that you are thinking of.

She was there as the *oldest* student in my class. (Passage 4-A)

For me, my mother was the *most beautiful* woman in the world. (Passage 13-A)

Quebec City is the *most joyful* place that I have ever been to. (Passage 5-C)

See the explanation in Section 2 of the postmodifier position.

Alternatively, you can use a possessive in the determiner position before a superlative adjective. The possessive itself defines the group to which the core noun belongs. For example, in Passage 14-F Lewicka writes about:

My *best* friend.

The group of friends referred to is adequately defined by the word *my*.

WHEN YOU ARE WRITING

Check your use of superlative adjectives by asking yourself these questions:

1. Which group is the noun described a member of?
2. Have you added a postmodifier in order to make that group clear to the reader?
3. If no, would it be better to use a base adjective instead?

You should only use a superlative if you want your reader to think of a ranked group.

1.2 Verbals as Premodifiers

Verbals are those verb forms that do not have tense. (See Chapter 10.) The verbals that end in *-ing* or *-d/t/n* are frequently used as adjectives, and so you can put them in the premodifier position in noun phrases. When you do so, remember that there is an important difference in meaning between the two kinds of verbals: those ending in *-ing* are generally **active,** while those ending in *-d/t/n* are always **passive.** This point is explained briefly below, but for further explanation see Chapter 10, Sections 3.2 and 3.3, and Chapter 11, Section 3.5.

1.2a Verbals with -*ing*

In Passage 10-A, the writer tells us:

The job had an *exciting* part.

In other words, part [of the job] was exciting—it <u>caused</u> excitement. Similarly, Passage 8-J includes the following sentence:

He did not stop for the *begging* dwarf.

This means that the dwarf was begging.

However, -*ing* verbals in the premodifier do not always describe what the core noun is doing. Consider, for example, this sentence:

It is not the *growing* or *harvesting* season on the big farms. (Passage 8-J)

This means that it is not the season <u>for</u> growing or harvesting.

These two different uses of -*ing* verbals as premodifiers do not seem to cause any difficulty. From your own knowledge of the world, you can tell what the relationship between the core noun and the verbal is.

1.2b Verbals with -*d/t/n*

A -*d/t/n* verbal is used as a premodifier in the following sentence:

I keep my diaries on my bookshelf, which has a *locked* glass door on it. (Passage 8-A)

This means that the door was locked by somebody—the door itself did not do anything. Other examples of -*d/t/n* verbals used as premodifiers appear in the following sentences:

"Yakitori" means "*grilled* chicken," so "Beef Yakitori" cannot exist. (Passage 8-H)

Sometimes *arranged* marriages don't work. (Passage 8-I)

Notice again the passive meaning: Somebody grilled the chicken and somebody arranged the marriage.

1.3 Nouns as Premodifiers

Nouns are often used to classify or describe other nouns, and then they are put in the premodifier position. One of the slogans quoted in Passage 6-A, "Class struggle is a key link," provides two examples:

0 <u>class</u> struggle   a <u>key</u> link
⟶   *   ⟶   *

Notice the difference between the noun that is a premodifier and the noun that is the core of the phrase: "class struggle" is a kind of struggle, not a kind of class; similarly "a key link" is a link (in a chain of events) and not a kind of key.

LEARNING STRATEGY

Forming Concepts: Analyzing many examples helps you understand relationships between words.

Look out for examples of two or more English nouns placed together. Think about what each example means, remembering that the last noun is the core noun, while any that come before it are premodifiers describing or classifying the core. You may want to write some of the examples down and discuss them with your colleagues in class or in a study group.

Examples that you might see include "pesticide ban," "college loan bill," "assassination bid," "war refugees," "furniture sale." (All these examples were found in the headlines on the first few pages of a single newspaper.)

1.4 Noun Phrases as Premodifiers

Occasionally a whole noun phrase can fill the premodifier position. The following example comes from Passage 6-B:

a computer operator course

"Computer operator" is itself a noun phrase with a premodifier and a core, although it does not have its own determiner:

computer operator

You may notice that the premodifier in this case is yet another noun, *computer.* Passage 6-B includes another example of exactly the same pattern:

a job placement agency

In such cases, where three nouns are strung together with no words or punctuation in between them, the last in the series is always the core noun.

A common kind of noun phrase in premodifier position is one that begins with a number. It is not like a regular noun phrase, however, because the noun following the number is always <u>singular</u> in form, and the number and noun are often linked by a hyphen. Note these examples:

a <u>three-*room*</u> apartment

a four-*cylinder* engine

Similarly, when a noun phrase beginning with a number combines with an adjective to make a premodifier, the noun following the number is singular:

a three-*year* old boy
a six-*foot* tall man

1.5 Order of Premodifiers

You can, in theory, use any number of premodifiers in a noun phrase, although it is unusual to use more than two. See the following example from Passage 6-A:

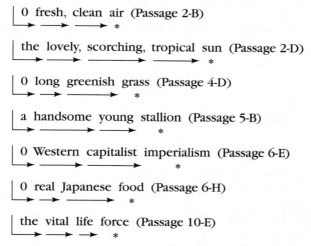

the Great Cultural Revolution

Examples from other passages in this book include:

0 fresh, clean air (Passage 2-B)

the lovely, scorching, tropical sun (Passage 2-D)

0 long greenish grass (Passage 4-D)

a handsome young stallion (Passage 5-B)

0 Western capitalist imperialism (Passage 6-E)

0 real Japanese food (Passage 6-H)

the vital life force (Passage 10-E)

The rules governing the order of premodifiers are complicated and subtle, and we can only give a simplified version here. In general, you can think of a series of three basic premodifier positions, any of which may be filled: The positions are for **emphasizers**, **describers**, and **classifiers**.

1.5a Emphasizers

Adjectives that emphasize or tone down the meaning of the rest of the noun phrase, and especially of the noun itself, are put first after the determiner. When used for this purpose, these adjectives cannot be made comparative, nor can they be used with a qualifier such as *very*. Such adjectives include:

absolute	entire	perfect	real
certain	extreme	plain	slight
definite	feeble	pure	total

CHAPTER 6: EXPANDED NOUN PHRASES

Emphasizers are used in the following examples:

the <u>unprecedented</u> Great Cultural Revolution (Passage 6-A)

the <u>so-called</u> revolutionary criticism (Passage 6-A)

<u>real</u> Japanese food (Passage 8-H)

1.5b Describers

These adjectives simply describe the noun. They can be made comparative and can be used with a qualifier. They are a large group that is further divided:

- <u>Evaluative</u> adjectives express the speaker's or writer's opinion or feeling about whatever is being described. They include words such as *beautiful, horrible, lovely, nasty,* and *wonderful.* When more than one describer is used, the evaluative one is put first.
- Adjectives that describe <u>size, length, or height</u> come next. They include *big, small, long, short,* and *tall.*
- Adjectives that describe other qualities follow, for example, *hot, cold, funny, sad, stupid, smart.*
- Adjectives that describe <u>color</u> come last.

1.5c Classifiers

This position may be filled by either adjectives or nouns.

FIGURE 6-7   The Order of Premodifiers Within a Noun Phrase

DETERMINER	INTENSIFIER/ MODIFIER	DESCRIBER			
		EVALUATIVE	SIZE	OTHER	COLOR
the		Great			
0				fresh, clean*	
the		lovely		scorching	
0			long		greenish
a		handsome		young	
0					
0	real				
the				vital	

* When two or more premodifiers of the same type are together, they can go in any order.

Adjectives in this position classify the core noun in terms of frequency, nationality or region, or area of activity or study. These adjectives usually follow the order given here:

- Frequency, e.g., *annual, monthly, weekly, daily.*
- Nationality or region, e.g., *African, Chinese, Spanish, western.*
- Area of activity or study, e.g., *educational, medical, political, social.*

When nouns are used as postmodifiers, they are always classifiers and come last before the core noun.

Figure 6-7 summarizes the rules about the order of postmodifiers and shows how those rules are applied in the examples quoted above.

WHEN YOU ARE WRITING

When you use a series of premodifiers, check the order in which you have put them against Figure 6-7. It is not a serious problem, however, if you cannot easily work out which category each of the adjectives you have used belongs to. The order of many adjectives is variable, and even when native speakers have a particular preference, it will not be considered a serious mistake if you get it wrong. The only effect will be that your writing will appear slightly foreign.

CLASSIFIER				NOUN
FREQUENCY REGION	NATIONALITY/ STUDY	ACTIVITY/	NOUN	
	Cultural		Revolution	
				air
tropical			sun	
				grass
				stallion
Western		capitalist	imperialism	
Japanese			food	
			life	force

1.6 Punctuating Premodifiers

When you use two or more describers, you can separate them from each other by commas:

> fresh, clean air (Passage 2-B)

Doing this has the effect of making each describer more emphatic. You should not, however, separate describers from other kinds of premodifiers, except when you have two describers before a classifier and the two already have a comma between them:

> the   lovely, scorching, tropical   sun (Passage 2-D)

The commas are not essential in either case, so when in doubt about whether they are appropriate, leave them out.

> You should not put a comma before the core noun.

LEARNING STRATEGY

Managing Your Learning: Keeping notes of examples that you read helps you understand grammatical structures.

Notice any strings of premodifiers that you come across when you read, and write them down, including any commas, in a notebook or on index cards. Then check them against Figure 6-7, noting which one fits into which premodifier position and how they are punctuated.

2. POSTMODIFIERS

You can also put a **postmodifier** after the core noun in a noun phrase. We discuss the three types of postmodifiers below.

2.1 Prepositional Phrases

A prepositional phrase is a phrase that consists of a **preposition** followed by a noun phrase. Passage 6-A gives several examples of noun phrases with this kind of postmodifier. Here, the prepositional phrase is underlined, and the preposition is in italics:

> all parts *of* China
> ⟶   *   ⟵

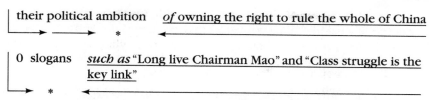

their political ambition   _of_ owning the right to rule the whole of China

0 slogans   _such as_ "Long live Chairman Mao" and "Class struggle is the key link"

You will nearly always find that a noun phrase that has a superlative adjective in the premodifier position also has a postmodifier. The postmodifier is often a prepositional phrase beginning with _in_. Consider again the following examples. We have underlined the whole noun phrase and put the preposition that begins the postmodifier in italics:

She was there as the oldest student _in_ my class. (Passage 4-A)

For me, my mother was the most beautiful woman _in_ the world. (Passage 13-A)

In each case, the postmodifier identifies the group with which the writer has compared the individual she is talking about. In Passage 4-A, Nakashizuka considers the woman's age in relation to that of the other people who were in her class. In Passage 13-A, Cioczek tells how, as a child, she thought of her mother in relation to all the other women in the world.

2.2 Verbal Phrases

A **verbal phrase** is the same as a predicate except that instead of a verb, it has a verbal, or a verb without tense (see Chapter 10). When used as a postmodifier in a noun phrase, a verbal phrase may begin with _to_ followed by the **base** form of the verb (that is, the verb itself with no ending added), or it may have the verb form that ends in _-ing_ or, less often, the _-d/t/n_ form of the verb. Passage 6-A contains an example where the postmodifier is a verbal phrase with the _-ing_ form:

0 students   _travelling_ from one place to another

In this example from Passage 5-A, the verbal phrase in the postmodifier begins with _to_ and the base form:

[Education] is . . . the main and basic program to achieve one's goal in life.

the   main and basic program   _to achieve_ one's goal in life

And in this example (from Passage 14-A), the postmodifier begins with the _-d/t/n_ form:

Some islands have volcanic soil strewn with ashes and lava.

0 volcanic soil   _strewn_ with ashes and lava

Notice that the verbal phrases that begin with *-ing* verbs are active in meaning: They describe what the things named by the core nouns <u>do</u>. Those that begin with *-d/t/n* verbs are passive in meaning: They describe what has <u>happened</u> to the things named by the core nouns. (See Chapters 8, 9, and 10.)

2.3 *Wh*-clauses (Relative Clauses)

A *wh*-clause is also called a **relative clause,** and it defines or identifies more precisely the core noun that it follows. It generally begins with *that* or with one of the following *wh*-words: *who, whom, which, when, where, whose.* Examples from Passage 6-A are:

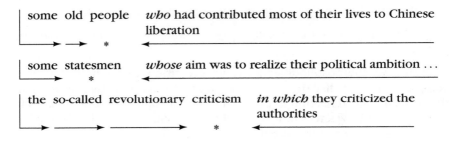

Another example appears in Gzik's essay about education (Passage 5-A):

<u>Children *who* live within two miles of school</u> are no longer qualified for bus service.

> 0 children *who* live within two miles of school

A *wh*-clause can be used, like a prepositional phrase, to define the group that you have ranked when you use a superlative adjective:

Quebec City is <u>the most joyful place *that* I have ever been to.</u> (Passage 5-C)

> the most joyful place *that* I have ever been to

2.3a Constructing *Wh*-clauses

A *wh*-clause is useful for identifying what you are talking about without making a new sentence. For example, if Gzik had not used a *wh*-clause, he would have had to make two sentences, like this:

In some cities, children live within two miles of school. Those children are no longer qualified for bus service.

He has two things to say about children. The first identifies which children he is talking about, while the second is new information about them:

	SUBJECT	PREDICATE
Identifying	children	live within two miles of school
New	children	are no longer qualified for bus service

He can combine these two statements by putting the identifying one into the new one as a postmodifier. To do this, he must go through three steps:

1. He deletes *children* in the identifying statement:

	SUBJECT	PREDICATE
Identifying	~~children~~	live within two miles of school
New	children	are no longer qualified for bus service

2. He inserts *who* after *children* in the new statement:

	SUBJECT	PREDICATE
Identifying	~~children~~	live within two miles of school
	who . . .	
New	children	are no longer qualified for bus service
	∧	

3. He puts what remains of the identifying statement immediately after *who:*

	SUBJECT	PREDICATE
Identifying	~~children~~	live within two miles of school
	who . . .	
New	children	are no longer qualified for bus service
	∧	

Thus, instead of two short sentences, he ends up with one long one in which the identifying information is given, but the new information is more prominent:

SUBJECT	PREDICATE
Children who live within two miles of school	are no longer qualified for bus service.

This example is relatively simple because the core noun described is the subject of the *wh*-clause, that is, of the identifying statement. Things get a little more complicated when the core noun is not the subject. Think about this sentence from Miura's essay in Chapter 1:

> The "English" that I learned in Japan didn't help much in New York. (Passage 1-A)

Miura has two things to say about "English," but in this case the word is in the **predicate** of the identifying statement, in the **object** position. (See Chapter 11, Section 2.)

	SUBJECT	PREDICATE
Identifying	I	learned "<u>English</u>" in Japan
New	The "<u>English</u>"	didn't help much in New York

To attach the identifying statement to the new one, Miura again goes through three steps:

1. She deletes *"English"* in the identifying statement:

	SUBJECT	PREDICATE
Identifying	I	learned "~~English~~" in Japan
New	The "<u>English</u>"	didn't help much in New York

2. She adds *that* after *"English"* in the new statement:

	SUBJECT	PREDICATE
Identifying	I	learned "~~English~~" in Japan
	that . . .	
New	The "<u>English</u>"	didn't help much in New York

3. She takes all that is left of the identifying statement and puts it after *that* in the new one:

	SUBJECT	PREDICATE
Identifying	I	learned "~~English~~" in Japan
	that . . .	
New	The "<u>English</u>"	didn't help much in New York

This leaves her with just one sentence:

SUBJECT	PREDICATE
The "<u>English</u>" that <u>I learned in Japan</u>	didn't help much in New York.

The same principle can be applied when what is described is in a prepositional phrase in the identifying statement. An example is given in Passage 8-C:

Another problem that we are faced with is that I have not yet met his parents.

Here the writer has two things to say about "another problem":

	SUBJECT	PREDICATE
Identifying	we	are faced with <u>another problem</u>
New	<u>another problem</u>	is that I have not yet met his parents

Notice that in the first statement, the words *another problem* follow the preposition *with*. When the writer turns this statement into a *wh*-clause, she goes through the three steps we describe above:

1. She deletes *another problem* in the identifying statement, but she keeps *with* where it is:

	SUBJECT	PREDICATE
Identifying	we	are faced with ~~another problem~~
New	<u>another problem</u>	is that I have not yet met his parents

2. She inserts *that* in the new statement:

	SUBJECT	PREDICATE
Identifying	we	are faced with ~~another problem~~
	that . . .	
New	<u>another problem</u>	is that I have not yet met his parents

3. She turns all that remains of the identifying statement into a postmodifier by inserting it after *that*. Notice that she leaves the preposition *with* where it is.

	SUBJECT	PREDICATE
Identifying	we	are faced with ~~another problem~~
	that . . .	
New	<u>another problem</u>	is that I have not yet met his parents

This gives her the following sentence:

	SUBJECT	PREDICATE
	<u>Another problem that we are faced with</u>	is that I have not yet met his parents.

WHEN YOU ARE WRITING

Learners of English may be tempted to put an extra pronoun in a *wh*-clause if the thing or person described is either in the object position or following a preposition in the identifying statement. For example, they might write:

The English that I learned <u>it</u> in Japan didn't help much in New York.

Another problem that we are faced with <u>it</u> now is that I have not yet met his parents.

Putting a pronoun into the *wh*-clause in this way is a mistake. To guard against it, check every *wh*-clause that you write, and ask yourself these questions:

1. Have you put *him, her, it,* or *them* in the *wh*-clause?
2. If so, what does the pronoun refer to?

If the pronoun refers to the noun that the *wh*-clause describes, you should cross it out.

Another kind of *wh*-clause begins with the *wh*-word *where*. An example is given in Chang's essay about Curaçao (Passage 3-H).

Curaçao is the island where I was born.

Chang has two things to say about "the island":

	SUBJECT	PREDICATE
Identifying	I	was born <u>on the island</u>
New	Curaçao	is <u>the island</u>

"On the island" is an adverbial telling us *where* she was born, so Chang deletes the whole adverbial and uses the *wh*-word *where*.

1. She deletes *on the island,* from the identifying statement:

	SUBJECT	PREDICATE
Identifying	I	was born <u>on the island</u>
New	Curaçao	is <u>the island</u>

2. She inserts *where* after *the island* in the second sentence:

	SUBJECT	PREDICATE
Identifying	I	was born ~~on the island.~~
		where . . .
New	Curaçao	is <u>the island</u>

∧

3. She puts the rest of the first sentence into the postmodifier that begins with *where:*

	SUBJECT	**PREDICATE**
Identifying	I	was born ~~on the island~~.

where . . .

| New | Curaçao | is the island |

So she finally has a sentence that ends with a long noun phrase:

	SUBJECT	**PREDICATE**
	Curaçao	is the island where I was born.

The word *when* can be used in a similar way to introduce a *wh*-clause that describes a time:

> There were moments *when* he talked very openly to us about himself, his family, and what he thought and in what he believed. (Passage 7-D)

2.3b When to Use Which Wh-word

The most common *wh*-words are *who, which,* and *that,* and another common option is to leave out the *wh*-word altogether. When you should use which of these options depends partly on what you are describing, partly on how formal you want to be, and partly on the position that the noun described fills in the identifying statement.

• *Who* can only be used to introduce clauses that describe people. It is the preferred *wh*-word when the person described is the subject of the identifying statement.

> They criticized the authorities and some old people *who* had contributed most of their lives to Chinese liberation. (Passage 6-A)

> [An adult immigrant] is afraid that he can't find a person *who* speaks his language. (Passage 7-F)

> Somebody *who* had this knowledge was considered to be an adherent to western capitalist imperialism. (Passage 9-A)

However, when the person described appears in the predicate of the identifying statement, it is better not to use *who.* In informal writing or speech, you should either leave it out or use *that* (see the last two parts of this section); in formal writing, you should use *whom* instead. (See Section 2.3c.)

• *Which* can only be used for clauses that describe things, but it does not matter whether the thing described is in the subject or the predicate of the identifying statement. Examples include the following:

> Today I must not only accomplish my today's homework, but also I shall write <u>one composition *which* should have been finished yesterday</u>. (Passage 4-B)

> At least I will have left them <u>something *which* money cannot buy</u>. (Passage 8-A)

- *That* can be used for either people or things, whatever their position in the identifying sentence.

> I gradually stopped postponing <u>the chores *that* faced me</u>. (Passage 4-B)

> <u>Those books *that* they absolutely need</u> they pay for out of their own pockets. (Passage 5-A)

> [Street entertainers] are <u>talented musicians *that* spend an average of eight hours a day on the streets</u>. (Passage 10-B)

- When what you are describing is in the predicate of the identifying statement, you can leave out the *wh*-word altogether—that is, use zero. You can use zero for either people or things. In informal speech or writing, it is better to use zero rather than *who* when you are describing a person that is in the predicate of the identifying statement. In the following example, we have printed a *0* where the *wh*-words would be:

> I listened to my cousin telling me about <u>the many places *0* she visited</u> and <u>the people *0* she met</u> while she was in Europe. (Passage 5-B)

Figure 6-8 summarizes the information on when to use which of these four options.

FIGURE 6-8   Using the Most Common *Wh*-words

Wh-WORD	USED FOR . . .
who	Introducing clauses that identify people only
which	Introducing clauses that identify things only
that	Introducing clauses that identify people or things
0	Introducing clauses that identify people or things, but only when they are in a predicate position of the identifying sentence

2.3c *Wh*-clauses in Formal English

In formal English, especially when you are writing, you may use two more *wh*-words not included in the above list: *whose* and *whom.* In addition, when you want to be formal, you must use prepositions in *wh*-clauses differently from how you treat them in informal writing or speech.

- *wh*-clauses with *whose*

  Use *whose* only when the noun you are describing is a **possessive** in the identifying statement. (See Chapter 5, Section 3.4, for a discussion of possessives.) Zhang uses *whose* in Passage 6-A:

  > This campaign was created by <u>some statesmen *whose* aim was to realize their political ambition</u>. . .

  She has told us two things about "some statesmen":

	SUBJECT	PREDICATE
Identifying	<u>some statesmen's</u> aim	was to realize their political ambition . . .
New	this campaign	was created by <u>some statesmen</u>

Notice that in the identifying statement, "some statesmen's" is a possessive beginning the noun phrase "some statesmen's aim."

To combine these two statements using *whose,* follow these steps:

1. Delete *some statesmen's* in the identifying statement:

	SUBJECT	PREDICATE
Identifying	~~some statesmen's~~ aim	was to realize their political ambition . . .
New	this campaign	was created by <u>some statesmen</u>

2. Insert *whose* after *some statesmen* in the new statement:

	SUBJECT	PREDICATE
Identifying	~~some statesmen's~~ aim	was to realize their political ambition . . .
		whose . . .
New	this campaign	was created by <u>some statesmen</u>
		∧

3. Insert what is left of the identifying statement after *whose* in the new one:

	SUBJECT	PREDICATE
Identifying	~~some statesmen's~~ aim	was to realize their political ambition . . .
		whose . . .
New	this campaign	was created by <u>some statesmen</u>
		∧

- *wh*-clauses with *whom*
  If a *wh*-clause is about a person, and the person is in the predicate of the identifying statement, you may use *whom*. For example, in Passage 10-B, the writer could have put

> A young man *whom* I know . . . developed a musical talent at eight years old.

In this particular essay, however, *whom* would not have been appropriate, since the style of the essay as a whole is informal.

- *wh*-clauses with prepositions
  In formal written English, a *wh*-clause should not have a preposition after the verb (whereas in speech or informal writing it is quite all right for them to do so). Consider again the example from Tineo's essay (Passage 8-C):

> Another problem *that* we are faced *with* is that I have not yet met his parents.

In formal writing, you use *which* instead of *that* to make the *wh*-clause. You should also shift the word *with* so that it is in front of *which:*

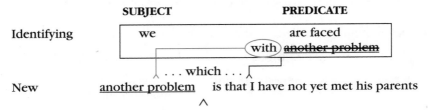

The resulting sentence will be like this:

> Another problem *with which* we are faced is that I have not yet met his parents.

Notice that Zhang's essay (Passage 6-A) has a *wh*-clause of this kind:

> [Students], along with workers, peasants and soldiers, . . . took part in the so-called revolutionary criticism *in which* they criticized the authorities and some old people who had contributed most of their lives to Chinese liberation.

It is in fact preferable to shift the preposition to the front of a *wh*-clause that begins with *which, whom,* or *whose,* but remember that the effect is formal. If you want to be less formal, use *that* or zero instead and leave the preposition at the end of the clause.

2.3d Punctuating Wh-clauses

You should never put a comma between a core noun and its postmodifier, even if it is a long *wh*-clause. If you do, you change the meaning of the *wh*-clause that follows the comma: Instead of being a postmodifier that identifies the noun, it becomes an **insert** that simply adds extra information about it. Consider, for example, this sentence from Passage 5-A:

> <u>Children who live within two miles of school</u> are no longer qualified for bus service.

This means that the buses will no longer pick up some children—the ones who live within two miles of school, but they will still pick up others—the ones who live farther away. But if we put in a comma, we convert the *wh*-clause to an insert and change the meaning of the sentence:

> Children, <u>who live within two miles of school</u>, are no longer qualified for bus service.

This means that the buses will no longer pick up any children. All the children live within two miles of school, so probably the authorities do not think it is necessary.
    (For more about *wh*-clauses as inserts, see Chapter 14, Section 3.)

LEARNING STRATEGY

Forming Concepts: Analyzing new information helps you understand it better.

    Look for *wh*-clauses when you are reading and notice the punctuation used. If there is no comma before the *wh*-word, try inserting one. How does it change the meaning? If there is a comma, try taking it out and asking the same question.

2.4 Singular and Plural Noun Phrases with Postmodifiers

You need to know whether the noun phrases you use are singular or plural, both for agreement between subject and verb and for choosing the right pronouns. This can be difficult when you use a postmodifier because you tend to lose sight of the core noun. So when you use a noun phrase with a postmodifier, ask yourself these questions:

1. What is the core noun of the phrase? (Remember, it will be the noun <u>before</u> the preposition, the verb without tense, or the *wh*-word.)
2. Is the core noun singular or plural? If the core noun in the phrase is singular, the whole phrase is singular, even when there is a plural noun in the postmodifier;

similarly, if the core noun is plural, the whole phrase is plural. It is only the core that counts.

a few sentences from the textbook = plural (Passage 1-A)

a dorm mistress for the sixth and seventh year seniors = singular (Passage 3-A)

the people of the island = plural (Passage 3-H)

0 many kinds of education = plural (Passage 4-D)

the smell of wild cornflowers = singular (Passage 7-B)

3. QUANTIFIER PHRASES

Quantifier phrases are like noun phrases except that the core word is a number or some other quantifier. This means that in this kind of phrase, the quantifier is not in the determiner position but in the core position. Below are two examples from Passage 5-A, with the quantifiers printed in italics and the whole phrases underlined. We have also analyzed the phrases to show the determiner, core, and postmodifier in each case. (It is rare for a quantifier phrase to have a premodifier.)

Every *one* of these trends is about to get worse . . .

every one of these trends

If a teacher has five classes and about 25 students in each class, and *each* of them uses one sheet a day, the teacher will run out of paper in about four weeks.

0 each of them

There are also several examples in other chapters of this book:

English was and is *one* of the main subjects at junior and high school in Japan. (Passage 1-A)

I am beginning to accept that New York is *one* of the Melting Pots . . . (Passage 8-H)

Scientists know *some* of the causes . . . (Passage 8-G)

Quantifier phrases are similar to noun phrases, but note that they have these special characteristics:

1. They never have *a* or *an* in the determiner position, and usually have zero there.
2. They usually have a postmodifier beginning with *of.*
3. The noun or pronoun that follows *of* in the postmodifier is always plural.

WHEN YOU ARE WRITING

If you use a phrase with *one* in the core position, ask yourself: How many is one? Singular or plural? It is singular, of course—so make everything that has to agree with it (verbs, pronouns) singular too.

ACTIVITIES

1. Understanding the Order of Premodifiers

Figure 6-9 on the next two pages is the same as Figure 6-7 except that all the spaces have been left blank. Look at Figure 6-7 again, and then fill in the blanks in Figure 6-9 by putting the words in each of the noun phrases listed below into the appropriate columns. If possible, do this with a partner or in a group.

1. the out-dated education system (Passage 1-A)
2. big mushroom-shaped trees (Passage 3-H)
3. a good, regular time . . . (Passage 4-B)
4. different educational systems (Passage 4-D)
5. the hot summer days (Passage 7-B)
6. a conservative school system (Passage 7-D)
7. special creative ability (Passage 8-H)
8. the beautiful big cranes (Passage 8-G)
9. an ancient Chinese medical technique (Passage 14-E)
10. measurable physiological changes (Passage 14-E)
11. recent medical reviews (Passage 14-E)
12. a bright new future (Passage 14-H)

2. Using Multiple Premodifiers

Insert one or more premodifiers in each of the noun phrases listed in Activity 1 above. Be prepared to explain to your classmates why you have put each

FIGURE 6-9   The Order of Premodifiers Within a Noun Phrase

DETERMINER	INTENSIFIER/ MODIFIER	DESCRIBER			
		EVALUATIVE	SIZE	OTHER	COLOR

premodifier in the particular place you have chosen. The first one is done for you as an example:

1. The <u>terrible</u> out-dated education system

   Terrible is placed before *out-dated* because it is an evaluative adjective.

3. Recognizing the Core Noun When There Is a Postmodifier

In the following passage, all the noun phrases that have postmodifiers are numbered and printed in italics. Underline the core noun in each case, and write above the phrase *sing.* if it is singular and *pl.* if it is plural. Your instructor may ask you to do the first paragraph together in class and then to finish at home.

Passage 6-B   **LOOKING FOR WORK**

by Vilma Villatoro

My first year in America was (1) *a year of struggles.* I first went to (2) *a school of languages* to learn English, but after six months I had to stop attending because (3) *the money I had saved for my education* was all spent. The next thing I did was to look for (4) *a job to support myself.* Since
5   I could speak very little English, I had to choose between working in a factory or in a cafeteria. After (5) *four and a half months working at the cafeteria,*

	CLASSIFIER			NOUN
FREQUENCY REGION	NATIONALITY/ STUDY	ACTIVITY/	NOUN	

my supervisor laid me off. Then I promised myself that I would never be unemployed again.

     I thought of improving my office skills because I wanted to get (6) *the same working status that I had in Honduras.* A secretarial school promised to help me get a job when I graduated. It was a good deal! In six months I would be making lots of money, I thought. A word processor specialist could start earning $21,000. I finished the course in five months. I made my own resumé, and then I went to the school personnel office to be interviewed. The personnel administrator was a very serious lady. She first looked at me from head to toe. Next she gave me a typing test. I gave her my resumé. It started with (7) *a short statement like this:* Objective: To obtain (8) *a position as a Word Processing Specialist.* She saw my resumé and said, "Your typing is excellent, but your accent is terrible. I think it won't be easy for me to get a job for you." She made me feel like a second class citizen. Although she said that, she sent me to a hospital for an interview. There were (9) *a lot of people applying for the same position,* and they all spoke English with an American accent. I didn't have (10) *any chance of getting a job there.* After that interview, I started looking for my own job. I went to a dozen places with no results. Finally I went to the Tap Center. The Tap

Center is (11) *a job placement agency for the unemployed.* There, they advised me to take a Computer Operator course. They told me that a hundred percent of all (12) *the people who take this course* get a well paid job. I attended classes from 9 to 5, and in the evenings I took a bookkeeping

30   course to get familiar with (13) *the accounting terminology in English.* In November 1989 I graduated from both courses; I got an "A" in bookkeeping and an award in computers.

My objective was to get (14) *a job as a bookkeeper;* I stated that in my resumé. I went to see the personnel administrator, who was a very nice lady.

35   During the interview the accent problem came out again; however, she promised to help me get a job. Three weeks passed, and she still did not show (15) *any signs that she was looking to place me in a job.* So I decided to mail one hundred resumés to (16) *all potential employers where I could get a job.* Finally, I got (17) *a bookkeeping position in a Spanish bank with*

40   *a starting salary of $18,000.*

4. Supplying Postmodifiers

In the following passage, all the postmodifiers have been removed and replaced by blanks. The postmodifiers are then printed, in random order, after the passage. You are asked to put each of them in its right place. (For the correct version of the passage, see Appendix 2.)

Passage 6-C   **WORKING IN CUBA**

by Nieves Angulo

What is a job? (1) The first thing _____ is (2) a place _____. But this is not the case sometimes. In Cuba, for example, students have jobs, and they do not earn money at all.

I began to work in agricultural farms at an early age. I did not do it because I had to earn money to support myself. It is (3) a requirement _____ after (4) the revolution _____. The government says that the young generation must contribute something to the revolution, so working on those farms is (5) one _____. Thus, at (6) the age _____, I was doing (7) the work _____.

POSTMODIFIERS

of them
for all Cuban students
of eleven
that comes to mind
at all
of a farmer
where people spend eight hours working and earning money
of 1959

5. Combining Statements Using *Wh*-clauses

The following pairs of statements have been adapted from various essays printed in this book. Originally the two statements in each pair were combined in a single sentence. Recombine the statements by changing the first one (the "identifying" statement) into a *wh*-clause and putting it into the second one (the "new" statement) as a postmodifier. Follow the procedure described in Section 2.3 of this chapter, and write the sentence you have constructed in the space provided beneath each pair.

1. Classmates were from different countries.

I had never lived in a foreign country before, so it was a new experience for me to have classmates. (Passage 4-A)

_____

_____

_____

_____

2. Many people could speak English, French, or German.

Many people denied the fact. (Passage 9-A)

_____

_____

_____

_____

3. A program entitled "Aspects of Shanghai Husbands" immediately became a tremendous hit and aroused widespread heated criticism.

About a year ago, Shanghai TV Station broadcast a program entitled "Aspects of Shanghai Husbands." (Passage 9-F)

_____

_____

_____

_____

4. She buys food.

   The food should be healthy food and should not cost much money. (Passage 8-D)

   _____

   _____

   _____

   _____

5. Scientists have not yet solved a mystery.

   Here is a mystery. (Passage 8-G)

   _____

   _____

   _____

   _____

6. People on the streets would give him donations.

   He began to support his family by the donations. (Passage 10-B)

   _____

   _____

   _____

   _____

7. Nearly everybody has said goodbye to old-fashioned, stereotyped thinking.

   The idea that a woman needs a husband in order to be happy is old-fashioned, stereotyped thinking. (Passage 11-A)

   _____

   _____

   _____

   _____

8. At a Japanese restaurant the owner was Australian and all the cooks and some waitresses were Koreans.

From 1985 to 1986 I was in Australia and was working at a Japanese restaurant. (Passage 8-H)

_____

_____

_____

_____

6. Constructing Your Own Wh-clauses

Working with a partner, make pairs of sentences that are true statements about things or people that are familiar to you. The first should be an identifying sentence, e.g. "We study at a college," the second, one that gives new information, e.g., "The college is at . . . [give the address]." Write each pair of sentences out in a framework like the one given below and as we have done in our explanation of *wh*-clauses in Section 2.3. Then combine the sentences in each pair by putting the identifying sentence into the new one as a *wh*-clause. Write the combined sentence underneath as suggested below.

	SUBJECT	PREDICATE
Identifying	We	study at a college
New	The college	is at . . .
Combined sentence	The college we study at is at . . .	

_____

_____

Pronouns

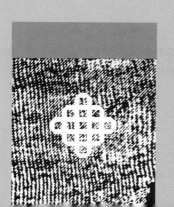

7

CHAPTER

When you use **pronouns**, you are usually telling your readers or listeners to think of people or things that they know about already. In the following passage, all the pronouns are underlined. As you read it, try to identify exactly what is referred to by each one. You should be able to do so easily except in those cases that are marked by an asterisk. (We will discuss those cases later in the chapter.)

Passage 7-A   **WHAT IS A PROFESSIONAL?**

by Satoko Asai

Several days ago, I read an interesting article in the newspaper. It was a correspondence column by a housewife. She was writing that a lot of married women were working these days, and the media had implied that just being a housewife was out-of-date. She commented that she was proud
5   that she was a housewife, because housewives were the professionals of housekeeping. Is she right? Is she really a professional? I don't think so.

A professional is a person who is faced with stressful circumstances, namely, if one* does not do good work, he/she* will not be allowed to continue that work. If one* makes a crucial mistake, he* or she* should not
10   survive in that field. That* is one of the measurements of a professional. But what if a housewife neglects her housekeeping job for a couple of days? Most likely, she will not be kicked out by her husband.

One day, I saw a homeless man in the subway. He was a little bit different from other homeless people. When he came into our car, he started
15   making a speech: how hard he had tried to find a job, how difficult it* was to do so, how hungry he was, and so on. Then he sang a song with a sad low voice. It sounded pitifully throughout the car. Moreover, his speech was so persuasive that people could not help feeling sympathy. As a result, most people there gave him some change, or even a dollar. His paper cup was
20   filled with money in a minute.

If we compare that homeless man and the housewife who wrote her contribution to the paper, which one seems to be more professional? Clearly, that homeless man is exposed to a much tougher world. If that man did not perform well in front of the people, he could not survive. Since the
25   housewife is not exposed to a severe situation, she is not a professional.

1. THE PRONOUN SETS OF ENGLISH

English, like other languages, has three basic sets of pronouns: **first person pronouns,** which people use for referring to themselves, **second person pronouns,** which people use for referring to those they are speaking or writing to, and **third person pronouns** for referring to other people or things. Except for the second person pronouns, each set has both singular and plural forms. In addition, the third person pronouns include masculine, feminine, and neuter forms, as well as an impersonal one. Finally, each set of pronouns includes different forms for use in different positions. In short, the pronoun system of English is quite complex, retaining distinctions that are no longer made in other parts of the language and reflecting ways in which the language is changing now. Figure 7-1 gives an overview of the whole system. We will then discuss each set in turn.

FIGURE 7-1   The Pronoun System

SET	SUBJECT	OBJECT	POSSESSIVE (DETERMINER)	POSSESSIVE (AS NOUN PHRASE)	REFLEXIVE
First person					
singular	I	me	my	mine	myself
plural	we	us	our	ours	ourselves
Second person					
singular	you	you	your	yours	yourself
plural	you	you	your	yours	yourselves
Third person					
sing. masc.	he	him	his	his	himself
sing. fem.	she	her	her	hers	herself
sing. neuter	it	it	its	—	itself
impersonal	one	one	one's	—	oneself
plural	they	them	their	theirs	themselves

2. FIRST PERSON PRONOUNS

2.1 Subject and Object Pronouns

The following examples, all taken from essays in this book, show how the first person pronoun forms are used in subject and object positions. In the subject position of a sentence or clause, use *I* or *we:*

Several days ago, I read an interesting article in the newspaper. (Passage 7-A)

From the windows we can see the St. Lawrence river . . . (Passage 5-C)

In the object or indirect object positions, or after a preposition, use *me* or *us:*

After her announcement, she asked me how I felt about leaving home. (Passage 3-A)

English for me was tedious memorization. (Passage 1-A)

. . . the teachers gave us a quiz once a week to know how many words we remembered. (Passage 1-A)

All of us are having a good time. (Passage 5-C)

When you use a first person singular pronoun together with a noun phrase and you join them together with *and,* you should, for politeness, put the pronoun second, after the *and.*

My uncle and I spent most of the time together in the backyard when I was a child. (Passage 5-D)

WHEN YOU'RE TALKING

You are quite likely to hear native speakers of English using *me* and *us* in the subject position.

Me and my friends went to the movies last night.

Using the pronouns in this way sounds natural and is perfectly comprehensible, but it is not technically correct, and it is associated with the way children talk. You should definitely avoid it in writing.

You will also sometimes hear native speakers using *I* in the object position:

The teacher didn't see my sister and I.

People do this because they have been taught not to use "me and my sister" in the subject position, and they do not realize that the problem is not the form "me" itself, but the position that it fills and the fact that it is placed before the noun phrase. The sentence should be:

The teacher didn't see my sister and me.

2.2   Possessive Pronouns

As you see from Figure 7-1, English has two kinds of possessive pronoun for each person. The first kind, which for the first person singular is *my* and for the first person plural *our,* is used in the determiner position of a noun phrase. (See Chapter 5, Section 3.4.) In the following examples, we have underlined the whole noun phrase and have put the possessive in italics:

> *My* favorite possession is an abacus. (Passage 9-D)

> *Our* teachers required us to memorize grammatical formulas and meanings of words. (Passage 1-A)

The second kind is used to replace a noun phrase that begins with a possessive in the determiner position. For example, if the remark about an abacus were made in a conversation, someone might reply to it as follows:

> Oh, mine is a computer!

Here, mine is used to replace "my favorite possession." Similarly, someone could reply to the remark about teachers, saying,

> Ours never did that, but they made us read and write a lot.

Ours is used in place of "our teachers."

Possessives used in place of noun phrases are not common, however, especially in writing, and the passages printed in this book include no examples.

2.3 Reflexive Pronouns

In all of the pronoun sets, reflexive pronouns have two different uses:

- They are used within the predicate to refer back to a person or thing mentioned previously, generally the subject of the sentence. So the first person reflexive pronouns refer back usually to *I* or *we,* and occasionally to *me* or *us.* In the following examples, both the reflexive pronouns and the pronouns that they refer back to are underlined:

  > I sometimes question myself, "How many years have I been learning English?" (Passage 1-A)

  > Of course, I might have tried to improve by myself, but I didn't even want to think about English. (Passage 1-A)

  > I did not do it because I had to support myself. (Passage 6-C)

  > Besides money, the job gave me confidence in myself. (Passage 10-A)

  > We had to get more information about the victims, arrange financial aid

for families, and especially, support <u>ourselves</u> and alleviate the prevailing distrust of each other. (Passage 14-H)

- Occasionally reflexive pronouns are used as inserts after noun phrases or pronouns in order to emphasize them. The student essays in this book contain no examples of *myself* or *ourselves* used in this way, so we have taken the following from a standard grammar book:

    I <u>myself</u> wouldn't take any notice.

    —*A Comprehensive Grammar of the English Language* by Randolph Quirk et al.

3. SECOND PERSON PRONOUNS

Choosing the correct second person pronoun for a particular position never seems to be a problem. What you have to think about is when it is suitable to use this pronoun set.

- In speech, you will use *you,* etc., all the time to refer to the person you are talking to.

- In writing, you will use the second person if you are giving direct instructions to your reader. Tsien, for example, uses it throughout her essay on "How to use time well":

    The first way to use time well is not to delay doing something until some future time. This is a terrible habit—procrastination. If <u>you</u> have a tendency toward procrastination, <u>you</u> are always doing yesterday's jobs today, and tomorrow <u>you</u> are doing today's unfinished work . . . (Passage 4-B)

- You may also use second person pronouns to refer, not to your readers or listeners in particular, but to people in general. That is how Sampson uses them in the following example:

    The primary customs that any immigrant coming into the U.S. should hold dear are their own. It makes no sense to change <u>your</u> ideas and beliefs if <u>you</u> think they are right. When it comes to <u>your</u> language, two languages are better than one. If <u>you</u> speak two languages, <u>you</u> could get special privileges when applying for some jobs. Having <u>your</u> own language and customs could be beneficial. (Passage 3-D)

This use is common in speech, but it is not considered proper in most academic writing. Moreover, in the above example, you can see that the writer has not been consistent: He uses *their* (from the third person plural set) in the first sentence and then switches to the second person. It would probably be more satisfactory for him to rewrite the passage like this:

> The primary customs that immigrants coming into the U.S. should hold dear are their own. It makes no sense for <u>them</u> to change <u>their</u> ideas and beliefs if <u>they</u> think those ideas and beliefs are right. When it comes to language, two languages are better than one. If people speak two languages, <u>they</u> could get special privileges when applying for some jobs. Having <u>their</u> own language and customs could be beneficial.

4. THIRD PERSON PRONOUNS

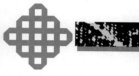

Third person pronouns are generally used to refer to people or things that have already been named. The important point is that it should be clear who or what you are referring to. When you are talking, of course, the people you are talking with will let you know if they have lost track of who or what you mean; when you are writing, however, it is easy to use pronouns ambiguously. You must edit your pronouns carefully, therefore, to make sure that you do not confuse your reader.

As Figure 7-1 shows, the third person pronoun set includes five different subsets. We discuss each of these below, with examples. In the examples, we have underlined the pronouns and have written what they refer to in italics.

4.1 Singular Masculine Pronouns

He, him, his, and *himself* normally refer to a person or animal that is male. Notice how, in Passage 7-A, Asai uses *he, him,* and *his* to tell us to keep "a homeless man" in mind throughout the following paragraph. (*He* is used in subject position, *him* in object position, and *his* as a determiner.)

> One day, I saw a *homeless man* in the subway. <u>He</u> was a little bit different from other homeless people. When <u>he</u> came into our car, <u>he</u> started making a speech: how hard <u>he</u> had tried to find a job, how difficult it was to do so, how hungry <u>he</u> was, and so on. Then <u>he</u> sang a song with a sad low voice. It sounded pitifully throughout the car. Moreover, <u>his</u> speech was so persuasive that people could not help feeling sympathy. As a result, most people there gave <u>him</u> some change, or even a dollar. <u>His</u> paper cup was filled with money in a minute.

Until the 1980s, singular masculine pronouns were also regularly used to refer to people or animals whose sex was not specified. Tsien uses *he* in this way at the end of her essay:

If *a person* uses time completely and well, <u>he</u> will be more successful than others. (Passage 4-B)

Nowadays, however, many people interpret masculine pronouns to exclude females, so they would understand the above sentence as applying only to male persons. To include both males and females in a generalization, do one of the following:

- If possible, make the noun phrase in which you name the group you are talking about, and the pronouns that go with it, plural, remembering to change the verbs, if necessary, as well:

  If *people* use time completely and well, <u>they</u> will be more successful than others.

Compare our editing, in Section 3 above, of the paragraph from Passage 3-D.

- You can simply repeat the noun phrase that you started with, changing the determiner to *the* if necessary:

  If *a teacher* has five classes and about 25 students in each class, and each of them uses one sheet a day, <u>the teacher</u> will run out of paper in about four weeks. (Passage 5-A)

However, you should use this tactic only if you do not have to refer to the same person many times; many repetitions would make your writing clumsy.

- Use the coordinated pronoun, *he or she:*

  Of course, this is a very natural process of learning, but we know today that *the child* cannot do it alone. <u>He or she</u> needs not only the presence of at least one adult person to provide care, but the baby needs also great support from this person. (Passage 8-E)

You may write *he or she* as *he/she,* or, alternatively, you may write *(s)he* or *s/he.* The problem with all these variations is that they are clumsy if you have to refer to the person many times. (Notice how the writer of Passage 8-E has used *the baby* to avoid having to use *he or she* again.)

A Note on Using *himself*

Himself, like *myself,* can be used in two different ways:

- Use it in a predicate or verbal phrase to refer back to the person responsible for the action in question. Typically, the person is named (or referred to as *he*) in the subject position, and then *himself* is used in the object position. (See Chapter 11.) Consider the following sentence:

  Ernest Hemingway killed <u>himself</u>.

This means that Ernest Hemingway committed suicide (unless, of course, it was an accident, but in Hemingway's case the killing was almost certainly deliberate).

Compare the following sentence:

Ernest Hemingway killed <u>him</u>.

This is a case, not of suicide, but of murder (or, maybe, of killing in war, which with Hemingway was probably the case): *Him* refers, not to the subject of the sentence, but to another person who must have been named earlier.

- You can also use *himself* to emphasize a particular person. For example, you might say:

  The president <u>himself</u> came to our class.

The point here is that the president did not send anyone else.

4.2 Singular Feminine Pronouns

She, her, hers, and *herself* are used to refer to female people or animals, as in Passage 7-A. Note that the same form, *her,* is used in both object and determiner positions:

> It was a correspondence column by a *housewife.* <u>She</u> was writing that a lot of married women were working these days and the media had implied that just being a housewife was out-of-date. <u>She</u> commented that <u>she</u> was proud that <u>she</u> was a housewife, because housewives were the professionals of housekeeping. Is <u>she</u> right? Is <u>she</u> really a professional? I don't think so.

You may sometimes use singular feminine pronouns to refer to a whole class of people, rather than to a specific person, provided every member of that class is female. Consider again Passage 7-A:

> But what if a *housewife* neglects <u>her</u> housekeeping job for a couple of days? Most likely, <u>she</u> will not be kicked out by <u>her</u> husband.

Feminine pronouns are also occasionally used to refer to countries, ships, or vehicles, but we have no examples of this use in this book.

A Note on Using *herself*

Herself is used in exactly the same ways as *himself.* Consequently there is a difference in meaning between these two statements:

Virginia Woolf killed <u>herself</u>.
Virginia Woolf killed <u>her</u>.

The first of these is a true statement: Virginia Woolf did indeed commit suicide. The second is almost certainly not true: Virginia Woolf never killed anybody as far as we know.

4.3 Singular Neuter Pronouns

4.3a Specific *it*

It and *its* are used to refer to specific things, whether concrete or abstract, that have already been named in singular noun phrases:

> Several days ago, I read *an interesting article in the newspaper.* <u>It</u> was a correspondence column by a housewife. (Passage 7-A)

> *Humanity* is in <u>its</u> childhood. (Passage 7-G)

WHEN YOU ARE WRITING

Its (without an apostrophe) is easily confused with *it's* (with an apostrophe). *Its* is the possessive, while *it's* is an abbreviation for *it is* or *it has*. So when you have written *it's,* ask yourself this question: Can I put *it is* or *it has* there instead? If you can, do so; if you cannot, then you probably mean to use the possessive *its* and should remove the apostrophe.

Because *it* can refer to any kind of thing, it is often used confusingly. Consider how Asai uses *it* in the following sentence:

> Then he sang *a song* with *a sad low voice.* <u>It</u> sounded pitifully throughout the car.

What sounded pitifully throughout the car, a song or a sad low voice? The reference is ambiguous, although in this case the ambiguity does not matter much since Asai's general meaning is clear.

WHEN YOU ARE WRITING

At the revision stage, check carefully on how you have used *it* in each case. Will your readers have any difficulty in telling what thing it refers to? If you think they might, try to substitute a noun phrase instead.

You should check your masculine and feminine pronouns for the same problem if at any time you are writing about more than one male or female.

4.3b General *it, this,* and *that*

This, that, and sometimes *it* can also be used to stand for a verbal phrase, clause, sentence, or even paragraph, that is, for an <u>idea</u> that the speaker or writer has just presented rather than a specifically named thing.

> *If one makes a crucial mistake, he or she should not survive in that field.* <u>That</u> is one of the measurements of a professional. (Passage 7-A)

That tells us, as readers, to think of the whole statement made in the previous sentence. See also how Tsien uses *this:*

> The first way to use time well is not *to delay doing something until some future time.* <u>This</u> is a terrible habit . . . (Passage 4-B)

Angulo uses *it* in a similar way:

> *I began to work in agricultural farms at an early age.* I did not do <u>it</u> because I had to earn money to support myself. (Passage 6-C)

WHEN YOU ARE WRITING

Just as with *it,* you should check each use of *this* or *that* to see that it is not ambiguous. When you use any of these words to refer to a whole sentence, clause, or verbal phrase, you can often make your writing clearer by using a noun phrase instead, e.g., "this problem," "that event."

4.3c Empty *it*

A third use of *it* is to put it in the subject position of a sentence when there is no real subject.

> <u>It</u> was mid-summer in New York, July 24, 1986, at 5:00 p.m. (Passage 8-B)

It does not refer to anything here; it is simply filling the subject position. The same is true when you "postpone" the topic of a sentence until the end, as you usually do when what you are talking about is expressed as a verbal phrase beginning with *to.* (See Chapter 10, Section 3.1.) Here is an example:

> <u>It</u> was a new experience for me to have classmates who were from different countries. (Passage 4-A)

(See Chapter 12, Section 6, for further explanation of this use of *it.*)

4.4 Impersonal Pronouns

One is used to mean "a person" when you have no particular person in mind. In American English, *one* or *one's* is only used to introduce the idea in the first place; after that, you are expected to use *he or she, his or her,* and *himself or herself.* See how Asai, a student in the United States, uses *one* in combination with *he or she* in Passage 7-A:

> If *one* makes a crucial mistake, <u>he or she</u> should not survive in that field.

The fact that you have to use compound pronouns after *one* makes the impersonal pronoun clumsy to use in American English. It is also very formal and if used too much, will make your writing sound stuffy.

In British English, *one* is not used in combination with *he or she,* etc. It is repeated instead, or the forms *one's* or *oneself* are used. So if she were studying in Britain, Asai would probably write:

> If *one* makes a crucial mistake, <u>one</u> should not survive in that field.

The British way of using *one* is less clumsy than the American, so *one* is more common and slightly less stuffy in British than in American English. Even in British English, however, the impersonal pronouns are characteristic of formal writing or speech.

4.5 Third Person Plural Pronouns

They, them, their, theirs, and *themselves* are used to refer to both people and things. Learners rarely have difficulty choosing the right one for a particular position in a sentence; the problem is in using these pronouns unambiguously. For example, we, the authors of this book, faced a problem when we decided to edit the following sentences from Passage 3-D:

> The primary customs that *any immigrant* coming into the U.S. should hold dear are <u>their</u> own. It makes no sense to change *your ideas and beliefs* if <u>you</u> think <u>they</u> are right.

To make the pronouns consistent, we decided that it would be better to make "any immigrant" plural and then to use third person plural pronouns throughout instead of second person ones. If we had done only that, however, we would have created an ambiguity:

> The primary customs that *immigrants* coming into the U.S. should hold dear are <u>their</u> own. It makes no sense to change <u>*their*</u> *ideas and beliefs* if <u>they</u> think <u>they</u> are right.

What is meant by *they* in the clause "they are right"? Readers would not be able to tell from the above version: *They* might refer to "immigrants" or it might refer to "their ideas and beliefs." From the original version, however, we knew that it must be "ideas and beliefs," so, to make the point clear, we did some further editing:

> The primary customs that *immigrants* coming into the U.S. should hold dear are <u>their</u> own. It makes no sense for <u>them</u> to change *their ideas and beliefs* if <u>they</u> think <u>those ideas and beliefs</u> are right.

This is a point that you have to watch carefully for when you edit your written work.

WHEN YOU ARE WRITING

When you write *their*, ask yourself this question: Do I really want the possessive pronoun here? *Their* is easily confused with *they're*, which is an abbreviation for *they are*. It is also easily confused with *there*, which is used, like *here*, to refer to a place. Another use of *there* is in the subject position of a sentence that introduces a new topic, as in the following example from Passage 11-A:

> <u>There</u> were only three occasions when [the woman I spoke to] wished she was married.

(See Chapter 12, Section 5, for a fuller explanation of sentences that begin with *there*.)

LEARNING STRATEGY

Managing Your Learning: Making a chart or diagram can help you remember differences.

FIGURE 7-2   *its/it's* and *their/they're/there*

POSSESSIVE PRONOUNS	ABBREVIATIONS	"PLACE" WORDS
its their	it's = it is / it has they're = they are	there is like here

A Note on Using *themselves*

Themselves is sometimes misused by learners of English. Consider the following examples:

> Romeo and Juliet loved each other.

This means that Romeo loved Juliet and Juliet loved Romeo. (If you know the story, you will see that this is an accurate statement—Romeo and Juliet are famous precisely because they did love each other.)

> Romeo and Juliet loved themselves.

This means that both Romeo and Juliet were selfish people: Romeo loved Romeo and Juliet loved Juliet (not an accurate statement, according to the story).

> Romeo and Juliet loved them.

This means that Romeo and Juliet both loved some other things or people. (The statement may be accurate, according to the story, if *them* refers to "parties.")

WHEN YOU'RE TALKING

You may hear speakers of some varieties of English using the form *theirself* (and also *hisself*). Although logically more consistent with the rest of the pronoun system than *themselves* and *himself, theirself* and *hisself* are not used in standard written English.

WHEN YOU ARE WRITING

Check the ending of the word *themselves* by asking yourself these questions:

1. Have you added the *-s* ending?
2. Have you changed the *-f* of *self* to *-ve* so as to make *selves?*

Students commonly encounter three major problems when using pronouns in writing:

- When they are making general statements, they tend to shift from one person to another, especially from *they/them* to *you*. This problem is discussed in Section 3 above.
- They often use third person pronouns (*he, she, it, they,* etc.) ambiguously—that is, it is not clear who or what the pronoun refers to. We have discussed this in various parts of Section 4, but we would like to emphasize here that the problem occurs with all third person pronouns. It is, perhaps, most frequently a problem with the plural ones.
- Student writers sometimes use a plural pronoun for a singular noun and vice versa. For example, it is easy when making generalizations about "a professional," as Asai does in Passage 7-A, to slip into using *they* to refer to the same idea. The mismatch can be quite troubling to a reader.

WHEN YOU ARE WRITING

Check each of your pronouns to make sure that they are consistent and unambiguous, and that they match the number of whatever they refer to. One way to do this is to start from the <u>end</u> of a piece of writing. Identify each pronoun and ask yourself these questions about it:

1. What does the pronoun refer to?
2. What other pronouns have you used for that referent? Do they all belong to the same set? If they do not, change some of them so that they are all consistent.
3. Is there any other noun phrase in your text that the pronoun could be referring to? If there is, change the pronoun to a noun phrase.
4. Does the pronoun match the number (singular or plural) of its referent? If it does not, change it from singular to plural or vice versa.

6. COMPOUND PRONOUNS

Another set of pronouns is used in place of noun phrases to refer to unidentified people or things. These pronouns are formed by combining a quantifier with *-one, -body,* or *-thing.* They are listed in Figure 7-3.

FIGURE 7-3   Compound Pronouns

FOR PEOPLE	FOR THINGS
everyone everybody	everything
anyone anybody	anything
someone somebody	something
no one nobody	nothing

The meaning of each compound pronoun depends on the quantifier on which it is based, and the rules about when to use the pronoun are the same as the rules for the quantifier. (See Chapter 5, Section 3.5.) The following examples demonstrate how the compound pronouns are used:

> Even though I was confused by those brand-new things [during my first English lesson], I was certainly learning <u>something</u>. . . . But my interest in English was being diminished day by day . . . We had to memorize a whole chapter to pass the examination. After the examination, I used to forget <u>everything</u>. Thus, I didn't learn <u>anything</u>. (Passage 1-A)

> If you check what you have done all day long, you will find you have done a lot of things which were not necessary. . . . Did you call <u>someone</u> up or talk with <u>somebody</u> without a purpose? (Passage 4-B)

> When I began to look for information about education, I found people who, instead of giving information, were trying to sell me things. <u>Nobody</u> explained to me the difference between two-year education and four-year education and the different kinds of financial aid that I could get . . . (Passage 7-F)

> I am surprised to see how much energy humans spend in destroying themselves. You must admit that they do <u>nothing</u> to better their mental power. (Passage 7-G)

Notice that *someone, somebody,* and *something* are used to make positive statements. If you want to make a negative statement, use *not . . . anyone/anybody/ anything,* or use *no one, nobody,* or *nothing.* Do not, however, combine these two kinds of negatives. It is considered a bad mistake in standard English to use *no one, nobody,* or *nothing* together with *not.*

All the compound pronouns are technically singular, but the gender of the ones used for people is obviously unknown, so English speakers are increasingly using *they/them/their* to refer to *everyone, everybody, someone, somebody, no one,* and *nobody.* See the following example:

> After *everyone* had told <u>their</u> own age, she looked at our faces with a warm smile and said joyously, "Oh, children!" (Passage 4-A)

Some people are still uncomfortable with this use, however, so it is better in formal situations to avoid the problem. For example, the above sentence could be edited in this way:

> After *we* had each told <u>our</u> own age, she looked at our faces with a warm smile and said joyously, "Oh, children!"

ACTIVITIES

1. Recognizing and Interpreting Pronouns

In Passage 7-B, underline every pronoun. Then write above the pronoun who or what it refers to, together with the number of the line in which that person or thing is first mentioned. Write *the writer* above *I, me,* etc., and in the one place where the pronoun refers to nothing (it is merely filling the subject position), write *nothing.* When the pronoun refers to nothing, you do not need to write any sentence number.

Check your answers with your classmates; you should all have the same ones.

Passage 7-B **A BEAUTIFUL PLACE**

by Anna Cioczek

There is one place in the world that I would like to visit again. It is a magic place—a small village in southeastern Poland where I spent a lot of time growing up. I can just close my eyes and think about this place. Memories come back to me, and I can see it with such clarity that it sometimes shocks

5   me that I am able to remember so many details.

This is my little paradise, a landscape of peace and harmony. There I am again, standing in the middle of the village like a ghost, brought by one of my memories of this place. I see my uncle's house, small but comfortable, very old-fashioned looking without bathroom and electric kitchen, surrounded by

10   the forest on one side and fields of corn on the other one. I am looking up to

the sky with white clouds and tiny birds singing incredibly beautifully. During the hot summer days, as soon as the sun goes up, they fly high to the sky and stay there all day long, keeping the farmers working in the fields company. There must have been a mystic relationship between them.

15   Warm fresh air brings the smell of wild cornflowers to me. They look delicate and fragile, like blue butterflies, so bright in color compared to the gold fields of corn that waves with the wind like a real ocean.

In my imagination, I can see the farm with my favorite animals—the horses. My uncle had four of them. One, in particular, called Kario, comes
20   back to my memories. He is a handsome young stallion with a powerful body, a little too massive and too big to be considered an example of beauty, but I like him anyway. So many times, I used to take him with me to the forest and spend hours and hours there, thinking about my problems, my happy times, my past, and my future dreams.

2. Using First and Second Person Pronouns

In the following passage, the writer has used a number of first and second person pronouns (including one instance of *myself*). We have printed and underlined the first pronoun that she uses from each of the two sets, but we have replaced the others by blanks. You are asked to fill in each blank with the correct pronoun. You may want to do this with a partner or in a group. (For a correct version of this passage, see Appendix 2.)

Passage 7-C   **AN IMMIGRANT'S EXPERIENCE**

by Martine Liney

America, the land of opportunities, the dream land. Is it really? For some people America is the land of opportunities, but for others it is the land of self-destruction.

I personally can say that America is the land of opportunity for the
5   people who already have family in the country like (1) _____. If you come to America as a young child with parents who are working hard to make it, (2) _____ are lucky, in fact very much so. (3) _____ have been here for three years. When (4) _____ came, (5) _____ didn't know English. With the right help, (6) _____ have graduated from high

10 school and am now continuing to pursue (7) _____ goals by attending
this college.

Life has been very easy for (8) _____ here. Unlike (9) _____
mother, (10) _____ do not have any responsibilities but (11) _____
school work and sometimes things that (12) _____ have planned and
15 what (13) _____ want to do. (14) _____ also didn't have to worry
about a permanent residence when (15) _____ came here, since (16)
_____ mother had already taken care of that. When (17) _____ came
here, (18) _____ went straight to school. To find a job was very easy. All
(19) _____ needed was to be the right age and to have (20) _____
20 working papers.

Yes, America is the land of opportunities, but not for a single working
parent like (21) _____ mother, who has been working very hard. (22)
_____ mom came here ten years ago to further her education and visit
the country so (23) _____ brother and (24) _____ could also come for
25 (25) _____ education. It has been ten years. Still, not once has she
stepped foot in a class room.

3. Using Third Person Pronouns

In the following passage, you are asked to fill in the blanks with third person
masculine, feminine, neuter, impersonal, or plural pronouns, according to the
sense of the passage. Again, you could do this with a partner or in a group. (For a
correct version of this passage, see Appendix 2.)

Passage 7-D   **UELI GERBER**

by Henriette Schoch

When Ueli Gerber was my teacher, (1) _____ was already in
(2) _____ fifties. Nevertheless, (3) _____ appearance was very well
groomed, and (4) _____ was quite tall and slender. . . . (5) _____
features were attractive and well proportioned. I suppose (6) _____
5 could have been said that (7) _____ was good looking if there hadn't
been those eyes. (8) _____ were close together and in deep sockets. The
color was a harsh blue. Maybe (9) _____ was this color which made
(10) _____ glance sometimes so cold, almost uncomfortable. Today I

think (11) _____ is true what a German poet once said: the eyes are the

10   windows of the soul. Ueli Gerber's soul evidently wasn't very pretty.

(12) _____ was always very correctly attired, never fancy but never without good taste. I never saw (13) _____ , for example, without a tie, although (14) _____ wasn't required for teachers to wear ties. (15) _____ used to say that (16) _____ knew, when (17) _____

15   wore (18) _____ tie, that (19) _____ was the teacher and no private person any more and that (20) _____ would feel naked without (21) _____. The tie was as important for (22) _____ as armor was for a knight when (23) _____ went for a fight. Apparently teaching was fighting; there was no doubt about (24) _____.

20   (25) _____ thought that (26) _____ had to fight, in order to force us to learn. In a rather conservative school system, as in Switzerland, (26) _____ is rather a usual attitude. In fact there are a lot of teachers who drill (27) _____ students with this attitude; and (28) _____ are successful, because (29) _____ are strong enough and, most important,

25   (30) _____ are fair. The students know exactly what (31) _____ have to do, and as long as (32) _____ stick to the rules, everything works pretty well. However, Ueli Gerber wasn't strong enough. (32) _____ personality was very ambiguous and unstable. There were moments when (33) _____ talked very openly to us about (34) _____, (35) _____

30   family, and what (36) _____ thought and in what (37) _____ believed. In other moments (38) _____ regretted (39) _____ open utterances, and (40) _____ behaved in a very reserved way, to the point of being impolite.

4. Substituting Pronouns for Noun Phrases

In the following passage, the 11 pronouns that the writer originally used have been replaced by the noun phrases that they refer to; as you see, it makes the writing very clumsy. Underline the noun phrases that you think must originally have been pronouns and write the appropriate pronoun above each. When you have finished, compare your interpretation with your classmates'. (For a correct version of this passage, see Appendix 2.)

Passage 7-E **HER LUCK**

by Parastoo Khorramian

(1) The little girl was a little girl who lived in a small town in Iran. (2) In the little girl's small town people were separated into two groups, lucky and unlucky. (3) No matter how hard the people worked, the results were the same. (4) Some could improve some people's lives by working hard and some could not. (5) In the little girl's case, the little girl's family could not improve the little girl's family's life. (6) The little girl's family wasn't lucky. (7) The little girl's mother and the little girl's father worked hard, but still there wasn't enough money at home. (8) Thinking of being unlucky forever would make the little girl sad, but one day everything changed.

5. Using Pronouns Clearly and Consistently

In the following passage, which is a powerful statement of immigrants' problems, the writer is not talking about specific people, but about a general group. It is difficult, when doing this, to use pronouns consistently; writers tend to shift from one pronoun to another, just as this writer has done. It is also difficult to use the pronouns unambiguously. Preferably working with two or three other people, edit the passage so that the pronouns are consistent and clear.

Passage 7-F **EDUCATION FOR IMMIGRANTS**

by Daysi Mendoza

In order for any person to succeed in America, they need to speak English and to have an education. For adult immigrants, it is difficult to succeed in America, because they have to be able to break certain barriers such as language and culture. It is more difficult when they cannot find the right help. An adult immigrant is like a disabled person in that he or she doesn't know the language and doesn't know where to go or how to get there. He is afraid that he can't find a person who speaks his language. What about when this education is not well developed and there is not enough information?

There are many education programs in America, but it is hard to get information about them. I will call this "Power Information," because without

it nobody can make it. It means that the programs are not appropriately advertised, and they are not informative. For example, when I began to look for information about education, I found people who, instead of giving
15   information, were trying to sell me things. Nobody explained to me the difference between two-year education and four-year education, and the different financial aids that I could get and their requirements.

Another problem is how long immigrants have to study to get a degree. There are a lot of obstacles in this university system for immigrants, such as
20   having to pass all remedial courses before taking regular classes. It does not matter if one is never absent and does all the assignments if you can't pass the exams. Also, in one class, there are students with different problems: for some it is grammar, for others it is organization, and for others it is a little of both. The professors can cover only one area, so what about the other
25   students who need help? In addition, you can pass the exams, but when you transfer to other colleges, they are not acceptable.

All these problems and many more make many adult immigrants give up learning English and getting an education. They feel frustrated and trapped by the system, and they prefer to be treated like a working human
30   machine, just another number, just another slave, just another fool.

LEARNING STRATEGY

Understanding and Using Emotions: When you become aware of other people's thoughts and feelings, you learn about other cultures.

6. Using Nonexclusive Language

The following passage is grammatically correct, but many people would object to it because the writer has used masculine nouns and pronouns to refer to people who might be women or girls. Edit the passage, preferably through discussion with classmates, so that the statements made do not exclude females.

Passage 7-G **THE NATURAL WORLD**

by Genevieve Troussereau

I am surprised to see how much energy humans spend in destroying themselves. You must admit that they do nothing to better their mental power. We struggle during our entire life to leave an inheritance to our children, but we are unable to transmit to them our knowledge, our experience, and our

5   wisdom. In regard to the evolution of human nature, we are still primitives.

The human being acts like a bull in the china shop of the earth, manipulating, observing without wisdom his own environment, and destroying it. When poetry begins, the natural world reveals its beauty and its subtleties, especially if the poet is a visionary, a man who doesn't use his strength but

10   the power of his mind. There are two ways to be generous, the child's way who wants to please his mother and makes a mess in the kitchen to prepare the dinner, or the delicate and attentive way of a lover who is sensitive to the needs of his love. Humanity is in its childhood.

Verbs with Tense: Active

8

CHAPTER

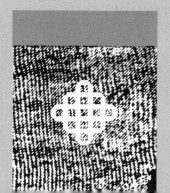

Every clause must have a **verb** at the beginning of the predicate, and the verb that fills this position always has tense. In the two passages below, the verbs with tense are underlined.

Passage 8-A   MY DIARIES

by Chien-Lun Yuan

I keep my diaries on my bookshelf, which has a locked glass door on it. When I read the earlier ones, the former times seem to appear again; I can see my first girl-friend talking with me; we go to have a picnic; we enjoy sweet days. The two years' life in the Chinese military is as clear as it was.

5   After my death, my grandchildren will read my diaries and they will know that their grandfather was once young and that he had many different experiences at that age. I do not care if they like my diaries or not. At least, I will have left them something which money cannot buy. Maybe these books are not as good as famous novels, but I value them. They are my own history.

Passage 8-B   MALAGA

by Daysi Mendoza

It was mid-summer in New York, July 24, 1986, at 5:00 p.m. My mother and I were on an airplane to Madrid, but our destination was Malaga. I could not believe that in a couple of hours my dream would come true and I would be in Spain. During the flight I fell asleep, and when I woke up, the airline

5   stewardess told us that we would be arriving in Madrid in thirty minutes. I could not believe that I had been sleeping for more than ten hours, because it was morning. At that time, I found that there was a six hour difference between Madrid and New York.

Madrid looked like New York, a big city with buildings, highways,

10   people and traffic; the only difference was the language. After we had gone through the whole procedure of immigration, we took another plane to get to Malaga. It took one hour to get there. Malaga was quite different from Madrid. Its airport was small, simple, and quiet. In one corner of the airport there was a small room with a sign that said "Monetary Change," and next to

15   this was another room with a sign that said "Tour Information," but it was closed. I went to the first room to exchange my dollars for Spanish currency and to get some information. A nice woman explained to me that the tour information office and all marketplaces were closed because it was the weekend. It reminded me that I was not in New York where everything is

20   always open.

178

The verb usually comes immediately after the subject. It may be either a **simple verb**—that is, one word—or an **expanded verb** (often called a **verb phrase**)—that is, more than one word. For every verb listed in the dictionary, there are three forms that are used for simple verbs and three forms that are used for expanded ones. The forms are shown in Figure 8-1.

In traditional grammar books, these forms are given a number of different names, according to how they are used. The following list shows all the different names:

OUR NAME	TRADITIONAL NAMES
base	stem; infinitive; present simple tense
base + -s	present simple tense (third person singular)
base + -ed	past tense
base + -ing	present participle; gerund
base + -d/t/n	past participle; passive participle

FIGURE 8-1   Verb Forms

FORMS USED FOR SIMPLE VERBS	FORMS USED FOR EXPANDED VERBS
base alone base + -s base + -ed	base alone base + -ing base + -d/t/n
EXAMPLES	
A regular verb	
wash washes washed	wash washing washed
Two irregular verbs	
keep keeps kept	keep keeping kept
eat eats ate	eat eating eaten

2. SIMPLE VERBS

Since simple verbs are both the most common and the easiest to use, we will discuss them first.

2.1 Simple Verb Forms

Simple verbs consist of one word only. Examples from the passages above are

PASSAGE 8-A	PASSAGE 8-B	
Line 1 keep, has	Line 1 was	Line 12 took, was
Line 2 read, seem	Line 2 were, was	Line 13 was
Line 3 go, enjoy	Line 4 fell, woke	Line 14 was, said
Line 4 is, was	Line 5 told	Line 15 was, said
Line 6 was, had	Line 7 was, found, was	Line 16 went
Line 7 like	Line 9 looked	Line 17 explained
Line 9 are, value, are	Line 10 was	Line 18 was
	Line 11 took	Line 19 reminded, was, is

Some of these simple verbs—*has, had, is, are,* and *was*—can also be used as auxiliaries to make expanded verbs. See the explanation of expanded verbs below.

Simple verbs (except for BE) have only three possible forms:

1. the **base** form of the verb, e.g., *keep, seem, enjoy, have, tell.*
2. the **base + -s** form, e.g., *keeps, seems, enjoys, has, tells.*
3. the **base + -ed** form, e.g., *kept, seemed, enjoyed, had, told.*

These are the forms shown on the left-hand side of Figure 8-1.

Form (3) is regular for most verbs—that is, you make it by adding *-ed* or (less often) *-d* to the base verb, e.g., *looked, explained, reminded;* but there are many verbs for which this form is irregular, e.g., *was/were, had, fell, woke, told, found, took, said, went.* The verbs with irregular forms are listed at the back of this book.

WHEN YOU'RE TALKING

The *-ed* ending on regular verbs is pronounced in three different ways:

1. Like a "d," e.g., *seemed, enjoyed, explained.* This is the most common pronunciation.
2. Like a "t," e.g., *looked, peeped, tossed, washed.* This pronunciation is used when the end of the base form is pronounced like "k," "p," "s," or "sh."

---

3. Like the word "id," e.g., *expanded, reminded, wasted.* This pronunciation is used when the base form ends with a sound like "d" or "t."

You may often find it difficult to hear the *-ed* ending on regular verbs, and in some dialects of English it is not always used. But it should never be dropped in formal speech or in writing.

2.2 Tense in Simple Verbs

Simple verbs have tense in themselves; that is, the end of a simple verb shows which time you are referring to. There are two possibilities: THEN, which usually means a past time, and NOW, which means the present period of time (whether that is a millennium, a year, an hour, or a moment). The two time frames are shown in Figure 8-2.

FIGURE 8-2   English Time Frames

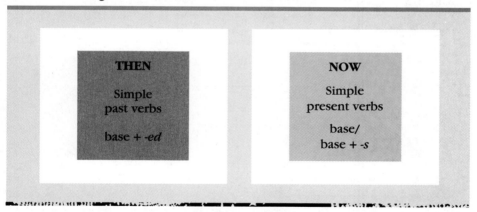

In Passage 8-A, Yuan is talking most of the time about NOW, so most of the simple verbs that he uses are in either the base or the base + -s form. In lines 4 and 6, however, he refers to THEN, that is, to the time when he wrote his diaries. In these places, he uses past tense forms:

Line 4—was
Line 6—was, had

All three are simple verbs.

In Passage 8-B, by contrast, Mendoza is talking most of the time about THEN, that is, July 24, 1986. So she uses the base + -ed form for each simple verb that is regular, and she uses the special past tense form for each simple verb that is irregular. In only one place does she refer to NOW, in line 19, when she speaks of New York. In that place, she uses the present tense form *is*.

2.3 Subject-Verb Agreement

When you are talking or writing about NOW, you have to choose between two simple verb forms: base and base + *-s*. Which of these two forms you should use in any particular sentence depends on the subject: Third person singular subjects must be followed by base + *-s*. To check whether your subject is third person singular, substitute a pronoun for it (unless there is a pronoun there already). Is the subject a *he, she,* or *it,* or is it a *they?* (If you have difficulty answering this question, see Chapter 5, Section 2; Chapter 6, Section 2.4; and Chapter 7, Section 4.) Once you have decided on the appropriate pronoun, apply the rule shown in Figure 8-3:

FIGURE 8-3   Agreement Between Subject and Verb

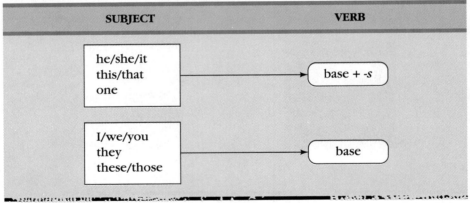

Examples from Passage 8-A are:

I <u>keep</u> my diaries on my bookshelf, which <u>has</u> a locked glass door on it.

SUBJECT	VERB
I ⟶	keep
my bookshelf = it ⟶	has

The former times <u>seem</u> to appear again

SUBJECT	VERB
the former times	
= they ⟶	seem

The two years' life in the Chinese military <u>is</u> as clear as it was.

SUBJECT	VERB
the two years' life in the Chinese military	
= it ⟶	is

When you are writing about THEN, you do not have to worry about agreement, except with the irregular past tense forms *was* and *were*. Notice how Mendoza uses these forms in Passage 8-B:

> It *was* mid-summer in New York, July 24, 1986, at 5:00 p.m. My mother and I *were* on an airplane to Madrid, but our destination *was* Malaga.

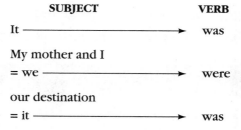

SUBJECT	VERB
It ⟶	was
My mother and I	
= we ⟶	were
our destination	
= it ⟶	was

Activities 1 and 2 at the end of this chapter provide practice in choosing the right kind of simple verb.

WHETHER YOU'RE TALKING OR WRITING

The -*s* ending on present tense verbs is considered important by many speakers of standard English, but it is often omitted, or used differently, by speakers of nonstandard dialects. Even in standard speech it is often hard to hear. Nevertheless, you should pay careful attention to it in your own speech as well as in your writing, since you may be judged as poorly educated if you omit it or use it in a nonstandard way.

3. EXPANDED VERBS

Expanded verbs consist of at least two words, that is an **auxiliary** and the verb itself. The two-word expanded verbs in Passages 8-A and 8-B are listed below.

PASSAGE 8-A				PASSAGE 8-B		
	AUXILIARY		**VERB**		**AUXILIARY**	**VERB**
Line 2–3	can		see	Line 3	could (not)	believe
Line 5	will		read	Line 3	would	come
Line 5–6	will		know	Line 4	would	be
Line 7	do	(not)	care	Line 5	would	arrive
Line 8	can	(not)	buy	Line 6	could (not)	believe
				Line 10	had	gone

Notice that immediately after the auxiliary, there is a position where you put the word *not* if you want to make the verb negative. We will call it the *not* **position.** You can also put other words in this position, such as *never* and *certainly* as in the examples below.

> I was *certainly* learning something. (Passage 1-A)

> I will *never* forget such a good teacher and friend. (Passage 3-A)

3.1 Auxiliaries Used to Begin Expanded Verbs

The first word in an expanded verb is always one of the auxiliaries listed in Figure 8-4. They are divided into four groups: the **DO** group, the **modals,** the **HAVE** group, and the **BE** group. These groups have different meanings or uses, which are discussed in Section 4.

FIGURE 8-4 Auxiliaries That Can Begin an Expanded Verb

	DO	MODALS	HAVE	BE
NOW	do does	will/would can/could shall should may/might must	have has	am is are
THEN	did	would could should might	had	was were

3.2 Tense in Expanded Verbs

The first word of an expanded verb is the only one that has tense; that is, it shows which time the sentence refers to. In Figure 8-4, each group of auxiliaries is divided into those that signal NOW (present tense forms) and those that signal THEN (past tense forms). Notice that a number of the modals can signal either NOW or THEN, depending on how they are used. (See Section 4.2.)

WHEN YOU ARE WRITING

It is unusual in writing to switch from NOW to THEN or THEN to NOW within a paragraph. So when you revise your work, notice the tense of each simple verb that you use and of the auxiliary at the beginning of each expanded verb. If you switch tense at any point, ask yourself: Do you really mean to switch time frames? Or have you just forgotten to use the right form?

3.3 Subject-Verb Agreement

There are four auxiliaries that can only be used with singular subjects. They are *does, has, is,* and *was.* For plural subjects, use *do, have, are,* and *were.* If you are not sure whether your subject is singular or plural, try replacing it with *he, she, it,* or *they.* Then check both expanded verbs and simple verbs for agreement by applying the rule summarized in Figure 8-5. (Note that the form after a *he, she,* or *it* subject, whether it is a simple verb or an auxiliary, always ends in *-s.*)

FIGURE 8-5   Agreement Between Subject and Verb or Auxiliary

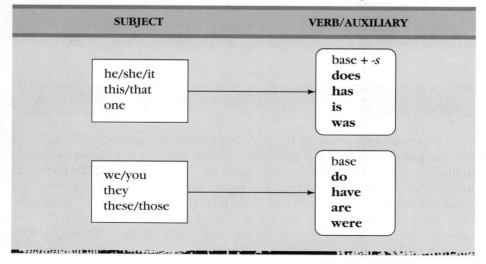

SUBJECT	VERB/AUXILIARY
he/she/it this/that one	base + *-s* **does** **has** **is** **was**
we/you they these/those	base **do** **have** **are** **were**

The pronoun *I* is an exception. For simple verbs and for most auxiliaries, you should use the same form after *I* as you do after *we*, but for BE use *am* in the NOW frame and *was* in the THEN one.

In Passage 8-A, there is only one verb phrase in which the writer had to worry about agreement. It is:

Line 7   I ——————————————→ <u>do</u> not care

In Passage 8-B, agreement is not a problem in any of the verb phrases.

WHEN YOU ARE WRITING

When you are in the NOW frame, you must check both simple verbs and auxiliaries for subject-verb agreement. Ask yourself these questions:

1. What is the subject of the verb?
2. Is the subject a *he, she,* or *it?*
3. If it is, have you put an *-s* on the verb or auxiliary that follows? Only the modals do not require an *-s* ending.

LEARNING STRATEGY

 Remembering New Material: Creating a chant helps you remember difficult forms.

Make a chant of the forms and say (or sing) it aloud to yourself, e.g., "he does, she does, it does, we do, you do, they do; he has, she has, it has, . . ." and so on.

3.4 Verb Forms After Auxiliaries

In a two-word expanded verb, the verb that follows the auxiliary has only three possible forms: base, base + *-ing,* or base + *-d/t/n.* The base form is the form listed in the dictionary. The *-ing* form is the base with *-ing* added. The *-d/t/n* form ends in *-ed* for most verbs and looks just like the simple past tense form, but there are some irregular verbs for which the *-d/t/n* form may end in *-t* or *-n,* e.g., *taught, kept, eaten, taken.* There are also a few other variations, such as *gone.* (See the back of this book for a list of irregular verbs, and see Chapter 9, Section 1.2 for a discussion of the variations on the *-d/t/n* form.)

Which of the three forms you use in any particular case depends on the auxiliary:

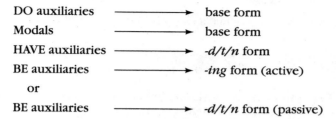

DO auxiliaries	→ base form
Modals	→ base form
HAVE auxiliaries	→ -*d/t/n* form
BE auxiliaries	→ -*ing* form (active)
or	
BE auxiliaries	→ -*d/t/n* form (passive)

Note that after auxiliaries of the BE group there are two possibilities, which mean quite different things. BE + -*ing* is **active**—the subject <u>is doing</u> something— while BE + -*d/t/n* is **passive**—the subject <u>is affected</u> by the action of something or someone else. (See Chapter 9.)

The rules for deciding which verb form should be used after any particular auxiliary are summarized in Figure 8-6:

FIGURE 8-6

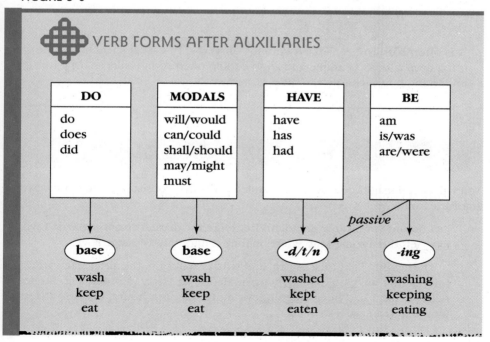

VERB FORMS AFTER AUXILIARIES

DO	MODALS	HAVE	BE
do	will/would	have	am
does	can/could	has	is/was
did	shall/should	had	are/were
	may/might		
	must		
↓	↓	↓	↓
base	**base**	-*d/t/n*	-*ing*
wash	wash	washed	washing
keep	keep	kept	keeping
eat	eat	eaten	eating

passive

In this book, you can find many examples of expanded verbs with one auxiliary. The following are taken from Passage 1-A:

I felt like I <u>would explore</u> an unknown world.

CHAPTER 8: VERBS WITH TENSE: ACTIVE

I <u>was</u> certainly <u>learning</u> something.

Thus I <u>didn't</u> <u>learn</u> anything.

Recently CUNY <u>has opened</u> a campus in the Hiroshima prefecture of Japan.

LEARNING STRATEGY

Remembering New Material: Making a picture in your mind and drawing it helps you remember.

Practice drawing Figure 8-6 from memory. Begin by drawing only the DO group with the arrow leading down to the base form. A day or so later, draw just the modals with the arrow leading to the base. After another day, draw the HAVE group with its arrow leading to *-d/t/n*. A day after that, draw the BE group with the two arrows leading to *-d/t/n* and to *-ing*. Finally, draw all the groups together.

WHEN YOU'RE TALKING

It is often hard to hear *-d/t/n* endings on verbs. In casual speech, people often drop a *-d* or *-t* ending, and an *-n* ending often sounds like an *-ing*. It is important, however, to write them correctly.

3.5 Expanded Verbs with Two Auxiliaries

You will occasionally come across expanded verbs that consist of three words: two auxiliaries and a verb.

I do not care if [my grandchildren] like my diaries or not. At least I <u>will have left</u> them something which money cannot buy. (Passage 8-A)

During the flight I fell asleep, and when I woke up, the airline stewardess told us that we <u>would be arriving</u> in Madrid in thirty minutes. I could not believe that I <u>had been sleeping</u> for more than ten hours, because it was morning. (Passage 8-B)

3.5a The First Auxiliary

In an expanded verb with two auxiliaries, the first word is always one of the auxiliaries listed in Figure 8-4. As with any other expanded verb, you must consider the following points when you decide which one to use.

Tense

If you are talking about NOW, choose one from the top half of Figure 8-4. If you are talking about THEN, choose one from the bottom half.

Subject-Verb Agreement

If the auxiliary you choose is *have/has, am/is/are,* or *was/were,* it must agree with the subject of the clause you are writing. Follow the rule given in Figure 8-5.

3.5b The Second Auxiliary

The second auxiliary in an expanded verb is always one of the following: *have, be, been,* or *being.* Which of these it should be depends on the auxiliary at the beginning. The rules are summarized below in Figure 8-7.

FIGURE 8-7   The Form of the Second Auxiliary in an Expanded Verb

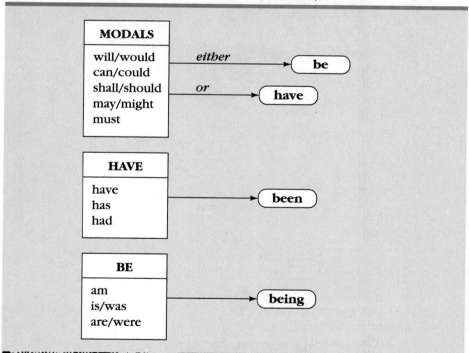

In other words, when two auxiliaries are used in an expanded verb, modals can be followed by either *be* or *have,* auxiliaries of the HAVE group can only be followed by *been,* and auxiliaries of the BE group can only be followed by *being* as the second auxiliary.

3.5c The Form of the Verb at the End

Only two verb forms are possible after the second auxiliary in an expanded verb: *-ing,* or *-d/t/n.* Which you choose depends on that second auxiliary: *Have* must be followed by *-d/t/n,* while *be, being,* or *been* may be followed by either *-ing* or *-d/t/n,* depending on whether you want the clause to be active or passive. (See Chapter 9.)

3.5d Summary

If we combine the last two points, we can summarize the rules for forming expanded verbs with two auxiliaries as in Figure 8-8.

FIGURE 8-8

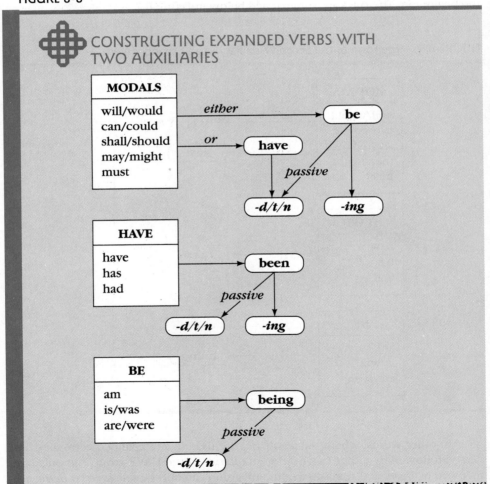

4. WHEN TO USE EXPANDED VERBS

The four groups of auxiliaries that are used with expanded verbs all have their own meaning. The meanings are explained briefly below, but to get a real sense of what each group does, you should observe carefully how auxiliaries are used in any English text that you read, and you should also listen for them when you are talking with native speakers.

4.1 The DO Group

There are only three reasons for using words from this group:

- To change sentences with simple verbs into questions. (See Chapter 2, Sections 2.1 and 2.2.)

  When <u>did</u> you <u>graduate</u>? (Chapter 2, Conversation 2)

- To make simple verbs negative.

  I <u>do</u> not <u>care</u> if they like my diaries or not. (Passage 8-A)

- To make simple verbs emphatic.

  I <u>do like</u> to write. (Passage 4-E)

4.2 The Modals

The modals are complicated because they are a large group of words that have different but often overlapping meanings, and they are used to make several distinctions. The major distinctions made by the modals are discussed below.

4.2a Modals Signaling Present and Past Time (NOW and THEN)

Every modal has tense, so it places the clause that it is in in either the NOW or the THEN time frame. In general, a modal looks ahead from that time frame to some expected future or possibility. The way the modals are related to the two time frames is illustrated in Figure 8-9.

FIGURE 8-9   The Time Relationship Expressed by Modals

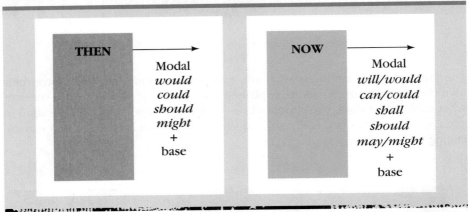

The most frequently used modals are *will* and *can*. These modals, together with their past tense forms *would* and *could,* express the time distinction most clearly:

- *will/would—Will* is used primarily for making predictions, that is, for talking about the future as seen from NOW. When you want to report a prediction or expectation in the past (THEN), use *would.* For example:

   After my death, my grandchildren <u>will read</u> my diaries and they <u>will know</u> that their grandfather was once young . . . (Passage 8-A)

   It was mid-summer in New York, July 24, 1986, at 5:00 p.m. My mother and I were on an airplane to Madrid . . . I could not believe that in a couple of hours my dream <u>would come</u> true, and I <u>would be</u> in Spain. (Passage 8-B)

Another use of *will* and *would* is for describing events that happen regularly, as a matter of habit. *Would* is often used in this way to describe regular events in the THEN frame.

   When I was in my senior year, [Sister Ida] became my dorm mistress. Every night when she came in and said goodnight, she <u>would ask</u> me to tell her what I did during the day or if I was homesick. From our conversation, she <u>would correct</u> my mistakes. (Passage 3-A)

- *can/could—Can* usually expresses the idea of ability. Use *can* for talking about ability in the present (NOW) and *could* for talking about ability in the past (THEN).

   When I read [my diaries], the former times seem to appear again; I <u>can see</u> my first girlfriend talking with me; we go to have a picnic; we enjoy sweet days. (Passage 8-A)

   It was mid-summer in New York, July 24, 1986, at 5:00 p.m. My mother and I were on an airplane to Madrid . . . I <u>could</u> not <u>believe</u> that in a couple of hours my dream would come true, and I would be in Spain. (Passage 8-B)

Both *would* and *could* can be used in the NOW time frame for certain purposes, which we explain below. *Will* and *can,* however, are never used in the THEN frame.

The relationship of the other modals to the two time frames is more complicated:

- *Shall* belongs to the NOW frame, but in modern usage it has no corresponding past tense form for THEN. It expresses expectation in the same way as *will* and is often used in British English after the pronouns *I* and *we.* It is rarely used in American English.
- *Should* was historically the past tense of *shall,* but now it can be used in either the NOW or the THEN frame. Its meanings are discussed below.
- *May* can only be used in the NOW frame. See the discussion below for what it means.
- *Might* is the past tense form of *may,* so it must be used in place of *may* in the THEN frame. It is often, however, used in the NOW frame. See below.
- *Must* can only be used in the NOW frame.

Figure 8-10 shows the time frames in which you can use the modals.

FIGURE 8-10   Time Frames the Modals Can Be Used In

NOW	will	can	shall	may	must
	would	could	should	might	
THEN	would	could	should	might	

WHEN YOU ARE WRITING

You need to check that you are using modals consistently with the time frame you are writing about:

1. When you are writing about THEN, you should not use *will, can, shall, may,* or *must.* Change them as follows:

will	→ *would*
can	→ *could*
shall	→ *would* (more usual than *should*)
may	→ *might*
must	→ *had to* (See Section 4.2g on semimodals.)

   It is especially important to remember to make these changes when you write reported speech. (See Chapter 13.)
2. When you are writing about NOW, check your uses of *would* and *could.* These words in the NOW frame suggest uncertainty. (See below.) So if you want to express a straightforward prediction, use *will.* If you want to describe a simple ability, use *can.*

4.2b Modals Expressing Certainty and Uncertainty (NOW)

Making Predictions

If you are sure about a prediction or are expressing a definite intention, you should use *will.* If you are less sure and think what you are describing is only a possibility, you can use *may.* For example, the writer of Passage 4-B suggests that in order to use time well you should make a schedule. She then predicts the results:

> This weekly schedule <u>may</u> not <u>solve</u> all of your problems, but it <u>will force</u> you to realize what is happening to your time. (Passage 4-B)

She is not sure about the first prediction, but she is sure about the second.

In addition, you can use the past tense forms *might* and *could* when you want to express even greater uncertainty. In the following examples (taken from Passage 3-D), we have written in brackets what is implied by the use of these forms:

> When people immigrate to the United States, they <u>might consider</u> themselves Americans. [But it is likely that they do not.]

> If you speak two languages, you <u>could get</u> special privileges when applying for some jobs. [But you will be lucky if you do.]

Finally, you can use *should* to show that you are not certain that what you are predicting will happen, but you think it is probable.

> I <u>should be</u> out of college in a year and a half. [If everything goes as I expect.]

In short, these modals make a continuum, as shown in Figure 8-11.

FIGURE 8-11   Modals for Making Predictions

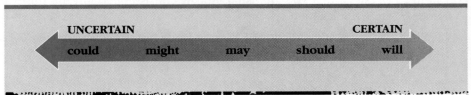

Making Inferences

Modals can also be used for expressing inferences, or guesses based on evidence. For example, in Passage 8-A, Yuan mentions "the two years' life in the Chinese military." From this reference, we can make an inference and express it this way:

Military service <u>must be</u> compulsory in China.

If we are not so certain, however, we can say:

Military service <u>may be</u> compulsory in China.

It would also be possible to use *might* or *could* to suggest even less certainty. So in expressing inferences, you can use a similar continuum, as shown in Figure 8-12:

FIGURE 8-12   Modals for Making Inferences

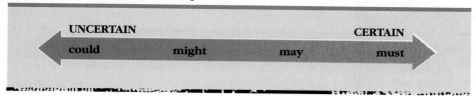

4.2c Modals Describing
Real Expectations or Imagined Situations

Real Expectations

When you make a prediction, you can use a clause beginning with *if* to define the situation in which you expect something to happen.

> If a person <u>uses</u> time completely and well, he <u>will be</u> more successful than others. (Passage 4-B)

> If a teacher <u>has</u> five classes and about 25 students in each class, and each of them <u>uses</u> one sheet a day, the teacher <u>will run</u> out of paper in about four weeks. (Passage 5-A)

The *if* clauses in these sentences show the conditions in which the predictions are expected to come true. That is why an *if* clause is often described as a **conditional** clause.

The use of tenses in *if* sentences is important. The writers quoted above have used present tense verbs in the *if* clauses and present tense modals (*will*) in the main clauses. This shows that they really expect what they are describing to happen. That is why this kind of *if* clause is often called a **likely conditional** clause. The possible combinations of verbs and modals in this kind of sentence are shown in Figure 8-13.

FIGURE 8-13 Verbs and Modals in *if* Sentences:
Real Expectations

EXPECTED SITUATION (*If* CLAUSE)		EXPECTED CONSEQUENCE (MAIN CLAUSE)
VERB		MODAL
If . . . base/base + -*s* *can/must* + base *have/has* + -*d/t/n* *am/is/are* + -*ing*		(then) . . . *will/shall* *can* *should* *may/might* *must*

Note:
1. Though you can use various kinds of present tense verbs in the *if* clause, *can* and *must* are the only modals that can be used there. The most common form in the *if* clause is the simple verb (base or base + -*s*).
2. *Will* is by far the most common modal in the main clause.
3. It is also possible to use a simple present tense verb in the main clause if you are describing some habitual activity.
4. In an *if* sentence that describes real expectations, you can never use *would* or *could*, either in the *if* clause or in the main clause.

Imagined Situations

The modals *would* and *could* can be used to describe events that have not happened, and are not likely to happen, but can be imagined.

In the following passage, for example, the writer describes some of the difficulties she is experiencing because her boyfriend comes from a different ethnic and religious background from herself. She uses the present tense most of the time to show that she is talking about NOW, but when she describes her wishes and fears, she uses *could* and *would*. By doing this, she shows that she does not expect these things to occur, at least not in the near future:

Passage 8-C **A FAMILY PROBLEM**

by Aida Tineo

Another problem that we are faced with is that I have not yet met his parents. His father, especially, is a very strict man. He wants to arrange his sons' and daughters' marriages. They are a big family, and the parents are now older. This makes me not want to push things, although my greatest wish is that
5 I <u>could meet</u> them and that they <u>could accept</u> me. Many times my boyfriend has felt the urge to let it all out and tell them, but the consequences may make things more difficult for us. The reason why he hasn't told his parents is that he is sure his parents <u>would be</u> highly upset; they <u>wouldn't</u> <u>accept</u> me or our relationship, and <u>would</u> most probably <u>throw</u> him out of the house.

An *if* clause is often used to set up the imagined situation. The verb in the *if* clause is always a past tense form (usually base + *-ed*). This shows that the situation is not really expected but only imagined, and so this kind of *if* clause is often called an **unlikely conditional** clause. For example, Tineo could have reworded the final sentence of the above passage in this way:

> If he <u>told</u> his parents, they <u>wouldn't accept</u> me or our relationship, and <u>would</u> most probably <u>throw</u> him out of the house.

Tadesse gives another example in her essay about working in a clothes store:

> If we <u>had</u> other colors, why <u>would</u> we <u>hide</u> them? (Passage 10-A)

The past tense form *had* after *if* indicates that they did not in fact have other colors.

Figure 8-14 summarizes the relationship between the past tense in the *if* clause and the modal in the main clause. Notice that you can never use *can* or *will* in this kind of sentence.

FIGURE 8-14   Verbs and Modals in *if* Sentences:
Imagined Situations

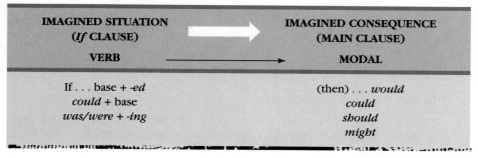

IMAGINED SITUATION (*If* CLAUSE)		IMAGINED CONSEQUENCE (MAIN CLAUSE)
VERB	→	**MODAL**
If . . . base + *-ed*		(then) . . . *would*
could + base		*could*
was/were + *-ing*		*should*
		might

Imagined situations can also be described in a **verbal phrase,** which has no tense, but the fact that the event is imagined is made clear by the use of *would* in the following clause. For example, in Christine Patouha's essay on street entertainers she describes a musician telling her why his group does not play in night clubs; we have underlined the verbal phrase at the beginning of the sentence as well as the expanded verbs with *would*:

> "<u>Playing in a night club</u>, we <u>would</u> not <u>make</u> as much money, and we <u>would</u> not <u>be</u> heard by as many people as in the streets." (Passage 10-B)

The musician clearly has no intention of playing in a night club, although he can imagine doing so. He could equally well have used an *if* clause:

> "If we <u>played</u> in a night club, we <u>would</u> not <u>make</u> as much money, and we <u>would</u> not <u>be</u> heard by as many people as in the streets." (Passage 10-B)

WHEN YOU ARE WRITING

It is easy to get the tenses in *if* sentences muddled up so that your reader cannot tell whether you are talking about what you really expect or what you only imagine as an unlikely possibility. To avoid such confusion, ask yourself these questions about any *if* sentence that you use:

1. What do you mean to convey to your reader? If it is a real expectation, refer to Figure 8-13. If it is an imagined situation, refer to Figure 8-14.
2. Is the verb in the *if* clause a present or past tense form? For a real expectation, it should be present; for an imagined situation, it should be past.
3. Is the modal in the main clause one of the corresponding set, as shown in Figure 8-13 (for present tense forms) or Figure 8-14 (for past tense forms)? If it is not, change it so that it does correspond.

4.2d Modals for Expressing Obligation, Recommendation, or Permission

You can also use modals to describe actions as being required (obligation), suggested (advice), or allowed (permission). You are most likely to come across the modals used in this sense when you are talking, and they all, even the "past" tense forms, refer to the present time (NOW). Examples are given below:

- Obligation: *must*

     The government says that the young generation <u>must contribute</u> something to the revolution, so working on those farms is one of them. (Passage 6-C)

- Recommendation: *should, could,* and *might*

     The schedule <u>should be</u> reasonable. . . . We <u>should catch</u> up with time from the beginning to the end. (Passage 4-B)

     Were you reading magazines or books while taking a bus or train? Did you call someone up or talk with somebody without a purpose? If the first question is answered "no" and the second question "yes," I can say that you wasted a lot of precious time, because you <u>could do</u> something on the train, and it was not necessary to call somebody or talk with somebody. (Passage 4-B)

- Permission: *may* or *can*

     <u>May</u> I ask a question?
     <u>Can</u> I open a window?

This set of modals again forms a continuum, from "permission," which allows the greatest freedom, to "obligation," which allows the least freedom. The continuum is shown in Figure 8-15.

FIGURE 8-15   Modals for Permission, Recommendation, Obligation

MOST FREE				LEAST FREE
can may	could might should			must
Permission	*Recommendation*			*Obligation*

4.2e Modals for Expressing Politeness

An important use of modals, especially in speech, is for making requests. We will consider two kinds of request: general requests and requests for permission.

Making General Requests

The most direct way of making a general request is to use an **imperative** verb, that is, the base form only. For example, a parent might say to a naughty child:

Come here at once!

In many social situations, however, such directness is not appropriate, even if you add the word *please*. You can make a request less authoritative and more polite by putting it in question form and using a modal. You can modify the degree of politeness by which modal you choose. For example, a student might say to a friend:

<u>Will</u> you <u>read</u> my essay, please, and tell me what's wrong with it?

A teacher might say to a student:

<u>Can</u> you <u>talk</u> to me about it after class, please?

Someone speaking to a stranger might say:

<u>Would</u> you <u>move</u> your car so that I can get out, please?

And a student might make a special request of a teacher in this way:

<u>Could</u> you please <u>write</u> me a letter of recommendation?

So again the modals form a continuum, which is shown in Figure 8-16:

FIGURE 8-16   Modals for Making General Requests

POLITE				DIRECT
could	would	can	will	[imperative]

Requesting Permission

A different set of modals is used for asking permission to do something: *can, may, could,* and *might*. They are all fairly polite, but *could* and *might* sound less confident and more polite than *can* and *may.* In addition, *can* and *could* are less formal than *may* and *might.* (Many teachers condemn the use of *can* for asking permission, but native speakers frequently use it this way all the same.) Following are some examples of requests for permission:

A student speaking to a friend:

> <u>Can</u> I <u>borrow</u> your pen please?

A student speaking to a teacher:

> <u>May</u> I <u>hand</u> it in later?

A library user talking to a librarian:

> <u>Could</u> I <u>make</u> a photocopy of this please?

A committee member at a formal meeting:

> <u>Might</u> I <u>make</u> a suggestion?

The continuum for requesting permission is shown in Figure 8-17.

FIGURE 8-17   Modals for Requesting Permission

Expressing Wishes and Making Offers

It is often not polite in English to say, "I want . . . ." The expression, "<u>I would</u> <u>like</u> . . ." is preferred instead. Similarly, it is more polite when making an offer to say, "<u>Would</u> you <u>like</u> . . . ?" or "What <u>would</u> you <u>like</u>?" rather than "Do you want . . . ?" or "What do you want?"

4.2f Summary of Modals

The various uses of modals that we have discussed are all shown together in Figure 8-18. As you study the figure, notice the following points:

- The "past" tense modals (those used for signaling THEN) are also used for expressing uncertainty, doubt, and politeness. In other words, when they are used in the NOW frame, these modals always suggest that the speaker or writer has some reservation or hesitation about what is being said.
- The meaning of a modal is affected not only by its place on one of the continua shown in Figure 8-18, but also by the tone of voice in which it is said. This point cannot be easily described, but it is something you should listen for when you hear native speakers talking.

FIGURE 8-18

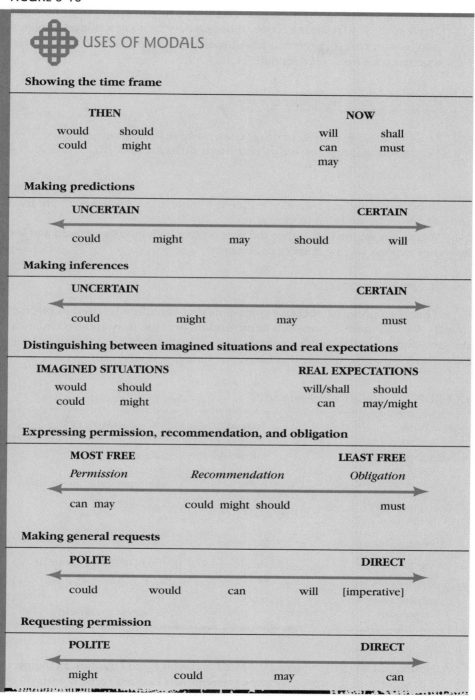

USES OF MODALS

Showing the time frame

THEN			NOW	
would	should		will	shall
could	might		can	must
			may	

Making predictions

UNCERTAIN   CERTAIN

could   might   may   should   will

Making inferences

UNCERTAIN   CERTAIN

could   might   may   must

Distinguishing between imagined situations and real expectations

IMAGINED SITUATIONS			REAL EXPECTATIONS	
would	should		will/shall	should
could	might		can	may/might

Expressing permission, recommendation, and obligation

MOST FREE   LEAST FREE

Permission   *Recommendation*   *Obligation*

can   may   could   might   should   must

Making general requests

POLITE   DIRECT

could   would   can   will   [imperative]

Requesting permission

POLITE   DIRECT

might   could   may   can

- Since *would, could, should,* and *might* are all used for expressing uncertainty and politeness, they do not signal THEN clearly, and *must* does not signal THEN at all. So to make inferences about past events, to describe an imagined past, or to express judgments about past actions, you have to use a modal together with *have.* (See Section 5.1.)

LEARNING STRATEGY

Managing Your Learning: Observing how native speakers use the language helps you learn difficult systems.

In both reading and listening, notice the context in which modals are used and pay particular attention to intonation.

When you are reading, notice the context in which modals are used and see how they express varying degrees of certainty.

4.2g Semimodals

There is a group of special expressions that can often be used in place of modals. We call these expressions **semimodals** because they are used in much the same way as modals and have similar meanings, but they are different in form. Figure 8-19 shows the modals that have corresponding semimodals:

FIGURE 8-19   Modals and Semimodals

PURPOSE	MODALS	SEMIMODALS
Making predictions	will/would	BE going to BE about to (for immediate future only)
Describing regular action in the past	would	used to
Expressing ability	can/could	BE able to
Giving advice	should had better	ought to (mainly British)
Expressing obligation or necessity	must	HAVE to HAVE got to (British)

Notice that all of the semimodals listed end with *to,* and they are all followed by the <u>base</u> form of the verb. For those semimodals that are formed with BE or

HAVE, you have to choose between *am, are, is, was,* and *were* for BE, and *has, have,* and *had* for HAVE. To choose the correct form, follow the same rules for tense and agreement as when you are using BE and HAVE as auxiliaries on their own. (See Section 3.3 in this chapter.)

The following explanations and examples show how the semimodals are used:

- *BE going to* is informal, so you are most likely to hear it in casual conversation. You may, however, use it in an informal personal essay, as in this example:

  As we approached [the old man], I <u>was going to</u> hand him the box of popcorn, but my cousin forcefully pulled me away before I had a chance. (Passage 5-B)

- *BE about to* can be used only for talking about the immediate future:

  Every one of these trends <u>is about to</u> get worse, as the states must choose between extra cops, extra classrooms, health care or welfare, higher taxes, or less of everything else. (Passage 5-A)

- *Used to* is a past tense form, so only use it when you are talking or writing about THEN. It means that the action was repeated or habitual. In the following example, Miura is referring to the time, some years ago, when she was in school in Japan.

  After the examination, I <u>used to</u> forget everything. (Passage 1-A)

Note that there is a *-d* at the end of <u>used</u> in *used to.* You cannot hear the *-d* in speech, but it is required in writing.

- *BE able to* is another way of expressing ability, and is especially useful for talking about the future.

  Most students <u>will be able to</u> pass the exam by the end of the course.

You can make this semimodal negative by using *BE unable to* instead of *BE not able to,* as the writer has in the following example.

  We struggle during our entire life to leave an inheritance to our children, but we <u>are unable to</u> transmit to them our knowledge, our experience, and our wisdom. (Passage 7-G)

- *Ought to* is more common in British than American English. It is a stronger way of making a recommendation than *should.* For example, we can extend the argument suggested in the quotation from Passage 7-G above:

  We <u>ought to</u> be concerned about passing on spiritual riches to our children rather than material ones.

- *Had better* is an informal expression used mainly in speech. Like *should,* it is used for giving advice. There are no examples in the essays in this book, so the following is taken from an informal conversation:

  We <u>had better</u> have something to eat before we go.

Depending on the tone of voice, *had better* can sound quite rude and even threatening.

You <u>had better</u> finish that job before I get back!

- *HAVE to* is especially useful because it has a past tense form, whereas the corresponding modal, *must,* has only a present tense. *HAVE to* is therefore used frequently to describe things that were compulsory or necessary in the past:

    [When I was in school in Japan], we <u>had to</u> memorize a whole chapter to pass the examination. (Passage 1-A)

    Since I could speak very little English, I <u>had to</u> choose between working in a factory or in a cafeteria. (Passage 6-B)

- *Would rather* is not listed in Figure 8-19 because, although it is a semimodal in the way it is used, it does not mean the same as any of the modals. It means the same as the verb *prefer.* It is used mainly in speech, but you may see it written on a bumper sticker, like this:

    I <u>would rather</u> be fishing.

Alternatively, you may see it in a shortened form:

    I'<u>d rather</u> be fishing.

The verb or auxiliary that follows *would rather* is always in the base form.

WHEN YOU'RE TALKING

Both modals and semimodals are often used in speech. They can be confusing because speakers tend to reduce them so much that you cannot hear them clearly. For example, all you can usually hear of *will* is "ll" and of *would* is "d." In the semimodal *had better, had* sounds like "d" too, if you can hear it at all, while *going to* often sounds like "gonna," and *had to* like "hadda."

Listen carefully when you hear native speakers using these forms, and notice how they reduce some of the words to almost nothing; but when you use the words in writing, be sure to write them out fully.

4.3 The HAVE Group

4.3a Using *had* + *-d/t/n*

When you are talking or writing about the past (THEN), use *had* to show action/events that happened before the main time that you are talking about. (Simple past tense verbs used earlier will have already put your reader or listener into the THEN frame.) The following sentence shows how an expanded verb with *had* works together with a simple past tense verb; the simple verb refers to the main time that the writer is talking about, while the expanded verb refers to the two years before that time:

> The prize, on which I <u>had spent</u> two years of my strength and energy, <u>was</u> in my hand. (Passage 3-E)

When *had* is used as an auxiliary with -*d/t/n,* it is often called the **past perfect** tense.

4.3b Using *has/have* + -*d/t/n*

Has or *have* can be used with a -*d/t/n* verb to mean two different things. In both meanings, the event referred to is past, but it is closely related to the present.

- Use *has/have* to show action/events beginning before NOW, but continuing up to NOW.

> I told Buddy: "Sweetheart, you'll find an Irish girl, and you and your family will be happy about it. Please, Buddy, leave me alone, from now on. I'll never forget you. You were my first friend in the U.S.A. And I had an excellent friend. You'll always be in my heart. Goodbye, be happy!" I <u>haven't seen</u> Buddy ever since.
>
> —Rosane Pires

- Use *has/have* to show action/events that happened before NOW but are relevant NOW. When you do this, you do not have to say when the thing happened and can stay in the NOW frame.

> Recently, CUNY [City University of New York] <u>has opened</u> a campus in the Hiroshima prefecture of Japan. (Passage 1-A)

> Her words released me from the "must-be-young disease." She maybe doesn't remember me since I was a very quiet student, nor does she know her words are still alive in my heart and <u>have affected</u> my thought. I think it will be fun to say, "Oh, children!" to a sixty-year-old person when I am eighty. (Passage 4-A)

These two uses of *has/have* with -*d/t/n* are often called the **present perfect** tense.

4.3c Summary of the HAVE group

Using the HAVE group of auxiliaries signals an event before the main time frame, as shown in Figure 8-20 on the next page.

FIGURE 8-20   The Time Relationship Expressed by HAVE + -d/t/n

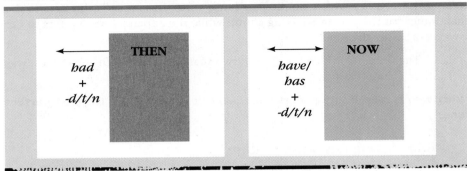

4.4 The BE Group

4.4a Using *am/is/are/was/were* + -*ing*

You can use auxiliaries of the BE group with -*ing* to show that the action represented by the verb is continuing through and beyond the main time (whether that time is <u>THEN</u> or <u>NOW</u>). This kind of expanded verb is often used to show actions going on at the same time as other actions that are expressed by simple verbs:

> I was <u>distracted</u> when I <u>noticed</u> an old man from afar off. He <u>was rummaging</u> through a garbage pail . . . (Passage 5-B)

> As we <u>step</u> on the boat, the atmosphere <u>is</u> very friendly and enjoyable. There <u>are</u> many musicians and singers, clowns and artists. The bands <u>are playing</u>, the singers <u>are singing</u>, and the whole crowd <u>is enjoying</u> the ride. (Passage 5-C)

In the NOW frame, *am, is,* and *are* can also be used with -*ing* to talk about the future:

> They <u>are coming</u> tomorrow.

The time relationship is shown in Figure 8-21.

FIGURE 8-21   The Time Relationship Expressed by BE + -*ing*

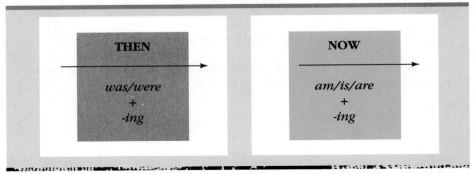

The combination of *am/is/are* with *-ing* is often called the **present progressive** or **present continuous** tense, while *was/were* with *-ing* is often called the **past progressive** or **past continuous** tense.

4.4b Using *am/is/are/was/were* + *-d/t/n*

When you use an auxiliary of the BE group with *-d/t/n*, you make the main verb **passive.** (See the explanation of passive verbs in Chapter 9.)

4.5 Summary of the Use of Auxiliaries

Figure 8-22 summarizes the way the different auxiliaries show time relationships.

FIGURE 8-22

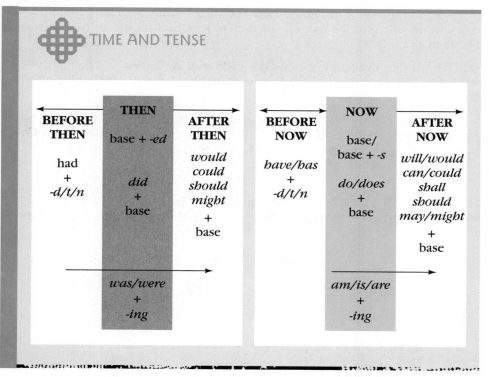

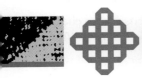

5. USING EXPANDED VERBS WITH TWO OR THREE AUXILIARIES

You are most likely to use more than one auxiliary when you are making a **passive** verb. (See Chapter 9.) Using two auxiliaries is relatively rare with active verbs, but it does give you a precise way of expressing how events are related to each other in time and of talking about events that never happened.

5.1 Modal + *have* + *-d/t/n*

5.1a Making Predictions

With the combination of *will* + *have,* you tell your reader or listener to think of a time later than your main time frame (i.e., in the future from the point of view of someone who is in the frame), and then to look back a little, to the time just before that future.

> After my death, my grandchildren will read my diaries . . . I do not care if they like my diaries or not. At least I <u>will have left</u> them something which money cannot buy. (Passage 8-A)

The future this writer wants us to think of is the time when he is dead; but obviously leaving the diaries will happen before his death, and this is made clear by the combination of *will* with *have.* The idea is illustrated in Figure 8-23.

FIGURE 8-23   The Time Relationship Expressed by Modal + HAVE + -d/t/n

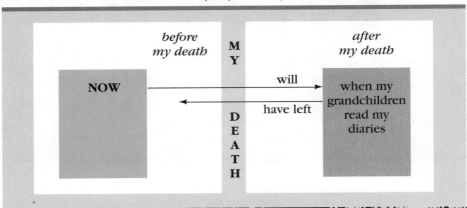

If you are less certain about your prediction, you can use *should* or *may.* In the following examples, the implication of the modal is put in square brackets:

I <u>should have finished</u> my school work by the time I start on the job. [I am fairly sure about it.]

They <u>may have done</u> the repairs by then. [But we cannot depend on it.]

You can express even greater uncertainty by using *might have* or *could have,* but it is potentially confusing to do this since both these combinations are more often used for making inferences or talking about an imagined past. (See below.)

5.1b Making Inferences

The modals used for making inferences can all be used with *have + -d/t/n* for making inferences about past events. The different modals express different degrees of certainty.

The traffic is backed up for miles. There <u>must have been</u> an accident. [That is the only explanation I can think of.]

I don't know where she is. She <u>may have gone</u> to a movie. [It is possible that this is the explanation, but I do not know for sure.]

You can use *might have* and *could have* for inferences you are even less sure about.

5.1c Describing an Unreal Past

Would, could, should, and *might* can all be used with *have* and the *-d/t/n* form of a verb to describe events that never happened and can never happen because the time for them is now gone. It is a way of imagining history as having been different from what it was.

Today I shall write one composition which I <u>should have finished</u> yesterday. [In fact, I did not finish the composition.] (Adapted from Passage 4-B)

Of course, I <u>might have tried</u> to improve by myself, but I didn't even want to think about English. [In fact, I did not try to improve by myself.] (Passage 1-A)

You can set up an unreal past by using an *if* clause, often called an **impossible conditional** clause (impossible because the past cannot in fact be different from what it was). The verb position in the *if* clause should be filled by an expanded verb with the auxiliary *had;* then in the main clause, the past tense modal + *have* + *-d/t/n* express the imaginary consequences of this situation. For example, we can say the following, based on what we know from Mendoza's essay in Passage 8-B:

If Mendoza <u>had been</u> to Spain before, she <u>would have known</u> that there

210

CHAPTER 8: VERBS WITH TENSE: ACTIVE

was a six-hour difference between Madrid and New York. [In fact, she had not been to Spain before, and so she did not know.]

The relationship between the verb in this kind of *if* clause and the modal in the main clause is shown in Figure 8-24.

FIGURE 8-24   Verbs and Modals in *if* Sentences: Unreal Past

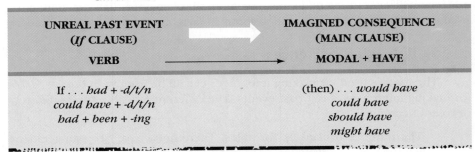

UNREAL PAST EVENT (*If* CLAUSE)		IMAGINED CONSEQUENCE (MAIN CLAUSE)
VERB		MODAL + HAVE
If . . . *had + -d/t/n* *could have + -d/t/n* *had + been + -ing*		(then) . . . *would have* *could have* *should have* *might have*

The modals used to make recommendations, *should, could,* and *might,* all suggest reproach or regret when they are used with *have.* This is because the *have* implies that whatever is recommended was not actually done. This sense of reproach is especially strong with *should have.* For example, in Passage 14-H, Stanislawska writes:

> We were fascinated by all these stories, but nobody had ever expected that we would be constrained to make use of those experiences which should have remained only history for us . . . .

5.2 Modal + *be* + *-ing*

The modals can be used with *be + -ing* in the same senses as they can be used with the base form of the verb. The difference is that *be + -ing* suggests that the action in question is continuous or in progress, often at the same time as another action. This example comes from Mendoza's essay (Passage 8-B):

> During the flight I fell asleep, and when I woke up, the airline stewardess told us that we would be arriving in Madrid in thirty minutes.

5.3 HAVE + *been* + *-ing*

By using this combination, you can tell your reader to think of the event you describe as happening before the main time frame but still relevant to that time, and also as happening continuously through a period. In this example, Mendoza continues describing what happened when she woke up:

> I could not believe that I <u>had been sleeping</u> for more than ten hours, because it was morning. (Passage 8-B)

5.4 Modal + *have* + *been* + *-ing*

This is an unusual combination, and you are unlikely to need to use it. It combines the sense of the modal (prediction, inference, or recommendation) with the past sense of HAVE and the continuous or progressive sense of BE + *-ing*. There is no example in the essays in this book, so we have made one up:

> I <u>should have been working</u> when you called, but actually I was asleep.

5.5 One or More Auxiliaries + BE + *-d/t/n*

Any combination of BE with *-d/t/n* makes the verb **passive**. (See Chapter 9.)

ACTIVITIES

1. Showing Tense in Simple Verbs

In the original version of the essay below, the writer correctly used present tense verbs in some places and past tense verbs in others. In the version given here, both present and past tense forms of each simple verb are given. Cross out whichever form is inappropriate in that particular part of the essay. You may want to do the first two paragraphs together with your classmates and then finish the exercise at home.

(For a correct version of this passage, see Appendix 2. The writer's original choices are given there, but some variation is possible because the choice depends on the meaning.)

Passage 8-D   **A CHINESE HOUSEWIFE**

by Lisa Tang

In Chinese society a housewife should be thrifty in order to help her husband to support the family. First of all, she (1) does/did her housework by herself and doesn't hire a maid to work with her. Secondly, when she (2)

goes/went shopping, she only (3) spends/spent money on daily necessities
5   and not on junk food. The food which she (4) buys/bought should be
healthy food and should not cost much money. Finally, she can't buy clothes
often except when she (5) has/had to go to a banquet. Mostly she (6)
makes/made her clothes herself and (7) wears/wore them at home. In this
way she (8) saves/saved money.

10   The word "thrifty" (9) means/meant something to me because my
mother (10) is/was a thrifty person. Also, it (11) reminds/reminded me of my
childhood in Hong Kong. I was raised in the middle class. I (12) have/had a
big family, and my parents (13) have/had five children. My father (14) is/was
the only one to earn money to support our family. He (15) goes/went to the
15   United States to work when we (16) are/were young. Our living (17)
depends/depended on the bill of exchange which he (18) sends/sent
monthly. I (19) guess/guessed that (20) is/was the reason why my mother
(21) becomes/became an economical person. . . .

I (22) remember/remembered one day I (23) ask/asked my mother to
20   buy me a pencil case which (24) has/had a Japanese cartoon character
design on the cover. She (25) refuses/refused because she (26) says/said she
had just bought me a new one a few months ago. I (27) tell/told her that the
one I (28) have/had (29) is/was out of style and the one which I (30)
want/wanted (31) is/was very popular now. Most of my school-mates (32)
25   have/had it. Therefore, I (33) want/wanted her to buy one for me. She (34)
rejects/rejected my request because she didn't want to spoil me and she
would not spend money on those luxury things. I (35) am/was really mad
and (36) cry/cried. The next two weeks I didn't eat my breakfast and (37)
try/tried to save money to buy the pencil case. Finally, I (38) buy/bought it
30   by myself. However, I (39) miss/missed my breakfast for two weeks.

2. Showing Subject-Verb Agreement in Simple Verbs

The following essay includes many simple verbs in the present tense, so the
writer had to choose the appropriate form to agree with the subject. Here, both
the base form and the base + -s is given in each case (except where the choice is
between *are* and *is*). Choose whichever form is appropriate and cross out the
inappropriate one. If you are not sure which to choose, check Figure 8-3. Then

read your version aloud to a partner, being careful to pronounce the *-s* endings distinctly. (For a correct version of this passage, see Appendix 2.)

Passage 8-E   **EARLY CHILDHOOD**

by Henriette Schoch

Among psychologists, especially in the field of developmental psychology, there is agreement about how important early childhood (1) are/is for a human being. A child (2) have/has to learn an incredible amount of very difficult and intricate things: even the action of taking hold of something (3) demand/
5   demands complete concentration and a lot of exercise, until the child (4) are/is able to control its movements without any observance. Before that, many rather complicated recognitions and conclusions (5) have/has to be made by the baby. The eyes, for instance, (6) have/has to learn to fix on something. Then, in an almost endless process of groping, touching, and taking into the
10   mouth, the baby (7) start/starts to distinguish between him- or herself and the surroundings. Months of active learning (8) pass/passes by until the happy and proud mother and father (9) observe/observes their baby creeping. Of course, this (10) are/is a very natural process of learning, but we (11) know/knows today that the child cannot do it alone. He or she (12) need/needs not
15   only the presence of at least one adult person who (13) provide/provides care, but the baby (14) need/needs great support from that person. Psychologists (15) say/says that the first two years of childhood (16) are/is the most important, and I (17) think/thinks they (18) are/is, because in this very short time a human being (19) acquire/acquires an important basis of
20   knowledge on which he (20) have/has to build.

3. Showing Tense in Simple and Expanded Verbs

This activity is best done in discussion with your classmates. In the passage below you are offered two choices for each simple verb and for each first auxiliary. Using Figures 8-4 and 8-22, decide which is the appropriate choice in each case, given the sense of the passage. Cross out the choice that you think is wrong.

As this is another long passage, you may be asked to do the work in two or three separate parts, any of which you may do on your own, in small groups, or in general class discussion. (For a correct version of this passage, see Appendix 2. In this case, again, the choice depends on what is meant.)

Passage 8-F   **MY FATHER**

by Igal Shilloh

My father (1) leaves/left his home when he (2) is/was only seventeen. He (3) kisses/kissed his widowed mother for the last time in his life and (4) goes/went on the frightening way to freedom. Two family pictures and a few pounds in his pocket (5) are/were the only things he (6) takes/took with him

5   along with the memories.

Of course, the memories. "I (7) remember/remembered," my father (8) tells/told me once, "that you (9) can't/couldn't take anything with you or the secret police (10) will/would suspect that you (11) are/were going to run away. I (12) don't/didn't take anything, just the smell of our home, the face

10 of my mother, the stove, the bed, the pictures on the walls, the sight of the neighborhood. Your mind (13) tries/tried to remember any small detail when you (14) know/knew that you (15) may/might not see any of this any more."

I (16) am/was looking at my father's picture when he (17) is/was eighteen. His eyes, smart and warm, (18) smile/smiled under his black hair

15 and his mouth (19) smiles/smiled gently. What (20) is/was inside this young man's head back then when he (21) is/was alone, in his new country, far away from his family? I (22) am/was trying to see into his eyes, to see what it (23) is/was like to fight the daily obstacles of getting a job, food, and a place to sleep. But the biggest struggle was probably with the memories, especially

20 the memories, which (24) are/were wounding the soul, and the longing for his family and his mother whom he (25) will/would never see again.

My father (26) is/was born in Syria in 1930. He (27) is/was the second child of a Jewish religious family. His father (28) dies/died when he (29) is/was young, and his mother (30) takes/took care of him and his older

25 brother. While he (31) is/was growing up, the state of Israel (32) is/was going to be born. The coming birth of Israel (33) is/was about to change my father's life forever.

When he (34) is/was seventeen, Syria and Israel (35) are/were at war, and he (36) has/had been called to join the Syrian army. The choice (37)

30 is/was clear. He (38) can't/couldn't join the Syrian army, which (39) is/was

fighting against his brothers and sisters in Israel. He (40) has/had to run away. His brother, who (41) is/was old enough to get away from the army, (42) stays/stayed with their weeping mother, who (43) sends/sent her younger son away from her to save his life.

4. Showing Subject-Verb Agreement in Simple and Expanded Verbs

In the following passage, you are given two alternatives for each auxiliary or verb that should show agreement with its subject. Cross out the one that is incorrect, using Figure 8-5 if you need to. Compare your answers with your classmates'. (For a correct version, see Appendix 2.)

Passage 8-G

WHY (1) DOES/DO WILD ANIMALS BECOME EXTINCT?

by Parastoo Khorramian

Everything in nature (2) is/are always changing. Some kinds of animals (3) is/are always dying out—becoming extinct. And, of course, new kinds (4) is/are always appearing.

There are many different things that may cause all the animals of one

5   particular kind to disappear. Scientists (5) knows/know some of the causes, but they (6) does/do not yet know others. For instance, they can tell part of the story about the whooping cranes. These (7) is/are very tall birds that (8) spends/spend the summers in northern Canada and the winters in southern Texas. Only about two dozen of the beautiful big cranes (9) is/are left. Soon

10   there may be none.

Hunters with guns (10) has/have helped to make the whooping crane almost extinct, but there (11) seems/seem to be something else going on too. Here (12) is/are a mystery that scientists (13) has/have not yet solved. In some years the flock (14) has/have no new baby whooping cranes along

15   when it (15) flies/fly south for the winter. (16) Does/do this mean that no eggs (17) has/have hatched, or that some disease or some wild enemy (18) has/have killed the young birds after they hatched? Or (19) does/do it mean that human hunters (20) is/are killing the young birds before they can fly? Nobody (21) knows/know.

5. Using the Right Verb Form After an Auxiliary

In the following passage, the auxiliary is given for each expanded verb. Choose which of the three forms of the verb that follows is the appropriate one. (Figure 8-6 will help you to make the choice.) Cross out the two verb forms that are not appropriate. (For a correct version of the passage, see Appendix 2.)

Passage 8-H   **THE MELTING POT**

by Kioko Miura

As a Japanese, I found it hard to understand the meaning of "the Melting Pot" when I learned the phrase about two years ago. But since I (1) have be/being/been in New York, I (2) am begin/beginning/begun to accept that New York is one of the Melting Pots, and I also remember that I (3) have
5   work/working/worked in the Melting Pot in Australia before coming to New York.

From 1985 to 1986 I was in Australia and (4) was work/working/worked at a Japanese restaurant where the owner was Australian and all the cooks and some waitresses were Koreans. At that time Japanese culture and food
10   were not familiar in Australia, and Australians (5) could not distinguish/ distinguishing/distinguished a Japanese from a Korean. The Australians' ignorance was an advantage for the restaurant, because even though those workers (6) were create/creating/created new Japanese-like food and (7) were serve/serving/served it as real Japanese food, Australians (8) were eat/
15   eating/eaten the imitation food satisfactorily and (9) were pay/paying/paid for it. Fortunately, the restaurant was always quite busy every night.

The owner and the other workers in this restaurant were completely strangers to Japanese culture, but they (10) could arrange/arranging/arranged "Japanese" food very well. Their special creative ability (11) could sometimes
20   cause/causing/caused a funny phenomenon. "Beef Yakitori" was one of their creations: "Yakitori" means grilled chicken, so "Beef Yakitori" (12) cannot exist/existing/existed. In this restaurant at least three countries' cultures (13) were blend/blending/blended in one place. Koreans who (14) did not know/knowing/known anything about Japan (15) were cook/cooking/
25   cooked Japanese food for Australians.

6. Using Modals

Pretend that you have won $500,000 in the lottery. Write down as many answers to the following questions as you can in five minutes:

What <u>would</u> you do?
What <u>could</u> you do?
What <u>should</u> you do?
What <u>might</u> you do?

You may find it helpful to consult Figure 8-18 while doing this.

Then compare your answers with your classmates'. Be prepared to explain such matters as why you <u>would</u> not necessarily do all the things that you <u>could</u> do, why you feel that you <u>should</u> do some things and whether you actually <u>would</u> do them, and what makes you uncertain about the things that you only <u>might</u> do. Your instructor may ask you to work in groups and present a summary of your group's answers to the rest of the class.

7. Exchanging Modals and Semimodals

There are two parts to this activity. For each part, you will find Figure 8-19 useful. If you work in pairs, one of you should consult the figure and the essays that the activity is based on while the other works on writing in the words.

A. The following sentences are taken from various essays quoted in this book. Each sentence contains a modal, which is underlined. Please write above it a semimodal that could replace it. You may find it easier to understand the sense of the modal if you read the whole passage, or at least the paragraph, from which the sentence comes.

1. In the morning I <u>would</u> wake up smelling fresh brewed coffee, fresh baked eggs, and toast. (Passage 3-H)

2. One day I <u>will</u> take a long vacation . . . (Passage 3-H)

3. Actually, I <u>couldn't</u> speak or understand English at all. (Passage 4-A)

4. If you have a tendency toward procrastination, you are always doing yesterday's jobs today, and tomorrow you are doing today's unfinished work. So, you <u>cannot</u> catch up with another person. (Passage 4-B)

5. One day, I determined to put away my homework which <u>would</u> be handed in to my teacher the next morning . . . (Passage 4-B)

6. I don't know which work I <u>should</u> give up, but I feel it is absolutely right to keep my baby. (Passage 4-C)

7. In each grade we <u>must</u> pass every subject . . . (Passage 4-D)

B. The following sentences have been chosen because they include semimodals. The semimodals are underlined. Write above each one a modal that could replace it. Again, consult the original passage if necessary.

1. After the examination I <u>used to</u> forget everything. (Passage 1-A)

2. I <u>have to</u> finish ordering fall and winter clothes before March. (Passage 4-C)

3. Every one of these trends <u>is about to</u> get worse, as the states must choose between extra cops, extra classrooms, health care or welfare, higher taxes, or less of everything else. (Passage 5-A)

8. Choosing Appropriate Modals and Semimodals

In the following passage, all the modals and semimodals have been replaced by blanks. Working on your own or in small groups, put an appropriate modal or semimodal in each place. In some cases, there is more than one possibility; choose what seems to you to be the best alternative and be prepared to explain your choice. (A correct version of this passage, i.e., the original one, is given in Appendix 2.)

Passage 8-I **MARRIAGE IN AFGHANISTAN**

by M. Daud Nassery

In Afghanistan, there is no such thing as dating, especially in high school. If a boy and a girl liked each other, they (1) _____ try to keep it secret. Almost all marriages were arranged by the families. Even today, in the countryside, nobody (2) _____ break the old rules. In the cities,

5 traditions are changing. Some of the younger generation have their own way of life. But they are not as independent as children in this country. You (3) _____ not date or see each other without the parents' permission.

My marriage was arranged by our families, who are distant cousins. My wife, Aqela, and I were engaged from the time that she was two or three

10 years old and I was six or seven. The reason for an early engagement is that families try to make their relationship stronger by sharing their children. My father worked in the Ministry of Finance, and Aqela's father was a schoolteacher. When I started high school, my parents told me that Aqela (4) _____ be my wife.

15 Sometimes arranged marriages don't work. But divorces are very few, because in our culture and religion divorce is considered shameful. If a

husband and wife are having problems, the family (5) _____ try to discuss and resolve their differences. Both sets of parents try to mediate, even if it means that the wife (6) _____ spend some time away, in
20 her father's house. I was very surprised, when I came to America, to find out the number of families that are broken and divorced.

—in *New Americans: An Oral History* by Al Santoli, Ballantine Books, 1988

9. Supplying Simple and Expanded Verbs

In the passage below, the first verb is underlined, and then you are given only the base form (in brackets) of each one that follows. In the blanks after each capitalized verb, you are asked to write in the appropriate simple or expanded form. The number of blanks indicates the number of words that are required, and when you need to put a word, such as *not,* after the first auxiliary, the word is given with the verb and a blank is provided for it. Notice that the passage deals with both present and past time, so you must think carefully about the sense in order to decide which tense and which auxiliary is appropriate. You may want to consult Figure 8-22 and also the list of irregular verbs inside the cover of this book.

Since this exercise is long, your teacher may divide it into several sections, and you may be asked to do some of it at home. (The original version of this passage is printed in Appendix 2.)

Passage 8-J   **CROSSING THE BORDER**

by Francisco Ramirez

We <u>left</u> Mexico for the United States in June 1985.

We (1) [begin] _____ walking north from the farm in Baja along the big road. We (2) [buy] _____ some Spanish bread and a can of orange juice. Our group (3) [be] _____ very small, just my
5 wife, the three children, and I. We (4) [be] _____ concerned about how we (5) [live] _____ _____ in the United States. We (6) [have] _____ no idea what to expect. And we (7) [save] _____ _____ only enough money to make the trip.

Many Guatemalans (8) [use] _____ Mexican "coyotes" to guide
10 them across the border, but many times these men (9) [take] _____ advantage of the people. They (10) [ask] _____, "Give me two hundred dollars, or five hundred." The Guatemalans say "Okay," because they (11) [be] _____ afraid. They (12) [have] _____ no idea what

220

CHAPTER 8: VERBS WITH TENSE: ACTIVE

to do once they (13) [reach] _____ the border. Sometimes there

15 (14) [be] _____ robberies, murders. We (15) [decide] _____

to cross the border without a "coyote." We (16) [not give] _____

_____ _____ our money to anybody.

When we (17) [be] _____ close to the border, we (18) [rest]

_____ alongside the road in the bushes. When we (19) [see]

20 _____ the Border Patrol, we (20) [get] _____ down and

(21) [hide] _____. The officers (22) [not see] _____

_____ _____ us. The problem (23) [be] _____ that

we (24) [run] _____ out of food and water, and we (25) [be]

_____ so exhausted from walking all night. We (26) [not want]

25 _____ _____ _____ to cross at the main point, near

San Diego. So we (27) [keep] _____ moving east, parallel to the

border.

Early in the next morning, we (28) [see] _____ the border

police capture a group of people as they (29) [try] _____ to cross.

30 Two or three trucks (30) [patrol] _____ _____ back and

forth. The area (31) [be] _____ very dry. There (32) [be]

_____ no fence, no grass, only scrub bushes and very small trees.

At 10:00 a.m., we (33) [still hide] _____ _____

_____. It (34) [be] _____ bright daylight, but we (35) [be]

35 _____ so hungry and thirsty in the hot sun that we (36) [decide]

_____ to take a chance. We (37) [huddle] _____ close

together and (38) [move] _____ as quickly as possible, though it

(39) [seem] _____ like forever. We (40) [look] _____ around

and (41) [not see] _____ _____ _____ any border

40 police, so we (42) [keep] _____ moving through the brush, off the

side of the road. We (43) [be] _____ very tired and (44) [have]

_____ no idea where we (45) [be] _____.

We (46) [not have] _____ _____ _____ any

bread or water. We (47) [look] _____ horrible and (48) [feel]

45 _____ like we (49) [die] _____ _____, especially the

children. It (50) [be] _____ an act of God that we (51) [meet]

_____ an American man. He (52) [talk] _____ to us in
English. We (53) [not understand] _____ _____
_____ his language, but he (54) [look] _____ like a good
man. It (55) [sound] _____ like he (56) [say] _____
_____, "Where (57) [you come] _____ _____
_____ from? Who (58) [be] _____ you?" We (59) [not
answer] _____ _____ _____ , but we (60) [try]
_____ talking in our language.

He (61) [say] _____, "Ahh. I (62) [understand] _____.
You (63) [be] _____ very poor people. I (64) [help] _____
_____ you." He (65) [give] _____ us some water and green
lime fruit from a bag that he (66) [carry] _____. He (67) [give]
_____ our small boy, Domingo, some candies.

After the man (68) [leave] _____, we (69) [pray] _____
and (70) [thank] _____ God. This man (71) [save] _____ our
lives. Then we (72) [continue] _____ walking. A few hours later, we
(73) [approach] _____ the city of San Isidro. A car (74) [pull]
_____ up to us, driven by a Mexican. We (75) [not have]
_____ _____ _____ any American money, but the
man (76) [offer] _____ to drive us near the town. Once there, we
(77) [meet] _____ another Mexican who (78) [drive] _____
us two hundred miles or more to Los Angeles. We (79) [never see]
_____ _____ _____ a big city before. It (80) [be]
_____ eleven o'clock at night when we (81) [arrive] _____.
All the lights (82) [be] _____ on, like a million stars. I (83) [say]
_____, "Thank God we (84) [be] _____ in Los Angeles."

—in *New Americans: An Oral History* by Al Santoli, Ballantine Books, 1988

10. Choosing Between Simple and Expanded Verbs

In the following passage, you are again given only the base form of each verb
that has tense (except for passive verbs, which have been supplied in full). Fill in
the correct form of the verb in brackets in the space provided. In this case, only
one blank is given for each verb, but sometimes it must be filled with more than
one word. In other words, besides thinking about tense and agreement, you must

also think about whether a simple or expanded verb is appropriate in each place, and if it is an expanded verb, you must think about which auxiliary you should use. Note that in two places in this passage, the auxiliary is a semimodal. This is another activity that is best done in groups or pairs.

(For a correct version of the passage, see Appendix 2. The answers given there are the original ones, but other answers are often possible.)

Passage 8-K   **WORKING IN EL PASO**

by José Urbina

My hometown (1) [be] _____ Juarez. Since I (2) [be] _____ nine years old, I (3) [come] _____ to El Paso to work. At first I (4) [do] _____ gardening in people's yards, but I (5) [stay] _____ in El Paso constantly since 1981, going out to the fields to do

5   farm work. I (6) [go] _____ to Juarez to visit my relatives at least one day each month, but in the last year, I (7) [not go] _____ because of the new immigration law. To visit Juarez I (8) [swim] _____ across the river.

During the past few months, the river (9) [be] _____ very high

10   and fast. That (10) [be] _____ one reason why not so many people (11) [come] _____ lately. I (12) [not work] _____ now, because it (13) [not be] _____ the growing or harvesting season on the big farms. On February 15, we usually (14) [begin] _____ to plant onions. That (15) [be] _____ when the main agricultural

15   season (16) [begin] _____ . We (17) [not pay] _____ our rent since December. If we (18) [be] _____ lucky, I (19) [find] _____ some part-time work to pay for food. Our baby (20) [be] _____ two months old. Because he was born in El Paso, he (21) [be] _____ an American citizen.

—in *New Americans: An Oral History* by Al Santoli, Ballantine Books, 1988

11. General Verb Problems

The following passage is from an early draft of an essay that a student wrote at the beginning of an English course. It is a good first draft, but there are a number of problems with the verbs. Go through the passage carefully, underlining all the verbs and writing the correct form above any auxiliary or verb form that is wrong. Put a check mark above any that is right.

(For a correct version of this essay, see Appendix 2; the essay could, however, be edited in many different ways.)

Passage 8-L   **MY GRANDMOTHER**

by Nieves Angulo

My grandmother has been the most wonderful person I had when problems struck me. Sometimes I would have problems with the principal of my school because of my desire to leave the country for political reasons. My grandmother would listened to me very quietly for hours, and then she
5   would suggested some solutions for the problems. But the most wonderful thing in her was that she won't imposed her suggestions on me. She said that one has to make her own final decision and no one should interfere. She helps me a lot in those days.

My grandmother is the biggest and most wonderful person I have in
10   this world. She has always been my great support in my rough times. She has always been there for me, very firm. I would like to be like her someday and to have that courage and that love that she has and give without asking anything in return. She inspire me, she guide me. Every day I pray that she could live many many more years.

Verbs with Tense: Passive

CHAPTER

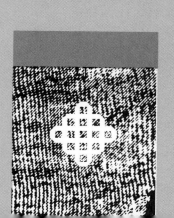

Passive verbs are expanded verbs of a special kind. The essay below includes a number of passive verbs. These verbs are underlined:

Passage 9-A **FOREIGN LANGUAGES IN POLAND**

by Dominika Stanislawska

There are many aspects of learning foreign languages. I am going to focus on the meaning of acquiring a second language in Poland after the Second World War. At that point, the country came into union with the communist countries.

5 During Stalin's era in the forties and fifties, knowledge of western languages was a real problem because it could cause a lot of trouble. Somebody who had this knowledge <u>was considered</u> to be an adherent to western capitalist imperialism and <u>was treated</u> like a spy and a traitor to communism. Many people who could speak German, English, or French

10 denied the fact. Very often somebody <u>would be imprisoned</u> without any trial, only for his knowledge of a western language.

Among those who experienced this were my parents. They knew German and English and that was what put them on "the black list" of suspects. They couldn't get good jobs. Once in a while, my father <u>was</u>

15 <u>arrested and interrogated</u>. Fortunately for us, we did not have any friends or relatives in Western Europe or in the U.S., so the police let him go free until the next time.

The only permitted foreign language was Russian though we <u>were</u> still <u>allowed</u> to speak Polish. . . .

1. THE STRUCTURE OF PASSIVE VERBS

A passive verb always has at least two parts: the auxiliary, which is usually a form of the verb BE, and the *-d/t/n* form of some other verb.

1.1 The Verb BE

BE is the most irregular of English verbs, having more different forms than any other. All of its forms are listed in Figure 9-1.

FIGURE 9-1   Forms of BE

Simple present	Base
am	**be**
is	
are	*-ing*
	being
Simple past	
was	*-d/t/n*
were	**been**

1.1a Basic Passive Verbs

Basic passive verbs are formed with the simple present or simple past forms of BE.

> Somebody who had this knowledge <u>was considered</u> to be an adherent to western capitalist imperialism . . . (Passage 9-A)

> The only permitted foreign language was Russian though we <u>were</u> still <u>allowed</u> to speak Polish. (Passage 9-A)

Stanislawska is talking about THEN, that is, "Stalin's era in the forties and fifties," so she uses the simple past of BE to indicate the time frame. In Passage 3-H, however, the writer is talking about Curaçao as it is NOW, so she uses simple present forms of BE:

> All these influences of French, Spanish, and Dutch <u>are reflected</u> in the language the folks speak, which is Papiamento. It is a mixture of all the languages mentioned and <u>is</u> also <u>mixed</u> with Portuguese and Indonesian. Although Papiamento <u>is spoken</u>, the official language is Dutch.

1.1b Expanded Passive Verbs

A passive verb, like an active one, can be expanded with an auxiliary from the modals, HAVE, or BE groups to show different time relationships. The auxiliary must be followed by an appropriate form of BE; that form of BE must then be followed by the *-d/t/n* form of the verb itself. See Figure 9-2 at the top of the next page.

The first auxiliary in an expanded passive verb means the same as it does in an active verb.

• A <u>modal</u> may indicate a prediction:

> If you read Japanese newspapers, you <u>will be surprised</u> by classified ads which read, "Hiring women under twenty-six years of age" . . . (Passage 4-A)

FIGURE 9-2   Constructing Expanded Passive Verbs

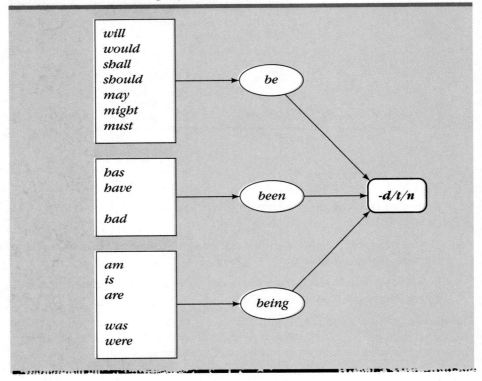

Or it may indicate habitual activity:

> Very often somebody <u>would be imprisoned</u> without any trial, only for his knowledge of a western language. (Passage 9-A)

It may also indicate an inference. (For a full discussion of the meanings of the various modals, see Chapter 8, Section 4.2.)

- An auxiliary of the HAVE group indicates an event before the main time frame:

> The thirteenth of December is a very significant day for me. On that day, in 1981, the Polish government set up the state of martial law which was supposed to smash and completely destroy the social and trade union movement called "Solidarity." Though formally registered, "Solidarity" <u>had</u> never <u>been approved</u> by the Polish and, especially, the Soviet authorities. (Passage 14-H)

(For a full discussion of HAVE, see Chapter 8, Section 4.3.)

- One of the simple forms of BE together with *being* and the *-d/t/n* form of a verb means that the verb is passive and the action described is continuous, or going on at the same time as something else. (See Chapter 8, Section 4.4.) For example, if you were to apply for a job and then call to ask about it, you might be given this response:

  Your application <u>is being considered</u>.

From this, you would know that the employers were still in the process of considering the application.

- You can also combine a modal with *have* and *been* and the *-d/t/n* form of a verb:

  Today I must not only accomplish my today's homework, but also I shall write one composition which <u>should have been finished</u> yesterday. (Passage 4-B)

The three auxiliaries in this example each suggest a different element of meaning: *Should* indicates that the writer is talking about what is right or preferable, rather than what actually happens; *have* shows that the writer is looking back to a previous time, that is, a time before "today"; and *been*, followed by the *-d/t/n* form, "finished," tells us that the verb is passive. (For more information on the combination of modal with *have*, see Chapter 8, Section 5.1.)

Passive verbs can therefore be used with almost all the combinations of auxiliaries that active verbs can. This means that every passive verb has an equivalent active verb that gives the same information about time. Figure 9-3 shows the whole range of active and passive verbs derived from the base word *eat*. Cats (typically) eat mice, so you can think of the active verb forms as describing what a cat does, and the passive verb forms as describing what happens to the mouse when the cat does it. Notice that each passive verb includes one more word than its equivalent active verb. The extra word is always a form of BE, and it appears last before the *-d/t/n* form of the verb itself, *eaten*.

FIGURE 9-3   Active and Passive Verbs

	ACTIVE	PASSIVE
NOW	eats/eat will* eat has/have eaten	am/is/are eaten will* be eaten has/have been eaten
THEN	ate would* eat had eaten	was/were eaten would* be eaten had been eaten

* Or any other modal belonging to the same time frame

1.2 The -*d/t/n* Form of the Verb

Passive verbs always end with the -*d/t/n* form of the verb; that is why this form is sometimes called the **passive participle.** Although often identical to the simple past tense form, the -*d/t/n* form does not mean past at all—it can be used in either time frame.

It is often hard to remember what the -*d/t/n* form of a particular verb is because it is derived from the base form in various ways. It may help you to remember if you think of verbs in groups, based on their -*d/t/n* forms.

Group 1: The -*d/t/n* Form Ends in -*d*

There are three categories within this group:

- The -*d/t/n* form is made by adding -*ed* to the base, or just -*d* if the base already ends in -*e*. This group includes all regular verbs.

BASE FORM	-*d/t/n* FORM
allow	allowed
approve	approved
consider	considered
imprison	imprisoned
treat	treated

- The -*d/t/n* form is made by adding just -*d* to the base, or changing the last letter to -*d.* Usually the vowel is changed too.

BASE FORM	-*d/t/n* FORM
have	had
hear	heard
say	said
sell	sold
tell	told

- For some verbs that already end in -*d*, the -*d/t/n* form is made by keeping the -*d* and changing the preceding vowel.

BASE FORM	-*d/t/n* FORM
bleed	bled
breed	bred
feed	fed
hold	held
lead	led
read	read

Group 2: The -*d/t/n* Form Ends in -*t*

This group includes four categories of verb:

- The -*d/t/n* form is made by changing -*d* at the end of the base to -*t*:

BASE FORM	-*d/t/n* FORM
bend	bent
build	built
lend	lent
send	sent
spend	spent

- The -*d/t/n* form is made by adding -*t* to the base and changing the preceding vowel. The final consonant of the base is sometimes changed too:

BASE FORM	-*d/t/n* FORM
deal	dealt
feel	felt
keep	kept
leave	left
mean	meant
meet	met
lose	lost

- The -*d/t/n* form is made by changing the vowel and changing the end of the base to -*ght*:

BASE FORM	-*d/t/n* FORM
bring	brought
catch	caught
fight	fought
teach	taught
think	thought

- For several verbs whose base ends in -*t*, the -*d/t/n* form is the same as the base:

BASE FORM	-*d/t/n* FORM
cast	cast
cut	cut
hit	hit
hurt	hurt
put	put
set	set
shut	shut
slit	slit
split	split

Group 3: The -*d/t/n* Form Ends in -*n*

This group includes four categories of verb:

- The -*d/t/n* form is made by adding -*n* to the base:

BASE FORM	-*d/t/n* FORM
blow	blown
grow	grown
know	known
mow	mown
sew	sewn
throw	thrown

- The -*d/t/n* form is made by adding -*n* to the base and changing the vowel:

BASE FORM	-*d/t/n* FORM
bear	borne/born
swear	sworn
tear	torn
wear	worn

- The -*d/t/n* form is made by adding -*en* to the base, or just -*n* if the base already ends in -*e*. The final consonant of the base must sometimes be doubled:

BASE FORM	-*d/t/n* FORM
beat	beaten
eat	eaten
forbid	forbidden
forgive	forgiven
give	given
see	seen
shake	shaken
take	taken

- The -*d/t/n* form is made by adding -*en* to the base and changing the preceding vowel:

BASE FORM	-*d/t/n* FORM
break	broken
choose	chosen
freeze	frozen
speak	spoken
steal	stolen
weave	woven

- The *-d/t/n* form is made by adding *-en* to the base, changing the preceding vowel, and usually doubling the consonant before *-en:*

BASE FORM	*-d/t/n* FORM
bite	bitten
drive	driven
forget	forgotten
hide	hidden
ride	ridden
write	written

1.3 Passives Formed with GET

Sometimes the verb GET is used to form a passive verb instead of BE. It is used particularly often when the verb to be made passive is either *marry* or *divorce:*

> After José and I <u>got married</u> and we found a place to live, I brought my children from a previous marriage.

Notice the difference between the verb form *married* and the noun *marriage*. *Marriage* is never used directly after GET.

2. WHAT PASSIVE VERBS MEAN

There is a fundamental difference in meaning between a passive verb and an active verb. In a clause with an active verb, the subject is "responsible" for the action described, as in this example from the second paragraph of Passage 9-A:

> Many people who could speak German, English, or French <u>denied</u> the fact.

Who did the denying? The answer is "many people who could speak German, English, or French"—that is, the subject of the sentence, and we know this because the verb is active. But see the difference in the following sentence where the verb is passive:

> Once in a while my father <u>was arrested and interrogated.</u>

Who did the arresting and interrogating? It was certainly not her father. He was not responsible for the action; he only suffered its effects. We know this because the verbs are passive.

The following examples illustrate the same point. As you read them, think carefully about who is responsible for the action described by the verb. Do you know? What is the relationship between the subject and the verb?

Most people there gave [the homeless man] some change, or even a dollar. His paper cup <u>was filled</u> with money in a minute. (Passage 7-A)

In her small town people <u>were separated</u> into two groups, lucky and unlucky. (Passage 7-E)

Acupuncture . . . <u>was devised</u> before 2500 BC in China, and by the late 20th century <u>was used</u> in many other areas of the world. [It] grew out of ancient Chinese philosophy's dualistic cosmic theory of the "Yin" and "Yang." The "Yin," the female principle, is passive and dark and <u>is represented</u> by the Earth; the "Yang," the male principle, is active and light and <u>is represented</u> by the heavens. Disease or physical disharmony <u>is caused</u> by an imbalance or undue preponderance of these two forces in the body, and the goal of Chinese medicine is to bring the "Yin" and the "Yang" back into balance with each other, thus restoring the person to health. (Passage 14-E)

3. WHEN TO USE PASSIVE VERBS

Passive verbs are useful for three different reasons.

- First, they enable you to keep a closely related set of noun phrases and pronouns in the subject position in a series of sentences. For example, in Passage 9-A Stanislawska is writing about the Polish people. By using passive verbs, she is able to keep this topic in the subject position and so add to the coherence of her essay. To show you how this works, we reprint the second paragraph again, underlining the passive verbs and putting the subject of each main clause in italics.

    During Stalin's era in the forties and fifties, *knowledge of western languages* was a real problem because it could cause a lot of trouble. *Somebody who had this knowledge* <u>was considered</u> to be an adherent to western capitalist imperialism and <u>was treated</u> like a spy and a traitor to communism. *Many people who could speak German, English, or French* denied the fact. Very often *somebody* <u>would be imprisoned</u> without any trial, only for his knowledge of a western language.

You see that most of these subjects are different ways of referring to her main topic, the people of Poland.

- Second, by using passive verbs, you can avoid saying who or what is responsible for the actions you are describing. For example, Stanislawska's use of passives means that she does not have to say who treated people like spies or imprisoned them (though we can guess it was the government). Thus she does not have to sound too accusing.

- Third, using a passive verb allows you to put the noun phrase that describes the person or thing responsible for the action toward the end of the sentence or clause instead of in the subject position at the beginning. Placed nearer to the end, the noun phrase is more prominent, so readers will notice it more. For example, the writer of Passage 14-E has been able to put a key idea at the end of a clause because she has used the passive:

> Disease or physical disharmony <u>is caused</u> by an imbalance or undue preponderance of these two forces in the body . . .

It is not, however, considered good style to use the passive too often. So only use it when you have a good reason: to keep the emphasis where you want it or to avoid having to give information that you are either unwilling or unable to give.

WHEN YOU ARE READING

You will often come across passive verbs in textbooks, especially in those about scientific or technical subjects. The following passage, for example, comes from a book about genetics, a branch of biology. The passive verbs are underlined:

> Both this book and the subject of genetics <u>are concerned</u> with understanding the mechanisms and controls of the process by which genes <u>are transmitted</u>, <u>are expressed</u>, direct the formation of the individual, and <u>are affected</u> in the course of evolution. In this section of the book we <u>are concerned</u> with the rules of transmission of genes, the units that control and determine the processes of development and the ultimate appearance of individuals.

—from *Principles of Genetics* by Robert H. Tamarind. (William C. Brown, 1986)

LEARNING STRATEGY

Forming Concepts: Analyzing the context of grammatical forms helps you understand when to use them.

When you are reading, listening to the radio, or watching TV, look out for passive verbs. Every now and then stop to consider why the writer or speaker has chosen to use the passive rather than the active form. Notice particularly how politicians use the passive: It is often a convenient way to avoid saying who is or was responsible for something.

I. Recognizing Passive Verbs

Identify the passive verbs in the following passage by underlining them. (You should find seven.) Be careful to underline all the parts of each verb: the first auxiliary, any additional form of BE that may be used, and the *-d/t/n* form of the verb itself. Then discuss with your classmates why the passive is used in each case. How would the essay be different if active verbs had been used instead?

Passage 9-B   **A "WOMB" OR A HUMAN BEING?**

by Xiao Ling Ding

One afternoon three months ago, I received a phone call from my friend Lin Hua in Zhang Village, where I had stayed for a year ten years before.

Over the telephone, I learned that Lin Hua had been forced to get divorced from her husband by her parents-in-law simply because she had
5   given birth to a daughter.

On hearing the tragic news, my heart was filled with righteous indignation. How could Lin Hua's parents-in-law behave that way? And where is the woman's legal status? "But you can hardly find any answer to these questions in the countryside," said Lin Hua. "There are some more
10   women who are just as unfortunate as I in our village." The following is also what I learned from Lin Hua that afternoon.

Zhang Village has a long history. The Confucian idea has been firmly rooted in the villagers' minds—the failure to produce a male heir was considered the most unfilial of all unfilial crimes. People have always
15   regarded it as the greatest blessing in life to have as many male descendants as possible. So their desire for a son is very strong. And the government's one-child family planning policy has just aggravated this problem. A married woman who fails to give birth to a boy is often ill-treated by her husband or by her parents-in-law. Lin Hua's story is only one example. There is a woman
20   named Fang Fang who is often beaten black and blue by her husband for having given birth to a daughter. Another woman named Li Ling was forced to have six induced abortions by her husband in order to produce a male heir! Though this couple has a son now, the wife's health has been ruined.

236

2. Choosing the Verb Form After an Auxiliary: Active and Passive Verbs

The following passage includes a number of two-word expanded verbs, some of which are active and some are passive. This means that when the auxiliary is *am, is, are, was,* or *were,* the next word may be either the *-ing* form or the *-d/t/n* form of the verb. To decide which is right in each case, you must think about the meaning of the expanded verb and of the sentence that it is in. Cross out the two forms that are not appropriate. (For a correct version of this passage, see Appendix 2.)

Passage 9-C   **THE KOREAN WRITING SYSTEM**
                                       by Jinny Yi

I (1) would like/liking/liked to introduce the Korean writing system because lots of people think that Korean, Chinese, and Japanese have the same writing systems. Chinese and Japanese have similar writing systems, but the Korean one is different.

5   First of all, the Korean writing system (2) was create/creating/created by Sejong, the fourth king of the Yi dynasty. He created the new writing system because of the common and lower class people, so that they (3) could learn/learning/learned to write better and easier. At that time, it was not easy to get an education for the lower class people; also, the slaves

10   (4) were not allow/allowing/allowed to learn to write. Furthermore, only people in the royal family (5) could get/getting/got an education, and it was not easy even for them to learn the Chinese loanwords. Chinese loanwords are very difficult to learn, because there are so many different ways of writing them. It is not an alphabet. So you must be highly educated to write

15   the Chinese loanwords.

The writing system (6) was introduce/introducing/introduced in 1446. It (7) was call/calling/called Han gul; it (8) is still call/calling/called Han gul in Korea today. Han gul (9) was design/designing/designed as an alphabet. There are 24 basic writing symbols. There are 14 consonants, and 10 vowels.

20   As I mentioned before, Han gul (10) was create/creating/created because of lower class people and (11) was use/using/used for lower class people, but now all Koreans (12) are use/using/used Han gul. But although Han gul (13) is much more commonly use/using/used in Korea these days, we (14) have keep/keeping/kept some Chinese loanwords. So we (15) can

25   say/saying/said that we have two methods of writing in Korea today.

Therefore, we, the people in our country, thank Sejong for creating our own writing system. Furthermore, we are very proud of having our own writing system.

3. Filling the Verb Position with Active or Passive Verbs

In the following passage, all the fillers of the verb position, except for the first, have been removed and replaced by blanks. The verbs, both active and passive, are then listed after the essay. You are asked to put each of them into its proper place. (For a correct version of this passage, see Appendix 2.)

Passage 9-D   **THE ABACUS**

by Chun-Chi Liu

My favorite possession <u>is</u> an abacus. It (1) _____ a traditional Chinese instrument that (2) _____ for calculation. It (3) _____ five thousand years of history and (4) _____ a great influence on the Chinese way of life. My personal character

5   (5) _____ by my abacus. It (6) _____ me feel competent and comfortable with numbers. Moreover, it (7) _____ me reach success in business.

In ancient times the abacus (8) _____ very popular in China. People (9) _____ it for trading their goods in the market. Later, the

10   structure and pattern of the abacus (10) _____, so there are some differences between the ancient and modern abacus. The ancient abacus (11) _____ by hand and was square, heavy, and black in color. It (12) _____ fifteen rows of beads and six bigger beads for each column. A bead (13) _____ 2" by 2". Now, the abacus

15   (14) _____ by machine; it (15) _____ rectangular, lighter, brown in color, with twenty-seven rows and five smaller beads for each column. A small bead (16) _____ 0.5" by 1".

The abacus (17) _____ into two parts, and there (18) _____ a space between each part . . .

measures	measured	is	has made	is made
used	was	has been changed	was made	has helped
is	had	were remodelled	is used	
is	has	is divided	has had	

4. Constructing Active and Passive Expanded Verbs

The writer of the following passage has used several expanded verbs, some of which are active and some passive. Here all the words in each expanded verb have been replaced by blanks, and the words themselves are listed after the essay. (No words have been added or subtracted, and each word is listed as many times as the writer used it.) You are asked to fill in the blanks from the three lists. The first blank in each phrase should be filled by a word from the list of First auxiliaries, and the last blank should be filled from the list of Verbs. For those expanded verbs that consist of three words, the middle blank should be filled from the list of Second auxiliaries. When you have finished, underline or circle each passive verb.

This activity is quite difficult, so it would be best to do it in groups or pairs. Figures 8-6 and 8-8 should be of some help. (For a correct version of the passage, see Appendix 2.)

Passage 9-E   **LUCK**

by Marius Stawoski

"Luck—that which happens, either good or bad, to a person by, or as if by, chance; fortune." I found this definition in the dictionary. In the story of "The Rocking-Horse Winner," Paul thought that if he knew the name of the horse which (1) _____ _____ the race, he (2) _____

5   _____ lucky. Is that the answer to the question that Paul asked his mother, "What is luck?" In her opinion she was unlucky and nobody ever knew why one person was lucky and another was not.

If I (3) _____ _____ _____ the same question as his mother was, I (4) _____ _____ _____ him the

10   tale which I (5) _____ _____ as a kid, that in ancient times there was a mother who had three sons. Two of them (6) _____ _____ wise and brave people. The youngest son (7) _____ _____ dumb because he was kind-hearted. One day, a king announced that he (8) _____ _____ his daughter's hand to

15   the man who killed the dragon which (9) _____ _____ his state. When the oldest son heard the news, he said, "I am the oldest son and the strongest one so I (10) _____ _____ the dragon." Next day, he set out. At the end of his journey, near the castle's gate, he saw a dwarf who asked him for a crust of bread. The oldest son (11) _____

20 not _____ attention to the hungry dwarf because he was afraid that
    somebody (12) _____ _____ him. The dragon became the
    winner in their fight and the wisest and bravest son (13) _____
    _____. The second son took his chance. Like his older brother, he
    (14) _____ not _____ for the begging dwarf. He also lost his
25 fight. The youngest son gave what he (15) _____ _____ for
    and the thankful dwarf gave him a special sword so that he
    (16) _____ _____ the dragon. He was lucky, but it happened
    to him because of his kindness.

        In my opinion, luck is the ability to take advantage of fortunate
30 circumstances. In other words, luck is a factor of our personality, and it stays
    with us even though circumstances (17) _____ _____ all the
    time. For example, "a hard little place at the center of her heart" was Paul's
    mother's bad luck.

        In the end, our luck depends on our personality, so if we want to
35 change our bad luck, we (18) _____ _____ out what we
    have   inside   ourselves   which   (19)   _____   _____
    _____.

FIRST AUXILIARIES		SECOND AUXILIARIES	VERBS	
are	was	be	asked	kill
could	was	been	asked	kill
did	were	have	be	killed
did	will		called	outstrip
had	would		changing	pay
must	would		considered	stop
should	would		devastating	told
was	would		find	told
was	would		give	win
was			improved	

5. Changing Active to Passive Verbs

    The following passage originally contained a number of passive verbs. We
have changed all but one of these into active verbs and have underlined the
clauses in which they appear. You are asked to rewrite these clauses so that the
verbs are again passive. When you do so, you will often be able to drop the word
or phrase that names the one "responsible" for the action described. In this way,

you can omit a number of vague expressions, such as "people" or "society," and you can make the clauses they occur in less clumsy. In number (1), however, the information about the one responsible for the action is important, so it must be kept; but changing the verb into a passive one will shift this information to the end of the clause where it will be more prominent. Number (1) has been done for you as an example:

1. The words for the theme song were composed by Sha Ye Xing, a contemporary playwright of high renown.

(For a correct version of this passage, see Appendix 2. Alternative wordings are possible, but Appendix 2 gives the writer's own version.)

Passage 9-F   **CHINESE WOMEN'S PLACE**

by Xiao Jun Su

About a year ago, Shanghai TV Station broadcast a program entitled "Aspects of Shanghai Husbands" which immediately became a tremendous hit and aroused widespread heated arguments. (1) <u>Sha Ye Xing, a contemporary playwright of high renown, composed the words for the theme song.</u> (2)

5 <u>They called the song "Where can a manly man be found?"</u>, but from its content and music it could be easily perceived that it was a rhetorical question rather than an ordinary one. One line from the song was particularly illuminating and penetrating: "When the wife growls, the husband trembles for three times on end." The program was vivid and effective in bringing

10 home to us the deplorable condition of those wretched Shanghai husbands (3) <u>who people tie down to housework and deprive of any financial power at home.</u> Thus the theme song uttered both an angry cry and a plaintive whine. It reflected the phenomenon (4) <u>that they hen-peck a rapidly increasing number of husbands nowadays</u> and that wives today are becoming as tough

15 and uncontrollable as tigresses or lionesses.

But why? For thousands of years (5) <u>people have eulogized Chinese women for their laudable virtues of being hard-working and being capable of enduring incredible sufferings.</u> During the feudal age (6) <u>society expected Chinese women to be unconditionally obedient not only to their fathers and</u>

20 <u>husbands but to their sons as well.</u> They had no say whatsoever at home, and (7) <u>people even forbade them to go outside their houses.</u> (8) <u>People would</u>

consider them bad-mannered and lascivious and would even punish them if they showed their teeth while smiling. (9) Society privileged a man to have several wives at the same time and he could divorce any of them at any moment

25   if he did not feel gratified, but a woman had to be loyal and "keep her body clean" even after her husband's death. Women had to work like slaves, and (10) people could buy them and sell them cheaply. Fettered tightly by the barbarian feudal system, (11) people treated them as ploughing animals or tools for reproduction, and they ranked among the lowest in the society. In a

30   word, (12) society oppressed and mercilessly persecuted them.

Verbals and
Verbal Phrases

10

CHAPTER

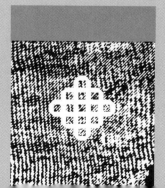

*I*n written English, there is a verb position at the beginning of every predicate, and that position is always filled by a simple or expanded verb. The verb must always have tense: That is, it must show which time frame (NOW or THEN) the sentence is in. But verbs can also be used in other positions, and then they do not have tense. We will call these kinds of verbs **verbals.** Verbals can sometimes be used as units on their own, but more often they are the first part of a **verbal phrase.** In the following essay, all the verbals are printed in italics, and the verbal phrases are underlined.

Passage 10-A   **A JOB IN A CLOTHES STORE**

by Sofia Tadesse

There are many minimum wage jobs for an unskilled person. Among them I have tried *baby-sitting,* *working* as a cashier, and *working* as a sales person. Last summer I worked for three months as a sales person in a boutique *located* on 34th Street and 6th Avenue. . . .

5   The job needed a lot of patience to *handle* all the customers. Not all the customers who came to the store were decent. Some came to *buy* things while others came only to *kill* some time outside their house. There were questions *asked* by my customers that annoyed me—such as if there were blue sweaters *hanging* on the rack, they would ask for red or some other

10   color with the same material and mode. If we had other colors why would we hide them? . . . Sometimes it was not enough to *know* where the things that were sold in the shop were located. Some customers also expected {me} to *know* the train or bus available around the store or the closest coffee shop, post office, etc. . . .

15   The job had an *exciting* part. It was *catching* shoplifters. In our store we occasionally found customers who didn't want to *trouble* a cashier with *ringing* up their money or *wrapping* up their merchandise. Instead, they considerately tried to *slip* purchases under their coats or into their *shopping* bags. Almost all the expensive clothes had alarms *attached* to them but there

20   were small items like underwear, stockings and scarfs that could be slipped out easily. If we spotted a shoplifter we were instructed to *signal* guards. There were times that I spotted shoplifters. The only thing I had to do was to *get* the attention of the guards by *calling* a number (my sales number) and the guards took the other *required* steps.

25   Although I may sound as though I disliked *working* in the store, I enjoyed it. Besides money, the job gave me confidence in myself, because whenever there was a misunderstanding between me and my co-workers or customers I managed to *control* my anger. Furthermore, I learned to *deal* with many people. In general for me it was a good experience.

244

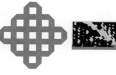
For every verb, there are three forms that can be used as verbals. They are shown in Figure 10-1.

FIGURE 10-1   Verb Forms Used as Verbals

NAME OF FORM	EXAMPLE (a regular verb)	EXAMPLE (an irregular verb)	EXAMPLE (an irregular verb)
(to) + base	(to) wash	(to) keep	(to) eat
base + *-ing*	washing	keeping	eating
base + *-d/t/n*	washed	kept	eaten

The forms used as verbals are the same as those used with auxiliaries to make expanded verbs. (See Chapter 8, Sections 1 and 3.)

When the base form of a verb is used as a verbal, it usually has the word *to* in front of it. This word distinguishes the verbal from the present simple verb that is used after plural subjects. (See Chapter 8, Section 2.3.)

In traditional grammar books, the verbals are given the following names:

(to) + base   =   infinitive
base + *-ing*   =   gerund
                 or present participle (depending on how it is used)
base + *-d/t/n*   =   past participle
                 or passive participle

The traditional use of the words *present* and *past* to describe the *-ing* and *-d/t/n* forms is confusing because these forms have no time reference by themselves. The time frame is established by the auxiliary when these forms are used in expanded verbs.

2. VERBAL PHRASES

A verbal phrase looks just like a predicate except that it begins with a verbal (a verb without tense) rather than a verb. Otherwise the phrase may have the same parts as a predicate. (See Chapters 11 and 12.) We have reprinted some of the verbal phrases from Passage 10-A below and have labeled the parts of each one.

| *verbal* | *adverbial* |
| working | as a cashier |

| *verbal* | *adverbial* |
| located | on 34th Street and 6th Avenue |

| *verbal* | *object* |
| to handle | all the customers |

| *verbal* | *object* | *adverbial* |
| to kill | some time | outside the house |

| *verbal* | *object* |
| catching | shoplifters |

Verbal phrases are useful because they enable you to name whole actions or events and to treat them as single units. They can be used in a number of different positions.

3. HOW TO USE VERBALS AND VERBAL PHRASES

3.1 *to* + Base

Verbals and verbal phrases formed with <u>to + base</u> suggest some future or expected activity. They usually express a purpose, either of an action or of a named thing or person. You can use these verbals in several different positions.

- In an **adverbial** position, a <u>to + base</u> verbal answers a question, "Why?" In Passage 10-A, for example, Tadesse uses two of them to tell us why customers came to the store:

    Some [customers] came <u>*to buy* things</u> while others came only <u>*to kill* some time outside their house</u>. (Passage 10-A)

Similarly, Law explains why she went to the Ursuline Convent School:

    When I finished my junior year in high school, I went there <u>*to continue* my education</u>. (Passage 3-A)

- You can also use <u>to + base</u> verbals in the **object** position after certain verbs. These verbs usually have some idea of purpose or expectation in themselves. In the following examples, we have printed these verbs in bold.

Of course, I might have **tried** _to improve_ by myself, but I did not even **want** _to think_ about English. (Passage 1-A)

A company **attempts** _to hire_ younger women. (Passage 4-A)

- A third way you can use a _to + base_ verbal or verbal phrase is to put it in the **postmodifier** position after a noun that names a thing or person. In this position, the verbal shows the purpose of whatever is named. Here we have printed the core noun in bold.

  [Education] is teaching or training a person's mind or character, the main and basic **program** _to achieve_ one's goal in life. (Passage 5-A)

  [A Chinese housewife] does her housework by herself and doesn't hire a **maid** _to work_ with her. (Passage 8-D)

- Similarly, you can make a statement about a purpose, ability, or wish by using this kind of verbal phrase in the **complement** position, that is, after the verb BE, or some other linking verb. (See Chapter 11, Section 3.5.)

  The purpose of education is _to help_ people achieve their goals in life.

- Finally, a verbal phrase that begins with _to + base_ can itself be the subject of a sentence, but then it is usually "postponed"—that is, placed at the end of the sentence, and the word _it_ is put in the subject position. (See Chapter 12 for a full explanation.) This structure makes a reader or listener notice the phrase, so it is a good way of emphasizing an important point.

  It was a new experience for me _to have_ classmates who were from different countries. (Passage 4-A)

  If people want to be successful, it is very important for them _to know_ how to use time well. (Passage 4-B)

3.2 Base + -*ing*

Verbals and verbal phrases that have the -*ing* form describe an action in progress rather than one that is expected. They are active in meaning—that is, they suggest that someone or something is "responsible" for the action. (See Chapter 9, Section 2.)

Verbals and verbal phrases with -*ing* can be used in two basic ways: to name an action or to describe someone or something.

3.2a -*ing* Verbal Phrases Used to Name Actions

By using an -*ing* verbal or verbal phrase, you can name an action and then treat it exactly as if it were a noun phrase. (In this use, traditional grammar books describe -*ing* verbals as gerunds.) Thus it can fill all the same positions as a noun phrase can.

- An *-ing* verbal or verbal phrase can be the **subject** of a sentence:

    Memorizing seemed to be the only way of learning English. (Passage 1-A)

    Having your own languages and customs could be beneficial. (Passage 3-D)

- You can also put an *-ing* verbal or verbal phrase in the **object** or **complement** position of a sentence, that is, after the verb:

    I have tried *baby-sitting, working* as a cashier, and *working* as a sales person. (Passage 10-A)

    As long as English teachers are not concerned with the importance of practical English . . ., they will continue *making* victims like me. (Passage 1-A)

    All I could do was some *reading*. (Passage 4-A)

When you use a verbal phrase in the object position, it is sometimes difficult to tell whether you should use a *to + base* verbal or an *-ing* one. For help on this point, see Chapter 11, Section 2.5.

- Occasionally you will find an *-ing* verbal used as the **core noun** in a noun phrase. In the following example, the verbal is in italics, and the noun phrase of which it is the core is underlined:

    Simple *dressing* makes Irena more comfortable. (Passage 14-F)

- A verbal phrase can also be used like a noun phrase or pronoun **after a preposition.** The verbal that follows the preposition *must* be the *-ing* form. In the following examples, the prepositions are printed in bold, and the verbals, as usual, in italics:

    [Some] customers . . . didn't want to trouble a cashier **with** *ringing* up their money or *wrapping* up their merchandise. (Passage 10-A)

    The only thing I had to do was to get the attention of the guards **by** *calling* a number . . . (Passage 10-A)

    In the old days, there was no limit **in** *choosing* any major or professional field that you wanted, regardless of what your grades were. (Passage 4-D)

A prepositional phrase that consists of preposition plus verbal phrase is often used in the front adverbial position of a sentence. In that case, the subject of the sentence as a whole is understood as being "responsible" for the action named in the verbal phrase. See the following example:

    U.N.E.S.C.O. has declared the islands "the cultural patrimony of the world." **By** *doing* so, U.N.E.S.C.O. can provide the support necessary to conserve this Galapagos garden intact. (Passage 14-A, Part 2)

Who is "doing so" ? The answer is U.N.E.S.C.O., the subject that follows the prepositional phrase.

WHEN YOU ARE WRITING

Be careful when you put a preposition followed by a verbal phrase in the front adverbial position. Does the subject that follows name the one responsible for the action you have just described? If it does not, you have created what is called a **dangling modifier.** To correct it, you should either change the prepositional phrase into a clause with its own subject or change the filler of the subject position that follows. For example, Tadesse might have written the following in an early draft of her essay:

In handling all the customers, the job needed a lot of patience.

Did the job handle customers? Not really—the writer did. She could have revised it to read:

Since I had to handle all the customers, the job needed a lot of patience.

Or she could have written:

In handling all the customers, I needed a lot of patience.

3.2b -*ing* Verbal Phrases Used to Describe People or Things

Verbals and verbal phrases with -*ing* can also be used to describe nouns. (Traditional grammar books call the verbal a present participle when it is used in this way.) Again, you can use the phrase in a number of different positions.

• You can **insert** an -*ing* verbal phrase, usually at the end of a sentence, separating it from the main part of the sentence by a comma:

The old man was rummaging through the garbage pail, *hoping* to find food or simply soda bottles. (Passage 5-B)

The human being acts like a bull in the china shop of the earth, *manipulating, observing* without wisdom his own environment, and *destroying* it. (Passage 7-G)

The land is in general barren, *having* craters that give it the look of the land on the moon. (Passage 14-A, Part 1)

In each case, the verbal phrase describes the subject of the sentence, telling the reader or listener what the subject is/was doing at the same time as the main action of the predicate.

You can also insert an *-ing* verbal phrase, or verbal alone, at the beginning of a sentence. For instance, you could rewrite the first of the above examples like this:

> _Hoping_ to find food or simply soda bottles, the old man was rummaging through the garbage pail.

Or you can insert the verbal phrase between the subject and the verb of the main clause:

> The old man, _hoping_ to find food or simply soda bottles, was rummaging through the garbage pail.

Notice that wherever it is inserted, the verbal phrase describes the subject of the sentence, and the action in the verbal phrase is going on at the same time as the action of the main clause. Notice also that the verbal phrase is marked off from the rest of the sentence by commas. (See Chapter 14, Section 3 on inserts.)

WHEN YOU ARE WRITING

Be careful about using an *-ing* verbal phrase at the beginning of a sentence. When you do, ask yourself this question: Who or what is the verbal phrase about, or who is "responsible" for the action? Is it the same as the subject of the main clause? If it is not, you have created a dangling modifier and should turn the verbal phrase into a clause with its own subject.

For example, there is a problem in the following sentence. (It has been adapted from a sentence in Passage 5-C.)

Getting back from the ride, it is 10 p.m.

Who is getting back from the ride? Clearly not "it," the subject of the sentence as a whole. Written like this, the sentence is confusing, because whoever is described in the verbal phrase is different from the subject of the main clause. You can solve the problem by changing the verbal phrase into a subordinate clause:

When we get back from the ride, it is 10 p.m.

This is how, in fact, the writer of Passage 5-C originally put it.

• You can also use an *-ing* verbal phrase as a **postmodifier** in a noun phrase. It describes whatever you have named in the core noun, so the core noun is understood as responsible for the action described. In the following examples, the core noun is printed in bold:

> If there were blue **sweaters** *hanging* on the rack, the customers would ask for red or some other color with the same material and mode. (Passage 10-A)

> The flowers were beautiful and attractive with **butterflies** *dancing* on them. (Passage 5-D)

When the verbal phrase is a postmodifier in a noun phrase, it is not separated from the noun by a comma.

• You can use an *-ing* verbal alone, like an adjective, in the **complement** position.

> Our war in 1981 was . . . painful and *confusing*. (Passage 14-H)

Like any other complement, the verbal describes the last preceding noun, in this case (and in most cases) the subject. (See Chapter 11, Section 3.)

• Finally, you can use an *-ing* verbal as a **premodifier** in a noun phrase. In this position, it is related to the noun in two quite different ways, depending on what the verbal and noun mean in themselves. In the following examples, the *-ing* verbal describes what the core noun does:

> The job had an *exciting* part. (Passage 10-A)

> Like his older brother, he did not stop for the *begging* dwarf. (Passage 9-E)

The core noun is understood as the one responsible for the action: A part of the job was exciting; the dwarf was begging.

In some cases, however, the core noun is obviously not responsible for the action. Consider this example:

> I remember that I have once worked in the *Melting* Pot in Australia . . . (Passage 8-H)

The pot was not melting, it was a pot <u>for</u> melting—in other words, *melting* is being used like a noun as a classifier. (See Chapter 6, Section 1.4.)

3.3 Base + -*d/t/n*

Unlike verbals with <u>to + base</u> or -*ing*, -*d/t/n* verbals and verbal phrases are **passive** in meaning. (See Chapter 9, Section 9.2.) That is, they suggest that someone or something "experiences" or is affected by the action described. They can be used to describe things or people named by nouns, in either the postmodifier or the premodifier position of a noun phrase, in the complement position in the predicate, or as inserts in sentences.

- When a -*d/t/n* verbal phrase is used as a **postmodifier,** it describes the "experience" of whatever is named by the core noun. Consider the following examples from Passage 10-A. (The core noun is printed in bold.)

    There were **questions** <u>*asked* by my customers</u> that annoyed me . . .

    Almost all the expensive clothes had **alarms** <u>*attached* to them</u>. . . .

Who did the asking? It was the customers, not the questions. Similarly, the alarms did not attach anything; they were attached by somebody.

- When you use a -*d/t/n* verbal as a **premodifier,** you again show that the core noun "experiences" the action, but is not "responsible" for it. For example:

    The guards took the other *required* steps. (Passage 10-A)

    I keep my diaries on my bookshelf which has a *locked* glass door on it. (Passage 8-A)

    "Yakitori" means *grilled* chicken, so "Beef Yakitori" cannot exist. (Passage 8-H)

The last example shows the point particularly clearly: Obviously the chicken did not grill itself! Nor did the door lock or the steps require anything.

- You will often see -*d/t/n* verbals and verbal phrases used as adjectives in the **complement** position. (See Chapter 11, Section 3.5.) If the linking verb is BE, the verbal looks just like a passive verb, except that the verbal may have a qualifier in front of it:

    I was <u>really *excited* by learning the language</u>. (Passage 1-A)

Notice that in English, a person or animal who feels something is thought of as being passive, as experiencing the feeling rather than doing it; so when a verb is used as an adjective to describe how someone feels, the verb is in the -*d/t/n* form, not the -*ing* one. Consider the following examples:

    I sometimes question myself, "How many years have I been learning English?" I am *shocked* when I count because I have been learning English more than eight years. Unfortunately, I'm not *satisfied* with my English skills . . . (Passage 1-A)

Here is a list of verbs that are commonly used to describe how people feel:

annoyed	interested
amazed	irritated
bored	satisfied
concerned	shocked
excited	surprised
frightened	terrified
frustrated	worried

Can you think of any more?

WHETHER YOU'RE TALKING OR WRITING

When you use a verb to describe a feeling, ask yourself this question: Are you talking about how the person (or animal) who is experiencing the feeling, or about what is causing it? If you are talking about someone's experience, you should use the *-d/t/n* form of the verb. If you are talking about what is causing the feeling, you should use the *-ing* form.

For example, you can describe people as either *interesting* or *interested:*

The students in this class are very *interesting.*

This suggests that the students have many good ideas and you would probably enjoy their company.

The students in this class are very *interested.*

This means that the students enjoy taking part in the class and learning whatever they are being taught.

- A verbal phrase with *-d/t/n* can be **inserted** in a sentence in the same ways as an *-ing* verbal phrase can. Like an *-ing* verbal phrase, it usually describes the subject of the sentence, but with this important difference: It describes what the subject experiences rather than what it does.

    <u>*Fettered* tightly by the barbarian feudal system</u>, women were treated as ploughing animals or tools for reproduction, and they ranked among the lowest in the society. (Passage 9-F)

    A car pulled up to us, <u>*driven* by a Mexican</u>. (Passage 8-J)

4. EXPANDED VERBALS

Verbals can be expanded by using *to have* or *having* with the *-d/t/n* form of a verb, *to be* with the *-ing* form, or *to be* or *being* with the *-d/t/n* form.

4.1 Verbals Expanded with HAVE

The combination of HAVE with *-d/t/n* means the same in a verbal as it does in a verb with tense—that is, it shows that the event described in the verbal phrase occurred before the main time you are talking about. The verb is active, not passive, and so the subject of the main sentence is assumed to be "responsible" for the verbal phrase.

to have + -d/t/n

You can use a verbal phrase that begins with *to have* + *-d/t/n* in the same places as you can use a simple verbal phrase beginning with *to*. The combination of *to* with *have* is like *will* with *have* in that it looks both forward to the future and back to the past. (See Chapter 8, Section 5a.)

By the end of next month, I want *to have lost* ten pounds.

Here the speaker is looking to the future and describing what he or she hopes will happen before that future date.

I'm pleased *to have met* you.

This suggests, "I am pleased now that I met you some time ago." The time is probably a short one; a person might say this, for instance, after meeting someone and talking for half an hour or so. The person would not say it immediately on meeting.

He is too big *to have gone* through that hole.

The speaker might be talking about a dog that has escaped—that is, a past event that is relevant NOW—and the sentence might be part of a conversation about how this event happened. Again, HAVE is used to look backward from the main time frame.

having + -d/t/n

This kind of verbal phrase is usually an insert at the front of a sentence (see Chapter 14, Section 3), but it can also be placed immediately after the subject or at the end. It describes something that the subject of the sentence did before the action described in the main clause, and it may give a reason for that action. For example, we could say about the experience described in Passage 10-A:

Having worked as a shop assistant, Tadesse knew how to control her temper.

254

4.2 Verbals Expanded with BE

4.2a *to be + -ing*

This expanded verbal has both the sense of purpose implied by *to + base* and the continuous sense implied by BE + *-ing*. It can be used in all the same places as a simple verbal or verbal phrase that begins with *to + base*.

It is a great pleasure *to be working* with you.

Right now I would like *to be sunning* myself on the beach.

She is too old *to be climbing* mountains!

4.2b *to be/being + -d/t/n*

Like any combination of BE with *-d/t/n*, these expanded verbals are always **passive.**

to be + -d/t/n

You can use a verbal phrase with *to be + -d/t/n* in all the places you can use any other verbal phrase that begins with *to*. Again, it looks toward the future or gives an explanation.

I went to the school personnel office *to be interviewed.* (Passage 6-B)

[Many adult immigrants] prefer *to be treated* like a working human machine . . . (Passage 7-F)

[Kario] is a handsome young stallion with a powerful body, a little too massive and too big *to be considered* an example of beauty. (Passage 7-B)

being + -d/t/n

You can use this combination like any simple *-ing* verbal. Its meaning, however, is passive.

Being interviewed is always stressful.

People will no longer stand *being treated* like machines.

4.3 Verbals Expanded with HAVE and BE

Both HAVE and BE can be combined with the *-d/t/n* form of a verb to make an expanded verbal. The form of HAVE may be either *to have* or *having,* while the form of BE is always *been.* HAVE shows that the event described is previous to the main time referred to, while BE shows that the verbal is passive.

For example, if you found that your old battered car had disappeared from where you parked it, you might say:

But it's too old *to have been stolen!*

Similarly, we could say of the experience described in Passage 1A:

Having been badly *taught* in Japan, Miura had difficulties with her English when she came to New York.

ACTIVITIES

1. Placing Verbals and Verbal Phrases

The writer of the passage below used all three kinds of verbals. In this exercise, the verbals and verbal phrases have been taken out and are printed in alphabetical order after the passage. You are asked to insert each one in the right place. (For a correct version of this passage, see Appendix 2.)

Passage 10-B   **STREET ENTERTAINMENT**

by Christine Patouha

New York City brings a lot of debates on the subject of work. For example, (1) _____ to some people is work but for others it is not work. The topic I will write about is street entertainment. For many people it is considered a job but for others it is not. Street entertainers I believe are

5 working. They are talented musicians that spend an average of eight hours a day on the streets (2) _____. They are entertaining people and whoever wants (3) _____ does. They work hard in (4) _____. A particular group that I know came here from Peru with a six month visa, as tourists. When their money ran out they started (5) _____. When

10 they noticed that people enjoyed their music, (6) _____, they continued (7) _____. Once, I asked one of the musicians, "Why don't you go and play in a night club?" His reply was "We are entertainers. We love what we do and we don't force anyone (8) _____. (9) _____, we would not make as much money and we would not be heard by as many

15 people as in the streets."

(continued in Activity 2)

begging
doing something they enjoy
entertaining in the street
played on hand-made instruments, such as wooden pipes which produce
    different sounds
playing in a night club
playing music
playing their music in subways and streets
to give them money
to listen to us.

2. Choosing the Appropriate Verbal

The following passage is a continuation of Passage 10-B above. This time, however, the verbals have been underlined and given in three forms: base, -ing, and -d/t/n. You are asked to choose which form is appropriate in each case and to cross out the other two. Note that the word *to* has not been underlined, so you are not to cross it out, but to choose the appropriate form to follow it. (A correct version of this part of the passage is also printed in Appendix 2.)

Passage 10-B   **STREET ENTERTAINMENT** (continued)
                             by Christine Patouha

There are many other advantages in street entertainment. A young man I know, (1) live/living/lived in Harlem, developed a musical talent at eight years old. He began (2) beat/beating/beaten a stick on a plastic can. He played in the streets of New York for many years, until he began to (3)

20   support/supporting/supported his family by the donations people on the street would give him. He was twelve years old at that time. Today this young man, about fifteen years old, has been in a music video clip with Maria Carey, in Pepsi and Levi's commercials, and in the movie "Green Card." Aside from all the television publicity, he has also had many offers by music producers

25   that would have given him the opportunity to (4) become/becoming/became famous if he had chosen to (5) quit/quitting/quit his street music. (6) Be/being/been still a young man, he has not taken their offers into great consideration, since the money (7) offer/offering/offered to him is not satisfactory. Nowadays, he does not play as much as he used to, but he is still

30   around and still (8) notice/noticing/noticed by the crowd.

Work is necessary in life. Everyone works, whether they are rich or poor. Poor people work harder and their jobs are less (9) <u>interest/ interesting/interested</u> to them, whereas rich people work in order to (10) <u>fulfill/ fulfilling/fulfilled</u> themselves. Without work people would be miserable and their lives would be dull. Work has become an everyday routine, just like (11) <u>take/taking/taken</u> a shower, (12) <u>eat/eating/eaten</u> and (13) <u>breathe/ breathing/breathed</u>.

35

3. Choosing the Appropriate Verbal

In this essay, the verbs without tense have again been underlined and given in three forms. The first of these forms, however, is given as *to + base*, so you will have to think about meaning a bit more in order to decide which is the appropriate form to use in each case. Remember that *to + base* suggests that the action named in the verbal or verbal phrase is expected or intended, whereas a verbal in the *-ing* form simply names the action. As in Activity 2, please cross out the two forms that are not appropriate. (A correct version of this passage is printed in Appendix 2.)

Passage 10-C   **CHOOSING A CAREER**

by Maria Vicco

In our western society (that is the only one I can account for) we are taught that we should be productive. So, when the time comes and if possible, we make a choice: either we get an education (1) <u>to learn/learning/ learned</u> and (2) <u>develop/developing/developed</u> the skills that will be applied later, or we learn on site. That is to say, we learn by (3) <u>to do/doing/done</u>.

5

I find myself in a critical situation, because I am in that process of (4) <u>to choose/choosing/chosen</u> what will be my occupation for the rest of my life. Well, maybe it sounds too dramatic. I'll say from now to the next ten years or so; and I find this choice hard but (5) <u>to fascinate/fascinating/ fascinated</u> at the same time.

10

I've already had a few (6) <u>to work/working/worked</u> experiences. Some of them I enjoyed, some I really hated. But they all helped me (7) <u>to see/seeing/ saw</u> more clearly what it is that I like (8) <u>to do/doing/done</u> best and, equally important, which activities I am good at.

I have found that (9) <u>to work/working/worked</u> in an office is definitely not my kind of job. I was a secretary in a bank. My duties were very simple:

15

I typed letters, answered phone calls, and reminded my boss of his daily activities. I hated the job. I am a very active person. I like (10) <u>to take/taking/taken</u> dance classes and (11) <u>to walk/walking/walked</u> around the city. There,
20 I had to stay (12) <u>to seat/seating/seated</u> for nine long hours, and the only light I saw was the one (13) <u>to come/coming/come</u> from the fluorescent lights.

On the other hand, I had two jobs (14) <u>to teach/teaching/taught</u> that pleased me very much, especially the one in the day care center. There I
25 looked after babies, and I shared duties with two other teachers. These duties included (15) <u>to make/making/made</u> breakfast in the morning, (16) <u>to change/changing/changed</u> diapers four times a day, <u>to go/going/gone</u> to the park (if it was a warm day), (17) <u>to cook/cooking/cooked</u>, (18) <u>to put/putting/put</u> the babies (19) <u>to sleep/sleeping/slept</u> and (20) <u>to dress/dressing/dressed</u>
30 them (21) <u>to go/going/gone</u> back home at six in the afternoon. Those were the duties. I also got (22) <u>to see/seeing/seen</u> how they grew up, how they learned (23) <u>to walk/walking/walked</u> by (24) <u>to investigate/investigating/investigated</u> the environment and their own bodies. I taught them words in Spanish and they amazed me by (25) <u>to remember/remembering/</u>
35 <u>remembered</u> them two weeks later. I felt (26) <u>to need/needing/needed</u> and, what was most (27) <u>to fascinate/fascinating/fascinated</u>, I learned from them.

4. Correcting Dangling Modifiers

Each of the following sentences, which have been taken or adapted from the passages in this book, begins with a verbal phrase in the front adverbial position. Some of these verbal phrases are used correctly, but others are not, because the subject of the clause that follows is not the one "responsible" for the verbal phrase. Discuss with your classmates which are correct and which are not. Put a check (✓) beside each that is correct and a cross (✗) by each that is not. For those that are incorrect, write in the space provided the adverbial clause that should be used instead.

1. <u>After making a schedule</u>, I followed it for each day. (Passage 4-B)

2. <u>Being in my senior year</u>, Sister Ida became my dorm mistress. (Passage 3-A)

3. <u>Dressed in tattered clothing</u>, the man was rummaging through a garbage pail hoping to find food or simply soda bottles. (Passage 5-B)

_____

4. <u>Stepping on the boat</u>, the atmosphere is very friendly and enjoyable. (Passage 5-C)

_____

5. <u>Coming into our car</u>, he started making a speech. (Passage 7-A)

_____

6. <u>Comparing that homeless man and the housewife who wrote her contribution to the paper</u>, which one seems to be more professional? (Passage 7-A)

_____

7. <u>After going through the whole process of immigration</u>, we took another plane to get to Malaga. (Passage 8-B)

_____

8. <u>Being seventeen</u>, Syria and Israel were at war, and he had been called to join the Syrian army. (Passage 8-F)

_____

9. <u>On hearing the tragic news</u>, my heart was filled with righteous indignation. (Passage 9-B)

_____

10. <u>Going to the square in front of the Chinese Theater</u>, there were a lot of tourists, and all of them were looking down eagerly. (Passage 13-B)

_____

The Three Most Common Predicate Patterns

11

CHAPTER

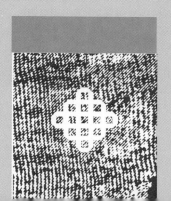

*E*nglish predicates have ten different patterns. This chapter describes the three most common ones. The other seven are explained in Chapter 12. Every predicate must have a verb, and the verb controls the form of the predicate. Many of the problems that students have in the predicate are mismatches between the verb and the form of the predicate.

In the following essay, we have underlined the predicates in the independent clauses.

Passage 11-A   **WOMEN AND MARRIAGE**

by Ralph Alcin

Once a woman reaches a certain age, she <u>realizes that there is nothing new under the sun</u>. The idea that a woman needs a husband in order to be happy <u>is old-fashioned, stereotyped thinking that nearly everybody has said goodbye to</u>. I <u>spoke to one woman who said that for the last nine years, there were only three occasions when she wished she was married</u>. The first
5   occasion <u>was when she was alone with a mouse in her apartment</u>. The second occasion <u>was the presence of a giant waterbug</u>. The third <u>was a terrible experience when she was with two crying children in the rain and she couldn't get a cab</u>.

If you have trouble identifying the predicate, see Chapter 3.

Here is a list of the independent clauses from these six sentences. In each clause, the main predicate is underlined, and the verb of the independent clause is printed in italics.

1. she *realizes* <u>that there is nothing new under the sun</u>
2. the idea that a woman needs a husband in order to be happy *is* <u>old-fashioned, stereotyped thinking that nearly everybody has said goodbye to</u>
3. I *spoke* <u>to one woman who said that for the last nine years, there were only three occasions when she wished she was married</u>
4. the first occasion *was* <u>when she was alone with a mouse in her apartment</u>
5. the second occasion *was* <u>the presence of a giant waterbug</u>
6. the third *was* <u>a terrible experience when she was with two crying children in the rain and she couldn't get a cab</u>

The examples show the complexity of the predicate. Each is a different length. The shortest one, number 5, has six words after the verb. The others have subordinate clauses in them, and each subordinate clause has its own predicate.

1. BASIC PREDICATE POSITIONS

Just as the written English sentence can be seen as having only four basic positions, the predicate in English can be divided into a series of six positions.

FIGURE 11-1 Positions in the Predicate

V	IO	Ptl	O	C	PA
Verb	Indirect Object	Particle	Direct Object	Complement	Predicate Adverbial

You will never find all of these positions filled in a single sentence. The only one that is required in every sentence is the first, the **verb.** The verb position may be filled by a simple verb or an expanded verb, and it may include **not** or another adverbial like **sometimes.** This verb must have tense. (See Chapters 8 and 9 for explanation about the verb forms.) The verb is the word that controls which other predicate positions must be filled, thus creating one of the ten basic predicate patterns. The following are the three most common patterns:

Verb and Object	V O
Verb and Complement	V C
Verb and Predicate Adverbial	V PA

1.1 Adverbials with Verbs

In many predicates, there is an adverb next to the verb. It comes before a simple verb or after the first auxiliary in an expanded verb. In the following examples, the adverb is underlined and the verb is printed in italics.

> I <u>sometimes</u> *question* myself, "How many years have I been learning English?" (Passage 1-A)

> . . . I *can* <u>clearly</u> *recall* how she looked and what she said. (Passage 4-A)

> . . . you *are* <u>always</u> *doing* yesterday's jobs today . . . (Passage 4-B)

> . . . my cousin <u>forcefully</u> *pulled* me away . . . (Passage 5-B)

> . . . I *can* <u>only</u> *turn* my head away . . . (Passage 5-B)

> . . . my mother *had* <u>already</u> *taken* care of that. (Passage 7-C)

263

... I *have* <u>not yet</u> *met* his parents. (Passage 8-C)

... "Solidarity" *had* <u>never</u> *been approved* by the Polish ... authorities. (Passage 14-H)

There are two groups of words which are regularly used in this position. One is a set of single words with no special endings.

even	never	perhaps	soon
first	next	rather	sort of
here	now	seldom	still
indeed	often	somehow	then
just	once	sometimes	(not) yet
later			

The other group is *-ly* adverbs. Here are some common ones.

actually	generally	rarely	repeatedly
apparently	gladly	really	surely
certainly	hardly	recently	undoubtedly
especially	nearly	regularly	usually
frequently	probably		

The problem that occurs occasionally with these words is misplacement. If the expanded verb has three elements, as in <u>had been approved</u>, the adverb usually goes after the first auxiliary, not after the second. For emphasis, it may come in front of the entire expanded verb. Almost never does it come after the verb.

Also, many of these words can go into the sentence adverbial positions, in front of or at the end of the entire clause. However, when some of them appear in the front, they require the auxiliary to move in front of the subject. <u>Not yet</u>, <u>never</u>, and <u>rarely</u> are examples of the adverbs that require the shift of the auxiliary. (See Chapter 14, Section 4.2.)

In the example sentences above, try moving the adverb to different places. Sometimes it will work nicely, but in other cases it changes the meaning of the sentence or it breaks the connections between neighboring words or phrases. Remember that the basic spot for these words is after the first auxiliary in an expanded verb or in front of a simple verb.

WHEN YOU ARE WRITING

Have you used one of these adverbs near the main verb? It should be placed in front of a simple verb or after the first auxiliary of an expanded verb.

The predicate pattern of **V O** is the primary one, used more frequently than any other. In the following examples, the **O** is underlined and the verb is in italics. From Passage 11-A:

S	V	O
she	*couldn't get*	a cab
she	*realizes*	that there is nothing new under the sun

Many verbs require that the object position (**O**) be filled. These verbs are identified in the dictionary by <u>t</u> or <u>vt</u>, for "(verb) transitive," written in italics. If you are not certain whether a particular verb is transitive, look in the dictionary.

The object position can be filled in six different ways: noun phrase, quotation, noun clause, pronoun, verbal phrase, and "subject" plus verbal phrase.

2.1 Noun Phrase in O

(S)	V	O
(she)	*couldn't get*	[a cab]

If you are not sure what noun phrases are or you want more information about them, see Chapters 5 and 6. Here are some examples from essays in this book.

From our conversation, she *would correct* my mistakes. (Passage 3-A)
                                           V   O

At the end of his journey, he *saw* a dwarf who asked him for a crust of bread. (Passage 9-E)

The Ecuadorian government . . . *has enacted* some laws forbidding introduction and use of modern things. (Passage 11-A)

2.2 Quotations in O

Verbs of saying and thinking can have quotations in the **O** position. Below is an example adapted from Passage 11-A.

One woman said, "During the last nine years, there were only three occasions when I wished I was married."

The problems with quotations arise from the verb tenses, the pronouns, and the punctuation. Everything must be the exact words that the speaker used, including the same verb tenses and pronouns. The quotation must be enclosed by quotation marks, and other punctuation marks follow certain strict rules. (See Chapter 13 for more information on direct and reported speech.)

2.3 Subordinate Clause in O

Subordinate clauses are common in the **O** position, especially after verbs of saying or thinking. They are called <u>noun clauses</u> because they fill positions that can also be filled by noun phrases.

A noun clause usually begins with one of the following subordinators: *that, if,* or a *wh*-word: *what, when, where, whether, which, who, whose, why,* or *how.* Here are examples from the essay at the beginning of this chapter and other essays in this book. In the following examples, the noun clause is underlined and the subordinator is printed in bold. The verb is printed in italics.

	V	*O*
she	*realizes*	**that** <u>there is nothing new under the sun</u> (Passage 11-A)

	V	*O*
I	*do* not *care*	**if** <u>they like my diaries or not</u>. (Passage 8-A)

	V	*O*
I	*can* clearly *recall*	**how** <u>she looked</u>
		and
		what <u>she said</u>. (Passage 4-A)

The introductory word *that* can often be omitted. It is usually the author's choice whether to use *that* or not.

	V	*O*
she	*wished*	<u>she was married</u>
she	*realizes*	**that** <u>there is nothing new under the sun</u> (Passage 11-A)

2.4 Pronoun in O

The **O** is usually filled by the object form of a pronoun. Occasionally the reflexive or the possessive form is used. (For more information about pronouns, see Chapter 7.) Here are examples from the essays in this book.

<u>object form</u>: . . . she kissed <u>me</u> at the taxi stand . . . (Passage 3-A)

<u>object form</u>: No person or country should take <u>them</u> away from you. (Passage 3-D)

<u>reflexive form</u>: I sometimes question <u>myself</u>, "How many years have I been learning English?" (Passage 1-A)

The problems that writers have with pronouns are:

1. agreement with the referent;
2. not having the pronoun last in a compound, such as "my mother and me."
3. ambiguity caused by a sequence of third person pronouns which have different referents.

(See Chapter 7, Section 5 for more discussion about these problems.)

WHEN YOU ARE WRITING

When you use a pronoun in the **O** position, you should ask yourself these questions:

1. Who or what does the pronoun refer to?
2. Is the referent singular or plural? Check that the pronoun is the same.
3. If the pronoun refers to the subject of the sentence, have you used the correct form of the reflexive pronoun? Check the spelling, especially if it is a plural form.
4. Is the **O** a compound? If it is, does the pronoun come last? If it is two or more pronouns, is the first person pronoun *(me, us)* last?

2.5 Verbal Phrase in O

Sometimes the filler of **O** is a group of words that looks like a predicate, but the verb at the beginning does not have a tense. We call these verbs **verbals** and the whole group of words a **verbal phrase.** (See Chapter 10 for more information about verbals and verbal phrases.)

Verbals in **O** have two forms: _to + base_ or _-ing_. Some grammar books have called _to + base_ forms **infinitives** and _-ing_ forms **gerunds.**

to + base verbal phrase:
Furthermore, I learned <u>to deal with many people</u>. (Passage 10-A)

-ing verbal phrase:
As long as English teachers are not concerned with the importance of practical English . . ., they will continue <u>making victims like me</u>. (Passage 1-A)

The form of the verbal phrase in **O** is controlled by the main verb. Some verbs require the _to + base_, others the _-ing_ form, and a third group can be followed by either form. We have adapted a sentence from Passage 1-A as an example of these three types of **V O.**

	V	O
I	didn't **want**	*to think* about English. (Passage 1-A)
I	didn't **enjoy**	*thinking* about English.
I	didn't **like**	*thinking* about English.
I	didn't **like**	*to think* about English.

In Figure 11-2, we present lists of some common verbs that follow each of these patterns. However, if you have any question about which pattern a particular verb follows, check the verb in a dictionary and look at the example sentences that are given.

FIGURE 11-2   Verbs Followed by Verbal Phrases

A. Verbs followed by *to + base*

Below is a list of some common verbs which **ALWAYS** take *to + base*, **NEVER** the *-ing* form in **O**.

agree	decide	learn	prepare	seek
ask	endeavor	long	promise	swear
beg	expect	need	refuse	want
claim	fail	offer	resolve	wish
consent	hope			

           V   *O*

I didn't **want** *to think* about English. (Passage 1-A)

B. Verbs followed by *-ing*

Below is a list of some common verbs that **ALWAYS** take the *-ing* in the **O**, **NEVER** *to + base*.

admit (to)	despise	finish	permit	resent
appreciate	detest	give up	postpone	resist
avoid	discuss	include	practice	resume
complete	doubt	keep (on)	put off	risk
confess (to)	endure	mention	quit	stop
consider	enjoy	mind	recall	suggest
defend	escape	miss	recommend	teach
delay	facilitate	object to	regret	tolerate
deny	favor	omit	renounce	

Six of these verbs have prepositions after them. Where the preposition is printed in parentheses, it is optional. If the preposition is printed without parentheses, it must be used, as in for example put off.

           V   *O*

I **kept on** postponing the chores that faced me. (Adapted from Passage 4-B)

FIGURE 11-2 (continued)

C. Verbs followed by _to_ + base or -_ing_

Below is a list of some common verbs that can take either _to_ + base or the -_ing_ form.

attempt	commence	fear	learn	propose
(can't) bear	continue	forget	like	remember
begin	decline	hate	love	(can't) stand
cease	deserve	help	mean	start
choose	dread	intend	prefer	try

With this group of verbs, the two forms often seem to have the same meaning. However, sometimes there is a clear difference in the meanings. The _to + base_ signals an action that is unfinished or not done yet, either because it will happen in the future or it is unlikely to happen. The -_ing_ verbal phrase shows something that is actual or definite. Look at the following examples.

John did not remember <u>to pay his phone bill</u>. Therefore, the phone company disconnected his phone.

This means that John never paid his phone bill, even after several threatening letters from the phone company. Finally, the company stopped John's phone service.

John did not remember <u>paying his phone bill</u>. Therefore, he worried that the phone company was going to turn off his phone.

This means that John did pay his bill, but he forgot that he had done it. Because he didn't remember his paying, he thought that the company might disconnect his phone service.

WHEN YOU ARE WRITING

Have you used a verb from one of these lists? Is it followed by a verbal phrase? If so, check the list to make sure that you have used the correct type of verbal phrase.

If you cannot find the main verb on these lists, but you think it might follow one of these patterns, check in your dictionary.

For example, in the _Longman Dictionary of Contemporary English_, <u>prefer</u> is listed as "1 [+to-v/v-ing/to]" This means that for the first meaning, it is followed either by _to_ + base or -_ing_. The writer of Passage 9-D might have written:

I prefer <u>to use</u> my abacus.

I prefer <u>using</u> my abacus <u>to</u> using a calculator.

LEARNING STRATEGY

Remembering New Material: Making up your own sentences helps you remember basic sentence patterns.

1. Make up sentences on your own. Make them about things that you know well or have happened to you. You might find that you remember humorous examples best. For example, you could take an unusual verbal phrase like "to count all the pennies in the jar" and "counting all the pennies in the jar." Then use someone's name as the subject, and go through the list of *Verbs followed by verbal phrases.*

   Bob promised to count all the pennies in the jar.

   Bob missed counting all the pennies in the jar.

   Repeat these sentences aloud so that you become familiar with how they sound.
   A variation on this is to use cards or small pieces of paper. Write the verb on one side and then put the example on the other side. Keep going through the entire stack until you have learned the patterns for all those verbs.

2. Try dividing all the words on each list into groups. You may group them in different ways, such as:

   (a) by meaning: *begin, commence,* and *start;*
   (b) by first letter: *learn, like,* and *love.*

   Note how many words are in each group and then learn each group separately.

2.6 "Subject" Plus Verbal Phrase in O

One of the most complex constructions that can be in the **O** is a verbal phrase with a "subject" of its own. Look at these examples:

$$V \qquad "S" + \qquad verbal\ phrase$$

Our teachers required **us** *to memorize* grammatical formulas and meanings of words. (Passage 1-A)

$$V \qquad "S" + \qquad verbal\ phrase$$

Some customers also expected **me** to know the train or bus available around the store the closest coffee shop, post office, etc. (Passage 10-A)

FIGURE 11-3

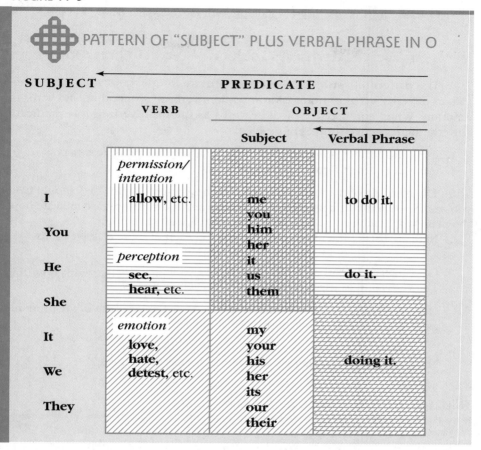

PATTERN OF "SUBJECT" PLUS VERBAL PHRASE IN O

SUBJECT	PREDICATE		
	VERB	OBJECT	
		Subject	Verbal Phrase
I You He She It We They	*permission/ intention* **allow**, etc.	me you him	**to do it.**
	perception **see, hear**, etc.	her it us them	**do it.**
	emotion **love, hate, detest**, etc.	my your his her its our their	**doing it.**

1. *Verbs of permission/intention:* if the "Subject" is a **pronoun,** use the *me, you, him, her, it, us, them* set of object pronouns; the **Verbal Phrase** form is *to + base;* the **vertical lines** go through the three areas of Verb, "Subject," and Verbal Phrase.

   Our instructor allowed **us** *to write* the exam in pencil.

2. *Verbs of perception:* the "Subject" **pronoun** must be from the object set; the **Verbal Phrase** form can be either the *base* without *to* or the *-ing;* the **horizontal lines** go across the three areas to show this matching.

   We saw **them** *capture* a group of people. (Passage 8-J)

   We saw **them** *capturing* a group of people.

3. *Verbs of emotion:* the "Subject" **pronoun** can be **either** the *me, you, him, her, it, us, them* object pronouns **or** the *my, your, his, her, its, our, their* possessive pronouns. In the **Verbal Phrase**, use only the *-ing;* the **diagonal lines** go through the three areas.

   Einstein's mother never imagined **him** *winning* the Nobel Prize.

   Einstein's mother never imagined **his** *winning* the Nobel Prize.

         V   *"S"* +   *verbal phrase*

I can see <u>my first girl-friend</u>   <u>talking with me</u>. (Passage 8-A)

2.6a Basic Patterns of "Subject" + Verbal Phrase in O

The pattern of **"subject" + verbal phrase** in O occurs after three main classes of verbs: verbs of permission/intention, verbs of perception, and verbs of emotion. When you use one of these verbs as the main verb in this predicate pattern, there are two sources of problems:

1. using the correct pronoun form for the "subject" if one is necessary;
2. using the correct form of the verbal phrase.

The meaning of the main verb controls these issues. Figure 11-3 should help you see the patterns. The lines around the verb and the verbal phrase indicate how the main verb, "subject," and verbal phrase match with each other.

Here are lists of the most common verbs in each of these classifications.

(1) Verbs of Permission/Intention
The verbs of permission/intention have several patterns.

- One group of permission/intention verbs take the object form of the pronoun as "subject" and *to + base* in the verbal phrase.

        V   *"S" + VP*

My abacus *has permitted* me to achieve success in business.

FIGURE 11-4   Verbs of Permission/Intention—Group I

allow	compel	get	permit	tell
authorize	expect	invite	persuade	train
	force	mean	teach	wish

- Other permission/intention verbs have two possible patterns. In the basic pattern, they take object pronoun as "subject" and *to + base* in the verbal phrase. Some of these verbs must have **for** in front of the "subject."

    They arranged *for* **him** to do it.
    They required   **him** to do it.

Some of these verbs can follow both patterns.

    They asked *for* **him** to do it.
    They asked   **him** to do it.

There is a difference in meaning between these two sentences. In the first one, "they" asked someone else to make the arrangements. In the second, "they" spoke directly to him.

In the other pattern, these verbs are followed by the subject form of pronouns and the base form of the verb without to. In this pattern, the main verb must be followed by *that*.

> We arranged *that* **he** do it.
> We <u>required</u> *that* **he** do it.

In the following list, *for* appears after certain verbs. If *for* is always required, there is an asterisk.

FIGURE 11-5   Verbs of Permission/Intention—Group 2

advise	desire (for)	prefer (for)	stipulate (for)*
agree (for)*	instruct	propose	urge
arrange (for)*	intend (for)	recommend	vote (for)*
ask (for)	order	request (for)	want
beg (for)	pray (for)	require	
command			

(2) Verbs of Perception

These verbs take the object form of the pronoun as the "subject" but can have either the base form without *to* or the *-ing* form in the verbal phrase.

$$V \qquad\qquad "S" + VP$$

My mother overheard **me** <u>*tell*</u> a lie to my cousin.
My mother overheard **me** <u>*telling*</u> a lie to my cousin.

FIGURE 11-6   Verbs of Perception

feel	notice	overhear	smell
hear	observe	see	watch

(3) Verbs of Emotion

These verbs can have either the object or the possessive form of the pronoun as "subject" but only have the *-ing* in the verbal phrase.

$$V \qquad\qquad\qquad "S" + VP$$

Benedict disliked **me** <u>*interviewing*</u> the Chief of Police about the crime.
Benedict disliked **my** <u>*interviewing*</u> the Chief of Police about the crime.

FIGURE 11-7   Verbs of Emotion

detest	imagine	miss	remember
dislike	involve	recall	resent
dread	justify	regret	risk
forget	(don't) mind	relish	(can't) stand

(4) Verbs That Do Not Fit the Basic Patterns

So far, we have described the basic patterns of <u>"Subject" plus verbal phrase</u>. However, there are 12 other very common verbs that do not follow the system. There are nine verbs of permission/intention and three verbs of emotion, which are discussed below.

- <u>Make</u>, <u>let</u>, and <u>have</u> NEVER have *to* before the verb in the verbal phrase after a "subject." They take the object form of pronouns as the "subject." Look at the following examples:

  His teacher   made   **him** *do* it.

  Let   **my people** *go*.

  Mr. Jones   had   **them** *sweep* the sidewalks.

Help can be used this way, but it sometimes has *to* before the base. The choice between the two forms is stylistic; it does not affect the meaning of the sentence.

His teacher helped **him** *complete* the exam.

His teacher helped **him** *to complete* the exam.

- Five verbs of permission/intention

  decide   demand   be determined   insist   suggest

  These verbs of permission/intention NEVER have *to* before the verb in the verbal phrase, and they require the subject forms of pronouns: *I, we, he, she, it, they.* In other words, the O looks like a noun clause except that the verb in the verbal phrase is in the base form.

	V	*"S"*	*VP*
His teacher	insisted	(that) **he**	*do* it.
His mother	suggested	(that) **she**	*meet* us the following day.

Notice that you can use **that** after these verbs if you want to.

• hate, like, love. These verbs of emotion take three patterns.

	V	*"S" + VP*	
They	love	**our** *doing* that.	(possessive form + *-ing*)
They	love	**us** *doing* that.	(object form + *-ing*)
They	would love	(for) **us** *to do* that.	(object form + *to* + base)

With these verbs, the object form of the pronoun as the "subject" can go with either an *-ing* or *to* + base verbal phrase. For example, in Passage 7-F, Mendoza writes about the difficulties that adult immigrants have in getting an education. We can summarize her conclusion by saying:

	V	*"S"* +	*VP*	+	*VP*
She	hates	**them**	*giving* up	and	not *getting* an education.
She	hates	(for) **them**	*to give* up	and	not *get* an education.

A variation on the pattern is that when the object pronoun as "subject" is matched with a *to* + base verbal phrase, *for* can be used to introduce the unit. In most cases, the *for* is optional.

Another variation is that a possessive pronoun can be used as "subject" with an *-ing* verbal phrase.

	V	*"S"*	*VP*	+	*VP*
She	hates	**their**	*giving* up	and	not *getting* an education.

WHEN YOU ARE WRITING

These 12 common verbs that do not fit the basic patterns of *"subject"* + *verb phrase* in O cause many problems. If you use one of them, compare the form of your sentence to the examples in our explanation.

1. Have you used the correct "subject" pronoun if you have a pronoun?
2. Is the verbal the correct form?

Suggest is a verb that often causes problems.

3. VERB AND COMPLEMENT (V C)

The second common predicate pattern is **V C**. The **C** occurs after a "linking" verb. The most common linking verb is *be* in all its forms: *am, is, are, was, were, be, being, been.* Here is a list of some other common linking verbs:

FIGURE 11-8   Linking Verbs

appear	go	prove	sound
become	grow	remain	stay
feel	keep	seem	taste
get	look	smell	turn

The **C** position can be filled by a wide variety of structures. In the following examples, the verbs are printed in italics and the **C's** are underlined.

V   C (noun phrase)
When I was in my senior year, she *became* my dorm mistress. (Passage 3-A)

V   C (noun phrase)
"Memorizing" *seemed* the only way of learning English. (Passage 1-A)

V C (prepositional phrase)
The islands *are* of volcanic origin. (Passage 14-A)

V   C (subordinate clause)
My duties *were* . . . I typed letters, answered phone calls, and reminded my boss of his daily activities. (Passage 10-C)

V C (adjective)
Things *are* not easy . . . (Passage 4-C)

V   C (-d/t/n form)
He   *was* always   very correctly attired . . . (Passage 7-D)
. . . most of them   *are*   covered with loose sand . . . (Passage 14-A)
They   *felt*   frustrated and trapped . . . (Passage 7-F)

V C (adjective phrase)
Things *become* more readily available. (Passage 5-A)

V   C (verbal phrase)
The only thing that I had to do *was* to get the attention of the guards. (Passage 10-A)

276

3.1 Noun Phrases in C

Noun phrases are very common in **C.**

The Ursuline Convent School *is* <u>a boarding school in the U.K</u>. (Passage 3-A)

. . . luck *is* <u>the ability to take advantage of fortunate circumstances</u>. (Passage 9-E)

The noun phrase in **C** usually qualifies the subject or emphasizes some feature of the subject. It does not usually cause any problems for writers.

However, one specialized type of noun phrase can create difficulties. This is the superlative form of adjectives.

$$V \qquad\qquad C$$

Taking care of a baby *is* <u>the hardest job that I have ever done</u>. (Passage 4-C)

$$V \qquad\qquad C$$

Quebec City *is* <u>the most joyful place that I have ever been to</u>. (Passage 5-C)

In the superlative phrases in **C,** there are three basic forms for the adjective premodifier, then the core noun, and then three forms of postmodifiers. The figure below shows the basic positions.

FIGURE 11-9　Superlative Adjective Phrase Positions

PREMODIFIER	CORE NOUN	POSTMODIFIER
the (adj) + *-est*	*	prepositional phrase
the most (adj)	*	verbal phrase
the least (adj)	*	*wh*-clause
For example:		
the happiest	place	that I have ever been to (Adapted from Passage 5-C)
the most joyful	place	that I have ever been to
the least boring	place	that I have ever been to
the most joyful	place	in the world
the most joyful	place	to have a vacation
the most joyful	place	that I have ever been to

Often, when a superlative adjective noun phrase is in **C,** the core position for the noun is empty because the context makes clear who or what is being described and what specific quality is the focus.

My uncle's backyard *was* not <u>the biggest in the neighborhood</u>.

Psychologists say that the first two years of childhood *are* <u>the most important</u>. (Passage 8-E)

This structure is used to highlight the idea that a named item is unique in a particular quality. (For more information about superlatives, see Chapter 6, Section 1.1d.)

However, there is a variation. When *one of* or another quantifier followed by *of* is used in front of a superlative, the core noun must be plural.

. . . education *is* <u>one of the most important things for us</u> (Passage 4-D)

WHEN YOU ARE WRITING

Often the superlative appears as an element in a larger noun phrase in **C**, after *one of.* There are two common difficulties.

- First, the writer might omit the determiner, but the superlative always requires some sort of determiner.
- Second, the writer might not make the core noun in the prepositional phrase plural, but this pattern signals that the reference is to a group.

When you have used a superlative adjective, make sure that you have a determiner or a possessive in front of it. If it is in a prepositional phrase that follows a quantifier and *of,* make sure the core noun in the prepositional phrase is plural.

3.2 Prepositional Phrases in C

Prepositional phrases are very common in **C**.

She *was* <u>from Russia</u>. (Passage 4-A)

The islands *are* <u>of volcanic origin</u>. (Passage 14-A)

She *is* <u>of medium build with short legs</u>. (Passage 14-F)

Prepositional phrases in **C** are used to focus on a particular quality of the subject. They usually do not create problems for writers.

3.3 Subordinate Clauses in C

Subordinate clauses are sometimes found in **C**.

Another problem that we are faced with *is* <u>that I have not yet met his parents</u>. (Passage 8-C)

My greatest wish *is* <u>that I could meet them and that they could accept me</u>. (Passage 8-C)

Subordinate clauses in **C** are needed for complex definitions of the subject. They do not often cause problems for writers.

3.4 Adjectives and Adjective Phrases in C

The **C** position is often filled by adjectives and adjective phrases because this predicate pattern is used for describing the subject of the sentence. In the following examples, the adjectives in **C** are underlined:

they . . . *looked* <u>expensive</u>. (Passage 4-A)

She *was* <u>about 60</u> (Passage 3-A)

The nature on our farm *is* <u>typically tropical</u>. (Passage 3-H)

The Chinese loanwords *are* <u>very difficult to learn</u> . . . (Passage 9-C)

The two years' life in the Chinese military *is* <u>as clear as it was</u>. (Passage 8-A)

3.4a Basic Structure of the Adjective Phrase

The adjective phrase has a structure that is similar to the noun phrase except that in the adjective phrase, an adjective forms the core element. There is a position before the core, and there is a position after the core adjective. If we symbolize the adjective phrase, it looks like this:

Pre . . .   adjective   . . . Post

Look at these examples with the symbols drawn under them.

They looked *expensive.* (Passage 4-A)

She was *about 60.* (Passage 3-A)

The nature on our farm is *typically tropical.* (Passage 3-H)

The Chinese loanwords are *very difficult to learn* . . . (Passage 9-C)

The two years' life in the Chinese military is *as clear as it was.* (Passage 8-A)

Qualifiers with Adjective Phrases
In some adjective phrases, only the premodifier and core positions are filled. The first element is a qualifier. (For a list of some common qualifiers that can be used with adjectives and adjectival phrases, see Chapter 6, Section 1.1.)

3.4b Two-part Adjective Phrases in C

In two-part adjective phrases, the core and the postmodifier positions are always filled, and the premodifier position is often filled too. The major types of two-part adjective phrases are **comparatives, quantitatives,** and **qualitatives.** In the following examples, the verbs are printed in italics, and the adjective phrase is underlined.

comparative
When it comes to your language, two languages *are* <u>better than one</u>. (Passage 3-D)

quantitative
I didn't answer because I *was* <u>too poor in English</u> at the time. (Passage 3-A)

qualitative
During my father's generation, the education system *was* <u>very different from my generation</u>. (Passage 4-D)

Figure 11-10 summarizes the major types of two-part adjective structures into comparatives, quantitatives, and qualitatives. The discussion of the major types that follows the chart uses the numbers from the figure to identify the sections.

FIGURE 11-10   Two-Part Adjective Phrases

TYPE	PRE-MODIFIER	ADJECTIVE	POST-MODIFIER	FORM
1. Comparatives				
		* + -er	*than*	noun phrase
	more	*	*than*	subordinate clause
	less	*		
	as	*	*as*	noun phrase
			as	subordinate clause
2. Quantitatives				
	too	*	*to*	verbal phrase
	so	*	*that*	subordinate clause
		* *enough*	*for*	prepositional phrase
			to	verbal phrase
			that	subordinate clause
3. Qualitatives				
		different	*from*	prepositional phrase
		similar	*to*	prepositional phrase

(1) Comparative Adjective Phrases

Look at the following examples:

If a person uses time completely and well, he *will be* <u>more successful than others</u>. (Passage 4-B)

It *is* <u>more difficult</u> [to succeed] when they cannot find the right help. (Passage 7-F)

The basic patterns for comparative adjective phrases are the following:

> * -er than . . .
> more * than . . .
> less * than . . .

The postmodifier position is filled by *than* followed by a noun phrase, verbal phrase, or a subordinate clause. This comparative structure is used to highlight a difference in a particular quality between two named items.

. . . younger women are always <u>*better than* older women</u> . . . (Passage 4-A)

Our war in 1981 was <u>much *more* painful and confusing *than* the ones of our parents and grandparents.</u> (Passage 14-H).

A noun, noun phrase, prepositional phrase, verbal phrase, or subordinate clause can come directly after the adjective and separate the two parts.

For some people,
> an opera is <u>*better* entertainment *than*</u> a pop music concert.
> an opera is <u>*better* to their ears *than*</u> a pop music concert.
> an opera is <u>*better* at providing complete entertainment *than*</u> a pop music concert.

In some situations, it is possible to omit the postmodifier *than* phrase or clause because the speaker or writer believes that the listener or reader already understands who or what is being compared.

When I was young, my cousin Sonia saw me as a spoiled child. Now that I am *older,* our relationship has changed. (adapted from Passage 3-F)

The comparison here does not need the subordinate clause <u>than I was</u> because the readers know that is the point of comparison. In addition to comparisons of age, <u>later</u> frequently does not have a than defining phrase. Everybody understands the comparison in "See you later."

WHEN YOU ARE WRITING

Be careful of the spelling of *than.* Some people confuse it with *then* because the two words sound the same in spoken English.

After an adjective that ends in -er, or *more* + adjective, or *less* + adjective, check to see that you have used *than.*

LEARNING STRATEGY

Remembering New Material: Focusing on the spelling of words that sound alike helps you not to confuse them.

Remember that *then* and *time* both have an *e* in them. If you are writing about a sequence of events, you must use *then*.

Also, *adjective* and *than* both have an *a* in them.

as * as . . .

The two years' life in the Chinese military is *as* clear *as* it was.

Maybe these books are not *as* good *as* famous novels, but I value them. (Passage 8-A)

The core position here is filled by an adjective or adjective phrase. The postmodifier position is filled by the second *as* followed by a noun phrase, prepositional phrase, verbal phrase, or a subordinate clause.

The structure is used to highlight equality in a particular characteristic between two named items. Also, if the structure is negative, with <u>not</u>, it points out some difference that is not defined completely.

Vilma Villatoro's experiences with job training were <u>not *as* beneficial *as* they might have been</u>. (Adapted from passage 4-F)

We do not know exactly what benefits were lacking unless we read her essay, but this sentence makes clear that there were some differences between what she was promised at the beginning of the training and what she really found at the end.

(2) Quantitative Adjective Phrases

Look at the following example:

I didn't answer because I was *too* poor in English at the time. (Passage 3-A)

Here are the basic structures for these patterns:

too	*	*for*	prepositional phrase
		to	verbal phrase
so	*	*that*	subordinate clause
	*	*enough for*	prepositional phrase
		to	verbal phrase
		that	subordinate clause

With *too* as the premodifier, the postmodifier is a prepositional phrase beginning with *for* or a verbal phrase beginning with *to + base*. The prepositional phrase and verbal phrase can occur together. This structure emphasizes an excess.

Victoria Wu discovered that she was *too* advanced *for* her conversation class. (Adapted from Passage 13-C)

Chun Ling Tsien thought that she was *too* tired *to* finish her homework. (Adapted from Passage 4-B)

I didn't answer because I was *too* poor in English at the time. (Passage 3-A)

Often a *too* adjectival phrase will not have a postmodifier. For example, the last example does not have a postmodifier *to + base* verbal because the writer believed that it was unnecessary. Also, the verbal would be "to answer the question," but putting it into the sentence would make the sentence clumsy and awkward.

WHEN YOU ARE WRITING

The *too* in front of adjectives sounds the same as the preposition *to* or the *to* used in front of the base form of the verb.

1. Look at every place where you have written *to* in front of an adjective.
2. Try to substitute *very* in place of *to*. If you can, then you should use *too* if you need it. Otherwise, put in *very*.

The adjective phrases that have *so* as the premodifier have a noun clause beginning with *that* as the postmodifier. This structure shows a result or outcome of the quality named after *so*.

. . . grown <u>so</u> strongly <u>that their huge amount of roots anchored the soil tightly</u> . . .

. . . it was <u>so</u> fresh <u>that I wanted to put my nose deep in the grass</u> . . . (Passage 5-D)

As a postmodifier, * *enough* . . . is followed by a *for* prepositional phrase, a *to + base* verbal phrase, a combination of both the prepositional phrase and the verbal phrase, or a subordinate clause. This structure is used to express sufficiency, that there is the correct amount of the quality that is named.

Chien-Lun Yuan believes that his diaries are <u>interesting *enough for* his grandchildren</u>.

He believes that his diaries are <u>enjoyable *enough to* read again and again</u>.

He believes that his diaries are <u>interesting *enough for* his grandchildren to read again and again</u>.

He believes that his diaries are <u>important *enough that* he plans to give them to his grandchildren</u>. (Adapted from Passage 8-A)

The structure can have the comparative *more than* added to show that the amount of the quality is beyond just adequate.

He believes that his diaries are **more than** <u>enjoyable *enough to* read again and again</u>.

(3) Qualitative Adjective Phrases

$$V \qquad\qquad C$$

That homeless man on the subway was <u>a little bit different from other homeless people</u>. (Passage 7-A)

Chinese and Japanese have similar writing systems, but the Korean one is <u>different</u>. (Passage 9-C)

The structures for qualitative adjective phrases are

> *different from* . . .
> *similar to* . . .
> *the same as* . . .

- The core adjective *different* is followed by *from*. It can be followed by a noun phrase, prepositional phrase, verbal phrase, or subordinate clause.

  Malaga was <u>different from New York</u>. (noun phrase)

  The prices of the curios on the streets were <u>different from in the shops</u>. (prepositional phrase)

  Speaking Spanish there was <u>different from speaking it here</u>. (verbal phrase)

  Malaga was <u>different from what I had imagined</u>. (subordinate clause) (Adapted from Passage 8-B)

WHETHER YOU'RE TALKING OR WRITING

You will hear **different than** used by many people. The meaning is clear, but it is not the standard form for formal speaking and writing. **Different from** is the standard form.

In your own writing, check carefully to make sure that *from* comes after *different*.

- *Similar to* functions in the same way as *different from*. It can be substituted for *different from* in the examples above. It also can take a qualifier in the premodifier position.

Madrid was <u>similar to</u> New York. (Adapted from Passage 8-B)

- *Same* already has a premodifier element, *the*. The postmodifier structure is *from, to,* or *as* followed by a possessive, a noun phrase, a prepositional phrase, a verbal phrase, or a subordinate clause. It can be substituted in all of the examples above where *different from* was used.

The prices in Madrid were <u>the same as</u> in New York. (Adapted from Passage 8-B)

3.5 Verbal Phrases in C

The **C** position is often filled by a verbal phrase. (See Chapter 10 for more explanation about the types of verbal phrases.) Look at these examples from essays in this book. The linking verb is printed in italics.

. . . the goal of Chinese medicine *was* <u>to bring the 'Yin' and the 'Yang' back into balance with each other</u>. (Passage 14-E)

The second way *is* <u>to be against time</u>. (Passage 4-B)

The first way to use time well *is* <u>not to delay doing something until some future time</u>. (Passage 4-B)

One thing I also miss *is* <u>waking up in the morning with the birds singing at my window</u>. (Passage 3-H)

Education *is* <u>teaching or training a person's mind or character</u>. (Passage 5-A)

The job had an exciting part. It *was* <u>catching shoplifters</u>. (Passage 10-A)

The examples above illustrate two major types of verbal phrase, the *to + base* form and the *-ing* form.

3.5a *-d/t/n* Forms in C

The *-d/t/n* forms are often used in **C**. Some of these describe emotions or states of mind. The linking verb is printed in italics.

I *was* <u>really excited</u> by learning the language . . . (Passage 1-A)

I *was* <u>very embarrassed</u> . . . (Passage 3-A)

I *am* <u>surprised</u> to see how much energy humans spend in destroying themselves. (Passage 7-G)

The *-d/t/n* verbal phrases in the examples above are passive in meaning. For example, in the second sentence above, she was embarrassed by **something;** she was not responsible for creating the feeling. She only experienced it; therefore, she was passive as far as embarrassment is concerned. (See Chapter 9 for more information about passives and Chapter 10, Section 3.3 for information about *-d/t/n* verbals.)

The *-ing* form of these same verbs can be used in the **C** position. The difference in meaning between the *-d/t/n* form and the *-ing* form is enormous.

A. The professor was boring.
B. The professor was bored.

This is the difference between **active** and **passive.** In example A, the professor caused the students to feel bored, so it was the professor's <u>actions</u> that created the feeling. He was responsible for the students feeling bored. In example B, something else caused the professor to feel bored; the professor is not actively creating the feeling, he is <u>experiencing the feeling</u>. He was not responsible for creating the feeling.

In these examples, <u>boring</u> and <u>bored</u> are not part of the verb phrase; they are in the **C** position and are functioning like adjectives. We can put emphasis on these words by putting *very* in front of them; if they were part of the verb phrase, we would not be able to do that.

Here are other examples of the passive use of the **C** position from Passage 1-A.

I am (very) <u>shocked</u> when I count how many years I have been learning English . . .

I'm not (very) <u>satisfied</u> with my English skills.

. . . as long as English teachers are not (very) <u>concerned</u> with the importance of practical English . . .

WHEN YOU ARE WRITING

When you use a form of a verb to describe a feeling, ask yourself these questions:

1. Are you talking about who or what is <u>responsible</u> for creating that feeling? Then you should use the *-ing* form of the verb. For example,

   Michael Jackson is exciting to watch.

2. Are you talking about who or what is <u>experiencing</u> the feeling? Then you should use the *-d/t/n* form of the verb. For example,

   Michael Jackson is excited about his next music project.

3. Have you written the *-d/t/n* form correctly? It is easy to leave off the last letter, especially the *-d*.

The *-d/t/n* form of the regular verbs must have the *-ed*, but in many cases you will not hear it pronounced when someone is speaking because it blends into the next word.

3.5b *un* + *-d/t/n*

Adding the prefix *un-* to a verb usually requires the *-d/t/n* form.

unannounced	unguarded	unmanned	unstudied
unbalanced	unheard	unnamed	untitled
uncaught	unimproved	unopened	unvoiced
undelivered	uninvolved	unprepared	unwed
unexpected	unknown	unqualified	unyellowed
unforgiven	unloved	unread	

The examples above function as adjectives. Nobody can "do" them. They simply describe a condition.

3.5c *get* and *become*

Two verbs cause particular difficulty: *get* and *become.*

A. . . . we <u>got reunited</u> in this huge country of the USA. (Passage 14-F)
B. My life <u>became</u> far less <u>complicated</u> . . . (Passage 4-B)

The basic meaning of these two sentences is passive, shown by the use of the *-d/t/n* form. The two friends did not reunite themselves; somebody else arranged the meeting, or else it happened by accident. In the second example, the writer's "life" itself did not do anything. The writer began using a schedule, which helped her use her time better. (See Chapter 10 for more information about verbals.)

The most common expressions that cause errors with *get* are:

To get <u>married</u>
To get <u>divorced</u>

The meaning of these two sentences is passive. When two people want to <u>get married</u>, they find a person who has the legal and perhaps religious authority to marry them. They do not do it by themselves. Likewise, if a couple decides that they no longer want to be married to each other, they cannot divorce themselves. They have to find an official, usually a judge, who will give them a divorce.

But *get* can also mean "to obtain." We can **obtain** <u>a divorce.</u> Therefore, *get* can be followed by the noun phrase in **O:** "a divorce."

$$V \qquad C$$

Today, when a couple has trouble, they *get* <u>divorced</u>.

$$V \qquad O$$

Today, when a couple has trouble, they *get* <u>a divorce</u>.

Both these forms are correct, and they mean the same thing. However, we cannot **obtain** a marriage. Therefore we must say, "The couple <u>got married</u>."

It is rare to find a predicate that is a verb alone. It is more common to find a verb followed by a predicate adverbial. In the following example, the expanded verb is in italics and the predicate adverbial is underlined.

V   PA

This general topic *can be divided* <u>into two categories</u>. (Passage 5-A)

The predicate adverbial position (**PA**) can be filled by a variety of structures, from single adverbs to prepositional phrases and verbal phrases, but it is most commonly filled by a prepositional phrase.

	V	PA
I	*had been sleeping*	<u>for more than ten hours</u>.
I	*went*	<u>to the first room</u> . . . (Passage 7-B)
My personal character	*has been changed*	<u>by my abacus</u>. (Passage 9-D)

The verbs in this pattern are either passive or "intransitive." (For an explanation of passive, see chapter 9.) Intransitive means that the verb never has an object (**O**). The verb is sometimes identified in the dictionary by a particular symbol such as <u>vi</u> or <u>I</u> written in italics.

The problem with the predicate adverbial (**PA**) is the choice of the preposition. The preposition is determined by the basic meaning of the preposition and also by the idiomatic tie to the preceding verb. There are no rules governing these ties. If you are not sure about the choice of preposition, look up the verb in the dictionary for suitable examples. The *Oxford Advanced Learner's Dictionary of Current English* explains the following combinations with the verb *look:*

look after	look back on	look in on	look over
look ahead to	look down on	look into	look through
look around	look for	look on	look up
look at	look forward to	look out for	look up to
look away from			

With each of these, the dictionary gives a definition and an example sentence. Some of them, like *look at,* have more than one meaning. For example, the *Oxford Advanced Learner's Dictionary of Current English* has four possible meanings for *look at:*

1. to refuse or reject	(They would*n't look at* my proposal.)
2. to examine	(We must *look at* the question from all sides.)
3. in polite requests	(Will you please *look at (read)* this letter.)
4. good/bad, etc., to look at	(This hotel is not much to *look at.*)

288

It is important to look at the examples to see how the verb plus preposition combination works.

LEARNING STRATEGY

Understanding and Using Emotions: Relaxing increases your chances of learning a language well.

There is no easy way to learn which prepositions go with particular verbs. Here are some techniques.

1. Relax.

2. Make a card for each verb plus preposition combination that you want to learn. Then go through the cards several times a week so that you can become familiar with the preposition.

3. Look up the different verbs in a dictionary, and make a card or a list of the prepositions that you find.

LEARNING STRATEGY

Overcoming Limitations: Using a dictionary helps you fill in gaps in your knowledge.

The second problem with adverbials occurs when they are placed between the verb and the object or complement. For example, compare the following pairs of sentences. The first one in each pair is incorrect.

Incorrect:	. . . they copied <u>from the textbook</u> a few sentences . . .
Correct:	. . . they copied a few sentences from the textbook . . . (Passage 1A)

Incorrect:	. . . I was filling <u>with popcorn</u> my stomach . . .
Correct:	. . . I was filling my stomach with popcorn . . . (Passage 5-B)

Incorrect:	It has made me feel <u>with numbers</u> comfortable and confident.
Correct:	It has made me feel comfortable and confident with numbers. (Passage 9-D)

1. Transitive and Intransitive Verbs

a. Using an English dictionary (not a bilingual one), find out whether the following verbs are transitive, intransitive, or both, depending on how they are used.

alarm	begin	call	charge	grow
order	reside	rest	tell	travel

b. Work with a partner and find ten verbs that you do not know well. Copy the example sentences from the dictionary. Try to have a variety of examples: some transitive, some intransitive, and some with two examples of the same verb.

Exchange papers with another pair of people. Decide whether the verbs in the example sentences are transitive or intransitive.

2. Verbs Followed by Verbal Phrases

a. Work in pairs. Use Figure 11-4. Ask each other questions using these verbs. Start with verbs from one of the lists, and gradually add a mixture. For example, your partner might begin by asking you:

What do you <u>enjoy</u> doing on the weekends?
What do you <u>object to</u> doing on the weekends?
What do you <u>suggest</u> doing on the weekends?

b. Work with a partner or in a group. Use Figure 11-4. Make up a paragraph using as many of the verbs as possible. Start with a single list. At a later time, mix the lists. (Don't worry about being logical in these paragraphs; the more unusual the ideas are, the easier it is to remember the form of the verbal phrase.)

> After college, we expect to become ambassadors to the U.N. We hope to prepare a new world order for the twenty-second century. We resolve to talk endlessly. We promise to make no decisions. (And so forth)

3. Verbs Followed by Verbal Phrases

Read the following essay. There are 16 verbal phrases in it, including five "subject" plus verb phrase ("**S**" + **VP**). Try to find them.

Passage 11-B   **PUNISHMENT WITH A CONVERSATION**
by Michelle Lee

One day my three sisters and I had a big fight, and we could not stop fighting until our father came home from his work. Since my father used to overlook our fights before, we thought that he would not blame or punish us. However, on that day, he was so angry that he would not let us off the hook easily. Since we would not talk to each other until the dinner was ready, we created an uneasy atmosphere, and that made my parents upset. As a punishment, my father ordered us not to have dinner and to come to the living room. I had never seen my father this mad for this kind of matter. He told us to raise our hands with straight arms and to hold them up until he told us not to. He even told us to kneel down on the floor, looking at each other. Without saying a word, we obeyed and accepted the punishment.

In the beginning, we glared at each other and blamed each other. Soon, we began to cry because of the pain. However, we could not cry aloud because we were afraid of having more severe punishment. Later, we could hear each other's rumbling sounds since we had not had dinner. After he finished dinner, he came to us and told us to make up. However, we were still staring hard at each other's eyes. Father became more furious at us and told us to think about what we had done to each other and the reason why he was punishing us.

After he had left the room, we soon became tired. We stopped crying because we had cried a lot and all our tears had dried out. We all looked at each other and, suddenly, burst into laughter. We looked terrible with tear-stained faces and tangled hair. Father came back to us after hearing our laughter and relieved us from the punishment.

He began to explain why he gave us the punishment. He told us his story which became an unforgettable and meaningful lesson to us. My father had a sister and a brother. However, during the war, he lost both his brother and sister. Ever since, growing up as an only child, he has been envious of people who have sisters and brothers. Whenever he missed his sister and brother, he said that he looked up in the sky and recalled the time that he shared with them. He emphasized that we should never fight with our sisters and should try to love each other. I guess this comes from his own experience and he regrets the fact that he could not give his siblings more affection.

After we heard this story, we all cried and felt ashamed of what we had

35   done. We promised to each other not to become apart and to help each
other out under any circumstances.

       Throughout our lives, we experience many unforgettable incidents
which may affect and change ourselves. My father's experience, as a child,
was unforgettable and painful to him. However, it made him realize the

40   importance of the existence of siblings. Even though the punishment hurt
me physically, it was not what taught me the lesson. It is the story that my
father told us that made me learn and realize the importance of sisterhood.
Therefore, from my experience, I believe that punishment is not the only
solution for teaching and guiding children.

4. Adjective Phrases

All of us have preferences—about the places where we live, the food we eat,
the clothes we wear. Pick a topic that is interesting to you and use Figure 11-9.
Describe your topic and use as many of the adjective phrases as you can.

5. *To* + Base Verbals

Francis is going on a six-week vacation next month. Unfortunately, he is not
a well-organized person. He has asked for your help. He wants you to prepare a list
of the things he should do before he leaves. Because he knows that the time is
short, he has asked that the list be divided into (1) **Things that he needs to do,**
(2) **Things that he should try to do,** and (3) **Things that he might get to do.**
Please try to be as complete as you can.

       After you have completed your list, compare it with one or two of your
classmates'. What are the differences between your lists? Is there anything that you
think you should add to yours?

6. *-ing* Verbal Phrases

All of us have things that we do (habits) that we would like to change. At the
end of December, many people write down some "New Year's Resolutions." For
most people, these are things that they would like to <u>stop</u> doing and other things
that they would like to <u>start</u>.

       Make your own list. The sentence is easy: "I would like to <u>stop</u> . . ." However,
you should also write down a couple of ideas about <u>how</u> you are going to do this.

       Also, for things that you would like to start, begin with the basic sentence, "I
would like to <u>start</u> . . ." Then add a couple of sentences explaining <u>how</u> you could
do this.

Less Common Predicate Patterns

12

CHAPTER

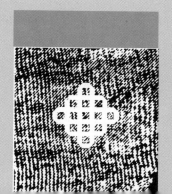

*E*nglish predicates have ten different patterns. This chapter describes the seven that are less frequent than the ones described in Chapter 11. They are complex, and they cause various types of difficulties for learners of English.

These are the seven less common predicate patterns that we will discuss in this chapter:

Verb with particle (**V Ptl**)
Verb with particle and object (**V Ptl O**)
Verb with indirect object and object (**V IO O**)
Verb with object and complement (**V O C**)
Verb with object and predicate adverbial (**V O PA**)
There as subject
It as subject

It is sometimes helpful to view the predicate in English as a series of six positions.

V	IO	Ptl	O	C	PA
Verb	Indirect Object	Particle	Direct Object	Complement	Predicate Adverbial

No single predicate will have all of these positions filled. The **verb** is the one position that must be filled, and it is the word that determines which other positions are filled. Therefore, our discussion of the predicate patterns focuses on the verb as the core.

1. VERBS WITH PARTICLES (PHRASAL VERBS) (V Ptl)

          V Ptl
That day I did not <u>go out</u>. (Passage 3-A)

          V   Ptl
. . . my homework which would be <u>handed in</u> to my teacher the next morning. (Passage 4-B)

          V Ptl
I don't know which work I should <u>give up</u>. (Passage 4-C)

          V Ptl
When their money <u>ran out</u>, they started . . . (Passage 10-B)

294

· 1. VERBS WITH PARTICLES (PHRASAL VERBS) (V PTL)

Some verbs have special meanings when they are combined with particles. *Hand in, give up,* and *run out* in the sentences above are three examples. Another name for them is **phrasal verbs.** We divide these verbs into two parts: the core verb and the particle. The verb and particle are closely joined; they carry their meaning as a unit, not as two separate words.

English has a variety of particles that are used in combination with certain verbs. The most common particles are:

FIGURE 12-1   Common Particles in English

about	at	into	through
across	away	off	to
after	back	on	together
ahead	by	out	under
along	down	over	up
apart	forward	past	upon
around	in	round	with

Here are some other examples from the passages in this book:

Next day, he <u>set *out*</u>. (Passage 9-E)

Some kinds of animals are always <u>dying *out*</u>—becoming extinct. (Passage 8-G)

Most likely, she will not be <u>kicked *out*</u> by her husband. (Passage 7-A)

During the interview, the accent problem <u>came *out*</u> again. (Passage 6-B)

After that, we <u>go *back*</u> to the hotel to <u>wash *up*</u> and to change our clothes. (Passage 5-C)

Often several particles can combine with a core verb, and each combination has a different meaning. For example, the verb *break* can take six different particles, each signaling a different meaning:

break away	=	separate from a group or mass
break down	=	stop functioning
break in	=	enter by using force
break off	=	stop, usually suddenly
break out	=	escape, or suddenly happen, as a disease
break up	=	destroy, usually with force or effort

The meaning of a **V Ptl** unit is often idiomatic, and many times the same combination has different meanings in different contexts. For example, you can say:

At 12:00 midnight the lights are <u>turned off</u>. (Passage 14-I)

This means that someone flicks a switch and all the lights go out. The meaning is different in:

> The students were <u>turned off</u> by the complex lecture.

This means that the lecture was so difficult that the students were not interested. Consult a good dictionary to find the meaning of the verb plus particle combinations that are unfamiliar to you. Even when you think you understand them, check with someone else (a native speaker if possible) to make sure.

Can you ever hope to learn all of these combinations? No, you can't, and you should not worry about it very much. People are creating new combinations all the time, especially in advertising. Fortunately, there are synonyms available for many of these verbs. For example, look at the three example sentences from the beginning of this chapter.

ORIGINAL	SYNONYM
That day I did not <u>go out</u>. (Passage 3-A)	That day I did not <u>leave my room</u>.
. . . my homework which would be <u>handed in</u> to my teacher the next morning. (Passage 4-B)	. . . my homework which would be <u>submitted</u> to my teacher the next morning.
When their money <u>ran out</u>, they started. . . . (Passage 10-B)	When their money was <u>depleted</u>, they started. . . .

Notice that using these synonyms makes the writing much more formal. You will therefore find that **V Ptl** units are particularly common in speech and in informal writing such as articles in popular magazines. You can also use them in academic writing, but if you want to show your control of formal language, use one word synonyms instead.

1.1 Verbs with Particles and Prepositional Phrases

Some **V Ptl** combinations have three parts: the core verb, a particle, and a preposition.

	V	*Ptl*	*PA*
I	am <u>looking</u>	<u>up</u>	<u>to</u> the sky with white clouds and tiny birds singing incredibly beautifully. (Passage 7-B)
Memories	<u>come</u>	<u>back</u>	<u>to</u> me. (Passage 7-B)

1. VERBS WITH PARTICLES (PHRASAL VERBS) (V PTL)

When we   <u>get</u>   <u>back</u>   <u>from</u> the ride, it is 10 P.M.
(Passage 5-C)

. . . the teacher   will <u>run</u>   <u>out</u>   <u>of</u> paper in about four weeks.
(Passage 5-A)

Many of these combinations of **V Ptl Prepositional Phrase** are very specific and have a particular meaning. For example, *catch up on . . .* means to learn the latest information about something. Here are some other examples of specific combinations that are used frequently.

FIGURE 12-2   Common Verbs with Particles and Prepositions

V PTL PREP	SYNONYM	V PTL PREP	SYNONYM
break up with . . .	separate from	get away with . . .	avoid punishment
catch on to . . .	understand	get back to . . .	return
catch up on . . .	discover the latest information	get down to . . .	concentrate
		give in to . . .	yield
catch up with . . .	overtake	give up on . . .	quit
check in on . . .	visit briefly	go in for . . .	try
check up on . . .	examine	keep up with . . .	maintain the same pace as someone
check out of . . .	leave		
close in on . . .	approach	look down on . . .	consider oneself superior to
come down with . . .	catch a disease		
come up with . . .	find	look in on . . .	visit
cut down on . . .	reduce	look up to . . .	admire
drop in on . . .	visit unannounced	make away with . . .	steal
end up with . . .	finish	pick up on . . .	realize
get along with . . .	be congenial	put up with . . .	endure
get away from . . .	leave	stand up for . . .	support

See *The Longman Dictionary of Phrasal Verbs.*

LEARNING STRATEGY

Managing Your Learning: Taking notes on idiomatic material and discussing it with native speakers helps you learn it.

The <u>verb with particle</u> pattern is used frequently in spoken English, and often it seems that new <u>verb with particle</u> combinations are being added daily.

1.2 Verbs with Particles and Objects

Some verbs can be followed by both a particle **(Ptl)** and an object **(O)**. With some verbs, the particle may also appear after the **O**. Look at these examples:

	V	Ptl	O	PA	
We were ordered to	fill	in	those blanks.		(Passage 1-A)
Every boarder had to	bring	up	her luggage	to her room.	(Passage 3-A)
I	found	out	why she wore those nice clothes.		(Passage 4-A)
I didn't forget to	set	aside	enough time for relaxation.		(Passage 4-B)

Here is a list of some common verbs with particles that take objects, with one synonym given in parentheses. However, these verbs with particles probably have more than one meaning. Refer to a dictionary of phrasal verbs for a more complete list of these combinations.

FIGURE 12-3   Common Verbs with Particles Followed by O

V PTL	SYNONYM	V PTL	SYNONYM
back up	support	get over	explain
blow up	cause an explosion	make out	understand
break off	stop suddenly	make up	invent
bring about	cause	put across	explain
bring up	raise	put off	delay
burn up	cause a fire	see off	say good-bye
draw up	write	turn off	extinguish
fill out	complete	turn down	reject
find out	discover		

In the set of examples at the beginning of this section, the particle can shift to the other side of the **O**. In fact, if **O** is a pronoun, the particle <u>must</u> come <u>after</u> **O**.

	V	Ptl	O	Ptl	PA
We were ordered to	fill		those blanks	in.	
Every boarder had to	bring		her luggage	up	to her room.
I	found		it	out.	
I didn't forget to	set		it	aside.	

Like the pattern in Figure 12-2, the meaning is idiomatic. For example, to <u>turn down the bed</u> is different from <u>turn down a job offer</u> and from <u>turn down the volume on the TV</u>. Also, <u>blow up a photograph</u> contrasts with <u>blow up a building</u>.

WHEN YOU ARE WRITING

Have you used a "preposition" after a verb? It might be one of these particles. Use our lists here, check your dictionary, or ask a native speaker about it if you are not certain that it is correct.

The editing problem is that if you have used a pronoun in **O,** the particle must come <u>after</u> the pronoun.

---

2. VERBS WITH INDIRECT OBJECTS AND OBJECTS (V IO O)

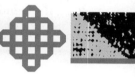

This pattern occurs with only a few verbs, but they are very common ones. They are listed later in this section.

	V	*IO*	*O*
The thankful dwarf	gave	him	a special sword. (Passage 9-E)
She	had bought	me	a new one. (Passage 8-E)
I	will have left	them	something which money cannot buy. (Passage 8-A)

The indirect object is the person or thing that receives the object. It usually comes between the verb and the **O.**

The "indirect object" information can also come after **O,** but then it requires a preposition. In American English, if **O** is a pronoun, the indirect object information must be expressed as a prepositional phrase.

	V	*O*	*PA*
The thankful dwarf	gave	it	to him.
She	had bought	it	for me.
I	will have left	it	for them.

The indirect object position is filled only when certain verbs are used. Here are the most common ones. The preposition that is needed when the information is shifted is given in parentheses.

FIGURE 12-4   Verbs That Can Have Indirect Objects

ask (of)	give (to)	show (to)
bring (to/for)	make (for)	take (to/for)
buy (for)	order (for)	tell (to)

WHEN YOU ARE WRITING

Have you used one of the verbs in the list in Figure 12-4? If you have, check the indirect object and the object.

If the indirect object is <u>between</u> the verb and **O**, it must <u>not</u> have a preposition.

If the indirect object information is after **O**, have you used the correct preposition?

3. VERBS WITH OBJECTS AND COMPLEMENTS (V O C)

This pattern is very rare. In these predicates, the complement is adding information about the **O**, not about the subject.

	V	*O*	*C*
They	might consider	themselves	Americans. (Passage 3-D)
. . . the consequences	may make	things	more difficult for us. (Passage 8-C)
UNESCO	has declared	the islands	"the cultural patrimony of the world." (Passage 14-A)

Usually the **object** is a noun phrase or a pronoun. The **complement** can be a single word adjective, an adjective phrase, or a noun phrase.

4. VERBS AND OBJECTS AND PREDICATE ADVERBIALS (V O PA)

The pattern occurs primarily with a small group of verbs. These are the most common ones:

FIGURE 12-5   Verbs That Take Object and Complement

appoint	elect	like	send
believe	find	make	think
call	get	prefer	turn
certify	hold	presume	want
choose	imagine	proclaim	wish
consider	judge	prove	
declare	keep	rate	
drive	leave	report	

Usually there is no editing problem with this pattern.

4. VERBS WITH OBJECTS AND PREDICATE ADVERBIALS (V O PA)

Although it is <u>always</u> possible to add an adverbial to <u>any</u> predicate, a few transitive verbs (**V O**) require that an adverbial be present.

	V	*O*	*PA*
Every boarder	had to bring	her luggage	**up to her room . . .** (Passage 3-A)
. . . they	would throw	him	**out of the house.** (Passage 8-C)
She only	spends	money	**on daily necessities.** (Passage 8-D)

The adverbials give information about place, condition, manner, time, reason, or purpose of the entire predicate. They are not merely attached to the **V** or to the **O** individually. Here is a list of some common verbs that follow this pattern:

FIGURE 12-6   Verbs That Take Object and Predicate Adverbial

bring	lead	send
drive	place	set
lay	put	take

Occasionally with these verbs the **PA** will not be filled. For example, we can say, "Tara brought her dog" or "We decided to take the train." This is possible only if the adverbial is understood; then the speaker does not have to include it.

WHEN YOU ARE WRITING

Have you used an adverbial in the predicate? It should almost always be at the end of the predicate, not between **V** and **O**. For example, avoid sentences like this one:

. . . we typed **at home** leaflets with patriotic poetry and slogans. (14-H)

If you have used an adverbial, do not put a comma between it and the rest of the sentence unless it is a long subordinate clause. (See Chapters 3 and 4.)

5. *THERE* AS SUBJECT

LEARNING STRATEGY

Forming Concepts: Knowing the purpose of a grammatical construction helps you understand when to use it.

This pattern is used for introducing a new topic or for giving emphasis to a topic.

There was no exception. (Passage 1-A)

There were many trees on the side of the river. (Passage 5-D)

There are 24 basic writing symbols. *There* are 14 consonants and 10 vowels. (Passage 8-G)

There were times that I spotted shoplifters. (Passage 10-A)

A sentence like "Many trees were on the side of the river" is not usual in English although it is grammatically correct. The phrasing in the example from Passage 5-D is normal.

These sentences have *there* as the grammatical subject. The complement in these sentences is usually a noun phrase. Sentences that begin with *there* highlight the complement element, giving focus to that topic and emphasizing it.

The problem that occurs with *there* as the subject is the verb that follows it. Should it be singular or plural? Here are the choices:

SINGULAR	PLURAL
is	are
was	were
has been	have been

The choice is controlled by the unit in the complement: if it is singular, then *was, is,* or *has* will be correct. If the complement is plural, then *were, are,* or *have* must be used. This is the only pattern where the verb agrees with what follows it. Look at the examples above. Only one of them is singular.

Also, if the complement is compound, the first item controls the choice of singular or plural. If that first item is singular, then the verb is singular.

There were many trees on the side of the river. (Passage 5-D)

There was a tree, a bench, and some flowers on the side of the river.

WHEN YOU'RE TALKING

In speech, you will hear *there's* for both singular and plural.

WHEN YOU ARE WRITING

Have you used *there* plus an auxiliary from the BE or HAVE group? If you have, check that you have the correct form of the auxiliary, either singular or plural. It depends on the complement.

One major use of *there* as subject is in questions, especially yes/no questions. If someone asks, "Is there a bus stop near here?" she expects more than, "Yes, there is." The responder should explain where the nearest bus stop is and give directions for getting to that stop. If there is no bus stop close by, the responder could suggest another means of transportation. A *there* yes/no question is an invitation to talk about something.

6. *IT* AS SUBJECT

Another common sentence pattern in English is the use of *it* as a subject, usually followed by *is, was, has, had,* or one of the modals.

> *It* is very important to make a schedule. (Passage 4-B)

> *It* will be fun to say "Oh children!" to a sixty year old person when I am eighty. (Passage 4-A)

One use of this pattern is for talking about the weather and the time: "It is raining" and "It is 8:30 in the evening right now."

This pattern is also used so that we can avoid having a complex grammatical unit as the subject. The topic of the "*it* as subject" sentence is "postponed" to the end of the clause, after the other elements of the predicate. Often this topic is a verbal phrase, a long noun phrase, or a clause.

S V	C	PP
It was	a new experience for me	to have classmates who were from different countries. (Passage 4-A)
Sometimes *it* was	not enough	to know where the things that were sold in the shop were located . . . (Passage 10-A)
It was	horrible	the way I was filling my stomach with popcorn . . . (Passage 5-B)

This pattern also occurs with other verbs, particularly *make* and *take*.

S V	O	PP
It makes	no sense	to change your ideas and beliefs . . . (Passage 3-D)
It took	one hour	to get there. (Passage 7-B)

Sometimes the verbal phrase in the postponed position has its own "subject." The form used is that of a prepositional phrase beginning with *for,* which usually appears at the beginning of the verbal phrase.

S V	C	PP
It was not	easy	for people to follow this one [schedule]. (Passage 4-B)
It won't be	easy	for me to get a job for you. (Passage 6-B)

304

WHEN YOU ARE WRITING

It is easy to omit this *it* in a sentence, especially if it occurs after a sentence adverbial. In spoken English, it is hard to hear because it is often part of a contraction and there is no clear "t" sound. However, in writing it is a serious error to leave out the *it*.

Check your sentences to make sure that each one has a subject. (If you cannot find the subject of sentences easily, see Chapter 3 for some helpful suggestions.)

 **ACTIVITIES**

1. Verbs with Particles

A. Take one of the following core verbs and try combining it with as many particles as possible from Figure 12-1. The verbs are *come, get, look, put, run,* and *take*. No verb will combine with all those particles.

Write down the combinations.

Exchange your list with a partner. Which combinations look "funny" to you? Challenge your partner about those. In any disagreement, look the core verb up in a good dictionary and look for examples of that combination. (Please remember that although one dictionary may not have it, the combination might still exist.)

B. Take a popular magazine like *Newsweek* or *People* or a newspaper. Spend 15 minutes looking only at the advertisements. Write down as many **V Ptl** combinations as you can find.

At the end of the 15 minutes, try to figure out another way to express the same idea, using a synonym for each of the **V Ptl** combinations.

Check your list with other members of your class.

C. Our most common everyday activities are usually described with verbs with particles.

Write out your typical daily routine, using as many of these verbs as you can. Then rewrite your routine, using verbs with no particles. You will probably have to use your dictionary to find these other verbs.

When you are finished, read your routine to some other people. (It will sound funny because we do not usually use such "formal" verbs for everyday activities.)

2. *There* as Subject

The following sentences all have *there* as subject, but they do not have any verb filled in. Decide what verb is appropriate and whether it should be singular or plural. In some sentences, there is more than one possible answer.

1. . . . there _____ too much homework to be done today. (Passage 4-B)

2. In our schools, there _____ many kinds of education and many ways of teaching. (adapted from Passage 4-D)

3. When I went for the interview, there _____ a lot of people applying for the same position. (Passage 6-B)

4. Apparently teaching was fighting; there _____ no doubt about it. (Passage 7-D)

5. At that time, there _____ not a lot of Asian students in our high school. (Passage 13-D)

6. Another problem is how long immigrants have to study to get a degree. There _____ a lot of obstacles in this university system. . . . (Passage 7-F)

7. Among psychologists, especially in the field of developmental psychology, there _____ agreement about how important early childhood is for a human being. (Passage 8-E)

8. Chinese loan words are very difficult to learn because there _____ so many different ways of writing them. (Passage 9-C)

9. Only about two dozen of the big beautiful cranes are left. Soon there _____ none. (Passage 8-G)

10. Later, the structure and pattern of the abacus changed, so there _____ some differences between the ancient and modern abacus. (Passage 9-D)

11. There _____ questions asked by my customers that annoyed me. (Passage 10-A)

12. Hunters with guns have helped to make the whooping crane almost extinct, but there _____ to be something else going on, too. (Passage 8-G)

13. Almost all the expensive clothes had alarms attached to them, but there _____ small items like underwear, stockings, and scarves that could be slipped out easily. (Passage 10-A)

14. . . . whenever there _____ a misunderstanding between my coworkers or customers and me, I managed to control my anger. (Passage 10-A)

15. . . . I noticed that there _____ a lot of hands and feet made of concrete on the ground. (Passage 13-B)

3. Non-pronoun *it* as Subject Contrasted with the Pronoun *it*

In the following section of a student essay, *it* is sometimes used as the "empty" subject followed by a postponed subject, and at other times as a pronoun. Each *it* is numbered. On a separate paper, make two headings: "Empty *it*" and "Pronoun." Write the number of each use of *it* under the appropriate heading.

Passage 4-B   **HOW TO USE TIME WELL**

Were you reading magazines or books while taking a bus or train? Did you call someone up or talk with somebody without a purpose? If the first question is answered "no" and the second question "yes," I could say that you wasted a lot of precious time because you could do something on the
5   train, and (1) <u>it</u> was not necessary to call somebody or talk with somebody. Of course, (2) <u>it</u> is very important to make a schedule if you want to keep on time. This weekly schedule may not solve all your problems, but (3) <u>it</u> will force you to realize what is happening to your time.

I have had tremendous success with this method. After making a
10   schedule, I followed (4) <u>it</u> for each day. I gradually stopped postponing the chores that faced me. My life became far less complicated, and each day was easier to face. Of course, the schedule should be reasonable because (5) <u>it</u> was not easy for people to follow this one. (6) <u>It</u> was filled in with committed time and time for relaxation.

4. Non-pronoun *it* as Subject

One of the most frequent uses of sentences with *it* as subject is to emphasize an adjective.

<u>It</u> is hard to get a good education.

However, it is possible to rephrase that sentence and use an *-ing* verbal phrase as the subject.

Get<u>ting</u> a good education is hard.

Or a rephrase can put a noun phrase or clause as the subject.

<u>A good education</u> is hard to get.

CHAPTER 12: LESS COMMON PREDICATE PATTERNS

All three of these versions are correct. Which alternative to use is decided by the emphasis that the writer wants for a particular paragraph.

Rewrite the sentences below in the two alternative styles. Do not try to change front or end adverbials.

1. There are many education programs in America, but it is hard to get information about them. (Passage 7-F)
2. At that time, it was not easy to get an education for the lower class people; . . . (Passage 9-C)
3. . . . it was not easy even for them to learn the Chinese loanwords. (Passage 9-C)
4. If people want to be successful, it is very important for them to know how to use time well. (Passage 4-B)
5. As a Japanese, I found it hard to understand the meaning of "the Melting Pot" when I learned the phrase about two years ago. (Passage 8-H)

NOTE   The following sentences can have only one other version. Also, notice that the front and end adverbials do not change.

6. . . . it is very important to make a schedule if you want to keep on time. (Passage 4-B)
7. It makes no sense to change your ideas and beliefs if you think they are right. (Passage 3-D)
8. I think it will be fun to say "Oh, children!" to a sixty-year-old person when I am eighty. (Passage 4-A)
9. I feel it is absolutely right to keep my baby. (Passage 4-C)
10. . . . and it will be an even greater achievement if I make it through college and get my degree. (Passage 4-E)
11. I think it won't be easy for me to get a job for you. (Passage 6-B)
12. . . . it sometimes shocks me that I am able to remember so many details. (Passage 7-B)
13. For adult immigrants, it is difficult to succeed in America because they have to be able to break certain barriers such as language and culture. (Passage 7-F)

Direct and Reported Speech

13

CHAPTER

*S*ometimes you need to include the ideas of someone else as you explain something. You might decide to use the other person's exact words, a **quotation,** to add power or beauty to what you are saying. At other times, you might want to give the other person's ideas, but the exact words are not important or you cannot remember them. Therefore, you **report** the information by paraphrasing it. English has various conventions about how to signal **direct speech** (a quotation) or **reported speech** (a paraphrase). Usually in oral English, there are no problems with direct and reported speech. However, there are several problems that occur in the written version.

LEARNING STRATEGY

Managing Your Learning: Experimenting with different ways of describing what people say will strengthen your writing and improve your comprehension.

1. DIRECT SPEECH

In Passage 13-A, the sentences with quotations have been numbered, the main verb of each is in italics, and the quotation is underlined.

Passage 13-A **DRAWING A PORTRAIT**

by Anna Cioczek

One day I was sitting in my room drawing my mother's picture. I spent a lot of time and energy on it, trying to make it as perfect as possible, because for me my mother was the most beautiful woman in the world and I wanted to show her how I felt about her.

5   After a while, my mother decided to check on what I was doing. She came to the room and sat beside my chair. As I looked at her, I realized that my work wasn't good at all.

(1) She *asked* me, "What are you doing, darling, for so long sitting here so quietly?"

10   (2) I *answered* with embarrassment, "Nothing special, just drawing."

(3) "Who is this?" she *asked,* pointing at my paper.

I didn't know what to say. I was ashamed of my work. (4)I *said,* "Oh, I really don't know. It can be daddy, since it cannot possibly be you."

This example shows how important and special she was for me when I

15   was a little girl. Many years later I still feel the same way. In the picture that I

310

have in my heart she is still young and beautiful. Her face has something special which is not easy to describe. Everything about her is sweet and makes you want to look at her.

The four examples of direct speech in the passage above show how quotations operate in English. <u>The quoted words</u> are marked at the beginning and the end by **quotation marks,** which are above the line. The quotation must be <u>the exact words</u> that the speaker said, with the same grammar, especially the pronouns and verb tenses.

1.1 Paragraphing

Often a piece of writing will be a record of what two or more people said to each other about a particular topic. This is called a **dialogue.** <u>Each change of speaker</u> in a dialogue is signaled by a <u>new paragraph</u>, especially when the writer gives no explicit identification of the speaker.

Direct speech usually has identification of the speakers, either their names or perhaps an identification of their relationship to the writer. In Passage 13-A, the asker of the questions was Cioczek's mother. Also, there should be some indication of when the conversation happened. Cioczek explains that this conversation took place many years ago, when she was a little girl. The verb and an adverbial can indicate the manner of speaking. The basic verbs are *say* and *ask.* However, there are 40 other verbs which are commonly used, such as *announce, exclaim, shout,* and *whisper.* There is a list of these verbs later in this chapter, under Section 1.3.

1.2 Punctuation

The boundaries of the direct speech are <u>marked by the quotation marks</u>. Quotation marks begin and end the entire statement, even if it is more than one sentence. Even the end punctuation—the periods, the question marks, and the exclamation points—go inside the quotation marks. All the other rules develop from this basic rule. For example, the following quotation is three sentences long, but it has only one set of quotation marks.

> Cioczek said, "In the picture that I have in my heart she is still young and beautiful. Her face has something special which is not easy to describe. Everything about her is sweet and makes you want to look at her."

The following examples show some of the basic rules about punctuating quotations.

These rules are affected by where the quotation is in the sentence. In these examples, the quotation is printed in bold type, and the verb that shows the manner of speaking is in italics.

- If the quotation is accompanied by the identification of the speaker, there are three different styles.

1. The quotation can come after the identification of the speaker. Notice:
   a. a comma is put before the quotation;
   b. the quotation starts with quotation marks and a capital letter;
   c. the quotation has a period, question mark, or exclamation point inside the quotation marks at the end.

   I *answered* with embarrassment, "Nothing special, just drawing."

   Pointing at my paper, she *asked,* "Who is this?"

2. The quotation can come first. Notice:

   • *Statement*
   a. a quoted statement will have a comma at the end, inside the quotation marks;
   b. the period will come at the end of the complete sentence. For example:

   "Nothing special, just drawing," I *answered* with embarrassment.

   • *Question or exclamation*
   a. a quoted question or exclamation will have the question mark or exclamation point at the end of the quotation, inside the quotation marks. The identification of the speaker will not start with a capital letter unless it is a proper name or *I.*
   b. a period will come at the end of the complete sentence.

   "Who is this?" she *asked,* pointing at my paper.

3. The single sentence quotation can be split by the identification of the speaker. Notice:
   a. a comma comes at the end of the first section of the quotation, inside the quotation marks;
   b. another comma comes at the end of the speaker identification;
   c. quotation marks start the second section of the quotation;
   d. the second section does not begin with a capital letter;
   e. the quotation ends with the appropriate punctuation mark inside the final quotation marks.

   "Nothing special," I *answered* with embarrassment, "just drawing."

• The quoted words might not be a complete grammatical sentence, but in a dialogue, each separate quotation always begins with a capital letter.

   I *answered* with embarrassment, "Nothing special, just drawing."

• In the identification of the speaker, the verb identifying the manner of speaking —such as *ask, answer, command, say,* or *shout* for example—is usually in the past tense.

1.3 Verbs of Speaking or Thinking

The most frequently used verbs of speaking are *say* and *ask.* However, there are a variety of verbs available. Some indicate a manner of speaking, such as *shout,* while others show a relationship of that utterance to the rest of the conversation, such as *answered.* Here is a list of some of these reporting verbs:

FIGURE 13-1   Verbs of Speaking or Thinking

add	comment	object	say
admit	conclude	observe	shout
announce	confess	order	state
answer	cry (out)	promise	tell
argue	declare	protest	think
assert	exclaim	recall	urge
ask	explain	remark	warm
beg	insist	repeat	whisper
boast	maintain	reply	wonder
claim	note	report	write

WHEN YOU ARE WRITING

Quoted dialogue can be very effective in an informal essay. The problem is to get the pronouns, verb tenses, and punctuation correct. It is best to check each feature individually.

1. Are the pronouns in the quotation correct, with the speaker referring to herself or himself as *I, me, my, mine,* and *myself,* and with the plural first person forms if needed? Is the listener referred to with the second person forms *(you)*?
2. Are the verb tenses in the quotation correct, the ones which the speaker used when actually saying those words?
3. Have you made a new paragraph each time a different person begins speaking?
4. Have you put quotation marks <u>above the line</u> at the beginning and the end of the exact words that each person said?
5. Does each of the quoted sentences end with a period, question mark, or exclamation point?

    (The only exception is if there is identification of the speaker after a quoted statement; then the quotation will only have a comma at the end.)

    "<u>Nothing special, just drawing</u>," I *answered* with embarrassment.

6. Is the final punctuation mark of the quotation <u>inside</u> the quotation marks?

2. REPORTED SPEECH

The verbs of saying, perception, and thinking are often followed by noun clauses that are **reports** of what someone said, asked, or thought. These clauses are not quotations; they are paraphrases or summaries of the person's statements, questions, or ideas. There are various levels of exactness and detail that the report can take. In this chapter, we focus on the level of reporting in which the reporter wants to give a partial paraphrase of the original speech, not just a brief summary of the major ideas.

In the following excerpt from a student essay, Goto's father probably told her many details about the American movie industry, but the conversation happened several years before she wrote the essay. She recalls in general what her visit to Hollywood was like and the questions that she had, but it would be impossible for her to remember the exact words that her father said. In this passage, the <u>reported</u> statements are underlined, and the main verb of the sentence is in italics.

Passage 13-B **HOLLYWOOD**

by Minako Goto

A couple of days later, I toured Hollywood with my family. When we went to the square in front of the Chinese Theater, there were a lot of tourists and all of them were looking down eagerly. I wondered why they were looking down; it looked very weird. At the same time, I noticed that
5 there were a lot of hands and feet made of concrete on the ground. I asked my father what this was for. He *told* me <u>that the movie industry developed excellently in Hollywood and American people had been making great movies for many years.</u> He *explained* <u>that there were very remarkable filmmakers, actors, and actresses in the U.S. and they were very creative.</u> He
10 *added* <u>that movies were the best part of culture in the United States.</u>

The major problem areas in reported statements are the pronouns, the verb tenses, and references to time and place.

2.1 Pronouns in Reported Speech

Look at these examples from other essays in this book. The reported statements are underlined, and the pronouns within them are in italics. We have also guessed at what the original conversation was like.

REPORTED: I asked my mother <u>to buy *me* a pencil case which had a Japanese cartoon character design on the cover.</u> She refused because she said <u>*she* had just bought *me* a new one a few months ago.</u> (Passage 8-D)

314

ACTUAL: "Mother, look at this beautiful pencil case. It has a Japanese cartoon character design on the cover. Will *you* please buy it for *me*?"

"No, *I* won't. *I* just bought *you* a new pencil case a few months ago."

REPORTED: The personnel administrator said that <u>*my* typing was excellent, but *my* accent was terrible. *She* didn't think that it would be easy for *her* to get a job for *me*</u>. (Adapted from Passage 6-B)

ACTUAL: The personnel administrator said, "Your typing is excellent, but it is hard to understand you when you speak. Your accent is terrible. It's not going to be easy for me to find a job for you."

- It is very rare to use second person pronouns *you, your, yours* in a reported statement. They are necessary only when the reporter is talking to the original speaker.

    "You told me <u>*you* were leaving on July 3</u>. Why are you still here?" Bob asked worriedly.

- In reported statements, a writer can easily confuse the reader because the third person pronoun forms (*he/him/his, she/her,* and *they/them/their*) must be used to refer to both the speakers and listeners. Look at this example adapted from Passage 6-B:

ACTUAL: The personnel administrator said, "*Your* typing is excellent, but it is hard to understand *you* when *you* speak. *Your* accent is terrible. It's not going to be easy for *me* to find a job for *you*."

REPORTED: The personnel administrator said that *her* typing was excellent, but *her* accent was terrible. *She* didn't think that it would be easy for *her* to get a job for *her*.

The reported version is confusing because *her* refers to different people. The writer must signal the change of referents. This passage should be revised so that each pronoun refers to the closest preceding name or identifying phrase:

REVISED: The personnel administrator said that *Vilma's* typing was excellent, but *her* accent was terrible. *The administrator* didn't think that it would be easy for *her* to get a job for *Vilma*.

WHEN YOU ARE WRITING

When you use reported statements, check the pronoun reference carefully. Change *you* and *I* and other second and first person pronouns to third person if necessary. Make sure that you do not have two third person pronouns in a row that refer to different people. Usually you should change the second one to a name or a phrase that identifies the person.

2.2 Verb Tenses in Reported Speech

The verb tense in reported statements is usually the past. In Passage 13-B, when Goto's father originally spoke to her in 1980, he used the NOW time frame for his direct speech. In the 1990s, when she reports what her father said, she uses the THEN time frame. Look at the examples below. The verbs are underlined, and the tense marker is in italics.

ACTUAL: "There *are* very remarkable filmmakers, actors, and actresses in the U.S."

REPORTED: He explained that there *were* very remarkable filmmakers, actors, and actresses in the U.S.

ACTUAL: "Movies *are* the best part of American culture."

REPORTED: He added that movies *were* the best part of American culture.

ACTUAL: "American people *have* been making great movies for many years."

REPORTED: He told me . . . American people *had* been making great movies for many years.

The reported statements usually require the THEN time frame. Also, except when we are talking about literature, we ordinarily use a past tense form for the "report" verb: *said, explained, added* and *wondered,* for example. It is usually a mistake to mix the THEN and NOW time frames in reported statements.

Changing *have/has* to *had*

Be particularly careful of HAVE + -*d/t/n*. When the quoted statement has the expanded verb *have/has* + -*d/t/n*, it is usually necessary to change *have/has* to *had*.

Original Version
I personally can say that America is the land of opportunity for the people who already have family in the country like me. . . . I *have* been here for three years. . . . I *have* graduated from high school and am now continuing to pursue my goals by attending this college. (Passage 7-C)

Reported Version
Martine Liney wrote that she believed that America was the land of opportunity for people who already had family in the country like her. At the time she wrote the essay, she *had* been in the U.S. for three years. She *had* graduated from high school and was attending college.

Changing Simple Past to *had* + -*d/t/n*

Often when the verb in the quoted statement is past tense, the reported version uses *had* + -*d/t/n*. (For more about this expanded verb, see Chapter 9.)

Look at the example below. The verbs are underlined, and the tense marker is printed in italics.

ACTUAL: "The movie industry _developed_ excellently in Hollywood.

REPORTED: He said that the movie industry _had_ developed excellently in Hollywood.

However, when the time relationships are clear from the context, it is not necessary to make this change. The reported statement can use the simple past.

ACTUAL: Sofia Tadesse said, "Last summer I _worked_ for three months as a sales person in a boutique."

REPORTED: Sofia Tadesse said that the previous summer she _worked_ for three months as a sales person in a boutique.

If the prepositional phrases "the previous summer" and "for three months" were not used, the verb would be _had worked_.

REPORTED: Sofia Tadesse said that she _had_ worked as a sales person in a boutique.

Changing Modals

The modals have their own rules governing their use in reported speech:

FIGURE 13-2   Modals in Reported Speech

DIRECT SPEECH	REPORTED SPEECH
can ⟶	_could_
will ⟶	_would_
may ⟶	_could_ (permission to do something) or _might_ (a possible action)
must ⟶	_had to_

ACTUAL: "I don't remember her name, but I _can_ clearly recall how she looked and what she said." (Passage 4-A)

REPORTED: Nakashizuka wrote that she didn't remember the woman's name but she _could_ remember the woman's appearance and what she said.

ACTUAL: "If you check what you have done all day long, you _will_ find you have done a lot of things which were not necessary." (Passage 4-B)

REPORTED: Chun Ling Tsien wrote that if people checked what they did during the day, they _would_ find that they had done a lot of unnecessary things.

ACTUAL: "In each grade we _must_ pass every subject. Otherwise, we _must_ repeat that particular grade." (Passage 4-D)

REPORTED: Nini Myint wrote that in Burma the students _had to_ pass every subject or else they _had to_ repeat the same grade.

(For more information about the modals, see Chapter 8, Section 4.2.)

Using the NOW Time Frame in Reported Speech

There are three conditions when the verb in the reported statement might be in the NOW time frame: (1) if the action is usual or habitual; (2) if it is happening at the time of reporting; or (3) if the action has not happened yet.

In his essay on the Galapagos Islands, Jaime Zaldumbide said that the Ecuadorian government _is attempting_ to keep the islands undeveloped and undamaged by passing laws to protect the environment. He added that UNESCO _is providing_ support. (Adapted from Passage 14-A.)

The use of the NOW time frame in this way is very rare.

WHEN YOU ARE WRITING

The safest rule about using the NOW time frame in reported statements is very simple: Don't use it. Even in the example given above, it would be correct to use the past tense.

2.3 References to Time and Place in Reported Speech

Certain place and time references that are used in conversation must be phrased differently in reported statements. For example, we can adapt information from Passage 8-D; perhaps the conversation went like this:

ACTUAL: "Mother, look at this beautiful pencil case. It has a Japanese cartoon character design on the cover. Will you please buy it for me?"

"No, I won't. I just bought you a new pencil case a few months ago."

"But the one I have is out of style, and this one is very popular now. Most of my school-mates have it."

"Lisa, I'm not going to buy <u>this</u> thing. I don't want to spoil you. We can't afford to spend money on such luxury things."

In a reported statement, reference words that indicate place such as *this* and *here* cannot be used because those words refer to the context where the original speaking occurred. The reported version must use *a . . ., that . . .,* or *that place*. If the name of the actual location is given, or if the place is clear from the context, the word *there* can be used in the reported version.

Similarly, words and phrases indicating time, like *now, a few months ago,* and *tomorrow,* cannot be used because they refer to the time when the original speaking happened. The reporter has to use a word or phrase that shows the time relationship: *at that time, a few months before,* or *the next day.*

In the reported version of the conversation given above, the changes in time and place references are underlined. There are only five.

REPORTED: Tang asked her mother to look at <u>a</u> pencil case which Tang felt was beautiful because it had a Japanese cartoon character design on the cover. Tang asked her mother to buy it for her.

Tang's mother said that she wouldn't because she had bought Tang a new pencil case <u>a few months before</u>.

Tang complained that the one she had was out of style, and <u>that</u> other one was very popular <u>at that time</u>. She said that most of her school-mates had it.

Her mother said that she was not going to buy <u>that box</u> because she did not want to spoil Tang. She added that they couldn't afford to spend money on such luxury things.

These five changes are in addition to the nine changes in pronouns and ten verb tense changes. However, these place and time references are especially important because each is connected to a specific item; an error can cause a lot of confusion for the readers.

WHEN YOU ARE WRITING

When you include reported statements in your writing, check the determiners, place references, and time references carefully. They cannot be the actual words of the speaker because the context has changed. Therefore, you must use the "reported forms" to make the context clear. See the suggestions in Figure 13-3 on p. 320.

FIGURE 13-3   Direct and Reported Speech:
Changing Place and Time Reference

DIRECT	REPORTED
Changes in determiners	
this ⟶	a, that
these ⟶	those
Changes in place references	
here ⟶	there, at that place
Changes in time references	
now ⟶	at that time, then
today ⟶	that day
tomorrow ⟶	the following day, the next day
yesterday ⟶	the previous day, the day before
next * ⟶	the following * , the next * , a * later
last * ⟶	the previous * , a * before
in three *s ⟶	three *s from then
three *s ago ⟶	three *s earlier,
	three *s before

* = week, month, year
*s = days, weeks, months, years

L E A R N I N G   S T R A T E G Y

Forming Concepts: Being aware of your reader's position in time and place helps you make your writing clearer.

Some verbs of speaking, perception, and thinking—like *ask, inquire,* and *wonder* —are often followed by a noun clause that is a <u>reported question</u>. The reported question begins with identification of who asked and then a verb such as *ask.* The question itself is paraphrased as a clause in **O.** (See Chapter 11, Section 2.3.)

Reported Information Questions

Reported questions differ from direct questions in two ways: position of the auxiliary and punctuation. They follow the rules of reported statements for pronouns, verb tenses, and references to time and place. Look at these quoted question forms adapted from Passage 13-B and compare them to the reported questions. The reported questions are underlined. The verbs are printed in italics.

QUOTED QUESTION	REPORTED QUESTION
I wondered, "Why *are* they *looking* down?"	I wondered <u>why they *were* looking down</u>.
I asked my father, "What *is* this for?"	I asked my father <u>what that *was* for</u>.

There are two major types of reported questions: information questions and yes/no questions. In reported information questions, the clause in **O** begins with a *wh*-subordinator (*what, when, where, whether, which, who, whose, why,* or *how*). It is often the same *wh*-question word that was used in the direct question.

Because yes/no questions do not have a *wh*-subordinator or <u>that</u> as an introductory word, the reported yes/no questions add a subordinator, often <u>if</u> or <u>whether</u>.

ACTUAL: Her uncle asked her, "*Do* you *have* any plans for the holidays?"
REPORTED: Her uncle asked her <u>whether she *had* any plans for the holidays</u>.

ACTUAL: "*Were* you *reading* magazines or books while taking a bus or train?" (Passage 4-B)
REPORTED: Chun Ling Tsien asked <u>if they *were reading* anything while taking a bus or train</u>.

In addition, rhetorical questions and tag questions have reported forms. (See Sections 3.3 and 3.4.)

3.1 Position of the Auxiliary in Reported Questions

In a reported question, the verb is different from the verb in a quoted question in two ways: the position of the auxiliary and the tense.

The first auxiliary is in the "statement" position, at the beginning of the predicate, <u>not</u> in the question position in front of the subject. In the first example above, the auxiliary comes in front of the verb *looking*. In the second example, *was* is the main verb.

Sometimes a reported question will not have an auxiliary at all because the question auxiliary was *do, does,* or *did.* In that situation, usually a simple past tense verb is used.

> ACTUAL: She asked, "How *do* you *feel* about leaving home?"
> REPORTED: She asked me <u>how I *felt* about leaving home</u>.

Sometimes, the reported question has the verb as the final item. This happens primarily when the question is asking for an amount, a place, a time, manner or method, or a reason.

> ACTUAL: She asked, "How old *are* you?"
> REPORTED: She asked me <u>how old I *was*</u>. (Adapted from Passage 4-A.)

Other questions require the addition of another verb like "tell."

> ACTUAL: She would ask me, "What *did* you *do* today?"
> REPORTED: She would ask me to tell her <u>what I *did* during the day</u>.

The same basic rules about verb changes that apply to reported information questions also apply to reported yes/no questions. The next example shows an addition to the verb change rule, namely that if there is a compound predicate, both verbs change. The verbs are printed in italics.

> ACTUAL: *Did* you *call* someone up or *talk* with somebody without a purpose? (Passage 4-B)
> REPORTED: She asked <u>whether they *called* someone up or *talked* with somebody without a purpose.</u>

The verb tense depends on the time of report, not the time of the original question; it is usually simple past or *had + -d/t/n.*

3.2 Punctuation of Reported Questions

One noticeable punctuation difference between the two forms is that reported questions do not have question marks. Nevertheless, they are still called reported questions because they are paraphrases of somebody's question. Usually the main verb of the sentence indicates a question. Here is a brief list of some common verbs that are used in reported questions: *ask; inquire; question; wonder.*

Also, reported questions do not have quotation marks because they are not the exact words that somebody spoke or wrote.

3.3 Summary of Reported Questions

Here is a summary of the differences between reported questions and quoted direct questions. In the following examples, the reported questions are underlined, the verbs in both the direct questions and the reported questions are printed in italics, and the subjects have a box around them.

Verb Form

1. For most quoted information questions and quoted yes/no questions, the auxiliary must come before the subject. In a reported question, the auxiliary comes after the subject. If the quoted question's auxiliary was *do, does,* or *did* without *n't*, the reported question will usually only have a main verb.

I wondered, "Why *are* they *looking* down?"	I wondered why they *were* looking down.
She asked, "How *do* you *feel* about leaving home?"	She asked me how I *felt* about leaving home.

2. In the quoted question, the time orientation of the verb is often NOW; in the reported question, the THEN frame is usually used.

I wondered, "Why *are* they *looking* down?"	I wondered why they *were* looking down.
She asked, "What *did* you *do* today?" and *Are* you homesick?"	She asked me what I *did* during the day and if I *was* homesick.

Punctuation

1. Do not use quotation marks for a reported question.

2. In a reported question, do not use a capital letter at the beginning of the question, on the *wh*-word or *if* unless it is the first word in the sentence.

3. Use only a period at the end of a reported question.

I wondered, "Why are they looking down?"	I wondered why they were looking down.
She asked me, "What did you do today?" and "Are you homesick?"	She asked me what I did during the day and if I was homesick.

3.4 Reported Rhetorical Questions

"Rhetorical questions" are ways of introducing a topic for examination and discussion. The asker does not want an answer; she wants to explain her own ideas on the topic. However, they do look like questions.

> ACTUAL: Michelle Saintilien asked, "Why should we be so reluctant or hesitant in helping people that are unfortunate, especially if the unfortunate are the homeless?" (Passage 5-B)
>
> REPORTED: Michelle Saintilien asked why we are so reluctant to help the homeless.

When rhetorical questions become reported questions, they follow the rules explained for the regular information questions. In addition, the paraphrased report must focus on the central topic. In the example above, the reported question has the main idea of her question, not the decorative phrases.

Notice that the reported form uses *are*. Usually, the reported question would have the past tense, but in this example the treatment of the homeless is a continuing issue.

Here is another example, but of a short question:

> ACTUAL: Jacek Gzik asked, "What is education?" (Passage 5-A)
>
> REPORTED: Jacek Gzik asked what education is.

If the speaker uses an introductory rhetorical question, and then he develops the topic and presents his own opinion, the verb *discuss* could be used in the reported version. Also, if the topic is very general, the reported question can be in present tense.

Rhetorical questions are rare, and reported rhetorical questions are very few and far between.

3.5 Reported Tag Questions

Tag questions are found more often in speech than in writing. (See Chapter 2 for more about tag questions.)

There are two ways to phrase tag questions in reported speech: They can be treated as yes/no questions, or they can be reported as statements that indicate the asker's view or intention.

If treated as yes/no questions, they follow the same rules as reported yes/no questions. For example, look at these questions adapted from the earlier examples in this chapter.

> ACTUAL: Her uncle asked her, "You don't have any plans for the holidays, do you?"
>
> REPORTED: Her uncle asked her if she had any plans for the holidays.

ACTUAL: Tsien asked, "You weren't reading magazines or books while taking a bus or train, were you?"
REPORTED: Tsien asked whether they were reading magazines or books while taking a bus or train.

ACTUAL: She asked, "You feel bad about leaving home, don't you?"
REPORTED: She asked me whether I felt bad about leaving home.

However, because the tag questions indicate the asker's opinion about the topic of the question, these tag questions can be reported statements.

ACTUAL: Her uncle asked her, "You don't have any plans for the holidays, do you?"
REPORTED: Her uncle hoped that she didn't have any plans for the holidays.

ACTUAL: Tsien asked, "You weren't reading magazines or books while taking a bus or train, were you?"
REPORTED: Tsien suggested that reading magazines or books while taking a bus or train was not a good use of time.

ACTUAL: She asked, "You feel bad about leaving home, don't you?"
REPORTED: She guessed that I felt bad about leaving home.

Notice that in these examples, the verbs of reporting are not question words; they indicate statements: *hope, suggest, guess.* In these examples, the reported version indicates a direction for the development of the topic: For the first example, her uncle had plans which he told her about; in the second example, Tsien would explain why reading on the bus or subway is not a good use of time; for the third example, the discussion would focus on her homesickness.

Any of these forms is correct. The choice depends on the writer's purpose for including the reported speech and the writer's plan for developing the essay.

WHEN YOU ARE WRITING

When you have used a verb of saying, seeing, or thinking—such as *ask, inquire, wonder,* or *announce, describe, explain, say,* or *state*—check any noun clause that comes next.

1. Where have you put the auxiliary, if you have used one? It should be after the subject.
2. What verb tense have you used? If you are reporting, it will probably be a past tense.
3. What pronouns have you used? You probably need the third person forms.
4. What punctuation have you used? The reported statement or question needs only a period at the end.

1. Quotations

In Passage 13-C, the punctuation around the direct quotations has been omitted. Identify the sentences that are direct quotations and insert the punctuation marks that are necessary.

You can see a correct version of this essay in Appendix 2.

Passage 13-C   **MICHELLE**

by Victoria Wu

She has huge, round brown eyes, dark brown curly hair, and her tiny face makes her normal size mouth look like it is grinning from ear to ear while she is laughing. Michelle impressed me not only because of her friendly and active teaching attitude but also because of her words that moved me very
5   much and have remained in my mind.

Are you sure you are in my class? Michelle asked me with her folding eyebrow. You should not be in this class. I don't know how you did on your placement test. These were the words she said to me in front of all the class 20 minutes after the first conversation class began in my first semester. She
10   told me I should have been in the conversation class two levels higher and she really did me a great favor: She went to the office, consulted with the director, and sent me to the correct class.

Our second encounter took place in my writing class one and a half years later. Michelle was my writing teacher then. When we saw each other
15   in the first class, we both opened our mouths widely, and suddenly she pointed her finger to me and said I remember you, Vicky. You were in my class two years ago. Are you still taking these ESL courses? Actually, I did not have a chance to explain why I was still taking the courses then. Through an essay she learned that an accident had happened to my family, so I returned
20   to my hometown and came back one and a half years later.

The third time I met Michelle was in her reading class. I performed poorly that term because I was attending classes in the day and working at night. I could not get enough time to review and do my homework. Furthermore, I was unable to take the final exam and consequently was not
25   allowed to leave the program. The director told me to ask Michelle if she

326

agreed that I was capable of passing the tests. The director decided to talk to her first. Michelle granted her approval, so I passed the class and was able to enter college.

30   I never saw Michelle after that final term, nor did I say thank you very much. I do not know whether I would have had the courage to say such simple words to her if I had seen her.

2. Direct Statements and Questions

In the following passage, the writer used several direct statements and questions. There is a blank line at each of those places. Each blank is numbered, and at the end of the passage is the list of these direct statements and questions with corresponding numbers, but we have left out the punctuation marks. For each blank, you must copy the statement or question from the list at the end of the exercise. You must put in the correct punctuation marks, including the paragraphing.

You can see a correct version of this essay in Appendix 2.

Passage 13-D   **LINDA**

by Thien Quan Duong

During the first few days of high school, I noticed a pair of friends who wore the same type of jacket and were walking down the hallway. I heard someone calling, "Linda, Linda," and one of them turned around and said hello. That was how I came to know Linda's name.

5   I seemed to see her around school every day in some of my classes. We had home room together for the freshman year. We sat close to each other because of our last names. At that time, there were not a lot of Asian students in our high school. I also couldn't speak English and understand it. I had to find out what the teacher said. The only Asian student sitting close

10   to me was Linda. I didn't want to disrupt the class. Therefore, I talked to her softly.

1. _____

She was so kind and explained everything to me. Our conversation carried on.

2. _____

_____

3. _____

_____

4. _____

5. _____

The bell rang and we had to go home.
The next morning, I saw her and we smiled at each other.

6. _____

_____

7. _____

_____

On the way to class, she met some of her friends and she introduced them to me. Then we went to class together because we had almost the same classes, except for Math, English and Science. She gave me her phone number and I gave her mine. She called me after school. We talked for a while.

8. _____

_____

9. _____

_____

10. _____

_____

She gave me the confidence to live in a foreign land and told me a lot about living in New York.

DIRECT STATEMENTS AND QUESTIONS

1. I had to ask her what did the teacher say
2. I asked her where are you from I am from Viet Nam, and how come you understand everything
3. She answered I am from China and my English is not good but the teacher uses simple English
4. I asked her how long have you been in the U.S.
5. She answered I have been here since 8th grade in junior high school
6. She said I am very surprised to hear you speak Chinese so fluently and without a Vietnamese accent
7. I said my parents are Chinese, and I was born in Viet Nam. I speak Chinese more often and better than Vietnamese
8. She asked me do you have any problem in classes that you don't understand
9. If I said yes she explained to me clearly and patiently in a friendly way
10. She called me up and said please call me any time if you need help

3. Direct and Reported Statements

The following essay contains places where the writer used statements in reported speech. Find those places and rewrite them as direct speech.

Which form is more effective in this essay? Why do you think so? Discuss your opinion with some other students.

Passage 13-E   **UNCLE TOY**
by Vanessa Cheong

Uncle Toy was my father's best friend. They knew each other since they were boys, so I knew him since I was born. My mother told me that he visited me on the second day of my birth.

He wanted to welcome his little sweetheart to this crazy world. He was
5   so happy. It seemed that he had just got his own daughter.

Uncle Toy was a very big man. He was about six feet and two hundred pounds. He had a full beard. I didn't like his mustache because it made me very uncomfortable when he kissed me. However, he loved his mustache. I remember that whenever I asked him to get shaved, he would say that he
10   wouldn't do that because nobody would know him without his beard. It was his symbol.

Uncle Toy lived in Hong Kong alone. All his family members had emigrated to Australia. Uncle Toy didn't want to leave Hong Kong. He said that he was born there and had grown up there. It was his home. He added that most of
15   his business was in Hong Kong.

Uncle Toy was a very special person in my life; besides a father, he was like my friend. He always listened to me. Sometimes he would ask me my opinion about something. That gave me a feeling that I was important and we were in an equal position. Whenever I asked him questions, he would
20   give me good answers. Unlike my father, he never said that I was too young to know those things. Therefore, I told him everything. I shared my secrets with him because he never laughed at my childish ideas.

4. Quoted and Reported Speech and Questions

Form a group with two other people. Decide on three interesting topics that you would like to talk about. Each person will have a role: one person will be the interviewer who asks the questions; the second person will respond to the questions with information and ideas, and the third person will be the "recorder," who is responsible for writing down what each person says. Set a time limit for the interview, starting with two minutes.

The recorder should not worry about correct grammar and punctuation until after the interview. The final edited version should have the correct punctuation and paragraphing.

After the edited version of the interview is finished, the recorder should rewrite the interview as reported speech, giving a summary of what was said.

The activity should continue so that each person has a chance to be interviewer, responder, and recorder.

Making Your Writing More Sophisticated

14

CHAPTER

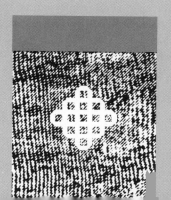

*S*ophisticated writing is a combination of many features, especially word choice and sentence structure. In this chapter, we examine six ways to make your writing more interesting: compounding, inserting additional information, embedding, shifting, inverting, and varying sentence structure. Five of these—compounding, inserting additional information, embedding, shifting, and using sentence variety— are common features of sophisticated writing. Inverting, however, is rare and performs a special discourse function.

The following essay is an example of sophisticated student writing.

Passage 14-A   **THE GALAPAGOS ISLANDS (Part 1)**

by Jaime Zaldumbide

Six hundred miles from the Ecuadorian coast, on the equinoctial line, there is a group of small islands called "El Archipelago de Colon" or, as the world knows them, "The Galapagos Islands." They owe their name to the giant Galapagos tortoises that inhabit the islands. . . .

5   1835 was a special year for the islands and for the world in general. Charles Darwin, on his trip around the world, landed there. He was so impressed by the fauna and the flora existing in this place that he presented the islands as the base of his theory of evolution; in 1859 he published a book, *The Origin of Species*. From that day on, the islands have attracted
10   scientists as well as simple tourists from all over the world.

The islands are alienated from modern life. The Ecuadorian government, which is trying to preserve them in their natural state, has enacted some laws forbidding the introduction and use of modern things. For this reason, also, UNESCO has declared the islands "the cultural patrimony of the world."
15   By doing so, UNESCO can provide the support necessary to conserve this Galapagos garden intact. With the creation of the Charles Darwin station, scientists can dedicate themselves exclusively, and in a scientific way, to the preservation and study of the islands' flora and fauna.

The archipelago has 2800 square miles of land, surrounded by 2300
20   square miles of water. It is formed of several small islands, thirteen medium ones, and a large one. The islands are of volcanic origin; most of them are rocky and covered with loose sand. The land is in general barren, having craters that give it the look of the land on the moon. Some islands have volcanic soil strewn with ashes and lava.

1. COMPOUNDING

You can put more information into your writing by making lists. In a list, you group ideas that are related by the process of addition. In writing, you can combine many different kinds of units into lists, but you must be careful about punctuation and about parallel structure.

1.1 Punctuating Lists

Compounding is usually done with *and*, occasionally with *but* or *or*. In American English, lists of two contain <u>no</u> commas, while lists of three or more have commas after each item except the last. Although the comma before the coordinator is optional in a list of more than two, some teachers insist on it. (For the rules about compounding independent clauses, which are different from the rules for all other lists, see Chapter 4, Section 1.)

Compounding Noun Phrases
. . . and it has <u>a beautiful bay</u>
    <u>*and* broken down craters</u> (Passage 14-A, Part 2)

It is formed of <u>several small islands,</u>
        <u>thirteen medium ones,</u>
        <u>*and* a large one</u>. (Passage 14-A, Part 1)

Compounding Predicates
She <u>was dorm mistress for the 5th and 7th year seniors</u>
    <u>*and* was also in charge of the school uniforms.</u> (Passage 3-A)

People <u>live in today,</u>
    <u>reflect about yesterday,</u>
    <u>*and* anticipate the tomorrow that is to come</u>. (Passage 4-B)

Compounding Verbal Phrases
The 13th day of every month we organized a church mass
    <u>to remember the day</u>
    <u>*and* to pray for the ones remaining in prisons</u>
        <u>*and* killed by the police.</u> (Passage 14-H)

We heard and read about <u>distributing political leaflets,</u>
        <u>harboring people,</u>
        <u>concealing our feelings,</u>
        <u>*and* covering up the truth during police interrogations</u>.
    (Passage 14-H)

Compounding Prepositional Phrases (rarely more than two)
1835 was a special year <u>for the islands</u>
<u>*and* for the world in general</u>. (Passage 14-A, Part 1)

Compounding *Wh*-clauses (rarely more than two)
But they all helped to see more clearly
<u>what it is that I like to do</u>
<u>*and*, equally important, which activities I am good at</u>. (Passage 10-C)

Compounding Subject-Predicates (inside a subordinate clause)
The Galapagos Islands, besides having one of the most spectacular
flora and fauna in the world, are perhaps the only place
<u>where men can be in contact with nature</u>
<u>*and* animals are not afraid of men</u>. (Passage 14-A, Part 2)

Compounding Independent Clauses
The rules for compounding independent clauses are given in Chapter 4. In modern American English, it is unusual to find more than two independent clauses in the same sentence (Example 1). Sometimes, however, it is appropriate to combine three independent clauses that are closely related in structure and content (Example 2). Occasionally, a series of separate sentences that are close in structure can create a powerful effect (Example 3).

1. <u>Bands are playing,</u>
    <u>singers are singing,</u>
    <u>*and* the whole crowd is enjoying the ride</u>. (Passage 5-C)

2. <u>*We collected* money for the families of the arrested</u>
    <u>*and* of those who lost their jobs;</u>
    <u>*we visited* each other;</u>
    <u>*we typed* at home leaflets with patriotic poetry and slogans</u>. (Passage 14-H)

3. Instead of this bright future,
    <u>*they gave us* coupons for food that we could buy after standing every day in long lines</u>.
    <u>*They gave us* the 20-year waiting period for our apartment</u>.
    <u>*They gave us* police to prevent our attempts at improving the situation</u>.
    <u>*They gave us* censorship to have even our thoughts under control</u>. (Passage 14-H)

1.2 Maintaining Parallel Structure

When writing a list, it is important that each item in the list be the same kind of structure, that is, all noun phrases, all *-ing* verbal phrases, all *wh*-clauses, etc. If your list has different structures in it, your reader will be confused about which items belong in your list. Often, but not always, the beginning item in a list signals the kind of parallel structure that follows.

- In the following list, the writer cannot decide whether she is making a list of prepositional phrases or of verbal phrases.

INCORRECT: We heard and read _about_ distributing political leaflets,
about harboring people,
concealing our feelings,
and covering up the truth during
police interrogations. (Passage 14-H)

CORRECT: We heard and read about distribut_ing_ political leaflets,
harbor_ing_ people,
conceal_ing_ our feelings,
and cover_ing_ up the truth during
police interrogations.

- In the following sentence, it is difficult to know what items the writer wants in his list. Is it a list of two or of three?

CONFUSING: It is common to see animals playing with men,
birds sitting on the shoulders of tourists,
and, sometimes, visitors have the opportunity to bathe
with seals. (Passage 14-A, Part 2)

From the content—the difference between _common_ and _sometimes_—the writer appears to want a list of two, followed by a second independent clause.

CORRECT: It is common to see animals playing with men
and birds sitting on the shoulders of tourists;
sometimes, visitors have the opportunity to bathe with seals.

- In the following sentence, the lack of parallel structure is distracting to the reader. In a later draft of the essay, which is not included in this book, the student corrected the problem.

DISTRACTING: I can do things comfortably,
and I don't have to worry what other people think of me,
to the way I act,
and to look or dress.

CORRECT: I can do things comfortably,
and I don't have to worry about _what_ other people think of me,
how I act,
and how I look or dress.

2. INSERTING ADDITIONAL INFORMATION

You can add information to the basic sentence by inserting additional material. Understanding how to use inserts will help you write more complex and interesting text.

2.1 Positions of Inserts

Although inserts can occur almost anywhere within the sentence, they are most frequently found in three positions: before the subject, after the subject, and after the predicate or adverbial. A caret (^) is used to indicate the common positions for inserts.

Adverbial, ^, Subject, ^, Predicate Adverbial, ^.

- before the subject

    Six hundred miles from the Ecuadorian coast, <u>on the equinoctial line</u>, there is a group of small islands called "El Archipelago de Colon" or, as the world knows them, "The Galapagos Islands." (Passage 14-A, Part 1)

- after the subject

    The Ecuadorian government, <u>which is trying to preserve them in their natural state</u>, has enacted some laws forbidding the introduction and use of modern things. (Passage 14-A, Part 1)

- after the predicate

    The land is in general barren, <u>having craters that give it the look of the land on the moon</u>. (Passage 14-A, Part 1)

2.2 Forms of Inserts

Although any construction can be used as an insert, the most common inserts are noun phrases, *wh*-clauses, and *-ing* verbal phrases. Noun phrases used as inserts are also called **appositives.**

- noun phrases

    The waters surrounding the islands are green, <u>a transparent green</u>. (Passage 14-A, Part 2)

    He published a book, *The Origin of Species*. (Passage 14-A, Part 1)

- *wh*-clauses

    On Santa Cruz, we have Puerto Oyora, <u>where the hotels are located</u>, the

Charles Darwin Scientific Station, and the Vann Straellen Center. (Passage 14-A, Part 1)

The Ecuadorian government, <u>which is trying to preserve them in their natural state</u>, has enacted some laws forbidding the introduction and use of modern things. (Passage 14-A, Part 1)

• *-ing* verbal phrases

The land is in general barren, <u>having craters that give it the look of the land on the moon</u>. (Passage 14-A, Part 1)

• other forms of insert

Water is found all year on San Cristobal Island, <u>thanks to rain</u>. (Passage 14-A, Part 2)

Today, the world can admire, <u>with the same wonder</u>, that nature that Charles Darwin marveled at more than a century ago. (Passage 14-A, Part 2)

This case is unique in the world because, <u>as is well-known</u>, penguins belong to icy climates. (Passage 14-A, Part 2)

WHEN YOU ARE WRITING

If you have written two sentences in a row that have the same subject, try combining them by making one into an insert.

• noun phrase insert

Shanghai is the leading industrial and commercial city in China. It is one of the world's largest ports. (from Passage 4-F)

Shanghai, <u>one of the world's largest ports</u>, is the leading industrial and commercial city in China.

• *wh*-clause insert

Shanghai is the leading industrial and commercial city of China. It is also the most important foreign trade center. (Passage 4-F)

Shanghai, <u>which is the leading industrial and commercial city of China</u>, is also the most important foreign trade center.

• *-ing* insert

There I am again. I am standing in the middle of the village like a ghost, brought by one of my memories of this place. (Passage 7-B)

There I am again, <u>standing in the middle of the village like a ghost, brought by one of my memories of this place</u>.

2.3 Functions of Inserts

Inserts always add something that is grammatically extra rather than something that is essential to the sentence. For that reason, you can always remove an insert, and the sentence will remain grammatically complete and correct, even though it will lose its "extra" information.

There are two kinds of inserts that are common: the writer's opinion and extra information. In the following examples, we have given the sentence without the insert first, followed by the sentence as the student wrote it, with an insert.

2.3a Writer's Opinion

An insert enables you to say briefly, but effectively, what you think about the information in your sentence.

The land is barren.

The land is, <u>unfortunately</u>, barren. (adapted from Passage 14-A, Part 1)

2.3b Additional Information

You can add additional information either to a part of the sentence or, if the insert is at the end, to the entire sentence.

- about a subject

    The Ecuadorian government has enacted some laws forbidding the introduction and use of modern things.

    The Ecuadorian government, <u>which is trying to preserve them in their natural state</u>, has enacted some laws forbidding the introduction and use of modern things. (Passage 14-A, Part 1)

- about an object

    In 1859, he published a book.

    In 1859, he published a book, *The Origin of Species*. (Passage 14-A, Part 1)

- about the entire independent clause

    The land is, in general, barren.

    The land is, in general, barren, <u>having craters that give it the look of the land on the moon</u>. (Passage 14-A, Part 1)

2.4 Punctuation of Inserts

There are four ways to punctuate inserts: with commas, colons, dashes, and parentheses. *Wh*-clauses require special attention.

2.4a Commas, Colons, Dashes, and Parentheses

• Commas are usually used to set off an insert from the rest of the sentence.

At 6:00 A.M. and 6:00 P.M., we can see one of the marvels of nature**,** the sunrise and sunset. (Passage 14-A, Part 2)

Charles Darwin**,** on his trip around the world**,** landed there. (Passage 14-A, Part 1)

• Colons most often indicate a list at the end of a sentence but may indicate an explanation of the previous independent clause.

The streets are full of talented people**:** musicians and singers, store owners, and people who enjoy walking and listening to others perform. (Passage 5-C)

So when the time comes, and if possible, we make a choice**:** Either we get an education to learn and develop the skills that will be applied later, or we learn on site. (Passage 10-C)

It started with a short statement like this**:** Objective: To obtain a position as a Word Processing Specialist. (Passage 6-B)

• Dashes set off lists inside a sentence or, especially in British English, are inserted at the end, where an American might use a colon. Dashes are becoming more common in American English.

This is a terrible habit**—**procrastination. (Passage 4-B)

I lived in a small and quiet city which never was in the mainstream of social upheaval in 1980 when "Solidarity" came into being, but the number of arrests and missing people were significant**—**75 percent of the active members. (Passage 14-H)

It was filled in first with committed time**—**eating, sleeping, dressing, school, etc. (Passage 4-B)

• Parentheses set off material that is extraneous to the surrounding sentence, especially author comments.

In our western society **(**that is the only one I can account for**)** we are taught that we should be productive. (Passage 10-C)

These duties included making breakfast in the morning, changing diapers four times a day, going to the park (<u>if it was a warm day</u>), cooking, putting the babies to sleep and dressing them to go back home at six in the afternoon. (Passage 10-C)

2.4b Punctuating *Wh*-clauses

One kind of insert, the *wh*-clause, causes punctuation problems for writers because it is easily confused with another kind of *wh*-clause that follows a noun. These two kinds of *wh*-clauses are traditionally called **nonrestrictive** and **restrictive.** The distinction between the two *wh*-clauses is difficult but important because the two kinds of clauses mean different things and are punctuated differently. (See Chapter 6, Section 2.3 and this chapter, Section 3.)

(1) *Wh*-clause as Postmodifier (Restrictive Clause)
A *wh*-clause after a noun is a modifier of the noun, making it more specific. It restricts, identifies, defines, narrows, or limits the noun it follows. It is required by the context: It is not an insert; it is not extra; it cannot be taken out.

Also, the number of people <u>who can visit the island</u> is limited by the Institute and the Ecuadorian government. (Passage 14-A, Part 2)

The *wh*-clause cannot be taken out without confusing the reader.

Also, the number of people . . . is limited by the Institute and the Ecuadorian government.

There is an information gap. What people?

This is the only place in the world <u>where both iguanas can be seen at the same time</u>. (Passage 14-A, Part 2)

If you try to take the *wh*-clause out of this example, the sentence becomes nonsense.

This is the only place in the world. . . .

"This is" certainly not "the only place in the world"! But it is "the only place where both iguanas can be seen at the same time."

Because the restricted clause is required, it is <u>never</u> separated from the core noun by commas.

(2) *Wh*-clause as Insert (Nonrestrictive Clause)
In contrast, a *wh*-clause that is inserted in the sentence adds extra information. It can be taken out because it does not specify, limit, or define what is being talked about. In the following examples, the sentence is given first with the *wh*-clause and then without it.

The Ecuadorian government**,** <u>which is trying to preserve them in their natural state</u>**,** has enacted some laws forbidding the introduction and use of modern things. (Passage 14-A, Part 1)

The Ecuadorian government has enacted some laws forbidding the introduction and use of modern things.

The insert can be taken out because it is not necessary to identify the Ecuadorian government. The Ecuadorian government is a known entity; there is only one national government in Ecuador.

On Santa Cruz, we have Puerto Oyora**, where the hotels are located,** the Charles Darwin Scientific Station, and the Vann Straellen Center. (Passage 14-A, Part 2)

On Santa Cruz, we have Puerto Oyora, the Charles Darwin Scientific Station and the Vann Straellen Center.

The insert can be taken out because Puerto Oyora is a known entity. The insert adds <u>extra</u> information about Puerto Oyora. You do not need that information to tell what the writer is talking about.

The distinction between an identifying *wh*-clause (restrictive) and an "extra information" *wh*-clause (nonrestrictive) can be difficult to make. Should you use a comma before the two *wh*-clauses in the following sentence?

But the biggest struggle was probably with the memories, especially the memories <u>which were wounding the soul</u>, and the longing for his family and his mother <u>whom he would never see again</u>. (Passage 8-F)

If you do not put a comma after *memories,* the sentence means that Shilloh's father is struggling with only <u>some</u> memories—those that were wounding his soul. If you do put a comma after *memories,* the sentence means that Shilloh's father is struggling with many more memories, <u>all</u> of which were wounding his soul.

If you do not put a comma after *mother,* never seeing her again becomes a defining property of his *mother.* If you do put a comma after mother, you have added information about her. Because the meaning of leaving out the comma is so subtle, you should probably put it in, because Shilloh's mother is a definite, identified person.

WHEN YOU ARE WRITING

When you see a noun followed by a *wh*-clause, ask yourself:

Do I need the information in the *wh*-clause to tell my reader what the noun is referring to?

If the answer is yes, do not use commas around the *wh*-clause.
If the answer is no, put commas around the *wh*-clause.

Embedding, putting units inside of other units, is a major way to make writing more sophisticated. In all writing, embedding often occurs in the object position. (See Chapter 11, Section 2.) In sophisticated writing, one particular kind of embedding, the expanded noun phrase followed by a clause, occurs occasionally. In the following examples, we have underlined first the noun phrase, then the clause that modifies it. The core noun is marked with an asterisk (*).

1. On that day, in 1981, the Polish government set up the state of <u>martial law which was supposed to smash and completely destroy the social and union trade movement called "Solidarity."</u> (Passage 14-H)

The underlined noun phrase is expanded with both a premodifier and a complex postmodifier.

> martial law <u>which was supposed to smash and completely destroy the</u>
> *   <u>social and trade union movement called "Solidarity"</u>

2. I lived in <u>a small and quiet city which never was in the mainstream of social upheaval until 1980 when "Solidarity" came into being.</u> (Passage 14-H)

The underlined noun phrase again is expanded with both a premodifier and a complex postmodifier.

> a small and quiet city <u>which never was in the mainstream of social upheaval</u>
> *   <u>until 1980 when "Solidarity" came into being</u>

3. This campaign was created by <u>some statesmen whose aim was to realize their political ambition of owning the right to rule the whole of China by praising Chairman Mao.</u> (Passage 6-A)

The underlined noun phrase is expanded with both a premodifier and an unusually complicated postmodifier, which is a *wh*-clause.

> some statesmen <u>whose aim was to realize their political ambition of</u>
> *   <u>owning the right to rule the whole of China by praising</u>
>   <u>Chairman Mao</u>

Such embedding is a mark of complex, sophisticated writing. (See Chapter 6, Section 2.3 for how to construct *wh*-clauses as postmodifiers.)

Who, which, or that

A *wh*-clause as a postmodifier can begin with a *wh*-word or *that*. (See Chapter 6, Section 2.3.)

• If the clause begins with *that*, it is clearly a postmodifier; it identifies and defines.

342

But the biggest struggle was probably with the memories, especially the memories <u>that were wounding the soul</u>, and the longing for his family and his mother, whom he would never see again. (Passage 8-F)

- If it begins with a *wh*-word, the clause can be understood either as defining the noun or as extra information. (See this chapter, Section 2.4.) If the writer wants to express clearly that the information is "extra," commas should be added.

But the biggest struggle was probably with the memories, especially the memories, <u>which were wounding the soul</u>, and the longing for his family and his mother, whom he would never see again.

- If a restrictive clause is separated from the noun, however, the clause usually begins with a *wh*-word. In the example, the noun phrase is underlined, the core noun is marked with an asterisk (*), and the *wh*-word is in italics.

Aside from all the television publicity, he has also had <u>many offers by music producers</u> *which* <u>would have given him the opportunity to become famous if he had chosen to quit his street music</u>. (Passage 10-B)

    *

4. SHIFTING AND INVERTING

Moving units out of their usual and expected place in sentences creates emphasis or special focus.

4.1 Shifting

You may put a unit at the beginning of a sentence for a variety of reasons related to emphasis, focus, and cohesion. In other contexts, a unit containing similar information could be found at the end of the sentence.

<u>Six hundred miles from the Ecuadorian coast</u>, on the equinoctial line, there is a group of small islands called "El Archipelago de Colon" or, as the world knows them, "the Galapagos Islands." (Passage 14-A, Part 1)

This time she is talking on a wireless telephone supported by one of her shoulders. <u>To save time</u>, her experienced hands are continuously cutting the carrots and tomatoes. (Passage 3-C)

This does not mean that they should forget their own language and customs. <u>Because their customs and language are something which they inherited through the passage of time and past generations</u>, they should not be dismissed lightly. (Passage 3-D)

The beginning of the sentence is the place to make clear how your sentence is related to the previous one. You often do this by careful use of transition words and phrases and of sentence adverbials. (See Chapter 4 and Chapter 3, Section 2.3.)

LEARNING STRATEGY

Forming Concepts: Studying how other people make transitions helps you improve your writing.

4.2 Inverting

On rare occasions, you will see inverted sentences. In an inverted sentence, the usual order of the subject and auxiliary or the subject and verb is reversed. In the examples, to show the special emphasis that inverting creates, we give first the writer's original sentence, then a version that is not inverted.

4.2a Inverting After Negatives

Subject-auxiliary inversion is required after three kinds of negative introducers.

1. after the negative coordinators: *neither* and *nor, not only* and *but also,* and *no sooner . . . than*

   She maybe doesn't remember me since I was a very quiet student,

   Neg   Aux   S

   <u>nor   does   she</u>   know her words are still alive in my heart and have changed my thinking. (Passage 4-A)

   She maybe doesn't remember me since I was a very quiet student, <u>and she does not</u> know her words are still alive in my heart and have changed my thinking.

       Neg   Aux   S

   <u>No sooner   had   Mr. Kean</u> stepped into the classroom than he noticed me. . . . (from a student essay not in this book)

   <u>Mr. Kean had no sooner</u> stepped into the classroom than he noticed me . . .

2. after negative adverbs: *never, rarely, seldom, hardly ever, only, barely, little*

     Neg   Aux   S

   <u>Never   had   Charles Darwin</u>   imagined such a sight.

   <u>Charles Darwin had never</u> imagined such a sight.

3. after negative phrases: *not once, not since, not for, not until, in no case, in no way, no way* (informal), *nowhere*

Neg   *Aux*   *S*

<u>On none of the islands</u>   can   we   find the comfort we are used to.
(Passage 14-A, Part 2)

<u>We cannot</u> find the comfort we are used to on any of the islands.

                                        Neg   *Aux*   *S*

It has been ten years. Still,   <u>not once</u>   has   she   set foot in a
classroom. (Passage 7-B)

It has been ten years. Still, <u>she has not once</u> set foot in a classroom.

4.2b Inverting for Emphasis

Inversion for emphasis is optional and rare. It is done for information structuring and for stylistic variety. The end positions in the sentence usually contain new information and have special prominence. Writers can play with these end positions to create special effects.

At sunrise we can see the rainbow in the sky reflected in the water, and finally <u>out comes the sun</u>. (Passage 14-A, Part 2)

. . . and finally <u>the sun comes out</u>.

<u>Across the river is a colorful spread: red, white, and green</u>. (Passage 5-C)

<u>A colorful spread—red, white, and green—is across the river</u>.

By inverting the sentences above, the writers have called attention to their topics. In the first sentence, the writer has emphasized the importance of the sun's appearance by putting *the sun* in the sentence final position. In the second example, the inversion has not only focused on the topic but has also enabled the writer to add a list of colors to her topic, *a colorful spread: red, white, and green.*

WHEN YOU ARE WRITING

Very occasionally when you are editing, try playing with your own style by inverting. Look particularly at your sentences that begin with *there*. Would any be more effective as inverted sentences?

<u>There</u> was a small waterfall with water running from the top of the hill into a river. (Passage 5-D)

<u>Running from the top of the hill into a river was a small waterfall</u>.

In addition, <u>there</u> were colorful flowers along the fence on both sides. (Passage 5-D)

In addition, <u>along the fence on both sides were colorful flowers</u>.

Do not use inversion very often. It is powerful because it is so rare.

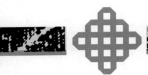

5. USING SENTENCE VARIETY

Sophisticated writing always contains a variety of sentence patterns, not just simple sentences. The two passages below are complicated in different ways, but one way is considered more sophisticated than the other. Compare the two paragraphs for compound units, inserts, embedded clauses, and adverbials at the beginning of the sentences. Also, look at how the transitions are made between sentences, especially the use of transition words and phrases and sentence adverbials. (For more about transition words and sentence adverbials, see Chapter 3, Section 2 and Chapter 4, Section 2.)

A. Passage 14-B   COMPUTERS (Part 1)

by Lai Kuen Wong

1. There is no doubt that the computer is a helpful invention in the twentieth century.
2. It helps people to save time, to search for information, and to do calculations accurately.
3. It is widely used in such businesses as department stores for keeping inventories, post offices for mailing letters, and gas stations for ringing up sales.
4. It is also used in schools.
5. The computer is a tool that can help students with their term papers.
6. The students can write and revise their essays easily.
7. They can benefit from computers as well as professors.

B. Passage 14-A   THE GALAPAGOS ISLANDS (Part 1)

by Jaime Zaldumbide

1. The islands are alienated from modern life.
2. The Ecuadorian government, which is trying to preserve them in their natural state, has enacted some laws forbidding the introduction and use of modern things.
3. For this reason, also, UNESCO has declared the islands "the cultural patrimony of the world."
4. By doing so, UNESCO can provide the support necessary to conserve this Galapagos garden intact.
5. With the creation of the Charles Darwin station, scientists can dedicate themselves exclusively, and in a scientific way, to the preservation and study of the islands' flora and fauna.

346

6. AN EXAMPLE OF SOPHISTICATED WRITING

Sophisticated writers use many devices at once to make their writing polished. Henry David Thoreau, a nineteenth century American writer, is well known for his sophisticated prose style. Below is the first paragraph from his famous essay on civil disobedience. Thoreau uses compounding, parallel structure, inserting, and inverting.

Passage 14-C   **RESISTANCE TO CIVIL GOVERNMENT**

by Henry David Thoreau

I heartily accept the motto,—"That government is best which governs least;" and I should like to see it acted up to more rapidly and systematically. Carried out, it finally amounts to this, which also I believe,—"That government is best which governs not at all;" and when men are prepared
5   for it, that will be the kind of government which they will have. Government is at best but an expedient; but most governments are usually, and all governments are sometimes, inexpedient. The objections which have been brought against a standing army, and they are many and weighty, and deserve to prevail, may also at last be brought against a standing government. The
10   standing army is only an arm of the standing government. The government itself, which is only the mode which the people have chosen to execute their will, is equally liable to be abused and perverted before the people can act through it. Witness the present Mexican war, the work of comparatively a few individuals using the standing government as their tool; for, in the
15   outset, the people would not have consented to this measure.

       —from *Walden and Civil Disobedience,* edited by Owen Thomas, Norton, 1966, p. 224

6.1 Compounding by Thoreau

Some of Thoreau's compounding and use of parallel structures are displayed below.

I heartily accept the motto, . . .
and I should like to see it acted up to more rapidly and systematically.

"That government is best which governs not at all" . . .
and . . . that will be the kind of government which they will have.

Government is at best but an expedient; but
most governments are usually
and all governments are sometimes inexpedient.

347

> The objections which have been brought against a standing army,
> and they are many
> > *and* weighty
> > *and* deserve to prevail
>
> The government . . . is equally liable to be abused
> > *and* perverted . . .

6.2 Inserting by Thoreau

All the inserts in the passage have been underlined.

> I heartily accept the motto,—"<u>That government is best which governs least</u>;" and I should like to see it acted up to more rapidly and systematically. <u>Carried out</u>, it finally amounts to this, <u>which also I believe</u>,—"<u>That government is best which governs not at all</u>;" and when men are prepared
> 5 for it, that will be the kind of government which they will have. Government is at best but an expedient; but most governments are usually, <u>and all governments are sometimes</u>, inexpedient. The objections which have been brought against a standing army, <u>and they are many and weighty, and deserve to prevail</u>, may also at last be brought against a standing government. The
> 10 standing army is only an arm of the standing government. The government itself, <u>which is only the mode which the people have chosen to execute their will</u>, is equally liable to be abused and perverted before the people can act through it. Witness the present Mexican war, <u>the work of comparatively a few individuals using the standing government as their tool</u>; for, in the
> 15 outset, the people would not have consented to this measure.

6.3 Inverting by Thoreau

Later on in his essay, Thoreau uses two inversions. First, we give the passage in which it occurs, then the normal or expected order of the elements, finally the inverted clause taken out of its context.

1. What makes this duty the more urgent is the fact that the country so overrun is not our own, but <u>ours is the invading army</u>.

	S	*V*	
normal order:	the invading army	is	ours

	V	*S*	
inverted order:	ours	is	the invading army

2. Thus, under the name of order and civil government, we are all made at last

to pay homage to and support our own meanness. <u>After the first blush of sin comes its indifference</u> and from immoral it becomes, as it were <u>un</u>moral, and not quite unnecessary to that life which we have made.

	S	V	
normal order:	<u>its indifference</u>	<u>comes</u>	<u>after the first blush of sin</u>

	V	S	
inverted order:	<u>after the first blush of sin</u>	<u>comes</u>	<u>its indifference</u>

In both of these inversions, the topic receives special emphasis by being put at the end.

In his sophisticated writing, Thoreau uses several of the features we discuss in this chapter—compounding, inserting, and inverting—as well as others, especially long sentences and elegant vocabulary. His style is characteristic of good writing of his time. Today, however, we have become much less formal in our writing, as we have in other areas of our lives. Many good writers today write more simply than Thoreau even though they use the same processes.

LEARNING STRATEGY

Forming Concepts: Studying classic texts helps you see the richness of English grammar.

 **ACTIVITIES**

I. Correcting Faulty Parallelism

Correct the faulty parallelisms taken from the early drafts of student essays. There may be more than one way to repair the sentence. Check your work with a partner.

1. He looks very young, handsome and has a strong body.
2. My older sister is tall, has medium length black hair, and she is not fat, not skinny.
3. She wears old-fashioned clothes, very long dresses, and usually colorful.
4. He chooses schools, friends for you, and tells you what kind of clothes you should wear.
5. I think that if they gave me a choice between writing a lot and reading a lot, I would choose writing, even though I have problems with spelling, forming paragraphs, or clearing up what I want to write about, or what my major point in the essay is.

2. Correcting Faulty Parallelism

The following paragraph from an early draft contains a number of problems with parallel structure. Working with a partner, discuss what you think the writer is trying to express. Then write your version of her essay, being careful to express parallel ideas in parallel structures.

Passage 14-D   **MY MOTHER**

by Valerie Lopez

When I converse with my mom on a certain topic and feeling uncomfortable nor able to find the proper words to say, she helps me out with what I'm trying to say by the questions she asks me and somehow the conversation turns into something easy and directed. She often advises me
5   softly and intelligently. Though she often scolds me for my misbehavior, especially my studies and going to mass, that I pursue pleasure before responsibilities, it is because of our differences in beliefs. I know she tries her best to bring me up properly and the way she was brought up taught to me is one conflict that we have.

3. Replacing Inserts

In the following essay, the inserts have been removed and placed at the end. Blanks (_____) show where the inserts were in the essay. Put the number of each insert in the appropriate blank, and indicate where commas are needed. (For the correct version of this essay, see Appendix 2.)

Passage 14-E   **ACUPUNCTURE**

by Yoon Ok Cha

Acupuncture was an ancient Chinese medical technique for relieving pain, curing disease, and improving general health. It was devised before 2500 BC in China, and by the late 20th century was used in many other areas of the world.
5   Acupuncture grew out of ancient Chinese philosophy's dualistic cosmic theory of the "Yin" and "Yang." The "Yin" _____ is passive and dark and is represented by the Earth; the "Yang" _____ is active and light and is represented by the heavens. Disease or physical disharmony is caused by an imbalance or undue preponderance of these two forces in
10   the body, and the goal of Chinese medicine was to bring the "Yin" and the "Yang" back into balance with each other _____.

An imbalance of "Yin" and "Yang" results in an obstruction of the vital life force in the body _____. The fundamental energy of the Oi flows through 12 meridians _____ in the body _____.

15   Acupuncture appears to be undeniably effective in relieving pain and is routinely used in China as an anesthetic during surgery. The evidence now indicates that acupuncture can induce analgesia and that its use is associated with measurable physiological changes. Recent medical reviews show that acupuncture is slowly beginning to be integrated into certain areas of
20   Western medicine.

INSERTS

1. each of which is in turn associated with a major visceral organ (liver, kidney, heart, etc.) and with a functional body system.
2. the female principle
3. or Oi
4. thus restoring the person to health
5. or pathways
6. the male principle

4. Placing Inserts

The inserts have been removed from the following essay and placed at the end. Read the essay through. Then decide where you think the inserts could be placed in the essay and how they should be punctuated. Work with a partner. Compare your work with that of another group. (For a correct version of this essay, see Appendix 2.)

Passage 14-F   **MY BEST FRIEND**

by Honorata Lewicka

The special person that I can easily talk about is my best friend. Our friendship started some twenty-five years ago in Poland. For the next eight years, we shared a school desk. After that, we went to different schools. We lost contact with each other for over a year. To our own surprise, we got
5   reunited in this huge country of the USA.

Irena is 32 years old. She is about 5'6" tall and has brown hair and eyes. She is of medium build with short legs. Her usual wardrobe is a pair of jeans or a skirt and a sweatshirt. Simple dressing makes Irena more comfortable, and it doesn't take time. Occasionally, she dresses with great elegance and

10 style. To the most simple dresses, she adds some touches that make the simplest dress look like it just came from a fashion magazine.

INSERTS

1. which she needs because she has five children and a husband
2. where we both started our education.
3. exchanging her everyday look for the glamour look
4. which were in far-away cities
5. who is one of a kind

5. Punctuating *Wh*-clauses

The following essay contains several underlined *wh*-clauses. Put commas around any *wh*-clauses that need them. Why do they need them? Do this with a partner or in a small group. (For a correct version of this essay, see Appendix 2.)

Passage 14-G   **MY HOMETOWN**

by Liyan Gu

I was born in Shanghai, but I moved to a little town with my parents when I was one year old. The town which was located 100 miles from Shanghai was a very pleasant place with approximately 2,000 people. That place left me the most wonderful memories and played an important role in
5   my life. I learned how to enjoy the wonderful world.

My house which stood at the corner of the widest street was on the most exciting street in that town. The other streets in the town were so narrow that people always went to the widest street to buy or sell things. During the day, this street formed a market. I think that is the reason why my
10   house was always full of people. My house which was two stories high was one of the biggest houses in town. The house itself which was shaped like a pyramid contained 14 rooms.

6. Punctuating *Wh*-clauses (Advanced)

The following essay contains several underlined *wh*-clauses. Put commas around any *wh*-clause that needs them. Why have you made the decision to use or not use commas? Remember: If you can take out the *wh*-clause and still identify the noun phrase, you do not need the *wh*-clause because it is an insert. If you cannot take a *which* clause out, try changing the *which* to *that*.

Do this exercise with a partner or in a small group. You can do this exercise over several class meetings. (For a correct version of this essay, see Appendix 2.)

Passage 14-H   **SOLIDARITY**

by Dominika Stanislawska

The thirteenth of December is a very significant day for me. On that day, in 1981, the Polish government set up the state of martial law <u>which was supposed to smash and completely destroy the social and union trade movement called "Solidarity.</u>" Though formally registered, "Solidarity" had

5   never been approved by the Polish and, especially, the Soviet authorities.

At that time I was one of ten million people belonging to "Solidarity." On December 13, 1981, many of my friends <u>who were activists of "Solidarity"</u> were arrested. Those <u>who escaped</u> went into hiding until police discovered the place. I lived in a small and quiet city <u>which never was in the mainstream</u>

10   <u>of social upheaval in 1980 when "Solidarity" came into being,</u> but the number of arrests and missing people were significant—75 percent of the active members. They were mostly men <u>who worked in "Solidarity's" administration</u> and those <u>who were additionally involved in the anticommunist political activity.</u>

15   In many cases these people were the only breadwinners of their families. The arrests left pregnant wives, children, and old parents without their support. Pensions, maternity and family benefits were insufficient to live on. After December 13 employers began to fire the remaining activists and wives of the arrested <u>whose names were entered on the special list that made any</u>

20   <u>employment for them impossible.</u> There were a few cases in my city <u>where fathers were arrested and mothers lost their jobs.</u>

After the first shock, the remaining members and sisters, wives, mothers, and daughters of the arrested gathered together to solve some of the problems. We had to get more information about the victims, arrange financial aid for

25   families, and, especially, support ourselves and alleviate the prevailing distrust of each other. We realized that any political activity at that time was impossible, but we had to raise our spirits. We collected money for the families of the arrested and of those <u>who lost their jobs;</u> we visited each other; we typed at

home leaflets with patriotic poetry and slogans. We tried to maintain the
feeling of solidarity among us. The 13th day of every month we organized a
church mass to remember the day and to pray for the ones remaining in
prisons and killed by police. Despite the ban on traveling, we tried to get to
different parts of the country to gain information and to inform others about
our activity. Step by step we were rebuilding the organization structure
under conspiracy.

I think the sense of conspiracy was in our blood. We inherited it from our
parents and grandparents <u>who used conspiracy during the Second World
War</u>. They were taught the means of conspiracy by their parents and
grandparents <u>who maintained Polish nationality against the attempts of
Russian, German, and Austrian invaders before World War I</u>. We heard and
read about distributing political leaflets, harboring people, concealing our
feelings, and covering up the truth during police interrogations.

We were fascinated by all these stories, but nobody had ever expected
that we would be constrained to make use of those experiences <u>which should
have remained only a history for us</u>. That was one of the most important slogans
of the communist government after World War II—"We will build a new
bright future for our children."

Instead of this bright future, they gave us coupons for food <u>which we
could buy after standing every day in long lines</u>. They gave us the 20 year
waiting period for our apartments. They gave us police to prevent our
attempts at improving the situation. They gave us censorship to have even
our thoughts under control. They imprisoned and ruined people <u>who were
telling them that something must be done about the future</u>.

Our war in 1981 was much more painful and confusing than the ones of
our parents and grandparents. They fought with strangers <u>who invaded
Poland</u>. We had to fight with our "brothers" <u>who were well-armed</u>. In our
defense we had only our strong desire to live better.

7. Interpreting Inserts

Although inserts are not grammatically necessary to have a correct sentence,
they add important information to a text. In the following selection, which is the
rest of the essay at the beginning of this chapter, the inserts have been underlined.

Try taking each one out. What is lost if you do? What kind of information is contained in the inserts? Discuss these questions with a partner or in a small group.

Passage 14-A   **THE GALAPAGOS ISLANDS (Part 2)**

by Jaime Zaldumbide

The Galapagos Islands are on the equinoctial line. This gives the idea of very torrid, hot weather. However, this is not so; <u>thanks to the cold Humboldt current</u>, the weather is springlike. The current gives the islands such changes of weather that we even find penguins. This case is unique in
25 the word because, <u>as is known</u>, penguins belong in icy climates.

We find two kinds of iguanas on the islands, <u>the sea iguana and the land iguana</u>. This is the only place in the world where both iguanas can be seen at the same time. There are land birds. They do not fly; they walk. The species change from island to island; they are totally different from the continental
30 species. Some of the species belong only to these islands.

The Galapagos Islands, <u>besides having one of the most spectacular flora and fauna in the world</u>, are perhaps the only place where men can be in contact with nature and animals are not afraid of men. It is common to see animals playing with men, birds sitting on the shoulders of tourists, and,
35 <u>sometimes</u>, visitors have the opportunity to bathe with seals.

As I mentioned before, there is a large island, <u>the Isabela</u>. This island in reality has not much importance. It is located far from the other islands, and the vegetation is poor. The main island is Santa Cruz, even though the capital is Puerto Baquerio Moreno, <u>on San Cristobal Island</u>. On Santa Cruz, we have
40 Puerto Oyora, <u>where the hotels are located</u>, the Charles Darwin Scientific Station, and the Vann Straellen Center. The last one is an information center for tourists. Water is found all year on San Cristobal Island, <u>thanks to rain</u>, and it has a beautiful bay and a broken down crater. On none of the islands can we find the comfort we are used to. For example, cars are prohibited, so
45 the tours are done on foot. Radios are also prohibited. At 12:00 midnight the lights are turned off. Also, the number of people who can visit the islands is limited by the Institute and the Ecuadorian government.

The waters surrounding the islands are green, <u>a transparent green</u>. At 6:00 A.M. and 6:00 P.M., we can see one of the marvels of nature, <u>the sunrise</u>
50 <u>and sunset</u>. At sunrise we can see the rainbow in the sky reflected in the water, and finally out comes the sun. At sunset it is the opposite, but after this, the evening is totally dark.

Fortunately, civilization has not yet touched, <u>or rather</u>, has not yet destroyed this paradise. Today, the world can admire, <u>with the same wonder</u>,
55 that nature that Charles Darwin marveled at more than a century ago. I hope future generations can have the opportunity to contemplate this marvelous and isolated Pacific world.

8. Correcting Mistakes in Inversion

The following sentences taken from early drafts of student essays each contain a subject and verb that should be inverted but are not. Can you find them and correct them? What is the word that determines that inversion must take place?

1. . . . I have looked at her photo album when she was young and in none of her photos she is wearing pants or short sleeves. I think it has to do with the way she was brought up by her parents.

2. Only if you happen to be the kind of person who can psychologically communicate with her you can be a good friend of hers.

9. Using Sentence Variety

Rewrite Passage 14-B on page 346, using a greater variety of sentences. Try to use coordinated and subordinated clauses, compound structures, and inserts. Pay particular attention to the beginning of your sentences. Share your work with a partner and compare your paragraphs. Which sentences do you particularly like?

10. Using Sentence Variety

The sentences below were taken from a continuation of Passage 14-B. Combine them in a variety of ways to make an interesting paragraph. Try to use coordination, subordination, compounding, and inserting. Work with a partner and compare your work with others in the class. What sentences are especially sophisticated? Why?

Passage 14-B   **COMPUTERS (Part 2)**

by Lai Kuen Wong

1. My writing teacher advises her students to use computers.
2. She said, "It is easier to make changes."
3. I agree with her.
4. I use the computer to write essays for the class.
5. As I type the essay on the screen, I can see my errors easily.
6. I can correct the errors without retyping the whole thing and wasting too much paper.
7. I can add words or spaces.
8. I can take away unwanted words on the screen at any time.
9. After I finish typing, I can check my spelling with the spell check in the computer.
10. The computer does a good job on editing.

11. Identifying the Processes That Make Writing Sophisticated

In the following paragraph, taken from the middle of an essay entitled "Chinese Attitudes Toward English," we have underlined several places where the writer has made the writing sophisticated. Can you identify the process the writer used: compounding, inserting, embedding, or using a sentence adverbial? Do this exercise with a partner or in a small group.

Passage 14-I   **CHINESE ATTITUDES TOWARD ENGLISH**

by Yuan Yan Liu

The greatness of China was proved in the Tang Dynasty. Its capital Chang An, <u>which is called Xian today</u>, was <u>a cosmopolitan city inhabited by a million people</u>. <u>The thriving economy of Tang, the advanced techniques, and the flourishing culture</u> were spread out to the world and, in the
5   meantime, attracted <u>vassals, merchants, missionaries, and visitors from other countries</u>. Unfortunately, the sense of superiority was carried on through the generations until in the Qing Dynasty (1646–1911), it was shattered to pieces by <u>the gunpowder that was invented by the Chinese people but used by the European countries</u>. <u>Being confronted with foreign cannons and</u>
10 <u>opium</u>, the government appeared <u>cowardly and incompetent</u>, and the Chinese people, <u>after putting their country almost at the bottom of the pyramid</u>, automatically found a related position for themselves. The sense of <u>humiliation and inferiority</u> prodded the Chinese to go out to learn from the west and reform China. This was <u>the first time that the Chinese government</u>
15 <u>sent students abroad to study</u> and <u>the first time that many Chinese people went abroad by themselves to learn, not to teach</u>. <u>When the door was forced to open</u>, for centuries the Chinese were put in an inferior position <u>in both their motherland and other countries</u>. <u>All the reforms that were trying to strengthen China</u> again led to fruitlessness. The once <u>great and strong</u>
20 empire was reduced to a <u>semi-colonial and semi-feudal</u> country. The Chinese people had no chance to know what superiority "tasted" like. They hated those foreign invaders, but in the meantime they felt <u>inferior to them and afraid of them</u>. The feelings of <u>hatred and fear</u> went down into history. Today, people over seventy still carry these feelings with them.

Punctuation Summary

1

APPENDIX

*P*unctuation conventions change over time. There are also a few differences between British and American usage. Below we give the punctuation conventions for contemporary standard written American English.

1. THE PERIOD

Use a period at the end of every sentence that is not a direct question or an exclamation.

> One day I was sitting in my room drawing my mother's picture. (Passage 13-A)

Use a period after abbreviations.

> Mr. Gerber's soul evidently wasn't very pretty. (adapted from Passage 7-D)

> These days the education system in the U.S. is "starving." (Passage 5-A)

> It was filled in first with committed time—eating, sleeping, dressing, school, etc. (Passage 4-B)

Use a period to write about dollars and cents.

> The homeless man had $2.35 in his cup. (adapted from Passage 7-A)

2. THE COMMA

2.1 The Five Most Important Commas

2.1a Between Independent Clauses

Use a comma between independent clauses joined by a coordinating conjunction: *and, but, or, for, yet, so, for, nor.*

> I don't remember her name, but I can clearly recall how she looked and what she said. (Passage 4-A)

> Class sizes are expanding, and the school year is getting shorter. (Passage 5-A)

EXCEPTION   If the two independent clauses are both short, you may leave out the comma.

I had a big family <u>and</u> my parents had five children. (Passage 8-D)

(See Chapter 4, Section 1.)

2.1b Following Introductory Adverbials

It is always correct to use a comma after an introductory adverbial. A comma is *optional* if the adverbial is short. A comma is *required* if the adverbial is long, if it is a verbal phrase, or if it begins with a subordinating conjunction.

Optional
<u>These days</u> the education system in the U.S. is "starving." (Passage 5-A)

<u>These days</u>**,** the education system in the U.S. is "starving."

Required
• long

   <u>During Stalin's era in the forties and fifties</u>**,** knowledge of western languages was a real problem because it could cause a lot of trouble. (Passage 9-A)

• contains a verbal

   <u>Hoping to find food or simply soda bottles</u>**,** he was rummaging through a garbage pail. (Passage 5-B)

• begins with a subordinating conjunction:

   <u>When I finished my junior year in high school</u>**,** I went there to finish my education. (Passage 3-A)

The comma *never* comes immediately after the subordinator. It *always* comes at the end of the subordinate clause.

INCORRECT: Although**,** I may sound like I disliked working in the store, I enjoyed it.

CORRECT: Although I may sound like I disliked working in the store**,** I enjoyed it. (Passage 10-A)

(See Chapter 3, Section 2.)

2.1c After Transition Words and Phrases

Use a comma after a transition word or phrase at the beginning of an independent clause. If the transition word "interrupts" the clause, put commas around it.

Furthermore, I learned to deal with many people. (Passage 10-A)

I learned, furthermore, to deal with many people.

(See Chapter 4, Section 1.2.)

2.1d Between All Items in a Series

Use a comma between all items in a series of more than two. British English does not require the last comma before *and*.

• series of two

apples and oranges

• series of more than two

American: apples, oranges, and bananas
British: apples, oranges and bananas

It is formed of <u>several small islands, thirteen medium ones, and a large one</u>. (Passage 14-A)

People <u>live in today, reflect about yesterday, and anticipate the tomorrow that is to come</u>. (Passage 4-B)

<u>Bands are playing, singers are singing, and the whole crowd is enjoying the ride</u>. (Passage 5-C)

2.1e Around Inserts

Use commas around inserts, that is, information that is added and "extra." Inserts are also called appositives and nonrestrictive clauses. The most common inserts are noun phrases, *wh*-clauses, and *-ing* verbal phrases.

• noun phrase:

The waters surrounding the islands are green, <u>a transparent green</u>. (Passage 14-A)

• *wh*-clause:

The Ecuadorian government, <u>which is trying to preserve them in their natural state</u>, has enacted some laws forbidding the introduction and use of modern things. (Passage 14-A)

• *-ing* verbal phrase:

The land is in general barren, <u>having craters that give it the look of the land on the moon</u>. (Passage 14-A)

• other inserts:

Water is found all year on San Cristobal Island, <u>thanks to rain</u>. (Passage 14-A)

Today, the world can admire, <u>with the same wonder,</u> that nature that Charles Darwin marveled at more than a century ago. (Passage 14-A)

This case is unique in the world because, <u>as is well-known,</u> penguins belong to icy climates. (Passage 14-A, Part 2)

Note that commas must be at **both** ends of an insert when the insert is in the middle of a sentence.

Do **not** use commas around restrictive clauses, which restrict, define, identify, limit or narrow the noun they follow. The information in a restrictive clause is essential, not extra.

Also, the number of people <u>who can visit the island</u> is limited by the Institute and the Ecuadorian government. (Passage 14-A, Part 2)

(See Chapter 14, Section 2.4.)

2.2 Less Frequent Commas

2.2a Setting Off Direct Quotations

Use commas when you identify the source of a direct quotation. The identification can come before, in the middle, or at the end of the quotation.

I said, "Oh, I really don't know. It can be daddy, since it cannot possibly be you." (Passage 13-A)

"Nothing special," I answered with embarrassment, "just drawing."

"Nothing special, just drawing," I answered with embarrassment. (Passage 13-A)

2.2b In Dates and Numbers

• Dates

Use commas in dates to set the year off from the rest of the date.

On <u>December 13, 1981</u>, many of my friends who were activists of "Solidarity" were arrested. (Passage 14-H)

• Numbers

Use commas in numbers longer than four digits. The comma is optional in four digit numbers.

2,500 [or 2500]
250,000
2,000,000

Do not use commas in telephone numbers, years, street numbers, or zip codes.

3. THE SEMICOLON

The semicolon is used mainly in formal writing.

3.1 Between Independent Clauses Before a Transition Word

In your formal writing, you will occasionally want to indicate that two independent clauses are closely tied by using a transition word or phrase preceded by a semicolon and followed by a comma.

> During the interview, the accent problem came out again; however, she promised to help me get a job. (Passage 6-B)

(See Chapter 4, Section 1.2.)

3.2 Between Independent Clauses Without a Transition Word

In your formal writing, you can occasionally connect two independent clauses with only a semicolon. This indicates that the two clauses are very closely tied in meaning.

> Most students were in their teens or twenties; only she was in her forties. (Passage 4-A)

(See Chapter 4, Section 1.2.)

4. THE COLON

Use a colon before several kinds of information at the end of a sentence: a list, a quotation, and an explanation or example.

4.1 Before a List

Use a colon before a list at the end of a sentence.

> I was unable to face all kinds of eyes: smiling eyes, curious eyes, jealous eyes, quiet eyes. (Passage 3-E)

364

When he came into our car, he started making a speech: how hard he had tried to find a job, how difficult it was to do so, how hungry he was, and so on. (Passage 7-A)

4.2 Before a Quotation

Today I think it is true what a German poet once said: the eyes are the windows of the soul. (Passage 7-D)

4.3 Before an Explanation or Example

My duties were very simple: I typed letters, answered phone calls, and reminded my boss of his daily activities. (Passage 10-C)

It started with a short statement like this: Objective: To obtain a position as a word processing specialist. (Passage 6-B)

5. THE APOSTROPHE

An apostrophe is used for two reasons: possession or contraction.

5.1 Possession

5.1a Nouns

• add *'s*

if the noun does not end in *s*

my uncle'<u>s</u> backyard (Passage 5-D)

men'<u>s</u> wear

the children'<u>s</u> hour

if the noun is singular and ends in *s*

my boss'<u>s</u> office

If adding *'s* makes the pronunciation awkward, you may use only an apostrophe: *'*. Both are acceptable.

> Moses' teachings

- add *'* only

if the noun is plural and ends in *s*

> my customers' tastes (Passage 4-C)

> the islands' flora and fauna (Passage 14-A)

- add *'s* or *'*

after the postmodifier at the end of a noun phrase

> the people next door's dog

5.1b Compound Pronouns and *One*

Add *'s* to *one* and to compound pronouns.

> It makes no sense to change one's ideas and beliefs if one thinks they are right. (adapted from Passage 3-D)

> After their discussion, Ayako Nakashizuka knew everyone's age. (adapted from Passage 4-A)

> (See Chapter 7, Section 6.)

5.2 Contractions

The apostrophe represents missing letters in contractions.

> How'd you like it there? (Conversation 2-2)

> I don't think it's an unusual statement that I'm making. (Conversation 2-5)

> *It's* always means "it is" or "it has." *They're* always means "they are."
> In formal writing, avoid using contractions.
> (See Chapter 7, Sections 4.3 and 4.5.)

6. QUOTATION MARKS

6.1 Direct Quotations

Use quotation marks around exact words from speech or writing.

> She asked me, "What are you doing, darling, for so long sitting here so quietly?" (Passage 13-A)

> [Malaga's] airport was small, simple, and quiet. In one corner of the airport there was a small room with a sign that said "Monetary Change," and next to this was another room with a sign that said "Tour Information," but it was closed. (Passage 8-B)

6.2 Punctuation Inside Quotations

- Put commas and periods inside quotation marks.

> "I remember," my father told me once, "that you couldn't take anything with you or the secret police would suspect that you were going to run away." (Passage 8-F)

- If you quote a question or an exclamation, put the question mark or exclamation point inside the quotation marks.

> "Who is this?" she asked, pointing at my paper. (Passage 13-A)

> Is the education system in the U.S. "starving"? (Adapted from Passage 5-A.)

- If a quotation is interrupted by identification of the speaker, capitalize the first word of the second part only if it starts a new sentence. Do not capitalize it if it continues a sentence started in the first part of the quotation.

> "Oh, I really don't know," I said. "It can be daddy, since it cannot possibly be you." (Passage 13-A)

> "I remember," my father told me once, "that you couldn't take anything with you or the secret police would suspect that you were going to run away." (Passage 8-F)

367

6.3 Words Used as Words

When you want to call attention to words, put quotation marks around them.

> The word "thrifty" means something to me because my mother was a thrifty person. (Passage 8-D)

> "Beef Yakitori" was one of their creations: "Yakitori" means grilled chicken, so "Beef Yakitori" cannot exist. (Passage 8-H)

> In November, 1989, I graduated from both courses; I got an "A" in bookkeeping and an award in computers. (Passage 6-B)

7. THE QUESTION MARK

Use a question mark after a direct question in a quotation.

> "Who is this?" she asked, pointing to my paper. (Passage 13-A)

Use a question mark after a direct rhetorical question.

> What is a job? The first thing that comes to mind is a place where people spend eight hours working and earning money. (Passage 6-C)

8. THE EXCLAMATION POINT

Use an exclamation point after a statement which expresses strong feeling. Use exclamation marks rarely in your writing.

> They promised to help me get a good job when I graduated. It was a good deal! (Passage 6-B)

9. THE DASH

You can use a dash in place of a colon to precede an insert at the end. The colon is more formal; the dash is more dramatic. The dash is more common in British than American English.

In my imagination I can see the farm with my favorite animal—the horse. (Adapted from Passage 7-B.)

This is a terrible habit—procrastination. (Passage 4-B)

It was filled in first with committed time—eating, sleeping, dressing, school, etc. (Passage 4-B)

(See Chapter 14, Section 3.4.)

10. PARENTHESES

Use parentheses around material that is supplemental to the text, especially author comments.

In our western society (that is the only one I can account for), we are taught that we should be productive. (Passage 10-C)

These duties included making breakfast in the morning, changing diapers four times a day, going to the park (if it was a warm day), cooking, putting the babies to sleep and dressing them to go back home at six in the afternoon. (Passage 10-C)

(See Chapter 14, Section 3.4.)

Correct
Versions of
Passages
Used in
Exercises

2
APPENDIX

APPENDIX 2: CORRECT VERSIONS OF ESSAYS

NOTE The passages below are the writers' own versions of the essays used in this book, except for a few editorial changes that we have made. The passages present correct solutions to the problems posed by the exercises, but in some of them a variety of solutions is possible.

Passage 3-D   OUR LANGUAGES AND CUSTOMS

by Freddy Sampson

When people immigrate to the United States, they might consider themselves Americans. This does not mean that they should forget their own language and customs. Because customs and language are inherited through the passage of time and past generations, they should not be dismissed
5   lightly.

The primary customs that any immigrant coming into the U.S. should hold dear are their own. It makes no sense to change your ideas and beliefs if you think they are right. When it comes to your language, two languages are better than one. If you speak two languages, you could get special privileges
10 when applying for some jobs. Having your own language and customs could be beneficial.

The fact that you must learn the American language and customs is acceptable. They should be assimilated to your own customs and language, not used to replace them. Since there are no perfect customs or languages,
15 to dismiss your own customs or language for those of the U.S. would be a fatal mistake. Because knowledge is power, you should not throw it away once you have it. Your language and customs are a part of you, your parents, their parents, and so on. They are the roots on which your past is built. No person or country should take them away from you.

Passage 3-E   A VALUABLE EXPERIENCE

by Than Than Oo Ma

Before the competition that night, my class teacher called me in and reminded me that I was not only going to represent my elementary grade but also my school's name. I went to sleep early that night, thinking and dreaming about the first prize.
5   The next day, my parents took me to the City Hall, where I had to compete with other students. The huge stage and the many people frightened me. When I arrived on the stage, my knees were shaking and my voice was trembling. I was unable to face all kinds of eyes: smiling eyes, curious eyes, jealous eyes, quiet eyes. Those eyes made me lose control. After finishing my
10 performance, I realized that all my hope was gone. When I came down from the stage, I saw my teacher's angry, reddish face. She yelled at me in front of the other students. "What have you done to me? What have you done to the school? You are a useless student."
On the way home, my mom cheered me up. She said there was nothing
15 that I couldn't do. I could even make a rod of iron into a fine, small needle.

Nevertheless, at the end of that day, I decided I must get the prize the next year.

The following year, I won the prize. At that time, I wasn't afraid to face all those eyes. I could control myself very well as a result of my experience the previous year. When I came down from the stage, I received big hugs, sweet smiles, and many kisses from my fifth grade class teacher, my parents, and also my fourth grade teacher. The prize, on which I had spent two years of my strength and energy, was in my hand.

My picture is hanging in the school library among the other honor students. Every time I see that picture, I remember the day that I lost the prize and the day that I won it.

Passage 3-H **CURAÇAO**

by Sou Chang

Curaçao is the island where I was born. It is situated just to the north of the Venezuelan coast. Curaçao had some French influence. Actually, if one looks at the name Curaçao, it is of French origin. Later in history when the slave trade flourished, it became a Dutch colony. Up to the present, Curaçao is still a Dutch colony.

All these influences of French, Spanish, and Dutch are reflected in the language the folks speak, which is Papiamento. It is a mixture of all the languages mentioned and is also mixed with Portuguese and Indonesian. Although Papiamento is spoken, the official language is Dutch.

The people from the island are so warm and friendly. The population consists of descendants of the original Indians from the island, descendants of slaves, Portuguese, Jews, Chinese, and Dutch. All these races get along well with each other. The people of the island are very helpful. If one is stuck with some problem, the people are ready to help you out. The people on the island like to make one feel at home.

One thing I also miss is waking up in the morning with the birds singing at my window. I grew up on a farm in Curaçao. In the morning I would wake up smelling fresh brewed coffee, fresh baked eggs, and toast. Later I would take a morning walk barefoot in the countryside. The plant life on our farm is typically tropical. We have coconut trees and big mushroom-shaped trees, which give shade against the lovely scorching tropical sun. A legendary site in the harbor of Curaçao is the Floating Market. It consists of Venezuelan boats. The merchants are there every morning selling and praising their fresh tropical fruits such as papayas, oranges, bananas, pineapples, and others. They also have vegetables such as tomatoes and cucumbers. There are also the fishermen selling their fish such as red snapper and shellfish, especially conch. The city made marble tables for them at the shore so they can display their goods. To make the scene more colorful, the merchants extend some multicolored drapes over their heads and tables. They use the drapes as a roof to protect them from the tropical sun.

Curaçao is a simple and yet colorful and happy island. I miss the island. Whenever I think of Curaçao, it brings back those nice and fond memories of the island. But one day I will take a long vacation, go back, relax, and I will enjoy every bit of it.

Passage 4-B   **HOW TO USE TIME WELL**

by Chun Ling Tsien

Time goes in only one direction—forward. It moves from the past to the present, from the present to the future. People live in today, reflect about yesterday, and anticipate the tomorrow that is about to come. If people want to be successful, it is very important for them to know how to use time well.

5   The first way to use time well is not to delay doing something until some future time. This is a terrible habit—procrastination. If you have a tendency toward procrastination, you are always doing yesterday's jobs today, and tomorrow you are doing today's unfinished work. As a result, you cannot catch up. For instance, I was supposed to finish two compositions for today,

10   but I only did one. Today I must not only accomplish my today's homework, but also I shall write one composition which should have been finished yesterday. However, I still have only as much time as the day before. In a word, there is too much homework to be done today.

The second way is to be against time. Many people complain that they

15   have no time to do this or that. In fact, if you check what you have done all day long, you will find you have done a lot of things which were not necessary. For example, were you reading magazines or books while taking a bus or train? Did you call someone up or talk with somebody without a purpose? If the first question is answered "no" and the second question

20   "yes," I could say that you wasted a lot of precious time because you could do something on the train, and it was not necessary to call somebody or talk with somebody. Above all, it is very important to make a schedule if you want to keep on time. This weekly schedule may not solve all your problems, but it will force you to realize what is happening to your time.

25   I have had tremendous success with this method. After making a schedule, I followed it each day. I gradually stopped postponing the chores that faced me. My life became far less complicated, so each day was easier to face. Of course, the schedule should be reasonable, and it was also not easy for me to follow this one. It was filled in first with committed time—eating,

30   sleeping, dressing, school, etc. Then I decided to put in a good, regular time for studying. I was sure to set aside enough time to complete work that I was normally assigned each week. By the way, I didn't forget to set aside enough time for relaxation. One day, I determined to put away my homework which would be handed in to my teacher the next morning because I was

35   extremely tired. I raised my head and stared at my schedule. I could see that it contained what I had written in my heart. I changed my mind and continued doing my homework. Thus, when I wanted to be lazy, my schedule gave me power and confidence to reach my aim.

In conclusion, a person cannot buy time. Now we should catch up

40   with time from the beginning to the end. If a person uses time completely and well, he will be more successful than others.

Passage 4-C   **MY WORK**

by Hye Soo Han

I have been doing four different kinds of work for two years.

First, I have my own retail shop for men's wear in Flushing. I work from Wednesday through Sunday until 8 p.m. I pick the style of clothes and order them directly from companies. Choosing the style of clothes and color
5   is a very difficult and important job for me. I have to finish ordering fall and winter clothes before March. I try to buy good quality clothes for a good price which will appeal to my customers' tastes. I display all my merchandise myself. The conduct of retail business is not that easy, but I'm enjoying my work.

10   My second job is being a housewife. My husband is a typical Korean type of man. Typical Korean husbands don't do housework such as cooking, dishwashing, cleaning, and laundry. They think housework is the duty of wives, and wives should be submissive. My husband has changed a little in the U.S., but he is still not really helpful with housework. Sometimes he just
15   helps me to vacuum my home and do laundry. Therefore, I'm always doing all the housework. I have a 10-month-old baby girl. She always scatters her toys and things all over the house. I make a constant effort to put the rooms to rights, but that is not easy to do.

The third job is school work. I'm taking four classes this semester. All
20   of the classes that I'm taking require a lot of work. I'm a foreigner, so I need more time to prepare the classes. But I don't have enough time to study. Homework and exams cause a lot of pressure all the time. Nowadays, I try to minimize my hours of sleep and prepare classes. However, I feel too tired, and it is hard to concentrate on studying.

25   My last job is being a mother. This work is the most difficult work. Taking care of a baby is the hardest job that I have ever done. Feeding, changing diapers, giving a bath, and soothing a crying baby all require love. Tuesday is the only day for spending full time with my baby. I feel very sorry for my baby. She is a good girl. She takes kindly to any strangers.

30   Nowadays, I feel the limitations on my ability to do four kinds of work together. I feel too tired to do all the work at the same time. I don't know which work I should give up, but I feel it is absolutely right to keep my baby.

Passage 4-D   **DIFFERENCES BETWEEN PARENTS' AND
                                    CHILDREN'S EDUCATION**

by Nini Myint

In order to live in this modern world, education is one of the most important things for us. There are many kinds of education and many ways of teaching. Every generation might have different educational systems, but they all have the same purpose. Moreover, there was a time that education
5   was not necessary, but as time goes by, things have changed. In Burma, there were many kinds of changes and differences.

During my father's generation, the education system was very different from my generation. Back in those days, most schools were provided by the British. In those days, people had a better education than nowadays because teachers had different ways of teaching. Most of the students were taught by British native teachers. Therefore, they spoke better English and had high standards in English. Also, they began learning English in primary school. Furthermore, all of the subjects were taught in English. The schools' rules were strictly followed, and they had punishment for every little thing.

In my generation, the educational system was far different from my father's. For example, all the subjects were taught in Burmese except for English. I myself and other students from my generation started to learn English in the fifth grade. In the fourth and eighth grades, the final exams are given by the state board of education, and in the tenth grade, the exam is the nation-wide exam. In each grade, we must pass every subject. Otherwise, we must repeat that particular grade. Therefore, it is really hard to graduate from high school. After tenth grade, we can enter college. In the old days, there was no limit in choosing any major or professional field that we wanted. Things are not easy in my generation. The students have fewer opportunities to learn.

Passage 4-E   **JOSÉ**

by José Mazariegos

My name is José. I came to the United States seven years ago. I've gone from the fifth grade in public school, to junior high, to high school, and now to college. I think this has been a great achievement for me, and it will be an even greater achievement if I make it through college and get my degree.

About myself, I'm 5'5". I weigh 127 pounds. I'm 18 years old. I live with my mother, my brother, and my sister. All of them speak two languages. Our first language is Spanish. We speak this language at home and all the times that we're together.

Writing seems easy for me. Even though I don't do a very good job of it, I do like to write. I think that if they gave me a choice between writing a lot and reading a lot, I would choose writing, even though I have problems with spelling, forming paragraphs, or being clear about the major point in my essay. I tend to confuse the person reading it, instead of having my thoughts in writing clear.

Passage 5-C   **QUEBEC CITY**

by Honorata Lewicka

Quebec City is the most joyful place that I have ever been to. Let me take you for a one-day tour around Quebec.

The day starts at 8 A.M., in a small room up on the fifth floor of a private hotel. The sun is very bright, the air is clean; it will be a great day. From the windows we can see the St. Lawrence river, which is full of white dots. The little dots are ships and boats on the river seen from a distance. Across the river is a colorful spread: red, white and green. You have to look very closely to see that the red spots are the roofs of houses, the white ones are the houses themselves, and there are green trees all around them.

10   First we take a ride outside of Quebec City, to the country, where we can see farms and animals that are not in the city. We stop at a farm where you can buy freshly picked strawberries, or you can pick them for yourselves. We pay for baskets and start to pick the strawberries, and we are allowed to eat them while we pick. These strawberries have soil on them, but they taste
15   great.

After that we go back to the hotel to wash up and to change our clothes. We are set to take a boat ride for a few hours. As we step on the boat, the atmosphere is very friendly and enjoyable. There are many musicians and singers, clowns and artists. Bands are playing, singers are singing, and the
20   whole crowd is enjoying the ride.

When we get back from the ride, it is 10 P.M. We take a walk along the streets where a festival is in progress. The streets are full of talented people: musicians and singers, store owners, and people who enjoy walking and listening to others perform.

25   All of us are having a good time. At about midnight, we walk back to our hotel where we can get some rest for the next day.

Passage 5-D   **MY UNCLE'S BACKYARD**

by Wan Lam

I liked my uncle's backyard. Although it was not big, it was beautiful and tranquil. It was in the back of a two-story Spanish style house, located in the countryside of Hong Kong.

The countryside was calm and elegant with few people living there. A
5   group of houses was built along the tiny river. There was a small waterfall with water running from the top of the hill into the river. There were many trees on the side of the river, grown so strongly that their huge amount of roots anchored the soil tightly and extended in all directions. My uncle's house was among those houses; and his backyard was facing the river. My
10   uncle and I spent most of the time together in the backyard when I was a child. Thus, it was more than a backyard.

The backyard was surrounded on three sides by fences which extended from one side of the house to the other end. It didn't occupy a large area, but it was big enough for children to play. The ground was covered with
15   long greenish grass; it was so fresh that I wanted to put my nose deep in the grass in order to breathe the air and enjoy the smell. It gave me a sense of refreshment.

In addition, there was a number of colorful flowers along the fences on two sides; tulips, daisies, lilies, sunflowers, and roses all showed off their
20   pretty dresses to attract one another. The flowers were beautiful and attractive with butterflies dancing on them.

APPENDIX 2: CORRECT VERSIONS OF ESSAYS

Passage 6-C   **WORKING IN CUBA**

by Nieves Angulo

What is a job? The first thing that comes to mind is a place where people spend eight hours working and earning money. But this is not the case sometimes. In Cuba, for example, students have jobs, and they do not earn money at all.

5   I began to work in agricultural farms at an early age. I did not do it because I had to earn money to support myself. It is a requirement for all Cuban students after the revolution of 1959. The government says that the young generation must contribute something to the revolution, so working on those farms is one of them. Thus, at the age of eleven, I was doing the
10 work of a farmer.

Passage 7-C   **AN IMMIGRANT'S EXPERIENCE**

by Martine Liney

America, the land of opportunities, the dream land. Is it really? For some people America is the land of opportunities, but for others it is the land of self-destruction.

I personally can say that America is the land of opportunity for the
5   people who already have family in the country like myself. If you come to America as a young child with parents who are working hard to make it, you are lucky, in fact very much so. I have been here for three years. When I came, I didn't know English. With the right help, I have graduated from high school and am now continuing to pursue my goals by attending this college.
10 Life has been very easy for me here. Unlike my mother, I do not have any responsibilities but my school work and sometimes things that I have planned and what I want to do. I also didn't have to worry about a permanent residence when I came here, since my mother had already taken care of that. When I came here, I went straight to school. To find a job was very easy. All
15 I needed was to be the right age and to have my working papers.

Yes, America is the land of opportunities, but not for a single working parent like my mother, who has been working very hard. My mom came here ten years ago to further her education and visit the country so my brother and I could also come for our education. It has been ten years. Still,
20 not once has she set foot in a class room.

Passage 7-D   **UELI GERBER**

by Henriette Schoch

When Ueli Gerber was my teacher, he was already in his fifties. Nevertheless, his appearance was very well groomed, and he was quite tall and slender. His features were attractive and well proportioned. I suppose it could have been said that he was good looking if there hadn't been those

5 eyes. They were close together and in deep sockets. The color was a harsh
blue. Maybe it was this color which made his glance sometimes so cold,
almost uncomfortable. Today I think it is true what a German poet once said:
The eyes are the windows of the soul. Ueli Gerber's soul evidently wasn't
very pretty.

10 He was always very correctly attired, never fancy but never without good
taste. I never saw him, for example, without a tie, although it wasn't required
for teachers to wear ties. He used to say that he knew, when he wore his tie,
that he was the teacher and no private person any more and that he would
feel naked without it. The tie was as important for him as armor was for a
15 knight when he went for a fight. Apparently teaching was fighting; there was
no doubt about that.

He thought that he had to fight, in order to force us to learn. In a rather
conservative school system, as in Switzerland, this is rather a usual attitude.
In fact there are a lot of teachers who drill their students with this attitude;
20 and they are successful, because they are strong enough and, most important,
they are fair. The students know exactly what they have to do, and as long as
they stick to the rules, everything works pretty well. However, Ueli Gerber
wasn't strong enough. His personality was very ambiguous and unstable.
There were moments when he talked very openly to us about himself, his
25 family, and what he thought and in what he believed. In other moments he
regretted his open utterances, and he behaved in a very reserved way, to the
point of being impolite.

Passage 7-E   HER LUCK

by Parastoo Khorramian

She was a little girl who lived in a small town in Iran. In her small town
people were separated into two groups, lucky and unlucky. No matter how
hard they worked, the results were the same. Some could improve their lives
by working hard and some could not. In the little girl's case, her family could
5 not improve their life. Her family wasn't lucky. Her mother and her father
worked hard, but still there wasn't enough money at home. Thinking of
being unlucky for ever would make her sad, but one day everything changed.

Passage 8-D   A CHINESE HOUSEWIFE

by Lisa Tang

In Chinese society a housewife should be thrifty in order to help her
husband to support the family. First of all, she does her housework by herself
and doesn't hire a maid to work with her. Secondly, when she goes shopping,
she only spends money on daily necessities and not on junk food. The food
5 which she buys should be healthy food and should not cost much money.
Finally, she can't buy clothes often except when she has to go to a banquet.
Mostly she makes her clothes herself and wears them at home. In this way
she saves money.

10   The word "thrifty" means something to me because my mother is a thrifty
person. Also, it reminds me of my childhood in Hong Kong. I was raised in
the middle class. I had a big family, and my parents had five children. My
father was the only one to earn money to support our family. He went to the
United States to work when we were young. Our living depended on the bill
of exchange which he sent monthly. I guess that is the reason why my
15   mother became an economical person.

        I remember one day I asked my mother to buy me a pencil case which
had a Japanese cartoon character design on the cover. She refused because
she said she had just bought me a new one a few months ago. I told her that
the one I had was out of style and the one which I wanted was very popular
20   now. Most of my school-mates had it. Therefore, I wanted her to buy one for
me. She rejected my request because she didn't want to spoil me and she
would not spend money on those luxury things. I was really mad and cried.
The next two weeks I didn't eat my breakfast and tried to save money to buy
the pencil case. Finally, I bought it by myself. However, I missed my breakfast
25   for two weeks.

Passage 8-E   **EARLY CHILDHOOD**

                          by Henriette Schoch

        Among psychologists, especially in the field of developmental psychology,
there is agreement about how important early childhood is for a human
being. A child has to learn an incredible amount of very difficult and intricate
things: Even the action of taking hold of something demands complete
5   concentration and a lot of exercise, until the child is able to control its
movements without any observance. Before that, many rather complicated
recognitions and conclusions have to be made by the baby. The eyes, for
instance, have to learn to fix on something. Then, in an almost endless
process of groping, touching, and taking into the mouth, the baby starts to
10   distinguish between him- or herself and the surroundings. Months of active
learning pass by until the happy and proud mother and father observe their
baby creeping. Of course, this is a very natural process of learning, but we
know today that the child cannot do it alone. He or she needs not only the
presence of at least one adult person who provides care, but the baby needs
15   great support from that person. Psychologists say that the first two years of
childhood are the most important, and I think they are, because in this very
short time a human being acquires an important basis of knowledge on
which he has to build.

Passage 8-F   **MY FATHER**

                          by Igal Shilloh

        My father left his home when he was only seventeen. He kissed his
widowed mother for the last time in his life and went on the frightening way

to freedom. Two family pictures and a few pounds in his pocket were the only things he took with him along with the memories.

5   Of course, the memories. "I remember," my father told me once, "that you couldn't take anything with you or the secret police would suspect that you were going to run away. I didn't take anything, just the smell of our home, the face of my mother, the stove, the bed, the pictures on the walls, the sight of the neighborhood. Your mind tries to remember any small detail
10   when you know that you may not see any of this any more."

    I am looking at my father's picture when he was eighteen. His eyes, smart and warm, smile under his black hair and his mouth smiles gently. What was inside this young man's head back then when he was alone, in his new country, far away from his family? I am trying to see into his eyes, to see
15   what it was like to fight the daily obstacles of getting a job, food, and a place to sleep. But the biggest struggle was probably with the memories, especially the memories, which were wounding the soul, and the longing for his family and his mother whom he would never see again.

    My father was born in Syria in 1930. He was the second child of a Jewish
20   religious family. His father died when he was young, and his mother took care of him and his older brother. While he was growing up, the state of Israel was going to be born. The coming birth of Israel was about to change my father's life forever.

    When he was seventeen, Syria and Israel were at war, and he had been
25   called to join the Syrian army. The choice was clear. He couldn't join the Syrian army, which was fighting against his brothers and sisters in Israel. He had to run away. His brother, who was old enough to get away from the army, stayed with their weeping mother, who sent her younger son away from her to save his life.

Passage 8-G   **WHY DO WILD ANIMALS BECOME EXTINCT?**

by Parastoo Khorramian

    Everything in nature is always changing. Some kinds of animals are always dying out—becoming extinct. And, of course, new kinds are always appearing.

5   There are many different things that may cause all the animals of one particular kind to disappear. Scientists know some of the causes, but they do not yet know others. For instance, they can tell part of the story about the whooping cranes. These are very tall birds that spend the summers in northern Canada and the winters in southern Texas. Only about two dozen of the beautiful big cranes are left. Soon there may be none.

10   Hunters with guns have helped to make the whooping crane almost extinct, but there seems to be something else going on too. Here is a mystery that scientists have not yet solved. In some years the flock has no new baby whooping cranes along when it flies south for the winter. Does this mean that no eggs have hatched, or that some disease or some wild enemy has
15   killed the young birds after they hatched? Or does it mean that human hunters are killing the young birds before they can fly? Nobody knows.

Passage 8-H **THE MELTING POT**

by Kioko Miura

As a Japanese, I found it hard to understand the meaning of "the Melting Pot" when I learned the phrase about two years ago. But since I have been in New York, I am beginning to accept that New York is one of the Melting Pots, and I also remember that I have worked in the Melting Pot in Australia before coming to New York.

From 1985 to 1986 I was in Australia and was working at a Japanese restaurant where the owner was Australian and all the cooks and some waitresses were Koreans. At that time Japanese culture and food were not familiar in Australia, and Australians could not distinguish a Japanese from a Korean. The Australians' ignorance was an advantage for the restaurant, because even though those workers were creating new Japanese-like food and were serving it as real Japanese food, Australians were eating the imitation food satisfactorily and were paying for it. Fortunately, the restaurant was always quite busy every night.

The owner and the other workers in this restaurant were completely strangers to Japanese culture, but they could arrange "Japanese" food very well. Their special creative ability could sometimes cause a funny phenomenon. "Beef Yakitori" was one of their creations: "Yakitori" means grilled chicken, so "Beef Yakitori" cannot exist. In this restaurant at least three countries' cultures were blending in one place. <u>Koreans</u> who did not know anything about Japan were cooking <u>Japanese</u> food for <u>Australians</u>.

Passage 8-I **MARRIAGE IN AFGHANISTAN**

by M. Daud Nassery

In Afghanistan, there is no such thing as dating, especially in high school. If a boy and a girl liked each other, they would try to keep it secret. Almost all marriages were arranged by the families. Even today, in the countryside, nobody can break the old rules. In the cities, traditions are changing. Some of the younger generation have their own way of life. But they are not as independent as children in this country. You cannot date or see each other without the parents' permission.

My marriage was arranged by our families, who are distant cousins. My wife, Aqela, and I were engaged from the time that she was two or three years old and I was six or seven. The reason for an early engagement is that families try to make their relationship stronger by sharing their children. My father worked in the Ministry of Finance, and Aqela's father was a schoolteacher. When I started high school, my parents told me that Aqela was going to be my wife.

Sometimes arranged marriages don't work. But divorces are very few, because in our culture and religion divorce is considered shameful. If a husband and wife are having problems, the family will try to discuss and resolve their differences. Both sets of parents try to mediate, even if it means that the wife must spend some time away, in her father's house. I was very surprised,

20   when I came to America, to find out the number of families that are broken
and divorced.

—in *New Americans: An Oral History* by Al Santoli

Passage 8-J   **CROSSING THE BORDER**

by Francisco Ramirez

We left Mexico for the United States in June 1985.

We began walking north from the farm in Baja along the big road. We
bought some Spanish bread and a can of orange juice. Our group was very
small, just my wife, the three children, and I. We were concerned about how
5   we would live in the United States. We had no idea what to expect. And we
had saved only enough money to make the trip.

Many Guatemalans use Mexican "coyotes" to guide them across the
border, but many times these men take advantage of the people. They ask,
"Give me two hundred dollars, or five hundred." The Guatemalans say "Okay,"
10   because they are afraid. They have no idea what to do once they reach the
border. Sometimes there are robberies, murders. We decided to cross the
border without a "coyote." We didn't give our money to anybody.

When we were close to the border, we rested alongside the road in the
bushes. When we saw the Border Patrol, we got down and hid. The officers
15   didn't see us. The problem was that we ran out of food and water, and we
were so exhausted from walking all night. We did not want to cross at the
main point, near San Diego. So we kept moving east, parallel to the border.

Early in the next morning, we saw the border police capture a group of
people as they tried to cross. Two or three trucks were patrolling back and
20   forth. The area was very dry. There was no fence, no grass, only scrub
bushes and very small trees.

At 10:00 A.M., we were still hiding. It was bright daylight, but we were
so hungry and thirsty in the hot sun that we decided to take a chance. We
huddled close together and moved as quickly as possible, though it seemed
25   like forever. We looked around and didn't see any border police, so we kept
moving through the brush, off the side of the road. We were very tired and
had no idea where we were.

We didn't have any bread or water. We looked horrible and felt like we
were dying, especially the children. It was an act of God that we met an
30   American man. He talked to us in English. We couldn't understand his
language, but he looked like a good man. It sounded like he was saying, "Where
do you come from? Who are you?" We couldn't answer, but we tried talking
in our language.

He said, "Ahh. I understand. You are very poor people. I can help you."
35   He gave us some water and green lime fruit from a bag that he carried. He
gave our small boy, Domingo, some candies.

After the man left, we prayed and thanked God. This man saved our
lives. Then we continued walking. A few hours later, we approached the city
of San Isidro. A car pulled up to us, driven by a Mexican. We didn't have any

APPENDIX 2: CORRECT VERSIONS OF ESSAYS

40   American money, but the man offered to drive us near the town. Once there, we met another Mexican who drove us two hundred miles or more to Los Angeles. We had never seen a big city before. It was eleven o'clock at night when we arrived. All the lights were on, like a million stars. I said, "Thank God we are in Los Angeles."

       —in *New Americans: An Oral History* by Al Santoli

Passage 8-K   **WORKING IN EL PASO**

                            by José Urbina

    My hometown is Juarez. Since I was nine years old, I've been coming to El Paso to work. At first I did gardening in people's yards, but I have stayed in El Paso constantly since 1981, going out to the fields to do farm work. I used to go to Juarez to visit my relatives at least one day each month. But in the
5   last year, I haven't gone because of the new immigration law. To visit Juarez I have to swim across the river. . . .

    During the past few months, the river has been very high and fast. That's one reason why not so many people have been crossing lately. I am not working now, because it isn't the growing or harvesting season on the
10 big farms. On February 15, we usually begin to plant onions. That is when the main agricultural season begins. . . .

    We haven't paid our rent since December. If we're lucky, I can find some part-time work to pay for food. Our baby . . . is two months old. Because he was born in El Paso, he is an American citizen.

       —in *New Americans: An Oral History* by Al Santoli

Passage 8-L   **MY GRANDMOTHER**

                            by Nieves Angulo

    My grandmother is the most wonderful person I have when problems strike me. Sometimes I used to have problems with the principal of my school because of my desire to leave the country for political reasons. My grandmother would listen to me very quietly for hours, and then she would
5 suggest some solutions for the problems. But the most wonderful thing in her is that she won't impose her suggestions on me. She says that one has to make her own final decision and no one should interfere. She helped me a lot in those days.

    My grandmother is the biggest and most wonderful person I have in
10 the world. She has always been my support in rough times. She has always been there for me, very firm. I would like to be like her someday and to have that courage and love that she has and to give without asking anything in return. She inspires me, she guides me. Every day I pray that she will live many many more years.

Passage 9-C   **THE KOREAN WRITING SYSTEM**

by Jinny Yi

I would like to introduce the Korean writing system because lots of people think that Korean, Chinese, and Japanese have the same writing systems. Chinese and Japanese have similar writing systems, but the Korean one is different.

First of all, the Korean writing system was created by Sejong, the fourth king of the Yi dynasty. He created the new writing system because of the common and lower class people, so that they could learn to write better and easier. At that time, it was not easy to get an education for the lower class people; also, the slaves were not allowed to learn to write. Furthermore, only people in the royal family could get an education, and it was not easy even for them to learn the Chinese loanwords. Chinese loanwords are very difficult to learn, because there are so many different ways of writing them. It is not an alphabet. So you must be highly educated to write the Chinese loanwords.

The writing system was introduced in 1446. It was called Han gul; it is still called Han gul in Korea today. Han gul was designed as an alphabet. There are 24 basic writing symbols. There are 14 consonants, and 10 vowels. As I mentioned before, Han gul was created because of lower class people and was used for lower class people, but now all Koreans are using Han gul. But although Han gul is much more commonly used in Korea these days, we have kept some Chinese loanwords. So we can say that we have two methods of writing in Korea today.

Therefore, we, the people in our country, thank Sejong for creating our own writing system. Furthermore, we are very proud of having our own writing system.

Passage 9-D   **THE ABACUS**

by Chun-Chi Liu

My favorite possession is an abacus. It is a traditional Chinese instrument that is used for calculation. It has five thousand years of history and has had a great influence on the Chinese way of life. My personal character has been changed by my abacus. It has made me feel competent and comfortable with numbers. Moreover, it has helped me reach success in business.

In ancient times the abacus was very popular in China. People used it for trading their goods in the market. Later, the structure and pattern of the abacus were remodelled, so there are some differences between the ancient and modern abacus. The ancient abacus was made by hand and was square, heavy, and black in color. It had fifteen rows of beads and six bigger beads for each column. A bead measured 2" by 2". Now, the abacus is made by machine; it is rectangular, lighter, brown in color, with twenty-seven rows and five smaller beads for each column. A small bead measures 0.5" by 1".

The abacus is divided into two parts, and there is a space between each part.

Passage 9-E   **LUCK**

by Marius Stawoski

"Luck—that which happens, either good or bad, to a person by, or as if by, chance; fortune." I found this definition in the dictionary. In the story of "The Rocking-Horse Winner," Paul thought that if he knew the name of the horse which would win the race, he would be lucky. Is that the answer to
5   the question that Paul asked his mother, "What is luck?" In her opinion she was unlucky and nobody ever knew why one person was lucky and another was not.

If I had been asked the same question as his mother was, I would have told him the tale which I was told as a kid, that in ancient times there was a
10 mother who had three sons. Two of them were considered wise and brave people. The youngest son was called dumb because he was kind-hearted. One day, a king announced that he would give his daughter's hand to the man who killed the dragon which was devastating his state. When the oldest son heard the news, he said, "I am the oldest son and the strongest one so I
15 will kill the dragon." Next day, he set out. At the end of his journey, near the castle's gate, he saw a dwarf who asked him for a crust of bread. The oldest son did not pay attention to the hungry dwarf because he was afraid that somebody would outstrip him. The dragon became the winner in their fight and the wisest and bravest son was killed. The second son took his chance.
20 Like his older brother, he did not stop for the begging dwarf. He also lost his fight. The youngest son gave what he was asked for and the thankful dwarf gave him a special sword so that he could kill the dragon. He was lucky, but it happened to him because of his kindness.

In my opinion, luck is the ability to take advantage of fortunate circum-
25 stances. In other words, luck is a factor of our personality, and it stays with us even though circumstances are changing all the time. For example, "a hard little place at the center of her heart" was Paul's mother's bad luck.

In the end, our luck depends on our personality, so if we want to change our bad luck, we must find out what we have inside ourselves which should
30 be improved.

Passage 9-F   **CHINESE WOMEN'S PLACE**

by Xiao Jun Su

About a year ago, Shanghai TV Station broadcast a program entitled "Aspects of Shanghai Husbands" which immediately became a tremendous hit and aroused widespread heated arguments. The words for the theme song were composed by Sha Ye Xing, a contemporary playwright of high renown.
5   The song was called "Where can a manly man be found?" but from its content and music it could be easily perceived that it was a rhetorical question rather than an ordinary one. One line from the song was particularly illuminating and penetrating: "When the wife growls, the husband trembles for three times on end." The program was vivid and effective in bringing home to us
10 the deplorable condition of those wretched Shanghai husbands who are tied down to housework and deprived of any financial power at home. Thus the

theme song uttered both an angry cry and a plaintive whine. It reflected the phenomenon that a rapidly increasing number of husbands are hen-pecked nowadays and that wives today are becoming as tough and uncontrollable as
15 tigresses or lionesses.

But why? For thousands of years Chinese women have been eulogized for their laudable virtues of being hard-working and being capable of enduring incredible sufferings. During the feudal age Chinese women were expected to be unconditionally obedient not only to their fathers and husbands
20 but to their sons as well. They had no say whatsoever at home, and they were even forbidden to go outside their houses. They would be considered bad-mannered and lascivious and would even be punished if they showed their teeth while smiling. A man was privileged to have several wives at the same time and he could divorce any of them at any moment if he did not feel
25 gratified, but a woman had to be loyal and "keep her body clean" even after her husband's death. Women had to work like slaves, and they could be bought and sold cheaply. Fettered tightly by the barbarian feudal system, they were treated as ploughing animals or tools for reproduction, and they ranked among the lowest in the society. In a word, they were oppressed and
30 mercilessly persecuted.

Passage 10-B   **STREET ENTERTAINMENT**

by Christine Patouha

New York City brings a lot of debates on the subject of work. For example, begging to some people is work but for others it is not work. The topic I will write about is street entertainment. For many people it is considered a job but for others it is not. Street entertainers I believe are working. They are
5 talented musicians that spend an average of eight hours a day on the streets playing music. They are entertaining people and whoever wants to give them money does. They work hard in doing something they enjoy. A particular group that I know came here from Peru with a six month visa, as tourists. When their money ran out they started playing their music in subways and
10 streets. When they noticed that people enjoyed their music, played on hand-made instruments, such as wooden pipes which produce different sounds, they continued entertaining in the street. Once, I asked one of the musicians, "Why don't you go and play in a night club?" His reply was "We are entertainers. We love what we do and we don't force anyone to listen to us. Playing in a
15 night club, we would not make as much money and we would not be heard by as many people as in the streets."

There are many other advantages in street entertainment. A young man I know, living in Harlem, developed a musical talent at eight years old. He began beating a stick on a plastic can. He played in the streets of New York
20 for many years, until he began to support his family by the donations people on the street would give him. He was twelve years old at that time. Today this young man, about fifteen years old, has been in a music video clip with Maria Carey, in Pepsi and Levi's commercials, and in the movie "Green Card." Aside from all the television publicity, he has also had many offers by music
25 producers that would have given him the opportunity to become famous if

he had chosen to quit his street music. Being still a young man, he has not taken their offers into great consideration, since the money offered to him is not satisfactory. Nowadays, he does not play as much as he used to, but he is still around and still noticed by the crowd.

30   Work is necessary in life. Everyone works, whether they are rich or poor. Poor people work harder and their jobs are less interesting to them, whereas rich people work in order to fulfill themselves. Without work people would be miserable and their lives would be dull. Work has become an everyday routine, just like taking a shower, eating and breathing.

Passage 10-C   CHOOSING A CAREER

by Maria Vicco

In our western society (that is the only one I can account for) we are taught that we should be productive. So, when the time comes and if possible, we make a choice: Either we get an education to learn and develop the skills that will be applied later, or we learn on site. That is to say, we learn by doing.

5   I find myself in a critical situation, because I am in that process of choosing what will be my occupation for the rest of my life. Well, maybe it sounds too dramatic. I'll say from now to the next ten years or so; and I find this choice hard but fascinating at the same time.

I've already had a few working experiences. Some of them I enjoyed,
10 some I really hated. But they all helped me to see more clearly what it is that I like doing best and, equally important, which activities I am good at.

I have found that working in an office is definitely not my kind of job. I was a secretary in a bank. My duties were very simple: I typed letters, answered phone calls, and reminded my boss of his daily activities. I hated the job. I
15 am a very active person. I like taking dance classes and walking around the city. There, I had to stay seated for nine long hours, and the only light I saw was the one coming from the fluorescent lights.

On the other hand, I had two jobs teaching that pleased me very much, especially the one in the day care center. There I looked after babies, and I
20 shared duties with two other teachers. These duties included making breakfast in the morning, changing diapers four times a day, going to the park (if it was a warm day), cooking, putting the babies to sleep, and dressing them to go back home at six in the afternoon. Those were the duties. I also got to see how they grew up, how they learned to walk by investigating the environment
25 and their own bodies. I taught them words in Spanish and they amazed me by remembering them two weeks later. I felt needed and, what was most fascinating, I learned from them.

Passage 13-C   MICHELLE

by Victoria Wu

She has huge, round brown eyes, dark brown curly hair, and her tiny face makes her normal size mouth look like it is grinning from ear to ear while she is laughing. Michelle impressed me not only because of her friendly and active

teaching attitude but also because of her words that moved me very much
and have remained in my mind.

"Are you sure you are in my class?" Michelle asked me with her folding
eyebrow. "No, you should not be in this class. I don't know how you did on
your placement test …" These were the words she said to me in front of all
the class 20 minutes after the first conversation class began in my first
semester. She told me I should have been in the conversation class two levels
higher and she really did me a great favor: She went to the office, consulted
with the director, and sent me to the correct class.

Our second encounter took place in my writing class one and a half
years later. Michelle was my writing teacher then. When we saw each other
in the first class, we both opened our mouths widely, and suddenly she
pointed her finger to me and said, "I remember you, Vicky. You were in my
class two years ago. Are you still taking ESL courses?" Actually, I did not have
a chance to explain why I was still taking the courses then. Through an essay
she learned that an accident had happened to my family, so I returned to my
hometown and came back one and a half years later.

The third time I met Michelle was in her reading class. I performed
poorly that term because I was attending classes in the day and working at
night. I could not get enough time to review and do my homework.
Furthermore, I was unable to take the final exam and consequently was not
allowed to leave the program. The director told me to ask Michelle if she
agreed that I was capable of passing the tests. The director decided to talk to
her first. Michelle granted her approval, so I passed the class and was able to
enter college.

I never saw Michelle after that final term, nor did I say, "Thank you very
much." I do not know whether I would have had the courage to say such
simple words to her if I had seen her.

Passage 13-D   LINDA

by Thien Quan Duong

During the first few days of high school, I noticed a pair of friends who
wore the same type of jacket and were walking down the hallway. I heard
someone calling, "Linda, Linda," and one of them turned around and said
hello. That was how I came to know Linda's name.

I seemed to see her around school every day in some of my classes. We
had home room together for the freshman year. We sat close to each other
because of our last names. At that time, there were not a lot of Asian
students in our high school. I also couldn't speak English and understand it.
I had to find out what the teacher said. The only Asian student sitting close
to me was Linda. I didn't want to disrupt the class. Therefore I talked to her
softly. I had to ask her, "What the teacher say?"

She was so kind and explained everything to me. Our conversation
carried on. I asked her, "Where are you from? I am from Viet Nam, and how
come you understand everything?"

She answered, "I am from China, and my English is not good, but the
teacher uses simple English."

I asked her, "How long have you been in the U.S.?"

She answered, "I have been here since 8th grade in junior high school."

The bell rang and we had to go home.

20   The next morning, I saw her, and we smiled at each other. She said, "I am very surprised to hear you speak Chinese so fluently and without a Vietnamese accent."

I said, "My parents are Chinese, and I was born in Viet Nam. I speak Chinese more often and better than Vietnamese."

25   On the way to class, she met some of her friends and she introduced them to me. Then we went to class together because we had almost the same classes, except for Math, English, and Science. She gave me her phone number and I gave her mine. She called me after school. We talked for a while.

She asked me, "Do you have any problem in classes that you don't 30 understand?"

If I said yes, she explained to me clearly and patiently in a friendly way. She called me up and said, "Please call me any time if you need help."

She gave me the confidence to live in a foreign land and told me a lot about living in New York.

Passage 14-E   ACUPUNCTURE

by Yoon Ok Cha

Acupuncture is an ancient Chinese medical technique for relieving pain, curing disease, and improving general health. It was devised before 2500 BC in China, and by the late 20th century was used in many other areas of the world.

5   Acupuncture grew out of ancient Chinese philosophy's dualistic cosmic theory of the "Yin" and "Yang." The "Yin," the female principle, is passive and dark and is represented by the Earth; the "Yang," the male principle, is active and light and is represented by the heavens. Disease or physical disharmony is caused by an imbalance or undue preponderance of 10 these two forces in the body, and the goal of Chinese medicine is to bring the "Yin" and the "Yang" back into balance with each other, thus restoring the person to health.

An imbalance of "Yin" and "Yang" results in an obstruction in the body of the vital life force, or Oi. The fundamental energy of the Oi flows through 15 12 meridians, or pathways, in the body, each of which is in turn associated with a major visceral organ (liver, kidney, heart, etc.) and with a functional body system.

Acupuncture appears to be undeniably effective in relieving pain and is routinely used in China as an anesthetic during surgery. The evidence now 20 indicates that acupuncture can induce analgesia and that its use is associated with measurable physiological changes. Recent medical reviews show that acupuncture is slowly beginning to be integrated into certain areas of Western medicine.

Passage 14-F   **MY BEST FRIEND**

by Honorata Lewicka

The special person that I can easily talk about is my best friend, who is one of a kind. Our friendship started some twenty-five years ago in Poland, where we both started our education. For the next eight years, we shared a school desk. After that, we went to different schools which were in far-away
5   cities. We lost contact with each other for over a year. To our own surprise, we got reunited in this huge country of the U.S.A.

Irena is 32 years old. She is about 5'6" tall and has brown hair and eyes. She is of medium build with short legs. Her usual wardrobe is a pair of jeans or a skirt and a sweatshirt. Simple dressing makes Irena more comfortable,
10 and it doesn't take time, which she needs because she has five children and a husband. Occasionally, she dresses with great elegance and style, exchanging her everyday look for the glamour look. To the most simple dresses, she adds some touches that make the simplest dress look like it just came from a fashion magazine.

Passsage 14-G   **MY HOMETOWN**

by Liyan Gu

I was born in Shanghai, but I moved to a little town with my parents when I was one year old. The town, which was located 100 miles from Shangai, was a very pleasant place with approximately 2,000 people. That place left me the most wonderful memories and played an important role in
5   my life. I learned how to enjoy the wonderful world.

The house, which stood at the corner of the widest street, was on the most exciting street in that town. The other streets in the town were so narrow that people always went to the widest street to buy or sell things. During the day, this street formed a market. I think that is the reason why my
10 house was always full of people. My house, which was two stories high, was one of the biggest houses in town. The house itself, which was shaped like a pyramid, contained 14 rooms.

Passage 14-H   **SOLIDARITY**

by Dominika Stanislawska

The thirteenth of December is a very significant day for me. On that day, in 1981, the Polish government set up the state of martial law that was supposed to smash and completely destroy the social and union trade movement called "Solidarity." Though formally registered, "Solidarity" had
5   never been approved by the Polish and, especially, the Soviet authorities.

At that time I was one of ten million people belonging to "Solidarity." On December 13, 1981, many of my friends who were activists of "Solidarity" were arrested. Those who escaped went into hiding until police discovered the

10 place. I lived in a small and quiet city that never was in the mainstream of social upheaval in 1980 when "Solidarity" came into being, but the number of arrests and missing people was significant—75 per cent of the active members. They were mostly men who worked in "Solidarity's" administration and those who were additionally involved in the anticommunist political activity.

15 In many cases these people were the only breadwinners of their families. The arrests left pregnant wives, children, and old parents without their support. Pensions, maternity and family benefits were insufficient to live on. After December 13 employers began to fire the remaining activists and wives of the arrested whose names were entered on the special list that made any employment for them impossible. There were a few cases in my 20 city where fathers were arrested and mothers lost their jobs.

After the first shock, the remaining members and sisters, wives, mothers, and daughters of the arrested gathered together to solve some of the problems. We had to get more information about the victims, arrange financial aid for families, and, especially, support ourselves and alleviate the prevailing 25 distrust of each other. We realized that any political activity at that time was impossible, but we had to raise our spirits. We collected money for the families of the arrested and of those who lost their jobs; we visited each other; we typed at home leaflets with patriotic poetry and slogans. We tried to maintain the feeling of solidarity among us. The 13th day of every month we organized 30 a church mass to remember the day and to pray for the ones remaining in prisons and killed by the police. Despite the ban on traveling, we tried to get to different parts of the country to gain information and to inform others about our activity. Step by step we were rebuilding the organization structure under conspiracy.

35 I think the sense of conspiracy was in our blood. We inherited it from our parents and grandparents, who used conspiracy during the Second World War. They were taught the means of conspiracy by their parents and grandparents, who maintained Polish nationality against the attempts of Russian, German, and Austrian invaders before World War I. We heard and 40 read about distributing political leaflets, harboring people, concealing our feelings, and covering up the truth during police interrogations.

We were fascinated by all these stories, but nobody had ever expected that we would be constrained to make use of those experiences, which should have remained only a history for us. That was one of the most important slogans 45 of the communist government after World War II—"We will build a new bright future for our children."

Instead of this bright future, they gave us coupons for food that we could buy after standing every day in long lines. They gave us the 20 year waiting period for our apartments. They gave us police to prevent our attempts at 50 improving the situation. They gave us censorship to have even our thoughts under control. They imprisoned and ruined people who were telling them that something must be done about the future.

Our war in 1981 was much more painful and confusing than the ones of our parents and grandparents. They fought with strangers who invaded 55 Poland. We had to fight with our "brothers" who were well armed. In our defense we had only our strong desire to live better.

Index

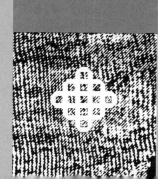

INDEX